Theoretical Inquiry

Theoretical Inquiry

Language, Linguistics, and Literature

Austin E. Quigley

Yale University Press
New Haven & London

Copyright © 2004 by Austin E. Quigley.
All rights reserved.
This book may not be reproduced, in whole or in part, including illustrations, in any form (beyond that copying permitted by Sections 107 and 108 of the U.S. Copyright Law and except by reviewers for the public press), without written permission from the publishers.

Set in Adobe Garamond type by The Composing Room of Michigan, Inc.
Printed in the United States of America by Sheridan Books.

Library of Congress Cataloging-in-Publication Data

Quigley, Austin E., 1942–
    Theoretical inquiry : language, linguistics. and literature / Austin E. Quigley.
        p. cm.
Includes bibliographical references and index.
  ISBN 0-300-10166-X (alk. paper)
1. Philology.   I. Title.
  P121.Q49 2004
  801—dc21
                                                                                                                               2003009885

A catalogue record for this book is available from the British Library.

The paper in this book meets the guidelines for permanence and durability of the Committee on Production Guidelines for Book Longevity of the Council on Library Resources.

10 9 8 7 6 5 4 3 2 1

For Patricia, Caroline, and Catherine

Contents

Preface, ix

Introduction, 1

1 Literary Theory and Linguistic Theory, 17

2 Saussure, Firth, and Bakhtin: Unity, Diversity, and Theory, 43

3 Chomsky and Halliday: Novelty, Generality, and Theory, 76

4 Wittgenstein: Facticity, Instrumentality, and Theory, 119

5 Literary and Cultural Studies: Theory, History, and Criticism, 156

Notes, 215

Bibliography, 249

Acknowledgments, 255

Index, 259

Preface

In the fifty years since René Wellek and Austin Warren published their influential book *Theory of Literature,* the theory movement in literary studies has acquired substantial momentum, achieved temporary predominance, and then lost almost entirely its hard-won credibility. In Frank Lentricchia's terms, theory-based literary criticism has become "a form of Xeroxing" in which texts are not so much read as "preread," with theoretical presuppositions dictating in advance the nature of critical conclusions. For Lentricchia, literary study in these terms involves simply the illustration of over-generalized presuppositions: "All of literature is x and nothing but x, and literary study is the naming (exposure) of x. For x, read imperialism, sexism, homophobia, and so on."[1] As Lentricchia has been one of the leading proponents of theory-based critical approaches, his defection from the cause has carried particular weight. But his counterargument is one against which Wellek and Warren warned us in their seminal study fifty years ago. Lentricchia now describes himself and his "discipline" as follows:

> I'm a teacher who believes that literature can't be taught, if by teaching we mean being in lucid possession of a discipline, a method, and rules for the

engagement of the object of study. I believe that the finest examples of the object of study cannot be ruled and that, therefore, professional literary study is a contradiction in terms. Great writing is a literally *unruly,* one-of-a-kind thing, something new and original in the world of literature, which (like all cultural worlds) is dominated by the conventional and the rule-driven: the boringly second rate.[2]

In their opening chapter, Wellek and Warren draw immediate attention to the dilemma that Lentricchia effectively redescribes, a dilemma that has haunted literary studies since its inception and literary theory throughout its evolution. On the one hand, they advocate a coherent general approach to literature, arguing that as "the true study of literature [is] at once 'literary' and 'systematic'" then "literary theory is the great need of literary scholarship today."[3] On the other hand, they emphasize the importance of the particularity of great works of literature and great authors with their consequent resistance to generalizations of any kind:

> Why do we study Shakespeare? It is clear we are not primarily interested in what he has in common with all men, for we could then as well study any other man, nor are we interested in what he has in common with all Englishmen, all men of the Renaissance, all Elizabethans, all poets, all dramatists, or even all Elizabethan dramatists, because in that case we might just as well study Dekker or Heywood. We want rather to discover what is peculiarly Shakespeare's, what makes Shakespeare Shakespeare; and this is obviously a problem of individuality and value.[4]

Recognizing the competing claims in literary studies of general literary knowledge and a knowledge of the unique characteristics of particular works, Wellek and Warren make two separate but related arguments. The first is the importance of our recognizing "that each work of literature is both general and particular, or—better, possibly—is both individual and general. Individuality can be distinguished from complete particularity and uniqueness."[5] The second is that, while literary theory must be conceived of in "universal terms," it is to be "systematic" not in the sense of providing a single overall method but in the sense of assembling "an *organon* of methods."[6] These insistences upon particularity in the context of generality and upon methodology in the context of multiple methods are insistences whose relationship begs many questions. Such questions are, however, left largely unanswered in a book in which the authors announce at the outset that "we [have not] undertaken to answer all the questions we raise."[7] The unanswered questions can readily be supplemented by others unasked, but it should not be overlooked that the subsequent theory movement flourished on claims to generality and foundered on the rocks of particularity; it also flourished by nourishing the expectation of a privileged understanding of methodologies, but foundered in practice by delivering mechanical applications of one privileged method at a time. The limitations of the latter became disturbingly apparent at the height of theory's claims to a central place in the literary discipline. As Wayne Booth put it in 1979, "Nothing is more self-destructive than the current fashion of cheering each new skyrocket as if it had finally given us all the light we need—and then sighing when it quickly fizzles out."[8]

Literary theory as a succession of methodological enthusiasms mechanically applied has managed, in effect, to provide us with the worst of both the worlds that Wellek and Warren sought to reconcile: it has been neither general enough to accommodate the complexity of the full range of literary works nor particular enough to clarify their distinctive individual character. It would thus be easy to follow Lentricchia in rejecting literary theory as a proven failure, but his readiness to revert to the argument that works of literature should simply be considered unique raises a different question not just about literary theory and literary studies, but also about a considerably wider set of concerns.

Though it may well be true that much of theory-informed literary criticism has become "a form of Xeroxing" in which works are not so much read as preread, we should nevertheless remind ourselves that the problem of moving unreflectingly from presupposition to conclusion is not one invented by literary theorists. And in deciding how to position ourselves relative to literary theory, we might first consider whether theory has failed us by providing us with impoverished instruments of investigation or whether we have failed theory by deploying them in impoverished ways. And when we look at the general development of literary studies in this century, the latter hypothesis becomes increasingly plausible.

Schematically summarized, literary study in the twentieth century has been dominated successively by historicists, New Critics, methodological critics, theorists, and cultural materialists. And in every case the dominant mode of inquiry has succumbed to the restrictive nature of its governing assumptions, which suggests that some of the problems of literary theory derive from presuppositions of more general consequence. Few would wish to deny, for example, the usefulness of situating a writer's work in the historical context from which it emerged. But some prominent historicists in the era before New Criticism (and some after) used their specialized knowledge of historical contexts to dictate what could possibly be said by any writer in a given period, instead of deploying that knowledge to provide a starting point for the exploration of an individual writer's imaginative excursions beyond the orthodoxies of the day. Presupposition, in effect, dictated conclusion.

The best of the New Critics, in turn, provided an appropriate realignment of modes of inquiry by insisting upon the virtues of close reading, relatively released from historical determinism, but their preferred techniques for enabling the imaginative work to speak for itself became, in the hands of lesser mortals, predictable and prescriptive, and writer after writer was reduced to exhibiting characteristic complexities of irony, paradox, and ambiguity. This form of presupposition, methodological rather than historical, likewise dictated a particular kind of conclusion.

Other models of textual analysis were subsequently borrowed from other disciplines, with Freudian critics, myth critics, phenomenologists, and Marxist critics, for example, providing new presuppositions that became anything but new in their mode of deployment. They simply provided further examples of interpretive methods that rediscovered their premises in their conclusions, illuminating what they thereby illuminated and obscuring what they obscured.

The underlying pattern here became visible enough to many, and part of the initial appeal of literary theory at this point was the potential for theorists to serve as analysts and advisors about the proliferation of critical monisms that new methodologies repeatedly supplied. But theorists soon became victims of the same disease, each promoting a new form of prescriptive reading so that the work of Barthes, Lacan, Foucault, Derrida, and others was pressed into largely similar service. And it is no surprise that the political imperatives of proponents of contemporary cultural studies have often encouraged them to follow suit, with confusing consequences for the ways in which the so-called "culture wars" are conceived on all sides. Essentialist conceptions of multiculturalism that relate generality to particularity by depicting cultural categories as largely homogenous within and somewhat opaque without effectively promote an oscillation between beliefs rather than an interaction of the kind that might promote intercultural exchange. And postcolonial studies finds itself as much constrained as enabled by the readiness to use as an informing paradigm for cultural interaction a uniform version of the colonial projects of Western imperialism.[9]

Literary theory is thus neither the first nor the last instrument of literary inquiry to reduce itself largely to rediscovering in literature what it presupposes to be there. Indeed, the disciplinary process of investing excessively in serial monisms has been so regularly repeated in literary studies that Graff has characterized it in terms of recurring methodological movements from "rags to riches to routine."[10] Whether this process is unique to literary studies is, of course, a necessary subsequent question, and Graff is inclined to answer it by arguing that the underlying problem is one of institutional organization in the academy rather than the malaise of a single discipline: "the routinization of critical discourses is a function of institutional arrangements that do not require these discourses to confront one another."[11] Like Wellek and Warren before him, Graff seeks to restore generality and flexibility to inquiry not by locating a privileged system or method but by bringing competing modes of discourse into some kind of conjunction with one another. Like Graff, we might well ask whether the problem is not just a problem of the collective mind-set of literature professors but whether there are even larger sociological pressures at work. For we would deceive ourselves if we believed that what we repeatedly encounter in literary studies as excessive investment in serial monisms is a shortcoming of this discipline alone or of this century alone.

In the middle of the nineteenth century, for example, John Henry Newman, in his *The Idea of a University,* lamented the tendency of undergraduates to "devour premiss and conclusion together with indiscriminate greediness."[12] His discontent with a faculty disposed to teach students in this way was such that he acknowledged that if forced to choose between having a faculty inclined to teach mechanically the orthodoxies of the day and having residential facilities within which students could learn in more varied ways from each other, he would settle for the residence halls.[13]

Newman struggled hard to characterize an alternative form of education that would enable students to acquire a historically informed but independent rather than mechanical voice. To achieve this, he argued, faculty need to cultivate the intellect, theirs and their students' alike, in such a way that education "consists, not merely in the passive reception into the mind of a number of ideas hitherto unknown to it, but in the mind's energetic and simultaneous action upon and towards and among those new ideas.... That only is true enlargement of mind which is the power of viewing many things at once as one whole."[14]

Given Wellek's and Warren's warnings, we might be appropriately wary of the relationship envisaged here between "many things" and "one whole," but it is instructive to see that for Newman, as for Wellek, Warren, and Graff, the path of resistance to mechanical thinking within one methodological framework is depicted in terms of relating and not simply equating multiple perspectives. But the nature of that process remains problematic in practice, whatever the investigative appeal of "the mind's energetic and simultaneous action upon and towards" whatever new ideas are presented to it. Ronald Crane, in fact, made the argument for coherent multiplicity of method at roughly the same time that Wellek and Warren made theirs. For Crane,

> Literary criticism is not, and never has been, a single discipline, to which successive writers have made partial and never wholly satisfactory contributions, but rather a collection of distinct and more or less incommensurable "frameworks" or "languages," within any one of which a question like that of poetic structure necessarily takes on a different meaning and receives a different kind of answer from the meaning it has and the kind of answer it is properly given in any of the rival critical languages in which it is discussed.[15]

Crane regards this "pluralistic view of critical languages" as crucially distinct from mere relativism, for "critical approaches of the most diverse sorts can coexist without implying either contradiction or inconsistency."[16] He also makes it clear that he does not wish to imply "that there are no general standards for distinguishing the better from the worse in the performances of critics or for making comparative valuations among the different existing languages of criticism."[17] But if we are to locate a single position outside of all other positions that enables us to regard each local language as a local language, we are well on our way toward a domain that is as appealing and as problematic as the one that literary theory initially sought to occupy, being somehow both generally applicable and generally above the fray. But that was precisely what Wellek and Warren warned us against when they argued for an organon of approaches rather than a single synthesis or summative combination of methods. The recurringly advocated alternative to global but deterministic theory is that of relating illuminatingly a variety of modes of inquiry.

The very term "pluralism" that Crane invokes invites us, of course, to ponder whether the appeal to ultimate unity is simply strategically deferred or more definitively acknowledged as either counterproductive or unachievable. For the rise and fall of literary theory inevitably raises the question of whether an excessive investment in single theories might be prevented by constructing, for example, an appropriately regulative theory of theory construction or, alternatively, a regulative theory of theory use. Or would such steps to govern pluralistic inquiry result not so much in the resolution of problems confronting literary theory as in their mere removal from one location to another?

The potential for resistance to mechanical movement from presupposition to conclusion that is provided by multiple methodologies is evident enough, as competing presuppositions are more likely to promote creative inquiry than to produce mechanical illustration. But the potential for creative inquiry is also accompanied by the possibility of generating merely relativistic perspectivism, in which interpretive ducks and rabbits are left to coexist along with myriad alternative kinds of favored fauna. Preventing pluralism of method from generating merely relativistic conclusions is no easy task, and one that is rendered even more difficult by Booth's recognition that a review of pluralistic practices and procedures itself reveals not so much a single understanding of pluralism as a "rivalry among pluralisms."[18] Booth tentatively explores the viability of the term "polymethodism" before conceding that "pluralism" is too entrenched to be avoided, however uncertain its implications.[19] But like Wellek and Warren before him and Graff and others after him he settles for invoking the principle of productively interacting methodologies rather than trying to provide it with a technically defined status.

These tentative excursions beyond the narrow confines of literary study and toward larger informative contexts become increasingly necessary steps if we are to make the most of the recognition that the diseases that undermined the health of literary theory are not unique to that project and are consequently curable only if we situate them in a much wider historical and methodological context. For the question that follows upon the questioning of literary theory for mechanically rediscovering its presuppositions in its conclusions is the puzzling question of how we can deploy theory as a means of discovery, in effect, how we can deploy theory to discover what it does not presuppose. And if we were to do that successfully, would we not, in effect, be falsifying any theory so deployed? Such questions begin to bring to the surface unexamined presuppositions about the nature and function of theory that a wider historical perspective will help clarify and refine, and their emergence in literary studies in the context of mechanical monisms, loosely related pluralisms, and unproductive relativisms effectively returns us to issues of large consequence that go back a very long way indeed. And the link between their reemergence in literary studies and in other modern disciplines is provided by the much remarked "linguistic turn" in a variety of disciplines in the twentieth century.[20]

The linguistic turn has often taken as its point of departure the Saussurean linguistics that emerged from the classroom lectures of Ferdinand de Saussure in the first decade of the twentieth century. Despite the radical steps taken by Saussure in shifting disciplinary priority from diachronic to synchronic perspectives, the linguistic turn in literary studies that eventually followed involved, in many ways, a return to unresolved historical issues in the philological approaches to literature that preceded the heyday of the [old] historicists.

And these philological issues themselves recapitulated arguments that go back to the earliest recorded debates about the structure and function of language.

There is, in effect, a continuum of debate that runs from ancient arguments over whether the world is one or many, through classical disagreements about whether language invokes a natural monism or implies a conventional chaos; Renaissance arguments over the relationship between fixity and change in a variety of key contexts; eighteenth-century arguments about the relationship between order and disorder; modern interest in the competing claims of structuralism and poststructuralism; contemporary cultural debate about the relative claims of similarity and difference in deploying the politically and socially sensitive categories of culture, race, class, and gender; and current puzzlement over how we might use theory in an investigative, nondeterministic manner. And to expand the historical and disciplinary contexts within which we consider issues arising in the construction and deployment of theory is to recognize that the mechanical methodological movement from inflexible presupposition to predictable conclusion is one embedded in a network of related issues of much wider consequence and even larger concern.

When Wellek and Warren fifty years ago raised questions about the status of method in literary studies they provided a precise formulation to a persisting question about the status of method when they asked whether we read Shakespeare to understand what he has uniquely to offer us, or to recognize the presence in his work of some of the unchallenged orthodoxies of his day. The recognition that there is more of a both/and here than an either/or, that particularity and generality can be reciprocally related, serves nevertheless to raise the question of how many "ands," how many forms of generality, are appropriately at issue. For the oscillation between unsatisfactory claims that only one approach can be right and similarly unsatisfactory claims that all approaches are equally right is an oscillation that has by now wearied everyone involved. Not many are now waiting eagerly for the dazzling flight of the next methodological "skyrocket" that Booth so aptly describes. The next one is just as likely to illuminate only briefly the methodological sky before fizzling out, like all of its recent predecessors, from structuralism to poststructuralism, by way of sudden and briefly sustained enthusiasms for the explanatory potential of the works of Freud, Marx, Frye, Jung, Sartre, Barthes, Lévi-Strauss, Lacan, Foucault, Derrida, and many others. As Booth also put it twenty years ago, what we need most is not yet another methodological skyrocket, yet another new mode of singular explanation, but a better understanding of how modes function so that we can use them effectively as instruments of inquiry.[21] And this inevitably requires us to revisit some recurringly problematic issues about the relationships among literary theory, history, and criticism, and the relationship among all three of them and works of imaginative literature.

The task remains a daunting one, however, as Carl Woodring's recently published *Literature: An Embattled Profession* confirms. Having lamented, like many others, the dispersion of members of the profession into rival camps, he argues, as others have argued before him, for the importance of some form of "commonality" that can readily accommodate, without seeking to eradicate, the differences that divide the profession: "Until a better theory is built than any we have now, the eclectic is the road to take. [It] should not ignore any feasible approaches, including those I have deplored in this volume."[22] An eclectic approach, he argues, is not necessarily a relativistic one, for it "need not imply that all procedures are equal" and "there is no necessity in literary studies to choose between belief in one immutable truth . . . and belief that all propositions are equally true or untrue."[23] Paul Cantor has also recently argued in similar terms: "'One theory fits all' may be the dream of mathematics and physics, but it is the nightmare of literary criticism."[24] While singular monistic approaches provide the potential advantage of apparently being applicable to everything, they also have the disadvantage of presupposing that everything important has probably already been said. Relativistic approaches, on the other hand, effectively presuppose that no one is listening anyway. The recurring appeal of the pluralism redescribed by Woodring, Cantor, and others has always been that of apparently promoting open-minded collective inquiry.

Unfortunately, however, the necessary point of departure for a renewed consideration of pluralistic approaches is that pluralism seems regularly to promise more than it is ever able to deliver. Repeated arguments in favor of pluralism have repeatedly failed to establish it as a viable mode of intellectual inquiry. Indeed, pluralism has even become the focus of accusations in recent years that, when it is not just a disguised form of relativism, it is a dangerously deceptive form of dogmatism and intolerance. But these arguments, too, are recurring steps in a lengthy historical process. No matter how persistent the claims for some productive intellectual position between the crude alternatives of monism and relativism, again and again over the centuries the monists and relativists have squared up for yet another confrontation, of which today's culture wars are simply the latest unhappy version. A key question about the current state of affairs, in which pluralism struggles to make headway against polarization, is thus not so much how did we arrive where we are today, but why are we still here? In its tendency to generate a relativism of successive monisms, literary theory, in effect, displays symptoms of problems with much broader intellectual implication and much longer historical relevance.

In historical terms, what we keep encountering is a recurring set of intellectual problems that emerge in related ways in different centuries and different disciplines. If we are to restore the viability of theoretical inquiry, what is needed is not a historically causal analysis of the emergence of particular theorists or theories but a case-by-case comparison of the recurring shape of theoretical arguments that repeatedly reach toward new terrain but, as often as not, relapse into the same historical dilemmas. The focus of interest is thus less upon the idiosyncratic historical circumstances of each theorist's encounter with recurring dilemmas than upon the implications of their widespread recurrence and upon the possibility of our moving beyond them.

To return in this larger historical and methodological context to the question of whether theory failed us or we failed theory is ultimately to ask not just what theory can do for us but also what we need to do for theory. To answer such a question we will need to reconsider in that larger context the nature and function of theory, which has so far served largely to recapitulate rather than resolve recurring historical dilemmas. Efforts to characterize a nondeterministic deployment of theory necessarily involve a clarification of the status of the several voices of theory, their relationship to other voices, notably those of historians and critics, and, in effect, the construction of a pluralistic investigative picture or pictures within which theory might more advantageously be positioned.

Such a procedure requires first of all, however, an understanding of how we might construct a nondeterministic and nonrelativistic big picture of pluralistic thinking that will resist its recurring collapse into an unacknowledged monism or a helpless relativism. The route forward does not necessarily involve the construction of a theory of theories or of a master theory of pluralism, both of which would be more likely to relocate than resolve current problems with literary theory. The alternative is a series of case studies, some of them lengthy, that will serve to juxtapose some of the illuminating but impoverished pictures of pluralism that have intermittently emerged as major theories in linguistics, literary studies, and elsewhere have developed, and in doing so have moved from initial formulations through subsequent deployment to consequent reconsiderations. Theories in such a context have their own historicity and instrumentality, each regularly taking on a variety of forms rather than achieving final and finished formulation. This pattern, it should be noted, is of no small consequence, for if we are to use theory as a means of discovery we must learn how to deploy it as a means of traveling with it beyond what it initially presupposes, and this, we might suspect, will require that theory, too, must somehow remain in motion. As case studies regularly reveal, the life of a theory is a topic worthy of consideration well beyond the narrow parameters of "rags to riches to routine."

What this book thus seeks to provide for literary theory is a regulative but open-ended big picture of pluralistic inquiry by constructing a conversation among disparate voices otherwise separated by historical time, cultural space, and disciplinary discourses. To approach the process of picture-building in this way is to acknowledge and confront one of the recurring challenges of pluralism (how to relate frames of reference without thereby creating a larger unified and inclusive frame that effectively subsumes all the others) and also to clarify one of its essential goals: to promote thinking across and not just within discrete frames of reference. If one of the recurring appeals of pluralism and also one of its recurring challenges is to demonstrate how we can advantageously think across and not just within various frames of reference, an inquiry into the viability of pluralistic thinking would not be well served by constructing a single frame of reference for it, by advocating a privileged version of it, or by incorporating into it an over-restricted set of voices. The picture-building must, in effect, be open-ended, bringing disparate voices into productive conjunction as a means of generating guidelines rather than rules for the further interaction of such voices.

This process of pluralistic picturing is not, however, merely methodological. As the widening of the context of investigation steadily reveals, there is much about literature as a linguistic construction that raises questions internal as well as external to literature about the relationship between unity and variety in each work and each genre, between fixity and change in their transmission, between belief and skepticism in their reception, and between order and disorder in their overall construction. Lentricchia would have been right to argue that there is a *potential* conflict between the uniqueness of major works of literature and any generality of approach that might characterize disciplinary thinking. But the actualization of the potential collision may be a consequence of an impoverished understanding of the complex and interactive nature of disciplinary inquiry. If we extend a pluralistic mode of inquiry to include not just theorists, historians, and critics, but also authors of literary works, we might well begin to rediscover what the profession briefly disdained or temporarily forgot: that those who exercise literary imagination in producing works of literature and those who exercise it in responding to works of literature have something useful to learn from each other.

The linguistic turn promoted by a less than adequate understanding of Saussure's work has helped precipitate this reciprocal isolation by promoting a significant shift in linguistic focus away from the literary works that attracted philologists and toward the spoken language and the process of speaking.[25] This was an important and necessary step for the discipline of linguistics, but it encouraged many subsequent linguists to reinvest in a theory of meaning based upon names, reference, and objects, in spite of Saussure's effectively discrediting such assumptions. The "linguistic turn" inadvertently promoted a return to longstanding concerns about the relationship between linguistic freedom and necessity, effectively reactivating some repeatedly discredited "common sense" assumptions about the relationships between word and world. And it is this set of assumptions that has provided the single most important thread that links the centuries-old conflicts between those of monistic and those of relativistic dispositions. The route taken by literary studies influenced by this linguistic turn is thus a route much traveled in centuries past, and literary theory has followed an equivalent path. Even those belatedly inclined to remind us that linguistic categories are social constructions oscillate between regarding this as confirmation (a) that categories are simply invented and therefore subject to relativistic reinvention or (b) that they are socially "given" and therefore unchangeable (except by social revolution).

Those inclined to ponder pluralistic alternatives and to envisage a conventionally controllable mode of linguistic multiplicity could do worse than seek recurring solace in Lily Briscoe's moment of culminating but fleeting recognition at the end of Virginia Woolf's *To the Lighthouse,* in which configurational reordering rather than referential pointing seems to produce illuminating relationships between the worlds of sight and sound.

> Quickly, as if she were recalled by something over there, she turned to her canvas. There it was—her picture. Yes, with all its green and blues, its lines running up and across, its attempt at something. . . . With a sudden intensity, as if she saw it clear for a second, she drew a line there, in the centre. It was done; it was finished. Yes, she thought, laying down her brush in extreme fatigue, I have had my vision.[26]

Like the "odd-shaped triangular shadow" thrown earlier on the scene by someone passing by, the line "altered the composition of the picture" in ways that reconfigured the relationship of its many parts, and the relationships of the many personalities with whom she simultaneously struggles.[27] In the esthetics of fleeting everyday experience Woolf and Briscoe locate a more illuminating relationship between word and world than any that can be captured by a reference theory of meaning, a deterministic theory of literature, or a politics of prejudicial presupposition. For pluralists, likewise, order and disorder, fixity and change, generality and particularity, convention and invention, esthetics and pragmatics, and skepticism and belief are not positioned as mutually exclusive concepts, or as a set of unrelated pairs, but as pieces on a board, which, in conjunction with many others, can be variously related and illuminatingly rearranged.

For the authors as well as the critics of works of literature, small changes of formulation can thus often have disproportionately large consequences. The literary imagination of those responding to works of literature must be no less flexible than the literary imagination of those who create it, and if literary theory is to serve us better than it has done so far, we must serve it better by understanding how to deploy it as a flexible instrument of inquiry, an instrument productively employed, in Newman's phrase, "in the mind's energetic and simultaneous action upon and towards" the new ideas it puts at our disposal. But whatever the appeal of such an approach to literary inquiry, it has proven strongly resistant to practical application, political acceptability, and institutional viability.

Though many have come to recognize the dangers of what Foucault calls "totalitarian theories"[28] and what others have invoked as privileged ideas, master tropes, universal methods, or ideological commitments, it is much less clear what the operational consequences are of Woodring's assertion that "there is no necessity in literary studies to choose between belief in one immutable truth . . . and belief that all propositions are equally true or untrue."[29] The attractiveness of some mode of controlled multiple thinking is a case more easily made than one that convincingly establishes its nondeterministic nonrelativistic viability. It would be misleading to try to deploy pluralism as a metaphysical concept, to view it, as the pedantic Casaubon might put it, as a "key to all mythologies,"[30] but some sophisticated conceptual awareness of its potential is needed if we are to position ourselves operationally between the seductive simplicities of monistic dogmatism and relativistic skepticism.

With the theory movement in literary studies having so far served more to illustrate than to resolve the problems that fueled enthusiasm for it, the challenges confronting the discipline remain much as Wellek and Warren described them fifty years ago:

> After all, we are only beginning to learn how to analyze a work of art in its integrity; we are still very clumsy in our methods, and their basis in theory is still constantly

> shifting. Thus, much is before us. . . . [Nevertheless] *a clear consciousness of a scheme of relationships between methods* is in itself a remedy against mental confusion, even though the individual may elect to combine several methods.[31] (my emphasis)

The status of methods, of their multiplicity, and of their relationships remains as problematic as ever and likewise the status of literary theory and the disciplinary viability of pluralistic inquiry.

Since the Renaissance ushered in its obsessions with time and change we have become steadily more comfortable with the notion that nothing lasts forever, locally or globally. But we are much less comfortable with the notion that nothing extends conceptually over everything, no matter how widely or narrowly we construct the frame. And if we are to enhance our expertise in conducting inquiry in such constrained temporal and spatial terms, we need not only to situate these issues in the context of the modern "linguistic turn" that has affected so many disciplines but also to situate that modern linguistic turn in the context of a historical return to unresolved issues in the discipline of linguistics of large and persisting consequence—not the least of which is its own tendency to oscillate between several of the polarities that continue to afflict literary studies.

Introduction

When Gustav Bergmann remarked that philosophy in the modern era had taken a "linguistic turn," he used a phrase that might be much more widely applied.[1] Whether we take it to imply an increased interest in language or an increased interest in linguistics (the science of language) is not, from case to case, as important as the general acknowledgment of a significant shift of attention. Language and linguistics moved in the twentieth century to the center of intellectual and aesthetic concerns. A steadily developing interest in humanity as a sign-using species enabled linguistic methodology to invade a variety of disciplines in the social sciences and the humanities. In literary studies in particular, successive fascinations with new critical hermeneutics, structuralist codes, deconstructive chasms, and discourse hybrids have kept interest in the nature of language at the center of disciplinary attention. Literary theory, indeed, has become inextricably intertwined with linguistic theory, and the problematic nature of sign systems has become a matter of ongoing, if not always rewarding, discussion and debate, with often confusing consequences.

The linguistic turn has been greeted in literary studies, as elsewhere, with alternating enthusiasm and dismay, and these reactions have been directly related to recurring struggles in the discipline to establish appropriate relationships among theory, history, and criticism, and between all three of them and ideology. Arguments about those relationships have been strongly affected by the increased attention to the problematics of language, but rather than being thereby resolved they have, if anything, been more fiercely renewed. From the point of view of academic critics, for example, if the New Critics, with their close scrutiny of linguistic structures, once earned congratulations for having rescued the discipline from the clutches of the historians, they then seemed to be subject to rebuke for having helped deliver it into the hands of the theorists. Situated in that once promising theoretical context, acts of interpretation developed an alarming propensity to become either predictable or indeterminate, or, in more recent years, with the advent of deconstruction, predictably indeterminate. Consequently, those struggling to keep literature at the center of literary studies have found themselves engaged in a defensive reaction that is now as much opposed to (disabling) theory as it once was to (disabling) history, without a clear understanding of alternatives.

The historicism that brought historical evidence into disrepute has a contemporary theoretical analogue in prominent versions of cultural studies, which confront literary studies with many of the same arguments. A broadly defined cultural context, characterized in terms of the political, social, and psychological forces that generate culture, is often deployed to dictate what is important about literary texts, so that one text serves as well as another, and literary texts are no more important than, nor even easily distinguishable from, other cultural documents, events, and processes. The context of cultural production writ large is allowed to dictate the significant parameters of artistic creativity and reader interest, just as the historicist version of specifically characterized eras did in its turn. With many cultural critics currently displaying an apparently inexhaustible readiness to illustrate a small set of presuppositions about race, class, gender, imperialism, and ethnicity in an indefinite set of cultural texts and cultural contexts, the contemporary clash between proponents of literary studies and proponents of cultural studies often recapitulates that between the New Critics and the earlier historicists.[2] In both cases the claim that literary texts have a special status and display an open set of interests is positioned against the claim that literary texts are indistinguishable from other cultural documents which register along with them a closed set of cultural conditions.

With the benefit of hindsight, of course, a consensus has developed that history, however problematic, is indispensable and that what the New Critics were really opposing was not history in general but a particular kind and a particular use of history (what we might now characterize as old historicism). Such a use of history reduced literary texts to illustrations of beliefs derived from elsewhere, and an abandonment of that use of history has enabled new historicists to claim, persuasively or otherwise, that their historical methods can facilitate rather than dominate literary criticism. The moment has arrived when the hegemonic claims of literary theory require adjustment in a similar way. The issue is not whether theory is needed, but whether it is possible to locate a particular kind and a particular use of theory that might also facilitate rather than dominate literary and cultural criticism.

In the broadest terms resistance to history and resistance to theory emerge when their presuppositions threaten to become not only necessary points of departure but also unavoidable destinations. In the context of disciplinary procedures, it matters little whether the set of convictions to be illustrated derives from a period construct, a political agenda, a religious commitment, or a theoretical position. If critics with an initial interest in such things as mythic archetypes, psychological neuroses, class constructions, gender stereotypes, structuralist oppositions, poststructuralist labyrinths, or intercultural conflicts simply locate in literary texts what has been presupposed, their activities serve primarily to renew a familiar discussion about whether we read to illustrate and confirm what we already believe or whether we read with an openness to the possibility of new belief. Lentricchia has characterized the former at its worst: "Tell me your theory and I'll tell you in advance what you'll say about any work of literature, especially those you haven't read."[3]

The recurring question is whether modes of investigation can offer not just a ground upon which to stand but a point of departure from which to proceed. How do we enable them to function as controlled means of discovery rather than as routine modes of confirmation? In particular, how can they help us locate the unexpected and not just rediscover what we presume in advance to be there? And how do we encourage people to use theory in particular and methodology in general in this more creative and less predictable manner? And then, in turn, how do we prevent such creative thinking from expanding into the arbitrary, resulting in difficult questions about the relative authority of critics and authors, and even more difficult ones about relativism itself?

Though there are certainly many positive examples of theoretically informed critical practice, the linguistic turn that literary inquiry did in fact take makes these questions difficult to answer in general theoretical terms. A version of language that was recovered from the lectures of Saussure, reinforced by subsequent developments in linguistics, extended by application in other disciplines, and reinforced by a variety of political imperatives has hampered our ability to think productively about theory as a useful means of discovering the unexpected. Even a theory like deconstruction whose goal was often to locate the unexpected soon began to produce a curiously predictable version of the unexpected. To restore our capacities in this regard we need to retrace our steps so that we can reconsider widespread presuppositions about the nature of language, theory, history, and criticism, and about their collective role in the study of literature in particular and culture in general.

Retracing our steps is particularly important, for theory, too, has its history and it makes no more sense to oppose theory to history than to oppose criticism to history. Like other modes of inquiry, theory, too, relies on evolving modes of discourse that have their own historical development, and in that evolving pattern, the questions raised by deconstruction are, in their own way, every bit as familiar as those raised by cultural studies. Just as important, however, is the recognition that successive enthusiasms for first deconstruction and then cultural studies are enthusiasms that recapitulate the discipline's tendency to oscillate between well-established alternatives: a close-reading emphasis upon the idiosyncratic texture of individual texts and a wide-ranging invocation of the claims of dominant cultural/historical contexts. A generation ago, as noted above, the alternatives were framed in such questions as, "Do we read Shakespeare because he is the most unusual writer of his time or because he is the most characteristic?" Though it was apparent then, as it is apparent now, that an inability to reconcile these two claims severely handicaps disciplinary inquiry, the discipline continues to oscillate between, rather than reconcile, the competing claims of generality and singularity, unity and variety, order and disorder, fixity and change. To retrace the path that the discipline has taken is, in effect, to put ourselves in a position to consider other paths it might have taken and indeed might still take.[4]

We should not overlook the fact that the reductive use of methodologies has long been a concern of practitioners in the discipline, who, having identified the problem as one of limited and limiting contextualization, have often sought to address it by expanding the contexts invoked in literary study. Although Graff is right to argue that the discipline's failure to bring history and criticism into fruitful alignment is symptomatic of "unresolved institutional tensions,"[5] it is also true that these tensions in turn reflect the older and larger linguistic problem of relating meaning to context in some consistent and persuasive manner. When theory is added to the brew it simply replicates the problem in another form, for it is precisely the selection of context that history and theory have both been asked to justify. But the oddity here is that historians, critics, and theorists regularly succumb to the same temptation even as they make sustained and sophisticated efforts to avoid doing so. For what keeps happening in each of the three domains is that attempts to avoid limiting contextualization by expanding the range of invoked contexts leads inexorably to claims to the authority of some newly established context, which quickly becomes, in its own way, as limiting and as ideologically charged as the context initially transcended. The result is a series of historical (re)contextualizations with competing claims to comprehensive applicability.

It is useful to recognize the insidious nature of this process in the three domains of history, criticism, and theory as each achieved a period of ascendance in the discipline. For it then becomes abundantly clear that the constant reemergence of monistic procedures is not just a consequence of the monistic inclinations that Graff so persuasively describes. The multiplicity of monisms has much larger implications. The standard critique of old historicism, for example, that helped give rise to new criticism, the theory movement, and, eventually, the new historicism, was that history so conceived required us to accept as coherent and comprehensive such reductive categories as the Elizabethan world picture and the medieval mind. This limited and limiting use of history served for a while to bring historical evidence into general disrepute, but the new historicism has sought to revive the claims to privilege of historical discourse by diversifying the historical contexts invoked and extending the range of historically important voices. In interpretive practice, however, as Pechter has so persuasively argued, this multiplication of historical information has tended to generate not new flexibility in the use of historical information but new forms of reductive contextualization that display localized political conflicts rather than a more general exchange among competing historical voices.[6] The new historicism thus begins to look like the old historicism multiplied many times rather than a new approach to the use of historical information. Instead of being resolved, the problem of contextual petrification is supplemented by the problem of contextual proliferation, and the odd result is that relativism of multiplying monisms that has become such a feature of the discipline writ large. And this promotion of relativistic monisms is as characteristic of critics and theorists as it is of historians.

If we look more closely at the modern evolution of modes of critical discourse, we encounter similar attempts to resist premature hermeneutic closure by seeking out new modes of contextualization, but with similar results. Modern critics have regularly turned toward other disciplines for new methodological procedures, larger contexts, and wider professional alliances. From the field of psychology, Freudian, Jungian, and Lacanian analyses of literature have emerged, from sociology Marxian analysis, from anthropology mythological analysis, from linguistics structural analysis, and so on. The failure of such external alliances to provide the prelude to more extensive agreement within the discipline derives largely from the fact that the various modes of contextualization seemed equally persuasive in their claims to interpretive privilege. Different modes of critical discourse generated different interpretations and, lacking effective means of adjudicating competing claims, practitioners were satisfied enough by the practical results of their own interpretive procedures to feel that no further proof was needed. Not yet fully alerted to the dangers of hermeneutic circularity, critical camps of various kinds lapsed into premature conviction about the validity and comprehensiveness of their own procedures. But we should bear in mind that such critical conviction emerged from an exploration of different terrain and did not, by and large, exemplify indifference to the problem of limited contextualization. As Hyman remarked in mid-century, modern criticism could be roughly described as "the organized use of non-literary techniques and bodies of knowledge to obtain insights into literature."[7]

The pursuit of external alliances nevertheless failed to provide an authoritative basis for a new internal coherence for the discipline, and those engaged in wider exploration ended up methodologically in the same position as those who did not: defending as adequate a contextualizing procedure that others saw as indefensibly narrow. The gains in procedural rigor that were often achieved as a consequence of these excursions into foreign terrain were vitiated by a general inability to address the implications of their collective multiplicity. The discipline began to settle for a pattern of local homogeneity and larger heterogeneity as, for conservatives and radicals alike, conviction and consensus became increasingly irreconcilable. It is in this context, by no means one of ignorance, inflexibility, or indifference, that each new mode of criticism became vulnerable to the temptation to become, as Graff so devastatingly argues, one of the carefully "self-protected methodologies, fully insured against error, backed by its own Fieldspeak, its own journals, conferences, and old-boy/old-girl network, and immune to criticism from outsiders."[8] For those entering the profession in the 1960s and 1970s, during the rise to prominence of literary theory, professional choice largely consisted in adopting and defending one of the major monistic methodologies or in making do with a relativistic eclecticism that sought to make stable wholes out of incommensurate parts.

It is thus not surprising that the 1970s saw a rapidly rising interest in literary theory. As a potential means of examining and adjudicating the contrasting claims of the competing voices of literary studies, literary theory offered some hope to those who felt the need to reconnect conviction with persuasion, to resolve the twin problems of contextual petrification and proliferation, and thus to provide the profession with a more fruitful form of coherence. Ironically enough, however, emerging modes of theoretical discourse served more to replicate than to resolve the problems exemplified in historical and critical discourse, and it too began to display the pattern of local homogeneity and larger heterogeneity. Literary theory soon became a means for each of the competing forms of critical discourse to advance its own claims, rather than a means by which the undecided might weigh or reconcile competing claims.

In pursuit of a voice of its own, literary theory thus began, ironically enough, to follow the example of literary criticism by widening its context of investigation and borrowing techniques and insights from other disciplines, particularly those advanced by European intellectuals from Nietzsche to Derrida. The consequence of this procedure for theorists was much the same as for critics, and it served not so much to reconcile existing divisions in the field but to multiply them. Theories proliferated and it quickly became apparent that literary theory had as much difficulty with evaluating competing forms of critical theory as it had with evaluating competing forms of critical or historical practice. Though theorists had once been people with a general interest in theories, there emerged a generation of theorists largely committed to single theories and to applying them with the enthusiasm and conviction that have now brought theory into disrepute.

In this situation of ever proliferating modes of critical, theoretical, and historical discourse, it seems logical enough that theoretical arguments would be advanced to make a virtue of necessity, to accept that conviction and consensus are necessarily opposed, and to reject the role of literary criticism, literary theory, and literary history as necessarily one of promoting more authoritative means of contextualizing literary texts. The burgeoning theory industry thus began to reject the integrative role it could no longer justify, to question the value of attempts to reconcile the claims of competing forms of criticism, and with deconstruction in the vanguard, to claim its virtues lay less in its larger instrumentality than in its relativistic local autonomy. The impulse to invoke new contexts in the expectation that consensus might thus be achievable was largely replaced by a self-validating claim to the intrinsic virtue of invoking new contexts. And it is but a small step from there to arguing that the selection of context is ultimately a self-serving matter of political interest and group empowerment.

Rorty and others have argued that literary theory has aligned itself with exploratory work in other disciplines in order to form a new genre of (textual) theory whose function Culler believes is "to make strange the familiar and to make readers conceive of their own thinking, behavior, and institutions in new ways."[9] But this emphasis on novelty generated in practice both more contextual monisms and more disciplinary skepticism, for the recurring goal here has not been one of promoting new means of reconciling differences but cf promoting further and irreducible multiplicity. The emphasis has been upon epistemological challenge, institutional disruption, and divisive novelty rather than upon a novelty that promotes the examination of belief, the consolidation of inquiry, or the extension of knowledge. Though there is no necessary reason for literary theory to pursue innovation to the exclusion of consolidation and, indeed, some reason to doubt the value of the former if it does not lead to the latter, the ease with which the term deconstruction achieved prominence aptly signaled the temper of the times.[10] And such has been the temper of the times that political imperatives and theoretical exigencies have combined to enable urgent claims to novelty to have the effect of making the old seem beyond justification and the new beyond critique, a combination with predictable consequences. Washington's perceptive, though often overemphatic, analysis of the "irregular union" between deconstruction, Marxism, and feminism, for example, provides a series of instances of ideological conviction picturing itself as a liberating alternative while establishing itself in practice as a new form of irreducible difference and unreflecting dogmatism.[11] The significant issue here is that the pursuit of novelty in such cases rapidly ceased, ironically enough, to be the pursuit of unexpected novelty, for narratives of oppression and liberation quickly acquired a characteristic shape. For better or worse, the pursuit of predictable novelty for political advantage has become the popular (and, paradoxically conventional) response to many real or imagined forms of oppression, both within the academy and without.

Given the pressing importance of many of these social concerns and the urgent problems of injustice needing to be addressed, their often inadequate politicization is unfortunate. But, whatever the political merits of such procedures, from a theoretical point of view they seem unpromising, at best. An adequate response to the oppressively monistic inclinations of others must go beyond that of inventing a newly oppressive monism of your own. More than a generation ago, Lionel Trilling rightly warned literary studies of the ease with which innovative ideas degenerate into unreflecting ideology, but no theorist today can afford to address monistic inclinations alone as the central cultural problem.[12] The disciplinary fascination with new techniques, the consequent proliferation of modes of interpretation, the increased suspicion of consensus as a useful goal, and a persisting interest in the problematics of language have all served to reinforce the claims of a relativism that sits uneasily alongside the recurring monistic practice of illustrated presupposition. As the development of historical, critical, and theoretical modes of discourse confirms, the key problem is the tendency of literary inquiry to oscillate uncontrollably between the reductive voices of monistic necessity and the equally reductive voices of skeptical relativism. As the discipline evolves, the problem simply migrates from one vocabulary to another, as Gandhi's positioning of contemporary postcolonial theory illustrates:

> Postcolonialism is caught between the politics of structure and totality on the one hand, and the politics of the fragment on the other. This is one way of suggesting that postcolonial theory is situated somewhere in the interstices between Marxism and postmodernism/poststructuralism. It is, in a sense, but one of the many discursive fields upon which the mutual antagonism between these competing bodies of thought is played out. Seen as such, postcolonialism shifts the scene of this long-standing contestation to the so-called "third world."[13]

It is in the context of these various disciplinary settings that renewed claims for the value of a conceptual pluralism must be situated, a pluralism whose scale of engagement is smaller than that of totality and larger than that of a fragment. This is not, of course, the soft pluralism of laissez-faire eclecticism, but the pluralism that seeks to restore viability to theory, history, and criticism by opposing their tendency to allow debate over appropriate contextualization to slide into either ideological monism or radical relativism. Thus Booth, seeking to keep radical relativism at bay, is moved to argue that "we do not lose our freedom by molding our minds in shapes established by others. We find it there."[14] Indeed, we may well do so, but the picture that satisfactorily relates inherited community constraint to enhanced individual freedom has proved persistently elusive, as Rorty's separation of private theorizing from public engagement illustrates.[15] And the difficulties the pluralist confronts, as Booth has pointed out, are most clearly registered in the apparent inconsistency between two imperatives: that of avoiding monism by affirming the irreducible variety of critical modes, and that of avoiding relativism by insisting that critical modes can interact in a manner that enables us to think productively across frames of reference and not just within them.

Our recurring inability to establish complementary relationships among history, criticism, and theory have culminated in the recognition that literary theory in its current forms seems more likely to exemplify the profession's problems than to resolve them. There is therefore good reason to ask whether a constrained pluralism, well informed about scholarship, language, and history, would be any more able to avoid the contextualizing problems exemplified in theory's oscillation between the pursuit of privileged truth and the promotion of uncontrolled signification. Though Graff is right to argue that these trends are, to some extent, the unexpected consequences of a limited form of institutional adaptability, the oscillations in literary theory between univocal authority and multivocal anarchy have another set of analogues which invoke a long and primarily linguistic history. The modern linguistic turn in literary studies marks, in its own way, a revival of longstanding concerns about the relationship between linguistic freedom and necessity, whose nature we would do well to reconsider in the context of enabling and disabling contextualization.

Though literary theory has taken many forms in the modern era and has emerged from many sources, the linguistic turn in the discipline has had major consequences for all of them. It has directly influenced in both fortunate and unfortunate ways what we expect a theory to do and be, and it has achieved this by directly influencing what we expect a language to do and be. It is, of course, no more likely that we can manage without a theory of language than that we can do without an understanding of history. Though Pavel has made an impressive case against the development of a master narrative from linguistic theory, a linguistic turn, in the context of modern thought, was probably unavoidable.[16] But what is just as important is that the particular linguistic turn that was taken was by no means unavoidable, for it was not the only one available. Literary studies might well have developed in other directions as a consequence of increased interest in language, directions that might have enabled us to ward off the excesses of structuralism and poststructuralism, avoid the premature rejection of history, resist the tendency to oppose generality to particularity, and adopt a very different notion of the potential role of theory in the discipline.

The linguistic turn in philosophy, as Rorty describes it, provides an instructive example for anyone pondering the implications of renewed interest in language in other disciplines: "The point about the so-called 'linguistic turn' in recent philosophy is supposed to be that whereas we once thought, with Aristotle, that necessity came from things, and later thought with Kant that it came from the structure of our minds, we now know that it comes from language. And since philosophy must seek the necessary, philosophy must become linguistic."[17] This emphasis on necessity is of some importance, for it both energizes and distorts the emerging linguistic perspective and the expectations about theory that accompany it. The notion that language is not so much a means of naming an independent world but of organizing the world of our experience is one that has had an increasing impact on western thought since Herder began to speculate in the eighteenth century about cultural and historical relativism. When Sapir and Whorf in this century argued in favor of a more specific linguistic relativity principle, they reinforced a growing belief that particular languages not only enable us to establish knowledge but also help constitute that knowledge and govern its very nature. As Sapir put it: "The fact of the matter is that the 'real world' is to a large extent unconsciously built up on the language habits of the group. No two languages are ever sufficiently similar to be considered as representing the same social reality. The worlds in which different societies live are distinct worlds, not merely the same world with different labels attached."[18] Wittgenstein had earlier claimed that "the limits of my language mean the limits of my world,"[19] and Cassirer had written persuasively about the instrumental status of concepts and categories that we too readily assume to be natural.[20] In ways whose larger implications are becoming ever more pressingly apparent, cultural relativism and cultural necessity are linked together in the context of an incipient linguistic determinism. In spite of their not being natural, linguistic categories turn out somehow to be both conventional and compelling. The world as ordered by the language we inherit is the world we live in and the world we live by. Necessity, it seems, is therefore linguistic.

It might, of course, be argued that if necessity is linguistic and language is conventional, then necessity is not as compelling as might otherwise be the case. Convention, after all, must surely have emerged over time and can surely be changed. But not linguistic convention as conceived by that most influential of modern linguists Ferdinand de Saussure. Conventions, in key components of Saussure's linguistic theory, are mutually defining, systematic, and fixed. But Saussure's theory was itself historically situated and designed to address existing problems in his own discipline. To separate it from that context is to assume, misleadingly, a transhistorical relationship between a theory and the facts it purportedly isolates and organizes. But just such an assumption has repeatedly been made, and it is here we encounter the second issue that links the linguistic turn to an apparently inflexible necessity. If the first issue is epistemological, the second is metatheoretical—it has to do with the demands we place upon and the expectations we have of theories in general. And these demands and expectations, already current in the physical sciences, moved decisively into the social sciences and humanities from the work of Saussure and the structuralist movement that followed upon it. In the famous words of Meillet, "*langue est un système où tout se tient.*"[21]

When a modern theory characterizes its data as a system of mutually defining terms, it tends to activate a conviction that the system is fixed and that a description of the whole is essential to an understanding of any of the parts. Saussure's monosystemic approach to key aspects of language promised exhaustive description, comprehensive explanation, and complete understanding. In the face of disciplinary disorder in fields as diverse as linguistics, aesthetics, and anthropology, explanatory order could be established to replace the apparent disorder. The well-known claims of Lévi-Strauss in anthropology serve to summarize the procedure and exemplify the hopes: "The customs of a community, taken as a whole, always have a particular style and are reducible to systems. I am of the opinion that the number of such systems is not unlimited and that . . . human societies, like individuals, never create absolutely, but merely choose certain combinations from an ideal repertoire that it should be possible to define."[22]

The possibility of locating the comprehensive order that underlies apparent disorder has extensive appeal, particularly to those working in the social sciences and in various branches of cultural criticism, and for a while it seemed axiomatic that theorists in every field of inquiry, structuralist or otherwise, should not only try to discover such underlying order but also succeed in doing so if they were to be taken seriously. But the counterarguments are by now equally well known. The monosystemic structuralist approach to order has difficulty accounting for human responsibility, individual creativity, and historical change, indeed for anything that is not already included in the presupposed system. Explanatory order is sustained not by its generality and capacity to include but by its readiness to exclude what it cannot accommodate. The consequent proliferation of structuralist ordering systems provoked an inevitable reaction: a theoretical fascination with the virtues of contingency and disorder.

In poststructuralist theory the emphasis has been on contingency, variability, diversity, and change, but so much so that durable forms of order become difficult to establish or explain. As far as literary studies are concerned, poststructuralism, in effect, revived the claims of critical creativity at the expense of its claims to authority. The inevitable consequence of theory's oscillation between limiting order and enabling disorder has thus been a growing disenchantment with both theory and method, a disenchantment vividly rendered in Vickers's *Appropriating Shakespeare*.[23] With structuralism seeming to enlarge our understanding and control at significant cost to our freedom, and poststructuralism seeming to enlarge our freedom at considerable cost to our understanding and control, the fruits of order and disorder as theory conceives of them, in the aftermath of the "linguistic turn," seem evenly and unattractively divided. Though the subsequent turn toward forms of order derived from politics, ideology, and social power provides us with the potential gains of contested forms of order, the gains are quickly lost when the structures and outcomes of the contests are treated as predetermined. What is missing overall is a regulatory understanding of the reordering that is involved in historical, critical, and theoretical processes of recontextualization.

There was, of course, a time when the virtues of order seemed much less problematic. A characteristic voice of the eighteenth century, for example, would be recognized in the following encomium to order and its implications:

> There is nothing in Nature that is great and beautiful, without Rule and Order; and the more Rule and Order, and Harmony, we find in the Objects that strike our Senses, the more Worthy and Noble we esteem them. I humbly conceive that it is the same in Art, and particularly in Poetry, which ought to be an exact Imitation of Nature. . . . As Nature is Order and Rule, and Harmony in the visible World, so Reason is the very same throughout the invisible Creation. For Reason is Order, and the Result of Order. And nothing that is Irregular, as far as it is Irregular, ever was, or ever can be either Natural or Reasonable. Whatever God created, he designed it Regular.[24]

This is the voice of unqualified conviction on the issue, but it is instructive to take note of the repeated appearance in modern literature of significant disagreement not only on the relative value of order and disorder, but also on the nature of their relationship. This is not just a matter of accepting help where we can find it, but of beginning necessary attempts to review relationships among criticism, history, theory, and literature. Modern literature is itself, of course, often theoretical in nature, in terms of its themes, ideas, and techniques. It should not, perhaps, be surprising that creative writers have often weighed complicated issues well in advance of the disciplinary theorists, and it is important that theory about literature keep up with the theorizing that literature itself includes and exemplifies. One recurring concern among modern authors has, for example, been to explore rather than presuppose the advantages and disadvantages of various kinds of order and disorder, thus inviting the kinds of complex consideration that theorists have been too quick to reduce to schematic choices.

The ambivalent appeal of an all-inclusive order has, for example, been displayed in the words of Joyce's Stephen Dedalus as he considers the attractions of the spiritual life: "Gradually, as his soul was enriched with spiritual knowledge, he saw the whole world forming one vast symmetrical expression of God's power and love. . . . So entire and unquestionable was this sense of the divine meaning in all nature granted to his soul that he could scarcely understand why it was in any way necessary that he should continue to live."[25] The irony in the concluding remark suffices to remind us how a putatively productive form of order can, if excessively relied upon, become disabling—an issue also exemplified in the crowd flowing over London Bridge in Eliot's "The Waste Land" ("I had not thought death had undone so many")[26] and in the regimented Big Brother society of Orwell's *Nineteen Eighty-Four*. Modern writers have dealt similarly with disorder, indicating that it, too, can be enabling or disabling depending on its relationship to residual or emergent forms of order. In Yeats's famous lines, disorder can lead to chaos ("Things fall apart; the centre cannot hold; / Mere anarchy is loosed upon the world"),[27] but it can also lead, as it led Yeats, to the discovery of more serviceable forms of order. In Forster's *Passage to India*, on the other hand, the muddle of disordered India provides access to mysterious multiplicity and thus offers an appealing alternative to the rigid ordering of English culture. We can even find the uncertain status of both order and disorder registered within the confines of a single poem, indeed, within what is arguably the most famous poem of the twentieth century. The debilitating uniformity of the crowd flowing over London Bridge in "The Waste Land" is matched by the debilitating disorder encountered on Margate Sands where the speaker "can connect / Nothing with nothing."[28]

It quickly becomes apparent that the relative merits of order and disorder cannot be usefully debated without careful clarification of the kinds and functions of the order and disorder at issue. When Stephen Dedalus turns his steps toward his father's house and toward the disorder established there, it is important to remember the limiting spiritual order with which this diminished realm is being contrasted: "The faint sour stink of rotted cabbages came towards him from the kitchengardens on the rising ground above the river. He smiled to think that it was this disorder, the misrule and confusion of his father's house and the stagnation of vegetable life, which was to win the day in his soul."[29] For

Stephen it is not disorder in general, but "this disorder" that wins the day against the kind of order exemplified by the religious life of the Jesuits (as he conceives it). But to speak of differing forms of order and differing forms of disorder is to acknowledge the multiplicity of things we call order and the multiplicity of things we call disorder. It is also to bring into question the nature of the contrast between them. Should we, in fact, regard them as opposites or as merely opposed?[30] Only at one extreme does order assign a single place for everything, and only at the other extreme does disorder dissolve into chaos. When other kinds of contrast are involved, things are much less simple to characterize.

Without recourse to some other perspective, we can make little sense of remarks by writers as various as E. M. Forster and Tom Stoppard. Forster commented that "Viewed realistically, the past is really a series of *dis*orders, succeeding one another by discoverable laws, no doubt, . . . but disorders all the same. So that, speaking as a writer, what I hope for today is a disorder which will be more favorable to artists than is the present one . . . there have been some advantageous disorders in the past . . . and we may do something to accelerate the next one."[31] And Stoppard's characters in *Arcadia* welcome some of the recent implications of chaos theory with similar enthusiasm: "We must stir our way onward mixing as we go, disorder out of disorder into disorder. . . . The future is disorder. A door like this has cracked open five or six times since we got up on our hind legs. It's the best possible time to be alive, when almost everything you thought you knew is wrong."[32] If we allow ourselves to treat order and disorder as opposed in principle and opposite in value, we will find such comments rather confusing. But if we place order and disorder on a continuum involving various degrees and kinds of contrast, we will be less inclined to make disabling judgments about either.

This point is, in its own way, obvious enough, but it is worth elaborating because of the more important point that follows upon it. If order and disorder are not treated as opposites and alternatives but as variously related states of affairs, how are we to find our way, as critics, theorists, and historians in heterogeneous domains that include irreducibly order and disorder in both productive and unproductive relationship to each other? What is the nature of literature, theory, history, criticism, ideology, and cultural relativism in such contexts? How do they relate not only to each other but also to the many linguistic theories, not just Saussure's, that have emerged in the modern era? And is there implicit here a different linguistic turn that the discipline might have taken, one that might promote a more satisfactory mode of contextualization than those of unfettered critical freedom and inflexible critical necessity?

It is the function of this book to shed some light on such matters and to provide an indication of another linguistic turn the literary discipline might have taken, one in which order and disorder, far from being viewed as mutually opposed, are regarded as both interdependent and mutually informing. This does not necessarily lead us to adopt the basic tenets of the oddly named chaos theory, but it does require us to recognize that theory in such contexts must play a more complicated role than that of seeking to locate underlying order or of trying to expose underlying disorder. It must help us understand how the Lévi-Strauss who argues for the importance of comprehensive systematic explanation in *Tristes Tropiques* can also confess in the same book that he has only a partial commitment to the principles and procedures implied by such general modes of explanation: "I have no aptitude for prudently cultivating a given field and gathering in the harvest year after year: I have a neolithic kind of intelligence. Like native bush fires, it sometimes sets unexplored areas alight; it may fertilize them and snatch a few crops from them, and then it moves on, leaving scorched earth in its wake."[33]

Such contradictory comments on the relative status and value of order and disorder return us to Saussure and to the linguistic turn that his work has promoted in so many disciplines. It was a turn precipitated by Saussure's apparent ability to establish order in the place of disorder, to locate explanatory perspectives in areas of puzzling complexity, to provide new and stable patterns for systematic thinking in disciplines characterized by conflict over change and weighed down by the intractable complexities of history. What stands or falls with received notions of Saussure's work is not just a particular linguistic theory, but a way of conceiving of theory and its relationship to practice that has had major and continuing consequences for literary studies, even among those who have not read a word he has written.

A return to Saussure's work will remind us that his theories were by no means as simple and programmatic as has often been thought, and a return to the larger context, both historical and modern, of linguistic theory will confirm that it has more things and other things to offer than those retrieved from a misleadingly selective reading of Saussure's seminal work.[34] Indeed, by following Saussure and others in situating the order and disorder of dialogue at the center of theoretical concerns, we can not only clarify the pluralistic issues affected by such an adjustment, but also reconsider the status of literary inquiry itself, as literary theory is repositioned in the context of many of the enthusiasms that have both promoted it and been promoted by it.

Chapter 1 Literary Theory and Linguistic Theory

Legend has it that, when the British Broadcasting Corporation resumed its television service after the Second World War, the first announcer to appear on screen (who had also been the last to appear some years before) began with the words: "As I was saying, before I was so rudely interrupted. . . ." With the decline in literary studies of deconstructive relativism and its replacement by the further contextual monisms of politicized cultural studies, a more constrained pluralism has resumed the task of trying to move the discipline forward, giving the current situation in literary studies a similar sense of restarting after interruption. Books by Booth, Scholes, Graff, Ellis, Armstrong, Damrosch, Woodring, and others have renewed attempts to reconcile creativity with control by characterizing critical pluralism as strongly constrained community inquiry and positioning it as an alternative to weakly constrained individual ingenuity on the one hand and cultural/historical/theoretical determinism on the other.[1]

To such pluralists the ability of skeptically inclined deconstructers to command attention on the basis of being relativistically interesting rather than monistically right could only be a fleeting interruption based upon misleading alternatives, for being interesting involves not just displaying figurative ingenuity but also achieving some form of persuasiveness. The latter does not necessarily involve being right, but it does mean coming publicly to terms with constraints that emerge from texts, contexts, and audiences. A reluctance to acknowledge those constraints is by no means equivalent to a freedom to ignore them, and it is helpful to no one to have complex issues involving linguistic order and disorder reduced to a simplistic choice between ideological necessity and quasi-romantic arbitrariness. The claims of generality and particularity require a more sophisticated form of reconciliation.

Although it was temporarily exhilarating for many of those committed to deconstruction to emphasize latent textual disorder as a means of promoting a process of interpretation that makes maximum room for critical creativity, even the most extreme argument in favor of multiple readings relies, as Booth points out, "on some sense of understanding that provides limits to multiplicity."[2] In avant-garde rhetoric, of course, such limits tend to be downplayed, and this can generate some confusion. In the case of deconstruction, advocates tended to emphasize the constraints that they wished to escape at the expense of those they were prepared to observe, so they purchased their iconoclasm at eventual cost to their credibility. By and large, they were more adept at theoretically distinguishing their position from that of despised monists than from that of radical skeptics. In the latter respect, however, their theorizing was not always matched by their practice, which was not entirely an exemplification of the kind of freedom their rhetoric suggested, a kind of freedom that Kant, as Booth reminds us, wryly critiqued many years ago: "The light dove, cleaving the air in her free flight, and feeling its resistance, might [well] imagine that its flight would be still easier in empty space."[3]

In practice, deconstructive ingenuity, like any other form of interpretive ingenuity, sought to balance its claims to freedom with the observance of certain regulative controls, but as the bulk of poststructuralist theorizing was directed against the various kinds of monistic foundationalism it attempted to transcend, it tended to underemphasize the procedures by which it sought to avoid being merely a radical relativism. Had it taken up the neglected task and sought to situate itself between monism and relativism, it would, of course, have been forced to portray itself in less radical terms, indeed, as an alternative attempt to occupy the terrain already claimed by pluralism.

Taking this course would, however, have put deconstruction at something of a disadvantage, for when compared to the pluralisms that preceded it and aspire to succeed it, deconstruction seems a somewhat impoverished form of pluralism. Having paid more attention to what it was against than what it was for, deconstruction tended to focus insufficiently on the significance of the constraints it acknowledged and consequently neglected to maintain their flexibility. An unfortunate result was that, although some deconstructive readings were as ingenious as the radical rhetoric would suggest, many came to seem, as several commentators quickly pointed out, rather predictable. Underacknowledged forms of control were allowed to atrophy into mechanical procedures and, ironically enough, a movement whose rhetoric made it vulnerable to charges of radical relativism managed to generate a practice vulnerable to charges of inflexible monism. As Graff put it:

> The deconstructionists' foreknowledge that all texts are allegories of their own unreadability (or that they necessarily foreground the problematic of representation, mask and reveal their rhetorical conditions of possibility, undo their claims of reference by their figurality, metaphoricity, and so forth) is made suspect by its monotonous universality of application. . . . To assume that, by some structural necessity of discourse or desire, all literature or all texts undo the logics of significations on which they operate only tends to make the revelation of that process in any particular text a foregone conclusion.[4]

This predictability, this lapse into formulaic appropriation of texts, is, ironically enough, precisely what deconstruction, and the pluralisms that preceded and succeeded it, set out to avoid. The emergence of formulaic readings from the putatively iconoclastic camp of deconstruction not only displays its limitations as a form of pluralism, but also exemplifies the recurring tendency in literary theory of rejected forms of monism to reassert themselves, even in the most unlikely places. Indeed the emergence of a dogmatic practice from deconstruction's skeptical theory provides the most spectacular example since the advent of vulgar Marxism and vulgar Freudianism of the problematic relationship between theories and theorists.[5] No matter how radical or idealistic the form of discourse, it threatens, if it is adopted as a privileged form of discourse, to lapse into a univocal interpretive method that encounters in texts only what it presupposes to be there. A predictable discovery of indeterminacy, whatever the importance of elements of indeterminacy, thus becomes as limited and limiting as any other forms of predictable discovery, including those of contemporary cultural materialism. It is just this tendency of modes of critical discourse to invite excessive commitment and thus promote programmatic procedures that prompted Booth to emphasize that the first principle of the pluralism that he derives from Crane, Burke, and Abrams is "that critical truth can never be exhausted in any one mode" of critical practice.[6] The recurring appeal of the pluralist perspective is that it recognizes and seeks to address the dangers to critical practice of unreflective monism while seeking also to avoid the alternative danger of uncontrolled relativism, but the recurring challenge is to characterize the nature of a compelling and controllable alternative.

For pluralism to make its case persuasive, it needs not only to acknowledge the coexistence of these two apparently opposed dangers, but also to clarify its intermittent recognition of their puzzling relatedness. And this turns out to be a task fraught with difficulty, for the pluralist, too, is vulnerable to their competing claims. If pluralism is to avoid being a disguised monism, it must, as Booth has argued, insist on the "*irreducible* variety of critical languages."[7] If it is to avoid being a species of radical relativism, however, it must claim that the various critical languages are not only irreconcilable but also capable of some kind of fruitful interaction with each other. The tendency of deconstruction to move back and forth between destabilizing theory and repetitive practice thus recapitulates the tendency of other forms of pluralism, and of literary studies in general, to be overcome by the insidious attractions of either relativism or monism. The example of deconstruction is salutary in this regard, however, for the movement's tendency to display not just one, but both of the vulnerabilities of pluralism underlines the peculiar relatedness of what we might have supposed to be alternative dangers. And this suggests in turn that we look more carefully at the implications of the complementary and not just contrasting relationship in literary studies between monistic necessity and relativistic arbitrariness. Renewed arguments in favor of a more constrained pluralism cannot be persuasive unless they can demonstrate means of avoiding the problems that initially generated and subsequently diminished enthusiasm for both aspects of the deconstructive movement.

It is not my purpose to add here to the series of critiques of poststructuralism, nor, in the light of their devastating culmination in Ellis's *Against Deconstruction,* does it seem necessary to do so.[8] What is of current importance is whether key limitations in deconstruction's procedures can be used to clarify general problems of pluralistic engagement in a manner that enables us to learn from previous difficulties. If we do not recognize and seek to understand the tendency of literary studies to oscillate between extremes, the demise of deconstructive relativism followed immediately by the emergence of new monisms in cultural studies will simply be the prelude to the emergence of yet another claim for unfettered critical freedom followed by yet another for privileged contextual control.

As has been widely remarked, so radical were the claims of deconstruction about the instability of language and the inevitability of misreading that they invited immediate questions about the consistency between the claims of the argument and the procedures by which it was advanced. Lengthy statements seeking to articulate and defend a position about linguistic instability seem curiously self-defeating. As this inconsistency was accompanied by unconvincing historical claims and apparent ignorance of earlier scholarship on key issues under discussion, deconstruction had serious problems to address. But these familiar problems are by no means the only points at issue. Just as important is the fact that dogmatic practice eventually emerged from skeptical theory in part because claims to a new logic encouraged proponents to dismiss rather than address counterarguments. Advocates of a putatively skeptical form of analysis were inclined, as advocates of other approaches are inclined, to require from potential practitioners a single leap of faith rather than an attitude of sustained inquiry, and this familiar procedure had in this case both predictable and less predictable results.

The success of deconstruction in attracting such support without addressing counterarguments had two important effects. One was to allow the individual voices of deconstruction to merge into a collective voice of choric conviction as claims to a new logic insulated the theory from (of all things) skeptical countervoices. The other was to turn unpersuaded commentators increasingly toward other kinds of response to the surprisingly large volume of work that the movement produced. The tendency was to widen the frame of reference by investing in sociological and institutional analyses in order to explain how a movement so widely viewed as suspect could have achieved, without apparently earning it, such a degree of prominence in the academic world. Though the intellectual and scholarly arguments against deconstruction seemed powerful enough, their initially limited effectiveness suggested to Graff that the rise and fall of deconstruction tells us more about the limiting institutional politics of literary studies than about its enabling procedures. The effect of sociological and institutional forms of analysis, however, has been to present further problems for the viability of deconstruction without establishing that even this frame of reference is, in fact, wide enough to explain just what went wrong. As we have noted, the issues that emerge in institutional and sociological analysis recapitulate issues with a much longer history, a history that suggests the linguistic nature of the further frame of reference that may yet be needed. The sociological and institutional analyses have, however, established a useful point of departure.

For Ellis the argument against deconstruction is primarily scholarly and logical, but it is in sociological terms that he registers his own puzzlement about the rise of deconstruction in the United States and its implications. Recognizing the destabilizing appeal of deconstruction in an authoritarian intellectual environment like that of France, Ellis wonders how it managed to flourish as a radically new position in the already diversified intellectual environment of the United States. Reconsidering in this light the movement's success in America, he argues that its prominence was not so much a consequence of its capacity to oppose some monolithic status quo as of its ability to give the already existing climate of multiple opinion "a new air of legitimacy."[9] Deconstructive relativism thus served initially not so much to undermine existing consensus as to confirm its absence by exploiting a widespread fascination with novelty that somehow coexists with an equally widespread suspicion of (other people's) dogmatism.

Graff explores the coexistence of dogmatism and skepticism further by arguing that, far from being a site of established authority, the morsellated literary domain in American universities has for a long time verged on chaos.[10] Its very openness to new kinds of thought not only grants all kinds of putative novelty a hearing but also makes it comparatively easy for them to acquire an institutional place. The institutional problem that deconstruction illustrates rather than resolves is thus the tendency of academic institutions to make places for competing modes of inquiry without encouraging, indeed, by discouraging, their interaction.[11] As Graff disturbingly suggests, the recurring consequence of demands from various intellectual and ideological groups that they be granted their own autonomous programs, research centers, or departments is not just that they acquire institutional status but also that they can be accommodated without being attended to.[12] And it is this institutional pattern that encourages skepticism and dogmatism to coexist rather than interact.

The indifference of proponents of deconstruction to charges of historical inaccuracy, scholarly ignorance, theoretical incoherence, and logical inconsistency is thus simply an extreme example of attitudes adopted by proponents of many modes of inquiry whose efforts to establish themselves within the academy are quickly followed by efforts to insulate themselves once the goal is achieved. In dismissing rather than addressing counterarguments, in claiming to have a logic of its own that is not answerable to the logics that preceded it or coexist with it, deconstruction seems, in this respect, as characteristic a phenomenon of the American academic world as it is, in its opposition to all kinds of authority, a phenomenon of the French avant-garde.

Recognizing the limited effectiveness of making logical arguments against a movement that claims immunity from the implications of any logic that fails to confirm it, Graff makes the institutional argument that if the academy is to flourish, it must reject this readiness to insulate modes of inquiry from each other and provide instead a context in which we can teach our differences rather than simply ignore them.[13] This is a solution very much in line with Booth's diagnosis of institutional problems in the United States. What is most urgently needed, he argues, is not yet more new modes of inquiry but a better understanding of how modes of inquiry function. In general, "we are more in need of attempts to understand than attempts to stir us up."[14] But it is by no means clear that the one will suffice without the other, nor is it clear what we do with differences once we have taught them. The strength of the pattern of institutionalized aggregation on the American academic scene derives in part from its capacity to serve the needs both of monists, whose conviction that they are right makes further argument unnecessary, and of relativists, whose suspicions about the desirability of social consensus make pursuit of it counterproductive.

This recognition can, of course, help us understand why the literary academy has become subject simultaneously to critiques that it is on the one hand monolithic and intolerant of diversity (witness the counterculture arguments of Marxists, feminists, and other cultural theorists) and on the other hand so overwhelmed by diversity that it has lost all capacity to function as a distinctive force in matters of national importance and national debate. Authority in the academy seems to coexist with kinds of anarchy that are themselves authoritarian.[15] Though there is thus good reason for Booth to argue that "we are more in need of attempts to understand than attempts to stir us up," there is also good reason to argue that we are in need of attempts to stir us up that will make a further contribution to our attempts to understand. Graff is right to argue that these disciplinary trends are, to some extent, the unexpected consequences of a limited form of institutional adaptability, but the oscillations in literary theory between univocal authority and multivocal anarchy have, as we have noted, another set of analogues with a long and primarily linguistic history. The modern linguistic turn in literary studies has also promoted an oscillating interest in the appeals of order and disorder, effectively reviving longstanding concerns about the relationship between linguistic freedom and necessity that will reward renewed and sustained attention. For it is in the complementary and not just contrasting historical relationships between linguistic freedom and necessity that we can recognize the depth and durability of issues that continue to generate widespread confusion.

In effect, if we are to make further progress in understanding issues of literary contextualizing we need to invoke a larger context than the institutional one provided by Graff, and consider more broadly both the implications of the "linguistic turn" in the discipline and the availability of alternatives. For directly related to the issue of literary contextualization is that of linguistic conceptualization, which, in various ways, shapes our view of the relationships among texts, readers, and contexts. We should, thus, remind ourselves that the critique of logocentrism provided by Derrida is simply the most recent of a long series of attempts to reconcile linguistic freedom with linguistic constraint that result not in reconciliation but in recurring oscillation between the claims of monistic necessity and relativistic anarchy. If renewed claims for a pluralism of collective inquiry are to establish their worth, such pluralism needs to demonstrate how it will address not only problems of contextual petrification but also problems of contextual proliferation, not only problems of institutional organization but also problems of linguistic presupposition. For finally it is problems of linguistic conceptualization that place order and disorder in such radical opposition, thereby promoting a relativism of competing monisms, and thus preventing literary history, criticism, and theory from establishing a more productive alignment. Though the followers of Derrida may well have misdescribed the problem, their sense of its location has, in many ways, been quite right.

What is at issue, for literary theorists as for others, in dealing with monism and relativism, is establishing contextual controls in linguistic realms that characteristically exhibit both order and disorder. And what influences the choice of controls are competing images of language as either (a) univocal, and therefore authoritative but potentially limiting, or (b) plurivocal, and therefore liberating but potentially unreliable. Though what is at stake for communities weighing univocal and plurivocal images of language has changed from era to era, the argument about whether linguistic contextualization serves us best when radically constrained or when radically diversified has a long and divisive history that goes back to classical times. And unless we develop pictures that can lead us beyond the well-established alternatives, the "linguistic turn" in the discipline will serve simply to renew rather than resolve the squabbles of the past.

The enduring form of the debate is one between those who argue that language is completely constrained by its role of reflecting a preexisting ontology and those who argue that it is free enough of prior constraint to enable us to invent an indefinite number of different modes of experience and awareness. In its earliest classical form the argument was related directly to the recurring question of whether the world was one or many, and as such it can be encountered in any basic introduction to linguistics:

> The Greek philosophers debated whether language was governed by "nature" or "convention." This opposition of "nature" and "convention" was a commonplace of Greek philosophical speculation. To say that a particular institution was "natural" was to imply that it had its origin in eternal and immutable principles outside man himself (and was therefore inviolable); to say that it was "conventional" implied that it was merely the result of custom and tradition. . . .[16]

Anything that resulted from custom or tradition was, of course, likely to be more variable, more vulnerable to change, and more subject to individual manipulation as a consequence of ongoing developments in customs and traditions. Anything that was "natural," however, offered possibilities of stable and coherent systematization which, while more resistant to social change and individual creativity, promised direct access to truths of enduring value. A "natural" language that reflects an external reality seems also to offer a dependable mode of control by relying upon a simple principle of operation, that of univocal reference: "The individual words in language name objects—sentences are combinations of such names.—In this picture of language we find the roots of the following idea: Every word has a meaning. This meaning is correlated with the word. It is the object for which the word stands."[17] This picture is as prominent in the minds of those who unreflectingly confirm it as in the minds of those who in recently denying it thought they had separated the signifier from the signified. A "conventional" picture on the other hand, which suggests that language registers our beliefs instead of reflecting what is given to us independent of belief, promises no such simple principle of control for us to accept or reject, for meaning is entangled in contexts, customs, conventions, and forms of life. The history of linguistic speculation has thus registered without finally resolving the competing claims of these two pictures of language while providing ever more sophisticated versions of each, and much of our unreflective thinking about language registers the continuing appeal of their contrasting claims.

Plato's notion of ideal forms, the interest of religions in preserving ancient truths in ancient languages, the Bible's depiction of Babel as punishment, the recurring conviction that etymological analysis will supply the true (because original) meaning of a word, the widespread resistance over the centuries to manifestations of linguistic change, the nineteenth-century pursuit of a foundational Indo-European language, the logical positivists' pursuit of an ideal language of reference, and modern scientists' interest in a neutral language of observation are all manifestations of the urge to hold onto the "natural" notion of a direct link between language and external reality in spite of the "conventional" recognition that languages display variety and register change. Language is repeatedly regarded as almost, but not quite univocal. All it apparently needs is a little help from its theorizing friends.

Repeated efforts over 2,500 years to establish that language can be a means of univocal access to stable truth and external knowledge register the appeal of one form or another of "natural" language, and this has enabled atomistic and referential theories of meaning to persist in spite of extensive evidence of the need for the contextual and relational theories of meaning that a "conventional" conception of language requires. And it is interesting in this respect to see as sophisticated a current theorist as Scholes describe the inherited problem as one of reconciling "difference" with "reference."[18] Such, indeed, is the strength of referential convictions that Wittgenstein accounts for them in terms of a picture that lies in our language, a picture of simple order that language seems to present to us whenever we use it, a picture that suggests that "proposition, language, thought, world, stand in line one behind the other, each equivalent to each."[19] It is just such a picture of epistemological necessity that induces Plato to conceive of essential Forms to which words must eventually refer and that induces logical positivists more than two thousand years later to conceive of ontological simples which, in an ideal language, words must necessarily name. And these are by no means matters of solely scholarly concern.

What is frequently overlooked is the weight of accompanying beliefs that referential convictions tend to bring with them. Assumptions that language is primarily in the business of making statements, establishing truth, communicating facts, and achieving self-transparency are all extensions of referential convictions about the nature of meaning, and they have, in turn, even larger implications. Indeed, a great many of our commonsense beliefs about language reflect centuries of effort to make sense of the notion of reference because it seems to offer both a simple explanation of how language works and a tempting confirmation of its capacity to provide direct access to the order of the world that surrounds us.

It is important to recognize that these are not merely technical matters. Over the centuries a great many philosophical, religious, and political conflicts have focused directly on the nature of language and its modes of control, and the residue of these conflicts continues to affect to this day issues of much larger scope. If language is controlled by something beyond us, we may feel blessed by the access we have to external truth or we may feel inhibited by the constraints of external necessity. If language is controlled by us, we may feel exhilarated by the power we share or restricted by its inability to lead us beyond ourselves. If language is partly controlled by us and partly controlled by external facts, we may feel we can enjoy the best of both worlds or we may feel it necessary to argue about who decides the appropriate alignment between what we contribute and what the world imposes. Such an argument will then be an argument about authority, about who has the ability and the right to authorize meaning on behalf of the community and in terms of accepted external constraint. The issue of linguistic contextualization is thus a crucial one for it inevitably involves someone or something being in control. Disputes about such authority go back at least as far as Plato's confrontation with the Sophists and have continued, off and on, ever since. Is language the means by which appropriate authority consolidates its community status and clarifies its capacity to reach authoritatively beyond us, or is language the means by which those of more dubious status achieve, by some sort of sophistry, of course, situational ascendancy and unpredictable power?

In these terms it is not surprising that what we first encounter as a conflict between Plato and the Sophists (one which logically enough led Plato also to advocate the exclusion of the poets from the city) has persisted over the centuries as a repeatedly renewed conflict between order and disorder, between necessity and novelty, between authority and anarchy. And to recognize the mutual implication of these apparently opposed alternatives is to recognize an ancient ancestor of the contextual and cultural conflicts revealed by Graff's analysis of modern academic institutions and embodied in Derrida's relativistic response to what he characterized as entrenched logocentrism.

With the stakes involved over the centuries in competing claims about the nature and function of language often running very high, it is also not surprising to encounter the frequency with which the movement of views runs from one extreme to the other. In his study of Renaissance manifestations of this problem, Waswo describes in detail how those advocating authoritative control and univocal languages attribute to Forms (Plato), scripture (Augustine), Latin (medieval scholars), ideas (Locke), symbols (Coleridge), and objects (empiricism) what he calls a "magic" capacity to align words with knowledge in a manner that precludes destabilizing slippage.[20] Alternative recognitions by the Sophists, the heretics, the advocates of vernaculars, and the proponents of "conventional" theories of language suggest that if language can change through time and across space and if it can open up room for legitimate disagreement and individual comprehension, then it must not be regarded as temporarily defective when it displays features of changing plurisignification. Such "conventional" arguments in favor of controlled multiplicity have, however, served over the years not so much to silence the claims of those seeking reliable forms of linguistic stability as to promote their more imaginative and more emphatic renewal.

The result, as Waswo has argued, is something of a seesaw effect in which each of the two opposing arguments drives the other toward further extremes.[21] Established authority views evidence of linguistic instability as incipient anarchy to which it must respond with renewed confirmation of linguistic controls. Such authority is then regarded as authoritarian, and threatened opponents adopt evidence of plurisignification to justify the anarchistic claims that are so often the final resort of the oppressed.

What binds together the monists and the relativists through the centuries is the misplaced ideal of a univocal image of language with all its implications for the status of knowledge, truth, certainty, and authority, an image that those of monistic inclination seem determined to sustain, an image that those of relativistic inclination seem determined to dismantle. And if we are to get beyond these limited and limiting options, we need to do some careful thinking about the reasons for their persistence.

The conflict between Latin and the vernacular languages in the Middle Ages is an instructive example. The longstanding preference for Latin in public affairs reflected not just the influence of the church on political events but the general conviction that the unchanging stability of Latin rendered it superior to rapidly changing vernaculars. A language dead in the sense of belonging to no existing community seemed paradoxically the most authoritatively alive. But the cost of maintaining it as the preeminent form of public discourse was the effective exclusion of the majority of the public. Only with the emergence of Renaissance fascinations with the temporal, the historical, and the changing and only in the context of heated debate did vernaculars come into their own. But upgrading the status of vernaculars to the equivalent of Latin promoted debate over the ideal form of each vernacular and led inexorably to the coexistence of contextual proliferation and petrification that we have encountered elsewhere.

Arguments over the status of vernacular languages provided, however, only one of the Renaissance forums for what Waswo calls "the dilemma of the age: the desire to arrive at certainties by means that are necessarily and increasingly recognized as contingent."[22] We are all, by now, aware enough of the untidiness of history to be wary of sudden moments of universal change.[23] The Renaissance dilemma clearly has its origins in classical debate and its analogues in modern disagreement. What happened in the Renaissance was one of the periodic intensifications of a persisting debate whose implications are always far-reaching but whose urgency varies from era to era. Major disagreements in the Renaissance about the importance of usage, contexts, and rules are the inevitable consequence of the readiness of Renaissance scholars to extend general interests in the temporal, the historical, and the changing into considerations of language. And the widespread significance of attempts to reconcile in linguistic realms the competing claims of conviction and contingency is registered in Renaissance arguments about the origins of language, the reliability of (particularly biblical) translations, the relationships among language, thought, and reality, the stability of meaning in biblical hermeneutics, the status of rules in grammar, the nature of imitation in literature, the importance of notions of linguistic decorum, the social function of rhetorical techniques, and the role of the reader in responding to scripture. Waswo summarizes thus the irreconcilable conflicts generated by Renaissance preoccupations with language:

> To have traced the development of the same systematic semantic ambivalence in three primary areas of the Renaissance preoccupation with language—humanist philosophy and rhetoric, vernacular polemics, and Protestant hermeneutics—in books that formed public tastes and trained its teachers, provides evidence, I believe, for a generally shifting consciousness of meaning that, by the later sixteenth century, is divided by conflicting assumptions almost to the point of schizophrenia. The reader is invited, on the one hand, to study in the classroom, to enjoy in literature, and to take with salvational seriousness in Scripture the proliferation of meanings in whose creation he participates with no apparent limit other than individual ingenuity. He is enjoined, on the other hand, that meaning resides only in realms of objective fact or divine ordination, access to which is arduous, to be rigorously controlled, and which exist quite apart from the power of him or his language to add or detract.[24]

The Renaissance tendency to employ language in one way while conceiving of it in another is thus testimony to the enduring conceptual appeal of a "natural" basis for language and a reference theory of meaning even to those displaying a serious interest in the claims of the historical, the temporal, and the contingent. What is at stake in this clash between conviction and contingency changes from era to era, but whether those concerns are religious, philosophical, political, sociological, psychological, institutional, or whatever, the enduring issues are ones of linguistic conceptualization, contextualization, and control. What keeps the monists and relativists in perpetual antagonism is a widespread reluctance to replace a simple theory of linguistic control with a complex one. For if standards for complex control are set at the same level as those of the presupposed simple one, then the complex, contextual, and contingent controls of "conventional" theories of language and meaning tend to look like no controls at all. And the inevitable result is an endlessly renewed oscillation between the unpalatable alternatives of established authority and antiestablishment anarchy.

We should thus be very much aware that the highly sophisticated modern arguments of Saussure and Wittgenstein for an other than referential linguistic theory are arguments that have illustrious ancestors. Illustrious may, however, be an inappropriate word. As a term of approbation it correctly conveys the scale of conceptual achievement of those who have thought their way beyond the limited and limiting alternatives of "natural" univocality and "conventional" arbitrariness. But the term seems hardly appropriate for the historical status of someone like Lorenzo Valla, who is little remembered for having made such arguments at all. As the issues have been debated with varying degrees of urgency between the advocates of linguistic authority and the advocates of linguistic anarchy, what history has repeatedly set aside are the complex claims of those seeking to occupy the middle ground. And before modern pluralism can make a convincing claim to that middle ground, it must confront the recognition that it has for centuries remained difficult terrain to conquer and inhabit.

It was in the fifteenth century, as Waswo, in a still controversial argument, points out, that Lorenzo Valla, an accomplished historical scholar, sought to replace the conflict between univocal authority and multivocal anarchy with a carefully articulated argument for a nonreferential form of controlled linguistic multiplicity. Demonstrating with detailed scholarly evidence that Latin, in spite of its claims to superiority in this regard, was, like the vernaculars, a changing and plurivocal language, Valla provided a series of arguments that challenged the claims of both authoritarians and anarchists. His views effectively renew and extend those of classical conventionalists when he suggests not only that linguistic conventions are the result of custom and tradition but also that language so conceived can register a controlled variation that should satisfy both sides' needs for stability on the one hand and flexibility on the other.

Valla, Waswo argues, effectively claims that meaning depends on usage, not on reference, that language changes because usage changes, that meaning is contextual, relational, and accountable to public convention, that truth and falsity are as much matters of affirmation as of confirmation, that language is a means of measuring possible knowledge rather than a means of referring to externally given knowledge, and that community agreement provides in general practice sufficient stability to prevent language sliding into a chaotic relativism and to preclude the need for invented foundations. As Waswo sees it, "In its subject, aim, situation, and strategy, Valla's effort is comparable to that of the most radical reconceiver of language in our time, the later Wittgenstein."[25] Like Wittgenstein, too, however, Valla found that his seminal work was preceded and succeeded by the continuing oscillation of the linguistic seesaw as old and new occupants of the extremities refused to engage with, much less refute, the claims of the occupant of the middle ground. The recognition that words somehow help constitute the realities we think we encounter beyond ourselves is a recognition that serves primarily to encourage those of a liberal frame of mind to concede that because anarchy seems possible, it must sometimes be necessary and those of a conservative frame of mind to argue that because anarchy seems possible, it must be systematically prevented.

What changed in the Renaissance as a consequence of Valla's work and that of sympathetic others was thus not the nature of the conflict between advocates of "natural" and "conventional" theories of language but the degree of its intensity. This level of conflict between contrasting linguistic theories and between linguistic theory and linguistic practice is a level of conflict that has increased, not steadily, but with no signs of diminution to this day. The conceptual complexity of the middle ground of conventionally controlled multiplicity has constantly proved vulnerable to the schematic simplicities of referential authority and relativistic skepticism.

To accept Waswo's thesis that "The intoxicating and terrifying possibility of *making* meaning, reacted to and against in a bewildering variety of ways, is . . . one of the principal defining energies of the entire Renaissance" is to recognize the continuity of a conflict shared by the modern era.[26] When Derrida argued that language is both unavoidably referential and as a consequence inexhaustibly deconstructable, he seemed not to be stopping the swing of the seesaw but to be moving back and forth as rapidly as possible between the two opposing ends.[27] By indicating how we might situationally resist logocentric uses of language while accepting that we can neither eradicate nor reform them, Derrida in effect conceded the battle to conquer and control alternative terrain. In order to perform its negative function, deconstruction was forced to retain whatever it subverted, for without something that claimed unyielding stability to subvert, there was nothing for deconstruction to deconstruct. In established historical fashion the advocate at one end of the seesaw rises only when an opponent descends on the other.

Far from being a manifestation of novelty or an agent of significant change, deconstruction thus served to recapitulate in its most graphic form the mode of renewal of a persisting conflict. When Derrida overlooked the work of Wittgenstein and returned scholarly discussion of language to pre-Wittgenstein positions, he followed a well-trodden path. For what deconstruction set to one side is what generations of earlier thinkers have been reluctant to provide room for: the determined occupant of the middle ground that modern pluralism seeks once more to conquer.

As we have seen, Booth is very much aware of the problems involved. Conceptually, he acknowledges the difficulty of establishing a pluralism that is neither a disguised monism nor a reluctant relativism. Institutionally, the problem is exacerbated by what he feels is "the natural drive of most scholars . . . either toward the triumph of a monism or the relaxation (or confession of defeat) implicit in eclecticism or skepticism."[28] And pragmatically he can see no way of making larger arguments in favor of pluralism than those provided by ethical claims about the importance of vitality, justice, and understanding in the field of literary studies. Convinced that critical understanding requires the use of more than one critical mode and committed to a belief in the fundamental importance of critical exchange and mutual understanding, Booth takes his stand finally on the basis of his own pragmatic beliefs.[29]

It is evident that Booth regards this as something of a concession, as it threatens to renew the tension between personal conviction and disciplinary consensus and to revive in another form the conflict between relativism and monism. But concern about the role of belief in critical activity serves to focus attention on the much neglected relationship between theory and theorist. Methodologies are, after all, as much dependent upon the skills of the user as upon the power of the methodological techniques, and it is important not to overlook the role of the theory user in negotiating between unpalatable theoretical alternatives, not the least of which are the competing claims of monism and relativism. There is no doubt that all claims to the adequacy of critical positions must eventually end where Booth's ends in asserting what it is better to believe. The question is, however, how soon and in what way arguments should move from observations about language, literature, history, and theory to arguments about pragmatic values, for it is often the case that the latter are sustained in part and indeed formed in part, by convictions about the former. And as far as issues of linguistic conceptualization are concerned, much of the influence is embedded in what pass for commonsense assumptions about language.

For the cultural relativist, of course, the fact that one has beliefs about the value of criticism and beliefs about the nature of language is an indication that both sets of beliefs are ideological and of a piece, and that the whole issue is one of polemical power. In one of the many ways in which modern relativism and modern monism become complementary, the relativist's assumption of other people's univocal ideologies is based as much as the monist's on the picture that Wittgenstein draws of proposition, language, thought, and world standing directly in line and each equivalent to each. The relativism of competing ideologies is, in effect, the relativism of competing monisms, and it is this that ties modern monists and relativists together. The notion that within an ideology or within a language there might be competing forces is one that causes dialecticians to go in search of teleological syntheses, cultural relativists to reduce multiplicity to the alternatives of supporting or subverting the status quo, and instinctive monists to seek ways of eradicating inconsistency. The idea of persisting and enabling multiplicity is a difficult one to hold onto, but without it the theorist will have little room for maneuver, and pluralism is likely to become what Booth fears—a thinly disguised monism or a reluctant relativism. But such a notion of enabling multiplicity is precisely what links issues of linguistic conceptualization to issues of contextualization and control. In these terms, the cultural/linguistic hybrid, far from being a distinctive postcolonial characteristic, is a much more widespread linguistic phenomenon, with implications also for the relationship between modes of critical discourse.[30]

Armstrong is the pluralist who has grappled most illuminatingly, if not entirely successfully, with the role of the theorist negotiating coexisting and coequal modes of critical discourse, and the strength and weaknesses of his argument point the way forward. And the way forward must include some sort of solution to the conundrum Booth assigned to pluralism of apparently having to affirm both the irreducible variety of critical languages and the capacity of irreducibly various languages to interact in some fruitful manner. Only if the former can modulate into the latter will we be enabled to think across and not just within the frames of inquiry that multiple languages provide. Armstrong's commitment to the former is soon clear but his ideas about the latter reveal without resolving the difficulties involved in reconciling exploratory investigation with enduring belief.

Acknowledging that no critical mode has a privileged claim to the revelation of critical truth, Armstrong argues, as Booth argues, that what comes first are theorists' beliefs whether they be pragmatic, ideological, historical, religious, sociological, psychological, anthropological, political, or whatever.

> Every interpretive approach has its own anticipatory understanding of literature, one that reflects its most basic presuppositions.... The characteristic hypotheses that a method of interpretation projects are the practical embodiment of more basic beliefs about human being, the being of the object it interrogates, and the being of the world as a whole. Psychoanalysis, Marxism, phenomenology, structuralism—each has a different method of interpretation because each has a different metaphysics, a different set of convictions that makes up its point of departure and defines its position in the hermeneutic field. If an interpreter believes with Freud, for example, that human beings are sexual animals and that literary works are the disguised expression of repressed libidinal desires, he or she will arrange textual details into configurations different from those of a Marxist critic who believes that we are social, historical beings and that art reflects class interests. To embrace a type of interpretation is to make a leap of faith by accepting one set of presuppositions and rejecting others.[31] (*Conflicting Readings*, pp. 4–5)

It is just such a leap of faith, we noted earlier, that advocates of deconstruction paradoxically required of potential practitioners of its skeptical procedures, but in doing so they were following a familiar pattern of behavior. To many, such a leap of faith suggests an immediate reduction of interpretation to ideology and of contextualization to imposed control. But the recognition that prior belief governs acts of interpretation does not, for Armstrong, exclude the claim for a degree of flexibility in their application. He insists that our capacity to be surprised by what we find in texts and our ability to recognize anomalies in our attempts to describe texts register our ability to see a little way beyond the limitations of any underlying set of beliefs. But Armstrong's attempts to clarify the consequences of the paradox that "Although I never leave my own world, I use its resources to implant an alien world within it" founder on the governing status of initial belief (*Conflicting Readings*, pp. 27–29). In describing the practice of reading and interpreting, Armstrong, in promising fashion, notes the importance of feedback, of texts challenging the hypotheses addressed to them and those challenges in turn changing the beliefs that precipitated them. The guiding image here is not one of insulated monism but of complex and gradual change (*Conflicting Readings*, pp. 29, 75–81). But in the process of his theorizing about critical modes, the pluralist promise disappears. The image here is one of definitive choice between preceding and fixed sets of alternatives. We must, it seems, "choose which presuppositions to adopt as the precondition for interpreting," and "interpretive conflict is... a contest between alternative beliefs" that are often "mutually exclusive and to a considerable degree self confirming" (*Conflicting Readings*, pp. 30, 97). Armstrong's theory thus accommodates a degree of interaction and reciprocal change between texts and the critical modes addressed to them, but it makes little room for such interaction and exchange between critical modes.

Instead of being a means of clarifying the role of the theorist in controlling the complex interaction of competing beliefs in the act of interpretation, Armstrong's pluralism thus becomes a means of clarifying the nature of choices about beliefs that literary theory makes available to the theorist: "If interpretation is a matter of deciding what it is better to believe, then an important role for theory is to increase the interpreter's self consciousness about the possible implications of various alternatives. . . . Although no theory can predict where any set of beliefs will lead, one value of studying hermeneutic conflict is that an interpreter may thereby understand more clearly the risks and powers of a particular mode by comparing it with others" (*Conflicting Readings,* pp. 156–57). Armstrong's local acknowledgments that methods can be adjusted in their application repeatedly give way to his larger conviction that, because fundamental beliefs underlie all methods of interpretation, we must, initially and finally, choose "what to believe" (*Conflicting Readings,* p. 156).

In a manner reminiscent of the picture Wittgenstein warns us against, belief, method, hypothesis, text, and world line up alongside each other with such consistency that the interpretive creativity Armstrong so clearly values is somewhat imperiled by hermeneutic necessity. In adopting any method of interpretation we are, Armstrong argues, wagering that "the insights made possible by its assumptions will offset the risks of blindness they entail" (*Conflicting Readings,* p. 7). Attempts to mingle methods viewed in such terms are fraught with danger for if, as he argues, "interpretation is based on beliefs" and these beliefs account for the "effectiveness and persuasiveness" of such interpretations, then efforts to combine significantly different methods are "not necessarily useful or advisable" (*Conflicting Readings,* p. 155).

In spite of his promising discussion of feedback during acts of interpretation between text, hypothesis, method, and belief, Armstrong's pluralism seems strongly to affirm only one of Booth's two claims and thus threatens to become a pluralism of largely insulated monisms. Though acts of interpretation may serve marginally to modify belief, theory seems primarily able to clarify modal choices and not to reconcile conflict. The flexibility and freedom attributed to the investigating mind are constrained by the method that establishes the domain of inquiry: "Understanding operates in the space of freedom between the basic beliefs defining an interpretive method and their particular, variable applications" (*Conflicting Readings,* p. 142).

Armstrong's pluralism thus does not fully address Booth's fears that pluralism may slide inadvertently into monism or relativism, for Armstrong's otherwise powerful argument tends to move back and forth between a monism of method and a relativism of methodology. His uncertainty about productive exchange between critical modes reflects Armstrong's justifiable conviction that choices must be made, but the choosing procedure seems rather limited and the choices premature. Critical pluralism so conceived displays some of the tendency registered in deconstruction to keep the linguistic seesaw oscillating rather than to bring it under control. We are confronted with an array of univocal languages whose relativistic implications require pragmatic decisions about which monism we think it best to believe in: "Anyone who accepts my theory is free to continue reading as he or she wishes" (*Conflicting Readings*, p. 156). This may enable us to address one, but not both of the current problems in the academy as Graff describes them, with the profession vulnerable simultaneously to charges of recapitulating "humanism's inability to tolerate differences" and to charges that its institutional organization is hostile to the pursuit of consensus.[32] We are still left with an argument that we need to teach our differences but without a conceptual context within which such a procedure might prove fruitful. Not quite managing to resolve the pluralist dilemma that Booth so precisely describes, Armstrong affirms the irreducible variety of critical modes but remains uncertain about their capacity for fruitful interaction. The challenge to characterize a pluralistic ability to think across and not just within frames of inquiry remains unmet.

For Armstrong, linking modes suggests combining modes, and he and pluralists in general are rightly wary of the danger of advocating a single all-embracing pluralistic methodology which provides a new and comprehensive mode of critical discourse. But most pluralists are equally wary of accusations that pluralism is only a laissez-faire philosophy in which anything can claim to be as valuable as anything else. Recognizing the importance of sustaining the twin claims of order and disorder in literary texts and critical methods, pluralists are reluctant to give priority to any fixed set of beliefs. Thus, to many pluralists, the New Critics' assumptions about unity emerging from apparent variety are no more or less reductive than poststructuralist assumptions about disunity appearing in the midst of apparent consistency.[33] To settle for either of these modes is to adopt either a univocal language of characteristic kinds of order or a univocal language of characteristic kinds of disorder. What is missing is some more flexible notion of the role of belief in critical activity, one more capable of promoting an enabling exchange among critical modes, an exchange in which modes can be related without being equated, thereby generating unexpected but not random discoveries in texts. And what is consequently required is a better understanding of the relatedness of order and disorder in both critical modes and literary texts. For it is the assumption of homogeneity within a frame of inquiry that renders it resistant to interaction with others and reduces it to ratifying rather than testing belief.

To move beyond the recurring polarization of beliefs and their self-confirming methodologies, the literary profession needs not yet another univocal mode, and not just a pluralistic acknowledgment of multiple univocal modes, but a recognition that modes can both remain different and interact because each of them has a capacity to be internally plurivocal and externally provisional, to be itself a means of relating rather than ratifying beliefs. Pluralism cannot function successfully as merely a commitment to invoking multiple modes, for if the modes invoked are treated as internally homogeneous they will also be largely impervious to external exchange, and pluralism will serve only to reinforce the current disciplinary structure of a relativism of competing monisms. For pluralism effectively to relate multiple modes there must be a sense in which each mode is itself conceived of as internally pluralistic. Such a shift in linguistic conceptualization would have direct implications for issues both of contextualization and of control. And this can only return us to the long line of arguments about the "conventional," contingent, and changing nature of language which from Valla to Wittgenstein and beyond have held out the promise of reconciling linguistic order and disorder through some form of controlled multiplicity. And this, in turn, will serve to reintroduce the issue of the controlling agent, and of the capacity of theorists, whatever their beliefs, to use theory to locate both the expected and the unexpected.

Armstrong derives much of his argument about the importance of belief from the philosophical work of C. S. Peirce, but for Peirce, the fixing of belief is an ongoing community activity that, whatever its capacity for convergence(s), is unlikely to congeal into tidy packages of unified convictions among which we must choose and upon which methods and hypotheses could firmly be based.[34] Some of Peirce's arguments about the community-based status of facts do, however, anticipate Kuhn's later arguments that the hermeneutic circle may serve to make hypotheses self-confirming, and part of the appeal of Armstrong's argument is that he does not wish to settle for that. Thus he argues at one point that "a belief is a guess about what we do not know [which] must consequently be both embraced with faith and questioned with skeptical detachment" (*Conflicting Readings,* p. 139). But his insistence on premature modal choice leaves little room within univocal critical languages for the role of skeptical detachment, or for the recognition that some beliefs are much more solidly entrenched than others, or for the possibility that our beliefs may form a heterogeneous rather than homogeneous set. Though Armstrong tries to make room for the latter point by distinguishing two levels of belief, they find themselves, in univocal languages, lined up behind each other too rigidly to allow unexpected discovery to flourish.[35] But the effort to accommodate the novelty of a new metaphor provides the point at which Armstrong's interest in univocal multiplicity reaches the brink of envisaging a plurivocal methodology and an alternative mode of linguistic conceptualization, contextualization, and control.

> The surprise of finding our preconceptions inadequate to make sense of the incongruous term may have several different results. We may reject as alien the beliefs on which the figure is based and reconfirm our own assumptions, perhaps with a better understanding of why we prefer them than we had before alternative convictions exposed their limits. . . . Or the new patterns and relations to which the metaphor has introduced us may become a lasting part of our own presuppositions about the world. We may reject some assumptions that we previously held but are inconsistent with the new figure, or we may find ways of expanding our preconceptions by grafting new beliefs onto them. Or, between the poles of self-delineation and personal redefinition, we may use the otherness of the figure as a challenge *to extend our ability to imagine different ways of seeing without firmly refusing or permanently adopting them. Even if we do not convert to new beliefs,* the experience of experimenting with alternative hypotheses about how to establish coherence *can increase our imagination for modes of vision other than our own.* (my emphases) (*Conflicting Readings*, pp. 78–79)

The possibility of entertaining beliefs that we do not necessarily hold, and the possibility of adopting multiple modes of vision are briefly acknowledged here, but in the absence of a framework within which they might function, they quickly recede from view. But it is precisely such recognitions that would lead us to move from univocal to plurivocal pictures of language and to reconceive the roles of theorists and their beliefs.

What is intermittently envisaged and repeatedly passed over in various forms of pluralism is the notion that the fit between belief, language, theory, idea, text, and world may be various and changing because language itself in any of its forms is various and changing. And it is just this form of linguistic conceptualization, one that seeks to accommodate the internal multiplicity of any linguistic mode, that is needed to get us beyond inherited alternatives of established authority and relativistic anarchy. Critical modes are not necessarily unified packages that demand affirmation of some basic set of beliefs, though they are often used that way. Nor is their potential internal multiplicity a signal that all affirmations of belief are self-dismantling. To conceive of using modes differently is to reconsider the relationship between belief and discovery and to open up the kind of space between theory and theorist that will enable the theorist to think creatively beyond and not just within adopted modes of inquiry.

When Graff points out that we tend to assume that "whether a critical method gets used creatively or mechanically depends less on institutional organization than on whether good teachers or poor ones are using it," he is quick to move toward his chosen target of institutional constraint rather than asking how it is that a teacher can use a method creatively or mechanically, how some teachers learn to avoid putting themselves to work for a mode of discourse and figure out, instead, how to put it to work for them.[36] For some critics, historians, and theorists, conviction and ideology are not equivalent terms, beliefs are not incompatible with an orientation toward change, and procedural frameworks serve to guide rather than govern intellectual inquiry. When Booth argues that what we really need is not new critical modes but new understanding of the nature of critical modes, he implicitly invites us to turn our attention not just toward particular critical languages, or toward language in general, but toward issues of linguistic conceptualization, toward inherited pictures we have of language that limit or enhance our capacities to use it both creatively and pluralistically.[37] For it is these entrenched pictures of language and its univocal mode of functioning that keep imposing on potentially flexible theory a rigidity that it does not necessarily require.

There is, in this respect, a direct analogy between the tendency of linguistic theory to degenerate into a mechanism for producing self-justifying descriptions and the tendency of literary theory to degenerate into a mechanism for producing self-validating interpretations. And when literary studies in the modern era made a linguistic turn, it was directly into the midst of an unresolved linguistic debate over the relationships between language, belief, and truth.

As Waswo, Graff, Armstrong, and others have argued, there are always religious, political, social, philosophical, and institutional pressures that drive us back toward the univocal use of languages, and these pressures seem to Wittgenstein, as we have noted, to be reinforced by the fact that "a *picture* held us captive. And we could not get outside it, for it lay in our language and language seemed to repeat it to us inexorably."[38] Only a better understanding of the nature of language can help us escape the limitations of this picture and the univocal consequences that drive us toward either a single self-enclosing monism or toward a relativistic choice between competing monisms. For the key issue is not whether particular modes of discourse require or encourage monistic or relativistic use, but whether the user has a disposition to use modes of discourse monistically, relativistically, or otherwise. Though this disposition will affect both the array of investigative instruments adopted and the techniques of applying them, it is not itself so much a theoretical position as a tendency to view theory in terms of pictures of language of one kind or another. For what is at issue here is not a theory of theory use but our capacity to situate theory in larger informative contexts. What is already apparent is that any attempt to establish a comprehensive theory of theory use would be a monistic move that would perpetuate rather than resolve the problems with which theory finds itself confronted.

If, however, we move from monosystemic univocal pictures of language to polysystemic plurivocal pictures, we can consider how linguistic order and disorder might productively coexist, we can reconceive the relationship between theorist and theory, and we can contemplate a solution to Booth's pluralist dilemma of apparently having to affirm and deny the claims of both monism and relativism. If we are to make the most of Graff's argument that an adequate pluralism will enable us to teach fruitfully our differences, of Armstrong's argument that clarification of differences will promote helpful choices, of Booth's argument that durable exchange between critical modes is as important as the pursuit of new modes, of Washington's argument that disinterestedness lies not in abandoning but in examining our interests, and of Ellis's argument that theory of criticism is best regarded not as a set of competing dogmas but as an active and ongoing reflection on the critical possibilities of communal inquiry, then we need some other pictures of language and linguistic control than those that keep reappearing on the cultural scene. And if we are to meet Graff's challenge to imagine a form of disciplinary coherence that neither invokes nor rejects consensus, we must begin by recognizing the continuing force of Wittgenstein's argument for linguistic reconceptualization, for a return to that excluded middle ground in which linguistic order and disorder are complementary rather than opposed alternatives: "A main source of our failure to understand," he argues, "is that we do not *command a clear view* of the use of our words."[39]

With the linguistic seesaw constantly swinging up and down, we find ourselves constantly choosing between alternatives we must learn to reconcile. Conviction and contingency, necessity and novelty, order and disorder, unity and variety, stability and change, belief and doubt, presupposition and discovery need to be relocated as reciprocally related oppositions rather than rigidly opposed alternatives. The claims of authority and anarchy may both be accommodated by a deconstructive picture that makes logocentrism a necessary condition of language, one that we can resist but not reform, but it leaves in place an image of language functioning in either univocal or unstable terms, and some more illuminating account is needed of the relationship between order and disorder in language. In the context of persisting linguistic heterogeneity, what binds contemporary monists and relativists both to each other and to their ancient ancestors is the tendency of the monists to overstate similarity so as to manufacture unity and of the relativists to overstate difference so as to manufacture division. Both overstatements together serve to create the familiar relativism of competing monisms that misaligns theory with fact, divides one theory from another, converts heterogeneous beliefs into unified ideology, and transforms theorists into illustrators rather than inquirers.

The "conventional" argument for plurivocal stability has long been that a language should be regarded as differently constituted rather than temporarily defective when, instead of monosystemic univocality, it displays features of changing plurisignification. The task for the pluralists who succeed deconstruction is thus the same task that confronted the pluralists who preceded it—to put to productive use in literary studies the notion revived intermittently from Valla to Wittgenstein that language is variously structured and variously functioning, that both its monistic use and its relativistic use are limited forms of practice, and that the fit between belief, theory, idea, language, text, and world is incipiently multiple and changing rather than uniform and mutually reinforcing. Indeed what is ultimately at issue in the interaction among polysystemic modes of discourse is the relationship between linguistic continuity and linguistic change. Instead of wondering how univocal languages can leave room for creativity and discovery, we might consider whether the more informative problem is that of linguistic change, its speed, its multiplicity, and its capacity to leave room for us to establish differing degrees and kinds of stability for different purposes.

In the modern period as in the Renaissance, pictures of controllable linguistic multiplicity have emerged from a variety of sources and in a variety of ways. If we are to keep these pictures from sliding into the obscurity of Valla's, and if pluralism is to offer the theory user the kind of understanding of critical modes that will advantageously affect critical practice, then we should look more closely at the work of some of those who have tried to establish alternative pictures to the misleading univocal ideal against which Wittgenstein so graphically warns us: "The ideal, as we think of it, is unshakable. You can never get outside it; you must always turn back. There is no outside; outside you cannot breathe.—Where does this idea come from? It is like a pair of glasses on our nose through which we see whatever we look at. It never occurs to us to take them off."[40] In modern linguistic theory, however, several attempts have been made to see beyond such univocal and monosystemic perspectives and it is to those alternatives, in all their complexity, that prospective pluralists might productively devote renewed and sustained attention. Without them, pluralism is likely to continue to promise more than it is able to deliver, but suitably informed by them, pluralism may yet enable literary theory to reconstitute itself as a viable mode of intellectual inquiry.

Chapter 2 Saussure, Firth, and Bakhtin: Unity, Diversity, and Theory

Ferdinand de Saussure did not write the book for which he is most well known. The text was compiled from notes taken in three lecture courses he gave at the University of Geneva between 1906 and 1911. As Saussure did not publish these ideas and left behind no lecture notes of his own, we have to rely on a creative synthesis of notes taken by several students. The authors acknowledge the difficulty of the task of reconstruction, taking particular note of the fact that the three lecture courses were delivered over a period of five years in which Saussure's ideas were themselves evolving. Whether that evolution was likely to be open-ended or teleological was prejudged by the principles of selection the authors felt impelled to apply: "We should need to identify every essential idea by reference to the system as a whole, analyse it in depth, and express it in a definitive form, unobscured by the variations and hesitations which naturally accompany oral delivery. We should then need to put each idea in its proper place, and present all the various parts in an order corresponding to the author's intentions, even if the intentions were not apparent but could only be inferred."[1]

The possibilities for error here are, of course, considerable, and it is important to note both the writers' determination to establish what they conceive of as "an organic whole" and their rueful acknowledgment that Saussure, had he lived, "perhaps might not have authorized the publication of this text."[2] Subsequent critical editions of the text provide access to some source material, but it is unlikely that scholarship will supply what Saussure's students and colleagues were unable to supply, a sense of the whole that will clarify all the puzzling remarks, remove the apparent inconsistencies, and fill in the obvious gaps. There is an editorial commitment to the principle of wholeness and homogeneity that certainly emerges from Saussure's work, but that principle may well be subject to various applications and situated in a variety of ways.[3]

What is very much apparent in Saussure's *Course in General Linguistics* is his recognition of the heterogeneity of the phenomenon we call language—a heterogeneity that, to his mind, precipitates a kind of disorder that constantly threatens to disable the discipline of linguistics. Although Saussure accepts that "Linguistics takes for its data in the first instance all manifestations of human language" (*Course*, p. 6),[4] he also argues that attempts to study the full diversity of what people say are doomed to inevitable failure: "Language in its entirety has many different and disparate aspects. It lies astride the boundaries separating various domains. It is at the same time physical, physiological and psychological. It belongs both to the individual and to society. No classification of human phenomena provides any single place for it, because language as such has no discernible unity. . . . Language in its totality is unknowable, for it lacks homogeneity" (*Course*, pp. 10, 20). Here we encounter what appears to be the Saussurean trademark: a dissatisfaction with manifest diversity and a pursuit of something uniform and unified with which to replace it. For only something that is homogeneous can, he argues, be fruitfully studied and provide the basis for a coherent discipline. But this unified entity is not to be established by studying language as a whole. Some more local part is to serve as the operational whole, and the full diversity of language is not, in fact, to be accommodated by any single strategy of description.

Given the multifaceted nature of language in general (*langage*) and the diversity of individual manifestations of speech (*parole*), Saussure sets out to subtract from the diversity a uniformity that is located somewhere within it: "Language as a structured system" stands out "amid the disparate mass of facts involved in language . . . as a well defined entity" (*Course*, p. 14). Consequently linguistics must isolate this well-defined entity and distinguish a linguistics of language structure (*langue*), which is devoted to it, from a linguistics of language (*langage*) or speech (*parole*): "Linguistic structure," as he describes it, is "language minus speech," and he proposes to focus linguistics primarily upon language structure conceived as something organized and unified "as a system" (*Course,* pp. 77, 21).

Thus when Saussure begins his pursuit of unified wholeness, he does so paradoxically by subdividing language into its several manifestations. And that subdivision is largely a matter of separating what is multiple, heterogeneous, and comprehensive from what is single, homogeneous, and of uncertainly general consequence. What is thereby set aside is much that has hitherto been of major importance. He proposes to move historical change, the prime focus of nineteenth-century linguistic attention, to one side by focusing upon particular states of a language at particular times (diachrony versus synchrony), and he proposes to move contemporary variation from the scene by distinguishing internal (systematic) linguistics from what is external (geographical, social, and individual variants). It is not, of course, claimed that these variants are completely unsystematic, but it seems clear that they are not systematic enough to be readily included in the linguistics of language structure. The principles of wholeness and harmony thus remain somewhat at odds for it is a subtracted operational whole that is to provide the order that Saussure locates in the midst of acknowledged disorder.

It is important to note, therefore, that along with his ideas on systematic wholes, Saussure, in spite of widespread impressions to the contrary, had much to say about linguistic disorder and linguistic diversity. Although he removed them from the center of attention, he made it clear (but not consistently clear) that he continued to regard the study of historical and external linguistics as important concerns, and he explored them both at some length. The book, and presumably the lectures, thus give extensive attention not only to the unity of synchronic linguistics, but also to the diversity of diachronic linguistics and geographical linguistics, with each topic providing one of the five main sections of the book. He is also at pains to indicate that they are interrelated. "Nothing enters the language," he notes, "before having been tried out in speech. All evolutionary phenomena have their roots in the linguistic activity of the individual" (*Course,* p. 167). At another point he notes that "external linguistics is . . . concerned with important matters, and these demand attention when one approaches the study of language" (*Course,* p. 21). Such remarks need to be borne in mind when we consider his strategy of setting aside variety, of focusing on the social side of language rather than the individual, of giving priority to the synchronic state rather than the diachronic succession, and of studying the systematic form rather than the heterogeneous substance. We should also remember that, far from dismissing it, he had promised to supply his students in a subsequent course with the very "linguistics of speech" (*Course*, p. 20) whose diversity he was now subordinating to a linguistics of social language states. This linguistics of speech is mentioned briefly in the book though its subsequent exploration was prevented by his untimely death.

To understand Saussure's reorganization of linguistic issues, we must thus bear in mind his concern for establishing a well-formed object that linguistics might study—an object whose well-formedness he regarded as essential if the discipline were to flourish. But in so establishing it, he was concerned less with eliminating the heterogeneous from linguistics than with clarifying the appropriate relationship between linguistic order and disorder, between homogeneous and heterogeneous aspects of language structure and speech. It is clearly the case that, for Saussure, the appropriate location of the heterogeneous is somewhere to one side of the center, while that which "gives language what unity it has" (*Course*, p. 11) is to be awarded the place of honor at the center of the discipline.

Efforts to establish the existence of the well-defined entity involve Saussure in what now look to be the weakest parts of his argument: the attempt to give language structure so defined the status of something found rather than made, something socially given rather than individually (re)constructed, something physiologically concrete rather than heuristically abstract. "A language, as a collective phenomenon," he asserts, "takes the form of a totality of imprints in everyone's brain, rather like a dictionary of which each individual has an identical copy" (*Course*, p. 19). Here, Saussure argues, is the communal linguistic heritage that underlies the diversity of community speech. Language as a shared structure is a "social institution" which "exists perfectly only in the collectivity," and it is in this state of collective perfection that language should centrally be studied by linguistics: "The actual object" of linguistic science "is the social product stored in the brain, the language itself" (*Course*, pp. 15, 13, 24). There is no mistaking the significance of the divisions Saussure wishes to establish. He seeks to locate a concrete and homogeneous object for the discipline to study, but it is to be something situated in not yet clearly defined ways in the midst of the otherwise heterogeneous linguistic data.

As Saussure reiterates his key distinctions, however, a significant shift in emphasis becomes increasingly apparent. The respect he registers elsewhere for the importance of what is heterogeneous (but not central) diminishes. "By distinguishing between the language itself and speech, we distinguish at the same time: 1, what is social from what is individual, and 2, what is essential from what is ancillary and more or less accidental" (*Course*, pp. 13–14). The second point is by no means an inevitable consequence of the first, but Saussure insists upon it several times, and that insistence is accompanied by sharper divisions between what is systematic and less systematic in language in general. Although "language has an individual aspect and a social aspect," and "one is not conceivable without the other," the interdependence of language and speech does not compromise "the absolute nature of the distinction between the two" (*Course*, pp. 9, 19). Although "Language at any given time involves an established system and an evolution," nevertheless the opposition between synchronic and diachronic viewpoints "is absolute and admits no compromise" (*Course*, pp. 9, 83). The study of each of these aspects of language becomes increasingly independent of the others, and efforts to situate linguistic order in the context of linguistic disorder give way to attempts to isolate the former from the latter.

The regular insistence on the importance of wholeness is thus one that emerges, ironically, in the context of an argument that divides the study of language not only into several parts but into several relatively autonomous parts. There is to be a separate "linguistics of speech" and a separate science of "evolutionary linguistics" to accommodate the demands of these aspects of language (*Course*, pp. 20, 81). And it becomes apparent that these other linguistics are not to enjoy equal status. When Saussure extends his distinction between what is social and what is individual into a distinction between what is essential and what is ancillary and more or less accidental, he is radically downgrading the lesser linguistic sciences that might study such heterogeneous phenomena in favor of "linguistics proper," which has the more highly ordered notion of language as "linguistic structure as its sole object of study" (*Course*, p. 20).

As the Saussure who has made such an impact on modern linguistics and other disciplines is not the Saussure who has much of interest to say about local synchronic variation and strands of diachronic change in language, but the Saussure who chooses to focus on homogeneous systematic wholes, it is important to note at the outset his ambivalence over the status of the heterogeneous aspects of language—important because what he has to say about heterogeneity is much overlooked, but also because there will be reason to return later to the uncertain relationship in his work between linguistic order and linguistic disorder, between linguistic unity and linguistic diversity. For the moment it will suffice to consider why Saussure was so interested in wholeness, homogeneity, and stability and what he was able to achieve by directing the discipline's attention to "linguistics proper," to a linguistics of fixed language states and consistent linguistic structures.

It might, of course, be argued that Saussure was a man of his time and as such displayed habits of contemporary thought. The dominant paradigm for acquisition of knowledge at the turn of the century was that provided by classical physics in its most advanced Newtonian form (one as yet untroubled by the imminent complexities of quantum mechanics and the emerging imponderables of relativity), and it would be possible to explain in these terms Saussure's interest in establishing an object of study as well-formed and concrete as that apparently supplied by the Newtonian universe. But this is not so much to explain Saussure's commitment to the homogeneous whole as to explain it away. Saussure, after all, was a man helping create the modes of thinking of his time and not just someone thinking in accord with patterns established by his predecessors. As a linguist, he was very much concerned with the limitations of the inherited discipline, with the need to change its assumptions, its procedures, and its status. A series of concerns that he registered about the fragmented nature of the discipline of linguistics, about its approach to language in general, about the role of history, the constitution of the sign, and the complexities of meaning all served to converge on this larger issue—the status of the discipline in general. And attempts to resolve all these concerns led Saussure inexorably toward the commitments to wholeness, homogeneity, and fixity that are so much a feature of his work.

Besides the epistemological paradigm provided by Newtonian physics, the other influential paradigm of nineteenth-century epistemology was that supplied by analogies with Darwinian theories of evolution. Linguistics in the nineteenth century had become preoccupied with establishing family trees displaying the historical relations of languages, and extensive attention was devoted to tracing the evolution of sounds through a series of linguistic environments. As some of the repertoire of distinctive sounds moved from one language to another through time, they exhibited shifts in pronunciation in apparently regular ways: ways regular enough to attract extensive attention and encourage some to formulate laws governing linguistic change.[5] The discipline that Saussure first encountered, though internally fragmented and in many ways diverse, thus had as its most prestigious concerns matters to do primarily with phonetics and with history. Saussure was soon ready to challenge it on both counts, but it is the relationship between his two objections that is most informative.

As Saussure discontentedly perceived it, "Since its beginnings, it would be true to say that modern linguistics has been entirely taken up with diachronic study" and this diachrony was troublesome because it was of a particular kind

(*Course,* p. 82). In emphasizing comparison of local components of several languages, it tended to preclude extended study of particular languages in all their internal complexity. This not only produced a discipline focused on linguistic bits and pieces rather than on languages as functional wholes, but also one that, in Saussure's eyes, gave the wrong priority to issues diachronic and synchronic. For Saussure this was not just a matter of personal preference but one of logical necessity—necessity dictated by the very nature of the linguistic sign. "It is a great mistake to consider a sign as nothing more than the combination of a certain sound and a certain concept. To think of a sign as nothing more would be to isolate it from the system to which it belongs. It would be to suppose that a start could be made with individual signs, and a system constructed by putting them together. On the contrary, the system as a united whole is the starting point, from which it becomes possible, by a process of analysis, to identify its constituent elements" (*Course,* p. 112). Far from synchronic matters evolving from diachronic ones, it seems that a synchronic study of systematic language states is a necessary prelude to appropriate diachronic comparison. And as we shall see, the decision to situate signs in systems makes it difficult for Saussure to conceive of systems as other than firm and fixed functional wholes.

Saussure is more than ready to call upon larger tradition to support his argument against more recent fashion. He offers a reminder that nineteenth-century diachronic procedure is a departure from a well-established tradition in the discipline of exploring the fixed states of particular languages at particular times—a tradition he characterizes as "quite flawless" (*Course,* p. 82). But Saussure's commitment to tradition is merely strategic, and he is quick to qualify his support for it. Though the method of earlier grammarians is, he feels, in this respect correct, its application leaves something to be desired. Earlier grammarians were in another key respect just like his immediate predecessors. In their concern to prescribe rather than describe linguistic forms, earlier grammarians tended to pay "no attention to whole areas of linguistic structure" and as a consequence make "no attempt at syntheses" (*Course,* p. 82). Though traditional and nineteenth-century grammarians differ in the priority they give to matters of "succession" and matters of "states," both end up focusing on linguistic bits and pieces (*Course,* pp. 80–82). For Saussure the approaches of both earlier and more recent grammarians fail fundamental tests of comprehensiveness and conceptualization. What needs to be addressed, he feels, is the recurring problem of fragmentation which has habitually emerged, though in various forms, from a discipline constantly unable to establish and circumscribe a well-defined object of study.

To see that there is a particular rather than a general reason for Saussure's fascination with wholeness and harmony is thus to recognize the key context of his thinking which is above all else, the status of the discipline of linguistics past, present, and future. And central to Saussure's attempts to reform the discipline of linguistics is a significantly larger role that it might play on the intellectual scene than had hitherto been the case. A suitably revised linguistics could provide a model for a new and ambitious science of semiology, a science of immense scope that would study "the role of signs as part of social life" (*Course*, p. 15). Such a science would "investigate the nature of signs and the laws governing them" (*Course*, p. 15). Although linguistics would be a relatively autonomous science in the midst of other semiological sciences emerging from social psychology and anthropology, it would have a place of honor among them.[6] For Saussure, "nothing is more appropriate than the study of languages to bring out the nature of the semiological problem," and among the various systems of signs used for "expressing ideas," language is "the most important" (*Course*, pp. 15–16). Consequently, "linguistics serves as a model for the whole of semiology, even though languages represent only one type of semiological system" (*Course*, p. 68).

These are grand claims on behalf of linguistics, but Saussure apparently sees no necessary inconsistency between his insistence that linguistics is best served by studying fixed language states and his attempt to reconstitute the discourse of linguistics by invoking its earlier and predicting its future forms. It is important, therefore, to remember once more that his emphasis on things social, homogeneous, and synchronic does not constitute a dismissal of things individual, heterogeneous, and diachronic. What matters but is not finally resolved is the relationship between them. Whether the most widely known relationship he envisages between them will serve to remove the appearance of inconsistency is something to be considered later when we return to its inherent instability. For the moment it is important to note not only that Saussure envisages a new role for linguistics and a new science of semiology, but also that both depend upon principles of wholeness and harmony. And it is on this basis that Saussure proposes to get the new process of semiological thinking under way.

What gives language a special place among semiological systems is, for Saussure, the fact that it displays, more clearly than others, the key recognition of semiology: the arbitrary nature of the sign. The fact that there is "no natural connexion" between that which signifies and that which is signified is, for Saussure, "the organizing principle for the whole of linguistics, considered as a science of language structure. The consequences which flow from this principle are innumerable" (*Course,* pp. 68–69). And indeed they are. The word "arbitrary" recurs throughout the argument, and its implications for the status of the sign quickly spread into every aspect of his approach to sign systems. That Saussure should take the principle of arbitrariness as the basis for his approach to order is an indication of the centrality to his work of the relatedness of order and disorder, and it is a principle that he develops at considerable length. For what gives Saussure's reconception of the sign such radical consequences is his insistence not only that the relationship between signal and signification is arbitrary, but also that both components, being conventional and contingent, are likewise arbitrary.

What Saussure is initiating here is an attack on the correspondence theory or reference theory of meaning—an attack which removes one principle of control from language and leaves Saussure in immediate need of another. In spite of the fact that there are obvious problems involved in attempts to regard the meaning of a word as the object or state of affairs for which it stands, this apparently commonsense belief has, as we noted earlier, persisted across the centuries.

Complications emerge very quickly when we remember that we can use different sets of words to "refer" to the "same object": for example, Diana Spencer, the Princess of Wales, the divorced wife of Prince Charles, the mother of the heir to the English throne after Charles, the princess killed in a Paris car accident, etc. And there seem to be many words that lack an apparently corresponding object: for example, tomorrow, sky, unicorn. Ellis develops the point further by considering the ways in which English and German relate and differentiate the terms cold, warm, and hot, and how differently, as a consequence, we might view the attractiveness of a hot bath:

> Even in a closely related language such as German, the concept *warm* is a different idea.... The English word gives the range of comfortable temperatures, but the German word reaches beyond that to the range of tolerable temperatures, only moving on to the historical equivalent for *hot* ("*heiss*"—but meaning "very hot") when tolerability is seriously in question.... At a particular temperature, we might indeed use appropriately both the German and the English word, but the temperature would have to be very high in the range of the one and low in the range of the other. Do the words at that particular juncture mean the same thing because they "refer" to the same temperature? No, because we have only to move a few degrees up the scale to find that while German is still using *warm,* English has moved on to *hot,* which shows that the words do not mean the same thing.[7]

As Saussure points out, those who insist upon regarding language as a naming process are assuming that ideas and objects exist in the form in which we encounter them *before* the words do with which we encounter them. The assumption is that we have ideas while the world has objects and states of affairs and we use language primarily as a device for naming those ideas, objects, and states of affairs. Hence the emergence of convictions that language is a means of expression and/or a means of representation. Saussure's radical reconstruction of the sign is based on his recognition that this is a misleading picture of language. He argues instead that what a linguistic sign connects is "not . . . a thing and a name, but . . . a concept and a sound pattern" (*Course*, p. 66). Both the concept (the signification) and the sound image (the signal) are conventional and taken together they constitute a sign. Though separable, the signal and signification are "intimately linked" (*Course*, p. 66).[8] Neither can exist without the other, neither would exist if language did not exist, and language exists only because communities of speakers exist. Consequently, both signal and signification are conventional.

But if both signal and signification are conventional, it becomes difficult to see how the sign can be a stable and viable unit. Reference to something outside of language has the apparent virtue of implying a reassuring form of control that gives language internal stability and external consequence. To insist instead on the conventionality of signal and signification in the context of an argument about arbitrariness is to open the door to chaos rather than clarity. It is here, however, that the necessity for and importance of Saussure's concept of a sign system becomes apparent. For Saussure, the system of relations between signs provides not only a clearer indication of what we do when we use language but also an adequate form of control. What language structure as a whole provides is a place for each sign in a system of signs that establishes a relative, but stable, value for each. The stabilizing characteristic of a sign in a system of signs is, in the simplest terms, "being whatever the others are not" (*Course*, p. 115).[9] Consequently, to move a sign from one system to another is to change its value, and to add or subtract one sign from a system of signs is to change the value of all the others.

Though this notion is by now well known, it has been sufficiently misunderstood to justify careful restatement, for only in the context of careful statement does the importance of system become as apparent as the importance of sign. And only in this context can we understand why the Saussure who so clearly recognized the heterogeneity of language became so obsessed with the possibility of a homogeneous linguistic structure.

If we consider, for example, a simple system like that of number, we can see the implications of Saussure's claims. In English the word *plural* exists in a number system consisting of two terms, "singular" and "plural." In Sanskrit, however, the number system has three terms, "singular," "dual," and "plural" (*Course*, p. 114). The differential meaning of the word "plural" in the two-term system is "not singular," that is, more than one. But the differential meaning of the word "plural" in the three-term system is "not singular or dual," that is, more than two. The system in each case is conventional; it assigns each item a value and it controls and guarantees that value. If the system is not fixed and reliable then neither is the value of its signs.

The implications of this switch from atomistic referential value of words to structural relational value are extensive, not just for linguistics, but for how we understand our use of language in the world. To recognize the conventionality of signal and signification and the system-based value of the sign is to recognize that language is not an atomistic naming device but a structural ordering device that involves a two-step process of grouping and distinguishing.[10] Each system provides the basis for grouping phenomena together and for distinguishing elements of the group from each other. The community of speakers of a language thus deals with the world not primarily in terms of "given" objects and relations but in terms of constructed and conventional objects and relations which are codified in the linguistic system they inherit. In the context of our example, people are disposed to deal with the world in terms of number because the language they inherit has a number system. They are likewise disposed to deal with the world in terms of two number categories or three because their language employs a two- or three-category number system. Issues to do with time, place, value, responsibility, individuality, and anything else of consequence to us are likewise prestructured by our language. The key contrast that emerges from Saussure's revision of the function of the sign is that the world connected with language in terms of the correspondence/reference theory is a world independent of the language that refers to it, while the world caught up in relational theory is partly constituted by the language that organizes it. Consequently language is not primarily a naming device but an ordering mechanism. We will explore later the degree to which we are merely influenced or largely compelled by the prestructuring such a view of language involves. At the moment it suffices to note both the power and the possible consequences of Saussure's reconstitution of the sign.

For linguistics, this reconstitution of the sign is the beginning of a reconstitution of the discipline's theoretical commitments and investigatory procedures. What Saussure in effect supplies is another principle for conceiving of the controls operating on and through language. Where the correspondence/

reference theory invokes controls established by the external world (and hence invites a great deal of discussion about true/false propositions), relational theory invokes controls derived from community activity in the past and inherited as a systematic whole by the present: "The structure of a language is a social product of our language faculty. At the same time, it is also a body of necessary conventions adopted by society to enable members of society to use their language faculty" (*Course*, pp. 9–10). Although subject to change, it is not subject to change by individual whim, for it has the weight of historical transmission behind it and the force of arbitrary convention: "It is because the linguistic sign is arbitrary that it knows no other law than that of tradition, and because it is founded upon tradition that it can be arbitrary" (*Course*, p. 74). Many who have borrowed Saussure's ideas about signs have overlooked his linking of the arbitrary with the force of historical and unyielding convention.

It might, of course, have been possible for Saussure to extend the implications of the notion of "a body of necessary conventions" in the direction of an aggregation of variously related systems or loosely related parts/wholes. But the twin desires to supply linguistics with a well-defined object of study and the reconstituted sign with a stable form of control reinforce his insistence on the integrated wholeness of the linguistic system. "A language as a structured system," we are told, "is both a self-contained whole and a principle of classification" (*Course*, p. 10). It is "a system of which all the parts can and must be considered as synchronically interdependent" (*Course*, p. 86). The pressures that drove Saussure to emphasize wholeness and harmony are evident enough. A theory of system-based rather than reference-based sign function seemed to demand the strong principle of control that only a fixed large system could supply. A convention-based system seemed likewise to need severe limits on the susceptibility of conventions to change. And a science of semiology based on the arbitrariness of the sign needed firm support if it were to become something other than an arbitrary discipline. But what is fascinating in watching Saussure at work is to encounter the intellectual rigor which drives him first to confront the features of language that generate its diversity and then to construct controls that might explain how something so potentially anarchic could serve as one of our principal means of organizing social life. It is this intellectual rigor that leads Saussure to overstate the need for wholeness and harmony, but his struggles to balance the claims of order and disorder in language and linguistics are far more informative than any of the apparent solutions he offers to their competing claims.

There are, of course, features of the systematic relationships among signs that render their solidarity less solid. And if we read Saussure's evolving ideas with care, we encounter attempts not just to eliminate potential disorder but to accommodate it in a variety of ways. The value of a sign, for example, is derived not just from its systematic relations with other items in the local system to which it belongs, but also from its interaction with other signs in a particular utterance. There are thus two axes of relationship and difference governing the value of a sign. There is the horizontal axis of sequence, chain, or presence to take into account the fact that a sign occurs in an utterance in the context of other signs that precede and succeed it. And there is the vertical axis of simultaneity, choice, or absence to take into account the fact that a sign occurs at a particular point in an utterance in contrast to other signs that might have appeared at the same point. Saussure calls the former syntagmatic relations and the latter associative relations, and he illustrates their relationship as follows: "Considered from these [syntagmatic and associative] points of view, a linguistic unit may be compared to a single part of a building, e.g. a column. A column is related in a certain way to the architrave that it supports. This disposition, involving two units co-present in space, is comparable to a syntagmatic relation. On the other hand, if the column is Doric, it will evoke mental comparison with the other architectural orders (Ionic, Corinthian, etc.), which are not in this instance spatially co-present. This relation is associative" (*Course*, p. 122).[11] What belongs in the linguistics of language structure (*langue*) are regular syntagmatic patterns that are widely used by speakers of the language and those regular associative contrasts that are likewise widely used. Idiosyncratic combinations and contrasts belong in the linguistics of speech (*parole*). As Saussure acknowledges, these distinctions are not easy to maintain, and the apparently secure notion of system becomes much less secure once the range of terms becomes a contextual variable. We see clearly here and elsewhere the strain involved in his efforts to separate the regular and homogeneous from the irregular and heterogeneous.[12] However, the principles of syntagmatic and associative relations are evident enough, and these are the primary controls on the value and signification of Saussure's reconstituted sign.

Though there are symptoms of strain in many parts of the argument presented in the *Course in General Linguistics,* the emphases that help bind it together rather than the strains that threaten to tear it apart have been the focus of attention of many who have sought to develop Saussure's thinking and apply it to other fields. Saussure's procedures for converting linguistic disorder into order have been given priority over his efforts to situate linguistic order in the context of linguistic disorder. The preferences for wholeness over fragmentation, homogeneity over heterogeneity, synchrony over diachrony, social *langue* over individual *parole,* and fixity over change proved to be key factors in the subsequent development of structuralism. They also helped reinforce demands in a variety of fields that theories be totalizing, explicit, and exhaustive. As a consequence, the very demands that once turned history into historicism have threatened to convert theory into ideology.[13]

Saussure's procedure of separating a unified *langue* from both diachronic change and synchronic variation reinforced a trend in which change and variation are not just relocated in theoretical schemas but to all intents and purposes are removed from them. And it is not difficult to recognize here the consolidation of the process that has led to contemporary theoretical dilemmas. Far from providing a point of investigative departure, theory so conceived tends to become both point of departure and destination, and the theorist who applies a monolithic and homogeneous theory is left, in effect, with no work to do. Structuralism, in particular, though internally various, dissolves speaking subjects into the codes they employ, and finds it difficult to give an adequate account of human creativity, individual responsibility, and social change. Necessity replaces freedom, unity replaces variety, certainty replaces doubt, and theory becomes the means of establishing the system of systems. Theory in such a context becomes a self-justifying machine for processing data rather than an instrument to be deployed in various ways by theorists pursuing differing kinds of inquiry. The gap between theory and theorist that allows for its creative use is, ironically enough, closed forever once a theory becomes (apparently) capable of converting all kinds of data, however ordered or disordered, into its own form of order. Like Joyce's Stephen Dedalus surveying a world apparently fully ordered by a benevolent God, theorists find themselves moving toward a devastating question about why any one of them should "continue to live."[14]

Such, in effect, has been the impact of the linguistic turn toward "necessity"[15] precipitated by Saussurean linguistic theory. But *within the discipline itself* other linguists soon began to speak out against the limitations of Saussure's theory as outlined in the *Course in General Linguistics.* It is instructive to look back at what two of them had to say and to note their efforts to build upon Saussure's attempts to situate order in the context of disorder rather than upon his attempts to separate the latter from the former. To reconsider their work is to envisage another linguistic turn that disciplines modeling their procedures on modern linguistics might have taken, and might yet take. For many of the difficulties currently afflicting literary theory were encountered and addressed by linguistic theory a generation earlier.

In 1949, some thirty years after Saussure's *Course* appeared, English linguist John Rupert Firth confirmed the new confidence and growing prominence of the discipline of linguistics, and his remarks registered the success of the revolution in the field that Saussure had sought to bring about. "Today," he remarked, "the linguistic disciplines are much surer of their own principles and philosophical outlook. Indeed, it is possible that during the next fifty years general linguistics may supplant a great deal of philosophy. The process has begun" (*Papers*, p. 168).[16] And indeed it had. Since the appearance of the book outlining Saussure's seminal reconstruction of the field, the notion that signs depend on systems of signs had become axiomatic in linguistics, and the conversion of data to systems had become a feature of intellectual activity in a variety of fields. But within linguistics the nature and function of such systems had quickly come under extensive review.

For Firth in the 1930s the key issue was not the function of the sign but the function of the system, and the key difference between Saussure's notion of system and the one that linguistics really needed was that between a system which mechanically repeats itself and a system which is dynamically reproduced. As we might expect, that difference is one between a sign system that has no room for variety and change and a sign system that seeks to accommodate both.

> Linguists and sociologists have to deal with *systems,* but systems very different from physical systems. Personal systems and social systems are actively maintained (with adaptation and change) in the bodily behavior of men. Most of the older definitions (and de Saussure's must fall in this category) need overhauling in the light of contemporary science.... Language and personality are built into the body, which is constantly taking part in activities directed to the conservation of the pattern of life. We must expect therefore that linguistic science will also find it necessary to postulate the maintenance of linguistic patterns and systems (including adaptation and change) within which there is order, structure, and function. Such systems are maintained by activity, and in activity they are to be studied. It is on these grounds that linguistics must be systemic. (*Papers*, p. 143)

This key contrast between systems which exist to be replicated and systems which exist because they are modified in replication is one which precipitates a revision of linguistics which is almost as radical as the one instituted by Saussure. Of major importance to Firth is the consequent reversal of the relationship between the general and the particular, between the social *langue* and the individual *parole,* between what we inherit as social convention and what we contribute as individual invention: "In emphasizing the systemic nature of language, I do not propose an *a priori* system of general categories by means of which the facts of all languages may be stated. Various systems are to be found in speech activity and when stated must adequately account for such activity. Science should not impose systems on languages, it should look for systems in speech activity" (*Papers,* p. 144). What Firth, in fact, offers is not unrelated to the linguistics of speech that Saussure had once promised to his students. But it is a linguistics of speech that, far from being subordinate to a linguistics of language structure (*langue*), renders the latter unnecessary and the distinction between the two counterproductive. For Firth, order and disorder in language are reciprocally related, and any attempt to study the highly ordered in isolation from the less highly ordered is likely to be misleading, for it separates order from the context in which it functions and in which it is enabled to function. No monosystemic procedure, for example, could ever account for the function of irony. What is needed is something more variable to supplement Saussure's notion of systemic value.

In Firthian linguistics signs not only have a value derived from internal systemic contrasts, they also have a function in the external contexts in which they are used. And this raises an issue, acknowledged as problematic by Saussure, which is of continuing consequence—the complex relationship between meaning derived from systemic contrast and meaning derived from both cotext and contextual use. For Firth a speaker makes systemic distinctions designed to achieve a particular purpose in what Firth calls a "context of situation" (*Papers,* pp. 27–28). And that context of situation is, for Firth, one best characterized not by considering a collective use of sign systems, nor by considering an individual using sign systems, but by considering complex social interaction involving the variable use of sign systems—in effect, by considering dialogue: "Neither linguists nor psychologists have begun the study of conversation, but it is here we shall find the key to a better understanding of what language really is and how it works. . . . That is what language really means to us—a way of doing things, of getting things done, a way of behaving and making others behave, a way of life" (*Papers,* pp. 32, 35). These two sentences are taken from two papers Firth published in 1935, the year in which he published the first major outline of a linguistic theory related to but radically different from Saussure's. Rightly perceiving that the relational linguistics that followed upon Saussure's reconstitution of the sign in fact involved a reallocation of priority between sign and system in favor of the latter, he began to explore the variable nature of systems.

Eventually Firth produced a theory of systemic linguistics in which meaning was not reducible either to Saussure's notion of the signification of the signal, or to the systemic value of a sign. Meaning instead is a function of a complex of systemic, collocational, and contextual relations that emerge from linguistic social interaction. As he puts it: "I propose to split up meaning or function into a series of component functions. Each function will be defined as the use of some language form or element in relation to some context. Meaning, that is to say, is to be regarded as a complex of contextual relations, and phonetics, grammar, lexicography, and semantics each handles its own components of the complex in its appropriate context" (*Papers,* p. 19). This dispersion of meaning into a variety of systemic, co-textual, and situational contexts exemplifies Firth's reconsideration of the systemic nature of linguistic structure: in effect the replacement of Saussure's monosystemic hypothesis with a polysystemic hypothesis and the relocation of order in the context of disorder. Rather than presupposing a unified whole consisting of a fixed set of systems with fixed relationships, Firth stresses the importance of considering language in terms of "a plurality of systems" whose relationships are contextually variable (*Papers,* p. 137). The notion that a single sign might make a variety of distinctions in a variable set of co-existing systems is one that not only recapitulates Saussure's rejection of word-idea or word-object approaches to the meaning of signs, but also rejects the "one morpheme one meaning" approach that succeeded it.[17] In Firth's view: "We must not expect to find one closed system. But we may apply systematic categories to the statement of the facts" (*Papers,* p. 187).

There is no mistaking the implications of these revisions to Saussurean linguistics—they are designed to restore a central role in linguistic theory to those elements of heterogeneity that Saussure was so keen to set to one side. Saussure's pursuit of a homogeneous, fixed, and unified *langue* is itself set to one side, even by a theory that seeks to build upon the Saussurean belief in the relational status of signs operating in sign systems. Systems, for Firth, are ordering mechanisms that function in the context of variability rather than uniformity. "Unity is the last concept that should be applied to language. Unity of language is the most fugitive of all unities, whether it be historical, geographical, national, or personal. There is no such thing as *une langue une* and there never has been" (*Papers,* p. 29).

Firth thus retains Saussure's notion of relational order while rejecting his efforts to separate *langue* from *parole,* synchrony from diachrony, internal linguistics from external, homogeneity from heterogeneity, and fixity from change. "Language, like personality, is a *binder of time,* of the past and future in 'the present.' On the one hand there is habit, custom, tradition, and on the other innovation, creation. Every time you speak, you create anew, and what you create is a function of your language and of your personality" (*Papers*, p. 142).[18] Such are the recognitions that precipitate Firth's distinction between systems that exist to be replicated and systems that exist because they are modified in replication. We can find systems and systemic relations in language use, but they are a function of the history of fluid and changing speech activity and not a consequence of preexisting or imposed schema that establish in advance what is possible for a language as a whole.

For Firth, the notion of a "language as a whole" (*Papers*, p. 71) is itself neither a necessary nor a desirable notion, and if we dispense with it we can restore the linguistic space within which human creativity, individual responsibility, and social change function. And it is Saussure's initial step of setting to one side linguistic heterogeneity that leads inexorably to the setting to one side of much that we value in language use. When Firth reintroduces the heterogeneous in language, he eliminates at a single stroke an apparently intractable problem, while, of course, giving new prominence to others. Not the least of the latter is that confronted by the theorist who must necessarily bring limited ordering principles to bear upon data whose modes of organization are both more varied and changing. In effect, the theorist has work to do once more, and has practical good reason, unlike Stephen Dedalus, to "continue to live." For neither the beliefs that promote the adoption of a particular theory nor the presuppositions embedded in that theory will serve to circumscribe what the data might have to offer.

What Firth in effect suggests is that linguistics should replace its efforts to find a well-formed object of study with efforts to institute systematic procedures for describing activity that is as ordered and chaotic as any other form of social practice. Such practice invokes the history of related practice and prepares its future. Its appropriate study not only involves abandoning the improbable notion of something socially constructed and deposited in the brain of each member of the community but also the notion that linguistics might be heuristically well served by hypothesizing such a construct. Firth's "pragmatic functionalism" (*Papers*, p. 36) is a linguistics in action studying a language in action, and its recognition of the irreducible heterogeneity of language in use is not a disabling recognition requiring evasive action but an enabling recognition that requires, as we shall see, a different kind of relationship between theory and theorist and a different sense of the relationship between theory and data.

Firth's was, however, by no means an isolated voice exploring the implications of linguistic diversity for linguistic theory in the period immediately succeeding the publication of Saussure's *Course in General Linguistics*. As Firth himself notes, the Russian formalists, too, were much concerned about the static formalism of Saussure's ideas. But the voice providing an even more radical critique of Saussure's ideas was another Russian voice, one only recently rediscovered by Western thinkers—that of Mikhail Bakhtin. As philosopher, literary critic, cultural historian, and linguistic theorist, Bakhtin covered extensive intellectual terrain.

Writing in Russia at a time of intense political turmoil, Bakhtin had great difficulty getting his ideas published at all. Arguments have been advanced that he published *The Formal Method in Literary Scholarship* (1928) and *Marxism and the Philosophy of Language* (1929) under the name of fellow members of the "Bakhtin Circle," P. N. Medvedev and V. N. Vološinov, but whatever the similarity of interests, the evidence does not currently justify that conclusion. Bakhtin's ideas on language are thus best known from his books on Dostoevsky (1929) and Rabelais (1965), and four essays on literature and aesthetics (1975), all of which have recently been translated into English (the latter as *The Dialogic Imagination*). The similarity of the ideas on linguistic diversity emerging from the works published under the names of Bakhtin, Medvedev, and Vološinov is evident enough, but the books by Vološinov and Medvedev overtly display a stronger Marxist influence. In Bakhtin's work an important context of understanding is that of the social situation of an utterance, but in the two books by the other authors mentioned above, the social context, in characteristically Marxist terms, often becomes the determining context, though the nature and degree of determinism remains ambiguous.[19]

In ways different than those of Firth, Bakhtin, too, takes issue with Saussure's attempts to distinguish between the collective language structure *langue* and the individual *parole,* and the social context of an utterance becomes one of dynamic exchange:

> Language, for the individual consciousness, lies on the borderline between oneself and the other. The word in language is half someone else's. It becomes "one's own" only when the speaker populates it with his own intention, his own accent, when he appropriates the word, adapting it to his own semantic and expressive intention. Prior to this moment of appropriation, the word does not exist in a neutral and impersonal language (it is not, after all, out of a dictionary that the speaker gets his words!), but rather it exists in other people's mouths, in other people's contexts, serving other people's intentions: it is from there that one must take the word, and make it one's own. And not all words for just anyone submit equally easily to this appropriation. . . . Language is not a neutral medium that passes freely and easily into the

private property of the speaker's intentions; it is populated—overpopulated—with the intentions of others. Expropriating it, forcing it to submit to one's own intentions and accents, is a difficult and complicated process.[20] (*Dialogic Imagination*, pp. 293–94)

This interaction between the voice of the speaker and the voices of previous speakers occurs in the context of interaction with the voices of other current speakers. For Bakhtin, as for Firth, "the word is born in a dialogue" and a linguistics unaware of the dialogic nature of utterances is poorly situated to clarify for us the nature of language (*Dialogic Imagination*, p. 279).[21]

This perspective leads Bakhtin, as it led Firth, to reject both Saussure's distinction between *langue* and *parole* (because the voices of the collective and the individual are not readily separable) and his distinction between synchrony and diachrony (because the individual voice is always mediating between an inherited language of the past and an emerging language of the future). An insistence on the irreducibility of the linguistics of the utterance also led both to focus on the centrality of dialogue and the necessity of giving priority to the contextualized utterance rather than the isolated sentence, for the speaker/writer must adopt words previously encountered elsewhere and adapt them to deal with an actual or potential hearer/reader: "All words have the 'taste' of a profession, a genre, a tendency, a party, a particular work, a particular person, a generation, an age group, the day and hour. Each word tastes of the context and contexts in which it has lived its socially charged life" (*Dialogic Imagination*, p. 293). Verbally expressed belief is here not so much a matter of initial and final decision but of ongoing adjustment to changing social contexts and evolving linguistic diversity, and in this respect at least, written forms of language and oral forms are the same. As Vološinov formulates it: "Language cannot properly be said to be handed down—it endures, but it endures as a continuous process of becoming. Individuals do not receive a ready-made language at all, rather, they enter upon the stream of verbal communication."[22]

Although the importance of context gives dialogue as significant a role for Bakhtin as it does for Firth, what we regularly regard as dialogue is only one exemplification of what Bakhtin regards as the dialogic nature of language that is characteristically multiple and constantly on the move. And for Bakhtin, as for Firth and Saussure, questions arise about the durable status of any theory addressed to such changing data. A language that is always in the process of being remade is not, of course, readily susceptible to large generalizations about its structure. Bakhtin, like Firth, prefers to think of language as an aggregate of local languages dialogically interacting rather than as a larger unity underlying the diversity of its many manifestations. "Language," he argues, "is never unitary," and what drives it toward heterogeneity is every bit as important as what moves it toward homogeneity (*Dialogic Imagination,* p. 288). And the contrasting demands of differing social groups renew and revise the crosscutting stratal organization generated by synchronic diversity and diachronic change.

> In any given historical moment of verbal-ideological life, each generation at each social level has its own language; moreover, every age group has as a matter of fact its own language, its own vocabulary, its own particular accentual system that, in their turn, vary depending on social level, academic institution (the language of the cadet, the high school student, the trade school student are all different languages) and other stratifying factors. All this is brought about by socially typifying languages, no matter how narrow the social circle in which they are spoken. . . . And finally, at any given moment, languages of various epochs and periods of socio-ideological life cohabit with one another. . . . Thus at any given moment of its historical existence, language is heteroglot from top to bottom.[23] (*Dialogic Imagination,* pp. 290–91)

Bakhtin's fascination with both multiplicity and change means that he cannot settle for a static heteroglossia. For Bakhtin as for Firth, synchronic variation and diachronic change are closely related forms of linguistic diversity, but the conflict between languages is a much more active force for change than is the case for Firth. The site of speech activity for Bakhtin's speaker is one of complex social and linguistic activity in an environment that is regularly constituted by competing forms of discourse. These offer not alternate ways of saying the same thing but contrasting ways of organizing social relationships, of adopting and distributing roles, values, and authority. To the extent that we become aware conceptually of what we do operationally, we constantly find ourselves in the position of "having to choose a language" from among many competing for our attention and having to adapt to our purposes whatever language we adopt (*Dialogic Imagination,* pp. 294–95).[24] What we are choosing is one of many ways of making meaning, one of many ways of organizing and controlling a situation, one of many ways of creating a social identity: "All languages of heteroglossia, whatever the principle underlying them and making each unique, are specific points of view on the world, forms for conceptualizing the world in words, specific world views, each characterized by its own objects, meanings, and values. As such they all may be juxtaposed to one another, mutually supplement one another, contradict one another, and be interrelated dialogically" (*Dialogic Imagination,* pp. 291–92).[25] There is thus no necessary inconsistency for Bakhtin between arguing that languages offer unique views of the world and arguing that languages can be dialogically interrelated. This dialogical interrelatedness is, of course, of the first importance, because it bears directly upon the relationship between modes of discourse and modes of belief and upon the reciprocal relationship between linguistic order and disorder. In such contexts, modes of discourse display both the capacity to become insulated monisms and the capacity to engage in pluralistic interaction.

What Bakhtin, like Firth, is offering is a very different picture of the role of systems in language than that offered by Saussure. Instead of a simple, static, monosystemic view of a language as a whole, he offers a portrait of a polysystemic, multiconstituted linguistic environment in which contrasting forms of social sharing are in constant interaction. There is, in effect, an ongoing struggle between speakers and other speakers and between one language and another for social ascendance. For Bakhtin, a linguistics that relies upon a notion of passive acceptance of language rather than active intervention is one that not only misdescribes the situation of the speaker, but one that misconstrues the nature of language and the issues involved in linguistic interaction.

> Linguistics and the philosophy of language acknowledge only a passive understanding of discourse.... In the actual life of speech, every concrete act of understanding is active: it assimilates the word to be understood into its own conceptual system filled with specific objects and emotional expressions, and it is indissolubly merged with the response, with a motivated agreement or disagreement.... [The speaker's] orientation toward the listener is an orientation toward a specific conceptual horizon, toward the specific world of the listener; it introduces totally new elements into his discourse; it is in this way after all, that various points of view, conceptual horizons, systems for providing expressive accents, various social 'languages' come to interact with one another. The speaker strives to get a reading on his own word, and on his own conceptual system that determines this word, within the alien conceptual system of the understanding receiver; he enters into dialogical relationship with certain aspects of this system. The speaker breaks through the alien conceptual horizon of the listener, constructs his own utterance on alien territory, against his, the listener's, apperceptive background.[26] (*Dialogic Imagination*, pp. 281–82)

It is this active interplay of competing and cooperating speakers of a variety of local languages from both the present and the past that provides the larger context of Bakhtin's notion of the dialogic nature of language. It is one far removed from Saussure's static synchrony, one that adds a further dimension of motion to Firth's active linguistic polysystemy, and one that has obvious implications for pluralists seeking to affirm both the autonomy and the interrelatedness of competing modes of discourse. Less clear, however, are the implications for the status of stable order and generalizable theory in a realm so irreducibly constituted by contestation, diversity, and change.

For Bakhtin the forces of cooperation and competition that characterize social activity in general are registered in the tension in large or local languages between the forces of fixity and the forces of change. Each exists in dynamic interaction with the other and linguistics must give simultaneous attention to both, not alternating attention to each. "Alongside the centripetal forces, the centrifugal forces of language carry on their uninterrupted work; alongside verbal-ideological centralization and unification, the uninterrupted processes of decentralization and disunification go forward.... The processes of centralization and decentralization, of unification and disunification, intersect in the utterance.... And this active participation of every utterance in living heteroglossia determines the linguistic profile and style of the utterance to no less a degree than its inclusion in any normative-centralizing system of a unitary language" (*Dialogic Imagination,* p. 272).

This is a much more radical version of the interaction between the forces of fixity and change in language than that provided by Firth or by the Russian formalists, and its implications become clear if we contrast it with the well-known alternative which Roman Jakobson developed to resolve the problems of his formalist predecessors. To avoid the problems posed by a static formalism, Jakobson argued that "every system necessarily exists as an evolution, whereas, on the other hand, evolution is inescapably of a systemic nature."[27] By taking this position, Jakobson could claim that change was both subject to systemic laws and open to variety. But what it was not open to, as are both Firth's and Bakhtin's approaches, is unexpected variety, and it is this that makes the work of Firth and Bakhtin of continuing importance. In spite of his efforts to avoid such problems, Jakobson, by making change itself systemic, continues to confront difficulties in accounting for human creativity, individual responsibility, and social and linguistic change. Change, in his terms, is reduced to variation within a set of predetermined options, and individual creativity is governed, not by unexpected interaction between systems, but by a "system of systems" with "its own structural laws."[28]

Such change, in effect, becomes regularized rather than unexpected and in an important sense ceases to be change at all. In the light of Firth's and Bakhtin's arguments, it is difficult to overstate the importance of a theory's capacity to accommodate unexpected change. This is an area of theory in which the problematic relationship between linguistic order and disorder comes most clearly into focus, and it is therefore one of the areas in which the nature and function of theory in general can most fruitfully be explored. But just as important are the implications of unexpected change for the pictures we construct of language and of the relative priority of linguistic fixity and linguistic change. Jakobson is thus quite right to raise the issue of interaction between systems, but Bakhtin's picture of that interaction is less predictable and more radical. If utterances are constantly dialogical, constantly involving the adaptation of old words to new purposes, and constantly registering the interaction between social languages, they will regularly generate different, but unpredictably different, forms of what Bakhtin calls hybridization. Such persistent rebuilding of language is a more complex form of the recurring linguistic renovation implicit in Firth's polysystemic hypothesis.

For Bakhtin as for Firth, language change and language fixity have to be studied together, but not within the framework of a system of systems. In the "crucible" of linguistic renovation, change, though retrospectively characterizable, cannot be prospectively circumscribed: "We may even say that language and languages change historically primarily by means of hybridization, by means of a mixing of various 'languages' co-existing within the boundaries of a single dialect, a single national language, a single branch, a single group of different branches or different groups of such branches, in the historical as well as paleontological past of languages—but the crucible for this mixing always remains the utterance" (*Dialogic Imagination,* pp. 358–59).

Emerging but not yet established change, far from being a separate or separable linguistic process, always coexists with ongoing but unstable fixity in every mode of discourse. In such a situation, what needs to be explained is not just how change occurs in the context of assumed fixity, but also how varying forms of fixity (however temporary) emerge in the context of ongoing change. Linguistic order, always located in the context of potential disorder, needs to be carefully situated in the persistently problematic contexts of contingency and sufficiency if order itself is to not to be misunderstood. And the challenge to generalizable theory is evident enough. There can be no system of systems because the forms of fixity against which change is measured are themselves changing.

Linguistic order and linguistic disorder, far from being opposed alternatives threatening to replace each other, are thus best treated as complementary and mutually informing forces. And the notion of discourse hybrids has consequently received increasing attention.[29] But in one brief phrase, Bakhtin suggests a very different way of conceiving the relationship between order and disorder than any we have so far discussed:

Unitary language constitutes the theoretical expression of the historical processes of linguistic unification and centralization, an expression of the centripetal forces of language. A unitary language is not something given [*dan*] but is always in essence posited [*zadan*]—and at every moment of its linguistic life it is opposed to the realities of heteroglossia. But at the same time it makes its real presence felt as a force for overcoming this heteroglossia, *imposing specific limits to it,* guaranteeing a certain maximum of mutual understanding and crystalizing into a real, although still relative, unity—the unity of the reigning conversational (everyday) and literary language, "correct language" (my emphasis) (*Dialogic Imagination,* p. 270).

The independent wholeness of Saussure's unitary *langue* (language structure) that sets to one side linguistic heterogeneity is here reconceived as an ordering force that serves not to oust, but to place "limits" on the forces of disorder. Instead of one supplanting the other, each is placed in ongoing interaction with the other, so that language remains a changing amalgam of persisting order and emerging variety, and, as such, requires us to study each component in the context of the other. Novelty and necessity become reciprocally related rather than radically opposed. As we will see, there is another famous linguist who makes just such an argument about order limiting rather than replacing disorder, and the convergence between their ideas lends peculiar force to this suggestion.

Bakhtin's picture of language activity as a process of continual development, "a process teeming with future and former languages" (*Dialogic Imagination,* p. 357), is one that offers a critique of Saussurean linguistics every bit as radical as that offered by Firth, and one that invites just as radical a reconception of the relationship between unity and diversity in language. But there is one further voice to be considered before we begin to contemplate the implications for other disciplines of an alternative linguistic turn that might be available to other disciplines as a consequence of the competing voices in linguistics.

This voice, too, is one committed to the exploration of linguistic diversity. Having argued that "the first thing that strikes one in studying languages is their diversity, the differences as between one country and another, or even one district and another" (*Course,* p. 189),[30] this voice goes on to provide one of the most concise and precise summaries of diversity among and within languages. But by now the scenario is reasonably familiar. The multiplicity of any synchronic state is invoked to explain the need for study of restricted or local languages, rather than of all a national language at once. The idiosynchronic discourse rather than the synchronic *langue* is the preferred object of study, for "Left to its own devices, a language has only dialects . . . [and] is destined to infinitesimal subdivision" (*Course,* p. 194).[31]

The manifest diversity of language is exemplified in the difficulty of distinguishing linguistically not only between related languages and related dialects but also between any single language and its dialects.[32] Rather than finding abrupt transitions between dialects or even between languages, the linguist often finds a series of almost "imperceptible transitions," with some linguistic features stopping where others begin but most spread unevenly around groups of variously related idioms (*Course*, pp. 200–202).

This uneven distribution of linguistic features across geographical space is matched by similar unevenness of linguistic features distributed across time. Language change, we are told, "will not be uniform over the whole territory, but will vary from place to place. A language has never been found to change in the same way throughout the whole area where it is spoken" (*Course*, p. 198). This picture of a multiform language undergoing constant but unevenly distributed change is a picture not of unified languages confronting each other uncomprehendingly across space and time, but of linguistic multiplicity evolving unevenly and unpredictably into other forms of multiplicity. Although unity is neither a presupposed point of departure nor an achievable goal, multiplicity is not randomness and it suffices to generate a recurring series of not necessarily unified but temporarily "coherent wholes" (*Course*, p. 206). And even if overall unity in a single language on a single territory were at some point achieved, it would, the argument continues, remain so only temporarily, for this language will eventually begin to display the characteristic heterogeneity of all linguistic systems:

> Whereas a single language was formerly in use throughout a given area, after five or ten centuries have elapsed people living at opposite points on the periphery of the area will in all probability no longer understand one another. On the other hand, those living at any given place will still understand the speech of neighbouring regions. A traveller crossing the country from one side to the other will find only slight differences between one locality and the next. But as he proceeds the differences accumulate, so that in the end he finds a language which would be incomprehensible to the inhabitants of the region he set out from. (*Course*, p. 199)

The forces that unify and the forces that diversify languages thus remain in constant conflict, and no form of language is either resistant to change or subject to only one kind of change. Synchronic variation and diachronic change are intimately intertwined, and the diversifying force they exemplify is one of continual but not consistent evolution. It is therefore important, the argument proceeds, for linguists to recognize that while the study of local forms of language will reduce the range of diversity they have to cope with, this restriction of attention will not eliminate it. The desire to locate uniformity is not to be satisfied by the restriction of attention to a social register, a local dialect, or a personal style. Such local forms of discourse are themselves internally multiple, unevenly changing, and unevenly differentiated from neighboring discourses. Regional dialects, for example, "have no natural boundaries," but neither do national languages, and what we think of as national languages are often separated as much by political as by linguistic boundaries (*Course,* pp. 200–203).[33]

As this linguist repeatedly insists, in every form of language, though in varying degrees in different situations, language diversity is very much apparent (an observation with evident implications for those advocating monistic modes of critical discourse). Syntagmatic and paradigmatic relations, far from being uniformly distributed, vary enormously, and collective norms are not always distinguishable from local variations: "Where syntagmas are concerned . . . one must recognize the fact that there is no clear boundary separating the language, as confirmed by communal usage, from speech, marked by freedom of the individual" (*Course,* p. 123). On the associative axis likewise, "the mind . . . grasps the nature of the relations involved in each case, and thus creates as many associative series as there are different relations" and "an associative group has no particular number of items in it; nor do they occur in any particular order. . . . Any given term acts as the centre of a constellation, from which connected terms radiate *ad infinitum*" (*Course,* pp. 123–24). Linguistic diversity so envisaged returns us to the problem of relating systemic and contextual meaning, but it is now possible to summarize the problem in an illuminating form. If the number of terms in a system is indefinite, how do we make sense of the claim that we can define any particular term in a system as "being whatever the others are not" (*Course,* p. 115).[34]

That final phrase is, of course, Saussure's, and it reintroduces the theme of fixed order to our discussion of linguistic diversity. But it is important to note that not only is the final quotation Saussure's, so also are all of the comments on linguistic diversity that have just preceded it. His acknowledgment that systems function not only in closed, but also in open sets is only one of many acknowledgments he makes of the immense diversity of linguistic systems, acknowledgments that register the tension in his work between a uniformity isolated and domesticated and a diversity reemerging and not clearly controlled.

Most of Saussure's comments on diversity are, of course, located in the sections of his book devoted to external rather than internal linguistics. But it is difficult, once one has read his views on diversity, to be persuaded of the distance the editors of his work seek to establish between unity and diversity in language. At times he seems to envisage other alternatives, and, as we have seen in several of his remarks, his views on diversity often parallel those of Firth and Bakhtin. He even recommends, as they recommend, that language be studied in the context of dialogue, though he prefers the more general term of linguistic intercourse to characterize contexts in which people speak to bridge rather than eliminate differences. It is in such contexts that for Saussure, as for Firth and Bakhtin, the monistic forces of linguistic unity and the relativistic forces of linguistic diversity, no longer mutually insulated, meet and interact:

> In any community, there are always two forces simultaneously pulling in opposite directions: particularism or parochialism on the one hand, and on the other the force of "intercourse," which establishes communication between men.
>
> It is parochialism which accounts for why a linguistic community remains faithful to the traditions it has nurtured. These habits are the ones every individual first acquires as a child: hence their strength and persistence. If they acted alone, they would give rise to endless linguistic diversity.
>
> But their influence is counteracted by the opposite force. If parochialism makes men keep to themselves, intercourse forces them to communicate with others. Intercourse brings a village visitors from elsewhere, brings together people from all around on the occasion of a celebration or a fair, unites men from different provinces under the same flag. In short, intercourse is a principle of unification, which counteracts the disuniting influence of parochialism. . . . So where [larger] areas are concerned, the two forces operate simultaneously but in varying degrees. . . . It is impossible to predict what the outcome from the joint action of these two forces will be. (*Course,* pp. 204–6)

In this context of unpredictable interaction between the forces of fixity and the forces of change, we are far from the context of a homogeneous and stable synchronic *langue.* Saussure places the speaker, as does Bakhtin, between a variety of languages, at home in some more than others, constantly striving to hold onto what is comfortable and known but also regularly seeking access to what is challenging, exciting, and not yet fully known. Saussure's speaker, like Firth's and Bakhtin's, has to learn not only how to choose an appropriate language for a particular context, but how to get others to accept the appropriateness or the necessity of the choice. Such a speaker, unlike the theorists depicted by Armstrong, is exploring the possibility rather than exemplifying the consequences of belief. For belief in a world of diversity and change is not something simple chosen once and repeated forever, but something complex that evolves in and is refined and ratified by ongoing social interaction.

In such passages, as we have noted, Saussure is no longer dealing with his internal linguistics of *langue,* but with his external linguistics of synchronic variation and diachronic change. Here the forces of fixity are not separated from the forces of change, unity is not separated from diversity, and order is not insulated from disorder. Whether internal linguistics as Saussure describes it seems a useful distinction or helpful abstraction from the external linguistics he so illuminatingly describes is a matter for debate. What is important to note is that the *Course in General Linguistics* itself offers a picture of diversity in language that is every bit as compelling as its picture of uniformity, and a picture in many ways compatible with the similar pictures of diversity offered by Firth and Bakhtin. But it is worth returning to Saussure's views on linguistic diversity after scrutinizing those of Firth and Bakhtin, because Saussure offers us an image of the relationship between order and disorder in language whose significance is enhanced by what we have learned about linguistic diversity from Firth and Bakhtin. It is a significance further enhanced when we remind ourselves of the sometimes debilitating consequences of the linguistic turn in the direction of order and necessity taken by so many disciplines.

As has so often been the case in the past, a renewed emphasis upon the order inherent in language leads inexorably toward renewed interest in linguistic disorder and instability. The modern conflict between structuralism and poststructuralism is, as we noted earlier, simply the most recent version of ancient conflicts between authority and anarchy, necessity and freedom, monism and relativism, conviction and contingency, and belief and doubt. But the initial turn in the direction of comprehensive, systematic order, in the direction of linguistic and structuralist necessity, is a turn that emerges from what might seem to be a selective and rather limited reading of Saussure's *Course in General Linguistics,* a turn that ignores much of what else happened not only in Saussure's book, but also elsewhere in the discipline of linguistics.

If we are to reconsider the significance of that turn and contemplate another, we might take as our starting point not Saussure's efforts to isolate linguistic order from linguistic disorder but the intellectual rigor that compels him to try to situate each in the context of the other and to try to base principles of order upon the recognition of the key role played by arbitrariness in linguistic systems. This will lead us to consider carefully the much neglected and radically different notion of the relationship between linguistic order and linguistic disorder that Saussure offers, one that bears a striking resemblance to something suggested also by Bakhtin.

As we have noted, Saussure insists, as a consequence of his reconstruction of the sign into a conventional signal and a conventional signification, that signs are not natural but arbitrary and that they exist not in isolation but in systems. Far from responding primarily to given entities in the world by assigning names, signs help constitute the world of our experience by grouping and distinguishing things, events, and processes that promote our own social activity.[35] Concepts are not arbitrary in the sense of random, but arbitrary in the sense of not being externally imposed.[36] This is, as we noted earlier, only one of the ways in which arbitrariness enters Saussure's linguistic theory. Indeed, he steps back at one point from his argument and observes that since Dwight Whitney insisted upon arbitrariness as a means of clarifying the institutional status of language and the sign, no one any longer opposed its truth, but not everyone recognized its larger consequences: "No one disputes the fact that linguistic signs are arbitrary. But it is often easier to discover a truth than to assign it to its correct place. The principle [of arbitrariness] is the organizing principle for the whole of linguistics, considered as a science of language structure. The consequences which flow from this principle are innumerable" (*Course*, p. 68).

This is, of course, a very strong statement, as Saussure selects an apparent principle of disorder as the "organizing principle" for the order inherent in linguistic structures, in the very realm of linguistics in which he had sought to maximize the function of comprehensive and stable order. And he insists upon it by exploring the function of arbitrariness in a variety of different ways. It should be noted therefore that when he eventually qualifies its role and its function, he does so by discussing degrees and kinds of arbitrariness: "The fundamental principle of the arbitrary nature of the sign does not prevent us from distinguishing in any language between what is intrinsically arbitrary—that is, unmotivated—and what is only relatively arbitrary.... In some cases, there are factors which allow us to recognise different degrees of arbitrariness.... *The sign may be motivated to a certain extent*" (*Course*, p. 130). Saussure has in mind here the way in which such terms as "*vingt*" and "*dix-neuf*" in French are differently motivated, with the former being quite arbitrary and the latter a motivated compound of two otherwise arbitrary terms. But just as arbitrariness has widespread impact on language, well beyond that of the arbitrary selection of the signal, so also does motivation, the recurring introduction of principles of order. And if the former is subject to differentiation in terms of kinds and degrees, so also must be the latter.

Saussure's shift from contrasting arbitrariness with motivation to contrasting arbitrariness with order in general is one that is made emphatically and at some length. But what is of major consequence is the picture Saussure offers of the relationship between arbitrariness and disorder on the one hand and motivation and order on the other. Just as Bakhtin was subsequently to suggest, Saussure argues that it is not the function of either order or disorder to replace the other, nor of one to take a privileged position over the other, nor of the two to form some sort of dialectical synthesis. Rather, order and disorder are placed in a complex relationship in which they are regarded not as exclusionary opposites but as two complementary and mutually informing forces. Order, far from being complete, is merely sufficient, and far from eradicating disorder, serves only to reduce it. Furthermore, it is not just in the context of discussing external linguistics but also in the context of discussing language's structural/systemic relations, that is, in the highly ordered internal linguistics of language structure (*langue*), that Saussure emphasizes the importance of the twin forces of order and disorder in language.

> *Everything having to do with languages as systems needs to be approached, we are convinced, with a view to examining the limitations of arbitrariness.* It is an approach which linguists have neglected. But it offers the best possible basis for linguistic studies. For the entire linguistic system is founded upon the irrational principle that the sign is arbitrary. Applied without restriction, this principle would lead to utter chaos. But the mind succeeds in introducing a principle of order and regularity into certain areas of the mass of signs. That is the role of relative motivation. If languages had a mechanism which were entirely rational, that mechanism could be studied in its own right. But it provides only *a partial correction to a system which is chaotic by nature. Hence we must adopt the point of view demanded by the nature of linguistic structure itself, and study this mechanism as a way of imposing a limitation upon what is arbitrary.* (my emphases) (*Course*, p. 131)

Such an approach to the limitation of arbitrariness had, indeed, scarcely received the attention of linguists, but the detailed descriptions contained in the work of Saussure, Firth, and Bakhtin of the irreducible diversity of language display them pondering it and inviting us to ponder it further. To do so will be to contemplate a very different linguistic turn than that toward necessity which has hitherto influenced so many disciplines. To study order not in the absence of but in the context of disorder, to study order as a means of controlling rather than replacing disorder, to study order as itself multiple and changing, but nevertheless stable and serviceable is to study something that requires theory, linguistic and otherwise, to make significant adjustments. For the key consequence of these alternative pictures of language is the different picture we are required and enabled to construct of the nature and function of theory.

It will not do in this context to privilege order over disorder and seek to establish monistic necessity. It will not do to privilege disorder over order and celebrate the unconstrained ludic potential of continuous contingency. And it will not do to place order and disorder in a dialectical context of antitheses, syntheses, and teleological schema. If an alternative linguistic theory is to provide an informative model for theory in other disciplines, it must be in terms that show how it can accommodate what it cannot yet predict, how it can provide access to what it cannot yet envisage, how it can supply instruments of discovery whose application it cannot fully control. Such a theory, seeking to link the inherited past to the emerging future, cannot restrict itself either to unity or to diversity or to any final accommodation they both might reach, but address itself to the task of clarifying how the two might interact in expected and unexpected ways. For the monistic impulse to exaggerate the role of order and the relativistic impulse to overstate the role of disorder are both simplifying gestures that function counterproductively. Both helped to promote a "linguistic turn" that served to renew the ancient conflict between necessity and novelty rather than to reconcile their competing claims. The key issue for theorists, therefore, is not just that they recognize the reciprocal relationship between order and disorder but that they find productive ways of picturing it. This will have large consequences for the ways in which we construct theories and deploy them, and it will directly affect the relationships both between theory and data and between theory and theorist.

A linguistic theory seeking to accommodate the reciprocal relationships between necessity and novelty, which Saussure, Firth, and Bakhtin in their different ways explore, would not only make problematic the relationship between theory and theorist and between theory and data, but also change quite radically, as the next chapter will suggest, presuppositions about the nature of theory that would have implications well beyond the boundaries of the discipline of linguistics. In their efforts to give formal and detailed shape to the theoretical principles of polysystemic, plurivocal linguistics, subsequent linguists explored to an advanced stage the problems that arise when attempts are made to reconcile the necessity derived from general principles of linguistic order with the constantly emerging disorder generated from a variety of sources. But to formulate the issue that way is to beg the key question with which linguists subsequently grappled: whether linguistic novelties are best treated negatively, as residual or emergent forms of disorder, or positively, as alternative forms of order. This issue, as we will see, has large implications for the nature of theory, for the role of theorists, and for the vexed relationship between language, belief, and truth. And directly bearing on those issues is the question unaddressed by the editors of Saussure's three lecture courses, which were delivered over a period of five years and left in important ways incomplete: whether there is as much to be gained by tracing the trajectory of a major theory's development as by seeking to establish its final or most fundamental form.

Chapter 3 Chomsky and Halliday: Novelty, Generality, and Theory

In the context of the pictures of language developed by Firth and Bakhtin, the work of Saussure looks decidedly different than it does in the context of the structuralist movement that sought to maximize Saussurean notions of order in semiotic systems. The nature and function of linguistic theory also look decidedly different as theory must seek to address data it can neither predict in advance nor circumscribe in retrospect. Any "linguistic turn" toward such reconstituted theory would mean for other disciplines not a turn toward the "necessity" described earlier by Rorty but toward an accommodation between the competing claims of necessity and novelty that theory must somehow make both possible and viable. Indeed, the pluralist's desire in literary studies to reconcile the competing claims of monists and relativists is directly analogous to the desire of linguists in the 1960s to reconcile the structuralist reification of Saussurean linguistics with the various relativizing reactions of other linguists to structuralism's excessive investment in totalizing principles of semiotic order.

To observe how post-Saussurean linguistic theory sought to reconcile novelty with necessity is to encounter sophisticated theory, at an advanced stage of articulation, struggling to find a means of controlling explanatory devices whose principal strength—their unifying descriptive power—threatened also to be their principal weakness. Their collective inclination to convert the unpredictable into the predictable inevitably misrepresented the nature of the unpredictable, while competing inclinations to describe the unpredictable as merely unpredictable were just as likely to mislead. Though advocates of different linguistic theories soon became adept at pointing out the weaknesses of competing theories, this did not serve to remove the problems of their own. The difficulty linguistic theorists thus encountered as tagmemic, glossematic, transformational, systemic, and stratificational models, among others, advanced their competing claims, was one of deciding how to evaluate and how to choose among a variety of theories, each of which dealt illuminatingly with some aspects of language and less illuminatingly with others. Here, choices between theories were not governed by the imperatives of belief that Armstrong assigned to literary theorists choosing among, say, Marxian, Freudian, or Lacanian interpretive perspectives, but by comparatively simple judgments about what constituted a better descriptive device. Simple though such judgments might seem at first glance, they soon confronted linguists with the difficulty of deciding what, about language, it is better to have described. And that problem serves ironically enough to reintroduce issues of belief that so radically affect the flexibility of the relationship between theorist and theory, issues that can only be satisfactorily addressed if some way can be found to make belief a point of departure and not just a preselected destination.

To disentangle the complexities of the relationship between theory and belief we need first to develop further the picture emerging in linguistics of polysystemic multivocal languages in which, to paraphrase Wittgenstein, the monistic assumption that belief, proposition, language, thought, and world line up alongside one another, each equivalent to each, is simply untenable. The reciprocal relationships in linguistic systems between order and disorder and between fixity and change suggest that the various sublanguages that constitute a national language are neither variants of some common system nor discrete and unified entities confronting each other uncomprehendingly across space and time. Rather they are distinct and related forms of linguistic multiplicity evolving unevenly and unpredictably into other forms of multiplicity. And if the order within and among such sublanguages is only sufficiently well established, in Saussure's phrase, to limit arbitrariness, then such order needs to be coherent enough to prevent disorder from becoming disabling but not so strong that it prevents creativity from promoting new forms of order within less than fully stable linguistic systems. Working with a language so conceived is not adopting a unified structure or accepting a unified package of beliefs but situating oneself in the context of guidelines that leave much room for maneuver. Conviction and contingency not only coexist, but are in some way correlated in linguistic systems based on both fixity and change.

Linguistic theorists attempting to describe such complex systems found themselves forced to focus directly upon the problem of reconciling linguistic necessity with linguistic novelty, and their efforts are instructive for anyone seeking to apply explanatory theory to similarly complicated data in other domains. The tensions that developed in the process of theory articulation register the general difficulties of relating theory to changing data, reveal something of the strengths and weaknesses of theory in general, and clarify the peculiar problems that emerge when anyone tries to develop criteria for choosing between competing theories. These problems for theory serve also to clarify and complicate the issues involved when pluralists in literary studies, seeking to affirm both the autonomy and the interrelatedness of competing modes of discourse, contemplate the possibility of combining elements selected from different theories.

Though those who take Saussurean linguistics as their point of departure for literary studies seem hardly aware of it, post-Saussurean linguistic theory turned not only to the development of structuralist theory and description but also to the puzzling implications of irreducible linguistic disorder. It is one thing, however, to acknowledge that language displays a changing variety of partially ordered patterns; it is quite another to incorporate such recognitions into explanatory theory and descriptive practice. A polysystemic language that displays irreducible variety and undergoes constant and unpredictable change will firmly resist attempts to reduce its various forms of ordering to a single mode of descriptive order. Efforts to establish such a form of order inevitably end up treating some of the elements of multiple order as symptoms of putatively unimportant disorder, while efforts to give the apparent disorder its due as another form of order increase both the number and variety of required descriptive techniques, making the resulting descriptive device more and more unwieldy. There thus seems to be an unavoidable conflict between the generality and the simplicity of any descriptive device. Difficult questions consequently arise about the ways in which we should choose between competing linguistic theories and between their always complicated and often uncertain methods of reconciling generality with novelty.

A standard account of selection procedure is provided by Davis, who describes theories in general as hypotheses with a capacity to predict the behavior of data. Theories so conceived consist of axioms, primitive terms, and definitions with which it is possible to provide descriptive accountings of data.[1] Choosing between competing theories then becomes, for Davis, a matter of applying three basic criteria: exactness, (self-consistent) generality, and simplicity. Such criteria appear at first glance to be reasonably objective and untainted by ideological conviction or potential prejudice. And they focus more upon the relationship between theory and data than upon the complexities of the relationship between theory and theorist. But their clarity is more apparent than real and Davis soon draws attention to the kind of problem we have already noted above. As each of these criteria is independent of the others, they may, in particular situations, be brought into conflict with each other: "Given two competing theories, the first may provide more exact accountings for restricted ranges of data whereas the second will provide less exact accountings of more extended ranges of data. Or, of two theories, the first may provide accountings covering some range of data but be less simple than a theory that accounts for data whose range is more restricted."[2]

Such cases of conflict between any two of the criteria, that is, between exactness and generality in the first case and between simplicity and generality in the second, can become even more complicated when, for example, exactness favors one theory but generality and simplicity favor another. When conflict between criteria is persistent and irresolvable, we have identified, Davis suggests, a point of flux in a discipline and a time when further research is required.[3] But the key question here would be further research into what?

In the case of language as Firth and Bakhtin (regularly) and Saussure (intermittently) envisage it, further research into the nature of language seems unlikely to help because what research itself has revealed is that the criteria of generality, simplicity, and exactness are likely to remain in persisting conflict given the complexity of linguistic data. We might then wish to consider, in the case of such persisting conflict, whether one of the three criteria should be regarded as more important than the other two. But lurking behind such abstract questions about the possibility of establishing criteria for selecting among criteria in deciding how best to describe data is the more concrete problem of deciding which data it seems most useful to have described. If the goals of a speaker/writer can range from saying just what is conventional and expected in a particular situation to saying something inventive and unexpected, the data to be described will be located at different points on the continuum that runs from the predictable to the unpredictable, and different linguistic models will treat this variety with differing degrees of success.

If we conceive the situation in these terms, choosing between various theories and their various modes of description is not merely a matter of descriptive tidiness; it also involves the persuasiveness of the theory's claims about the nature of language and the capacity of the descriptive method to illuminate language so conceived. In an important sense, the significance of which will become more apparent later, theories help constitute the data that the descriptive devices describe. And this recognition lends a peculiarly modern twist both to the persistent problem of relating language to belief and truth and to the emerging problem of situating theorist relative to theory.

Theory, in this sense, is a rather strange phenomenon. It wins adherents not only on the basis of its generality, simplicity, and exactness but also on the basis of its capacity to apply inductive and deductive logic in contexts that make it appear otherwise convincing. This involves, among other things, a capacity to clarify and resolve contemporary problems in the discipline whose precise nature and larger significance may or may not have been recognized hitherto. There is thus a historical dimension to theory selection, and in the case of linguistics in particular, the great challenge to the discipline since Saussure both emphasized and explained its lack of coherence has been to provide some modes of informative ordering that might unify the discipline while also providing what linguistic diversity will inevitably demand—some means of addressing related forms of disorder. Such concerns quickly take us beyond the criteria of simplicity, exactness, and generality and leave us groping for other criteria of adequacy. This leads inevitably toward questions about the *kinds* of simplicity, exactness, and generality that will serve our needs and to a recognition of the dangers involved in the excessive pursuit of any one of them. And in post-Saussurean theory, there have been few problems more vexed than those that emerge from often brilliant but always precarious attempts to address the apparently unexceptionable but ultimately unsatisfiable demands of generality. It is that problematic process that is clarified by efforts to trace something of the trajectory of a theory's development rather than to establish its final form. Indeed, as the impulse of theory is always to overreach itself, there is much to suggest that its final form might not be its most productive form.

The key question we inherit from Saussure, however, is not only whether it is possible to establish an illuminating form of generalized order in evolving realms of order and disorder but also whether his conceptions of the sign system and of the relationally defined sign give rise to a notion of order that is not flexible enough to accommodate the complexities and novelties of social and linguistic data. For the literary theorist, too, this is an important question as such novelties may well reach their limiting case in literary texts, particularly if they are considered, as Hirsch provisionally suggests, as language games distinguished by the characteristic of being played only once.[4]

Subsequent linguists have intermittently grappled with this problem, and it is helpful to theorists in other fields to recognize the ingenuity of their efforts and the intricacies of the issues that arise. Beginning in the 1950s two major attempts to accommodate the competing claims of generality and novelty were mounted by Noam Chomsky and his associates and by Michael Halliday and his associates. Radical revisions of the theories emerged during the 1960s and 1970s, and the repeatedly revised theories provide compelling examples of theory evolution in the face of intractable problems. The work of the two linguistic theorists most visibly committed to the task of reconciling novelty and necessity inadvertently reveals the difficulty of restraining the imperatives of generality, the irresistible appeal of apparent truth, and the insidious nature of the hermeneutic circularity they both set out so assiduously to avoid. And to trace the trajectory of these theories from a fascination with novelty to a relapse into necessity is to see something about the nature of theory that cannot be as clearly displayed in any other way.

Chomsky began by addressing directly the issue of relating the apparent disorder produced by creativity to the inherited order of an established system. In doing so, the most famous linguist of the modern era confronted directly the problem of reconciling necessity with novelty and he set the discipline a direct challenge. Its key task, he argued, was to explain and account for understandable novelty, specifically for the peculiar ability of a native speaker "to produce and understand new utterances, while he rejects other new sequences as not belonging to the language" (*Syntactic Structures*, p. 23).[5] The native speaker seems to have the ability to distinguish between an apparent disorder that belongs in the language and an apparent disorder that does not.

To accommodate such recognitions of order and variety in the language, Chomsky envisaged a more sophisticated form of linguistic description than the one he found in the work of Saussure and his structuralist successors. The basic problem with their work, he argued, was a deficient conception of descriptive method registered in an excessive reliance on "taxonomic principles of segmentation and classification" (*Aspects*, p. 47).[6] The apparently all-powerful descriptive device of the sign system as conceived by Saussure restricts linguistics, in Chomsky's view, to the elementary operations involved in "segmentation, classification, substitution procedures, filling of slots in frames, association, etc." (*Aspects*, p. 57). This is, of course, a less than adequate version of

Saussurean linguistics, but Chomsky argued persuasively that systems operating one at a time in a hierarchical relationship cannot, no matter how carefully applied, account for the ordered knowledge of language a speaker displays or for the fact that such knowledge is acquired through encounters with the order and disorder of other people's speech. A relationally defined sign, he concluded, must surely occupy a more sophisticated grammatical environment than that in which structuralists have tended to locate it, particularly if generality is not to exclude unjustifiably a variety of kinds of linguistic novelty.

For Chomsky an understanding of that environment involves a radical reconsideration of the nature and function of linguistic levels in linguistic description. It has long been an accepted principle of linguistic description, as of other forms of description, that if you wish to describe something that is very complicated, it is better to produce a series of descriptions of a series of parts which can then be recombined to cover the whole than to try to describe all of a complex whole at once. In its most elementary form, this amounts to no more than recognizing what it is that we do when we think of language as having words with characteristic structures, phrases (word groups) with other kinds of structures, and clauses, sentences, and paragraphs with their own characteristic structures too. In more sophisticated contexts, however, the success of a theory of language depends on its capacity to select imaginatively the levels at which linguistic patterns will be isolated and the mechanisms with which they will subsequently be combined. And it is in this sense (and others) that a theory helps constitute the facts it confronts. It is in this sense too that theorists have to decide at some point whether to present their techniques of analysis as heuristic instruments imposed on the data for pragmatic purposes or as ontological clarifications of the nature of linguistic systems. And it is important to keep that emerging problem in mind, for it, too, bears upon the issue of reconciling novelty with generality in some noncircular manner.

A characteristic structuralist analysis, is, for Chomsky, seriously limited in its construction and combination of descriptive levels for it insists on analyzing sentences in terms of their most immediately visible grammatical features (immediate constituent analysis) and then relating those features in a solely hierarchical manner (e.g., sentence structure consists of clause units, clause structure of phrase units, phrase structure of word units, word structure of morpheme units). Such a procedure keeps repeating the same kind of analysis at each level, and it is this rigidity, Chomsky argues, that restricts its capacity to deal with the novelty and not just the necessity of linguistic systems. He points out how such descriptive analysis encounters considerable difficulty in dealing with discontinuous structures and even greater ones in capturing the relatedness of dissimilar structures, like active and passive sentences. Even more important, it finds itself helpless in the face of Chomsky's demand that an adequate linguistics be able to account for "the speaker's ability to produce and understand instantly new sentences that are not similar to those previously heard in any physically defined sense or in terms of any notion of frames or classes of elements, nor associated with those previously heard by conditioning, nor obtainable from them by any sort of 'generalization' known to psychology or philosophy" (*Aspects*, pp. 57–58).

What Chomsky offers instead is a much more abstract notion of linguistic level, one that requires different modes of description at different levels, one more capable of accommodating both regularity and variety. In its original conception this consisted of a set of phrase structure rules that generate simple phrase structures, a set of transformational rules that construct more complicated structures from the simple ones, and a set of morphophonemic rules that convert the abstract sentence structures (morpheme sequences) derived from the first two sets of rules into actual instances of sentences (phoneme sequences). It is the nontaxonomic asymmetry between levels that enables the theory to account for a speaker's ability to produce and understand new sentences. A limited number of transformational rules that can add, delete, and rearrange elements of simpler structures are capable of repeated application to produce more and more complex sentences. Such novelty and complexity are, however, achieved by means of a mechanism that is itself entirely regular.

It is this notion of rule-governed creativity that attracted the admiration of a generation of linguists. Here was a new theory that persuasively identified a recalcitrant problem in the discipline and offered a promising solution. Chomsky appeared simultaneously to have demonstrated the insurmountable problems of taxonomic structuralism and the capacity of a reconceived transformational linguistics to accommodate linguistic novelty by reconciling order and disorder within a new and more flexible mode of ordering.

With a few simple assertions in his first major work, *Syntactic Structures*, Chomsky seemed to have permanently reconstituted the field of linguistics. First, he argued, "syntax is the study of the principles and processes by which sentences are constructed in particular languages." Second, "syntactic investigation of a given language has as its goal the construction of a grammar that can be viewed as a device of some sort for producing the sentences of the language under analysis." Third, language is to be conceived as "a set (finite or infinite) of sentences, each finite in length and constructed out of a finite set of elements."

Fourth, "the grammar of [a language] will . . . be a device that generates all of the grammatical sequences of [the language] and none of the ungrammatical ones" (*Syntactic Structures,* pp. 11–13). In four simple sentences, Chomsky reshaped the linguistic discipline by redescribing the linguistic scene within which the linguist operates. He focused linguistics on sentences (which Saussure had banished to *parole* because of their structural heterogeneity), reconstructed grammars into sentence-producing devices, built creativity into the very definition of language as a potentially infinite set of sentences constructed transformationally from a finite set of elements, and insisted that creativity in language use is quite compatible with a definitive and comprehensive set of rules and regulations. As Chomsky later put it, the time had come to "attempt an explicit formulation of the 'creative' processes of language" (*Aspects,* p. 8).

The phrases "all and only" and "infinite use of finite means" rang like clarion calls through the linguistics of the 1960s.[7] Chomsky appeared to have solved the problem of reconciling necessity with novelty and to have successfully rebuilt "the vast complexity of the actual language more elegantly and systematically by extracting the contribution to this complexity of several linguistic levels, each of which is simple in itself" (*Syntactic Structures,* p. 42). Simplicity, generality, and exactness seemed, for a moment, to be advantageously reconciled in a theory that focused explicitly on the nature of linguistic novelty.

There were some problems, however, with the original model and with claims that what was being so elegantly and flexibly ordered was "actual language." Chomsky was soon attacked on the one hand for focusing upon problems of syntax when the discipline had yet to resolve recalcitrant problems in phonemics and morphology and on the other hand for having focused on syntax without reference to the equally longstanding problems of semantics. Failure to address such issues must surely undermine claims that the theory would deal with "actual language" and that it could address "all and only" the sentences of a particular language. Some wondered whether Chomsky's claims to generality had produced yet another example of the procedure of exclusion by which linguists describe what they can describe and then reject the rest as someone else's business. Chomsky's response to such challenges was, however, characteristically intelligent and curiously inconsistent. Addressing the phonemics and morphology issues he argued as follows: "It is quite true that the higher levels of linguistic description depend on results obtained at the lower levels. But there is also a good sense in which the converse is true. . . . The grammar of a language is a complex system with many and varied interconnections between its parts. In order to develop one part of grammar thoroughly, it is often useful, or even necessary, to have some picture of the character of a completed system" (*Syntactic Structures,* pp. 59–60).

Heuristically this makes eminent sense, as the precise function of any part can be explored more advantageously in the context of an embryonic whole. Such a conception of the relationship between part and whole mobilizes the cycle of investigation to which Chomsky refers approvingly elsewhere, a cycle in which part and whole continually adjust to the demands of each other (*Aspects,* p. 46). The envisaged trajectory of theory development appears increasingly inclusive and increasingly general. But this relationship between part and whole seems not to function at the interface between grammar and meaning, and at this level the "completed system" seems not only incomplete but uncompletable. For the Chomsky of *Syntactic Structures* the study of grammar and the study of meaning are separate issues. Here there is no big picture of which they are both informative parts. This linguistic theory is, as he puts it, "completely formal and non-semantic" (*Syntactic Structures,* p. 93). The set of sentences that such a grammar can generate is precisely that—a set of grammatical sentences established on a purely formal basis. The fact that there are correspondences between formal and semantic features of a language is not, for him, a justification for studying both aspects of language simultaneously: "Grammar," he argues, "is best formulated as a self-contained study independent of semantics" (*Syntactic Structures,* p. 106). Though he can envisage a more comprehensive linguistic theory than his own, subsequently incorporating both "a theory of linguistic form and a theory of the use of language as subparts," the autonomy and priority of formal matters remains quite clear: "Having determined the syntactic structure of the language, we can study the way in which this syntactic structure is put to use in the actual functioning of language" (*Syntactic Structures,* p. 102). In arguing that "phrase structure and transformational structure appear to provide the major syntactic devices available in language for organization and expression of content," Chomsky first separates form from content and then anticipates reconnecting them not with an interactive cycle of discovery but by casting content in the shape of the already posited form (*Syntactic Structures,* p. 102). Theory development, though readily acknowledged as necessary, is, almost from the outset, severely restricted by initial presuppositions about the priority and generality of the formal order that characterized the first stage of the theory.

These efforts to keep the problems of semantics at bay are understandable enough. It is generally recognized that the complexity of language increases exponentially as description moves up the scale from phonology through syntax to semantics and its contextual relations. But Chomsky's determination to marginalize semantics diminished the admiration he had earned for insisting on the centrality of complex sentence structure. Chomsky's tactics for dealing with the messiness of semantics tend to oscillate between initial procedures of exclusion (semantics should be studied separately) and subsequent procedures of absorption (semantics is simply extended form). In both cases the appeal of the "all and only" claim is considerably diminished and the attempts to situate part and whole in an ongoing cycle of investigation abruptly terminated.

This response to the claims of semantics is oddly inconsistent with the response to the claims of phonemics and morphology, but the manifest desire to achieve apparent generality by imposing premature closure on the cycle of investigation is also visible elsewhere, even in the investigation of syntactic patterns. When, for example, such formal patterns appear confusing and it is unclear whether or not a particular sentence is grammatical, Chomsky recommends that the rules of grammar be derived from the clear cases and then the grammar, rather than the native speaker, be allowed to make decisions about grammaticality (*Syntactic Structures,* p. 14). Novelty and necessity in such a context seem more likely to be at odds with each other than to be productively reconciled. Indeed, an alarming circularity threatens to emerge as the generalizing mechanism for describing all and only the sentences of a language is itself allowed to dictate what is and is not a sentence of the language.

As subsequent critics of Chomsky's work never tire of pointing out, the initial promise of that work to accommodate novelty into linguistic description is accompanied by a disappointingly contradictory tendency to claim comprehensive generality by excluding important kinds of novelty. The grammar that promised to include all and only the sentences of a language finds itself struggling both with problems of inclusion and with problems of exclusion. It seems unable, for example, to include some of the most elementary kinds of everyday creativity. Some of the sentences of advertising language ("Only two Alka-Seltzers ago, you were feeling downhearted and low") and some of the sentences of literary language ("He danced his did"—e. e. cummings) have to be categorized as ungrammatical. And one of the key reasons for this is that once the notion of a grammar as a mechanical device for producing sentences is accepted, we have to deal with its mechanical readiness to generalize indiscriminately from all idiosyncratic cases. As Grinder and Elgin put it:

> If you are going to allow a grammar to generate a line of poetry like "He danced his did," and you are going to treat that as acceptable, how are you going to prevent a se-

quence like "He danced his paper bag"? On the surface it appears that "He danced his paper bag" should be a lot less deviant than "He danced his did," since it is at least structurally identifiable as a proper expansion of an English sentence. No Phrase Structure Grammar of English, however, offers as a possible expansion the following rules:

R1 (a) S→NP VP
    (b) VP→Verb Determiner Verb

It is precisely these two rules that would be required to generate "He danced his did."[8]

To designate such a sentence grammatical, of course, is to begin to make a comparatively simple grammar increasingly unwieldy. To designate it ungrammatical is to display a rigidity that brings into question the nature of the grammar, the function of its decisions about grammaticality, the relationship between grammaticality and acceptability, and the diminished role of the linguist in operating such a device.[9]

To deal with these and other issues that register a disposition to exclude variety rather than accommodate creativity, Chomsky made renewed attempts to include more elements of language and more of their novelty. In *Aspects of the Theory of Syntax,* he offered a revised version of his transformational generative grammar, and the trajectory of the theory's development is informative. This revision made way for the previously excluded semantic component, but in doing so it made even clearer the tension in the theory between an impulse to avoid descriptive circularity by accommodating novelty and an imperative to achieve descriptive closure by excluding it. And the apparently reconciled claims of simplicity, generality, and exactness became subject to renewed tension as the larger generality produced more complex levels of description and more complex relationships among them. Such a price might be well worth paying, if the achieved generality seemed persuasively inclusive, but if problems of exclusion begin to recur, then the costs to the model's simplicity are not likely to be outweighed by the gains in its generality.

The three levels (phrase structure, transformations, morphophonemics) of the original formal model evolved into a model with three major components: the syntactic, the phonological, and the semantic. But this effort to make the model more inclusive is limited by a gesture of containment as the developing theory retains its initial commitment to the priority of the syntactic component. The all-powerful syntactic component is required to specify for each sentence "a *deep structure* that determines its semantic interpretation and a *surface structure* that determines its phonetic interpretation. The first of these is interpreted by the semantic component; the second, by the phonological component" (*Aspects,* p. 16). The limitations of a formally determined semantics, however, become as quickly apparent as those of a mechanically generated form. A linguistic model initially admired for its capacity to accommodate novelty, variety, and creativity soon found itself trying to promote descriptive closure by establishing the meaning of words on the basis of fixed semantic features and rigid empirical signification. The imperatives of a certain kind of order continue to restrict the reach of a generality that was already in conflict with the claims of simplicity.

Katz and Fodor, with Chomsky's initial approval, approached semantics by seeking for each word "a decomposition of the sense it represents by breaking down that sense into its component concepts."[10] In these terms, Katz, comparing his theory of meaning to Democritean atomic theory, provided a famous list of the semantic features of the word "chair": "(Object), (Physical), (Non-living), (Artifact), (Furniture), (Portable), (Something with legs), (Something with a back), (Something with a seat), (Seat for one)."[11] In a suitably puzzled review, Harrison asked whether it is "a semantically important fact about chairs that they are portable, for example? My own intuition says no, on two grounds: first, that one can tell whether something is a chair without knowing whether it is portable or not, and second, that many chairs are not in fact portable."[12] He cites as an example the stone chair in which Lincoln sits in Washington, and it would not be difficult to suggest others. But the difficulty of semantic feature analysis does not end there. As Harrison also points out, Katz, seeking to constrain combinations of semantic features to prevent the grammatical device from generating "The reflection chased the bandit" and "The stick chased the dog," finds himself excluding what appear to be perfectly good English sentences such as "The clouds chased each other across the sky" and "The thought of bed chased all concern with linguistic theory from my mind."[13]

Harrison's humor captures the more general recognition that the problems of order and disorder in language seem likely to exceed the reach toward inclusive generality of even so original and brilliant a linguist as Chomsky. The initial gesture of inclusiveness embodied in attempts to account for a native speaker's ability to produce and understand new sentences steadily gives way to generalizing attempts to justify the exclusion of a great deal of variety and change in language. The initial decision to exclude semantics from the grammar was succeeded by a courageous attempt to include it. But the delayed attempt to include it meant that efforts had also to be made to contain it: in effect, to restrict it to what the already established formal devices of the grammar could readily accommodate. Instead of a fruitful cycle of investigation in which the demands of formal and semantic patterning adjusted to each other, the earlier formal commitments provided severe restraints upon the possibilities of describing in an illuminating manner matters of semantic function.

With some disappointment we recognize, in Davis's terms, an irreconcilable conflict between efforts to achieve generality and efforts to sustain simplicity and exactness in the context of linguistic novelty. The distinction between a semantic deep structure and a phonological surface structure separated by and related by a variety of transformations is a simplifying attempt to allow the diversity of semantics into the system while keeping it under preconstituted formal control. If the basic strings that provide the semantic deep structure fully account for the semantic component of the grammar, semantic considerations can be excluded from the variations wrought by the transformational level and from the variety exhibited in the surface structure. Requirements of simplicity dictate that (optional) transformations cannot affect meaning and consequently cannot add or delete meaningful terms.

Such tidiness in the theory is, however, being bought at a considerable price. The theorist who claimed to be able to cover all and only the sentences of a language, to accommodate the remarkable variety of sentence structures, and to account for a native speaker's ability to produce and understand new sentences now sought to ratify a limited kind of generality and sustain simplicity by making a disturbingly familiar move. Chomsky unapologetically grasps and wields to devastating effect a cruder version of the Saussurean axe: "Linguistic theory," we are told, "is concerned primarily with an ideal speaker-listener, in a completely homogeneous speech community, who knows its language perfectly" (*Aspects,* p. 3). And what the linguist is to describe is no longer "actual language" but a speaker-hearer's linguistic competence. The focus is upon the idealized "knowledge of his language," rather than upon the particular linguistic performances that exemplify "actual use of language in concrete situations" (*Aspects,* p. 4). A grammar is now an account of an ideal speaker-hearer's formal knowledge of an ideal language in an ideal community, and it does not seek to account for nonideal use of a nonideal language in a nonideal community. The ambitious attempt to account for a nonfinite set of sentences derived from finite elements now turns out to exclude as much as it seeks to include.

Simplicity, even when purchased at such a price, soon proved unsustainable. The strategies of exclusion, however radical, proved insufficient to contain the complexities of the semantic component now incorporated into the grammar. Within a short time transformational generative grammarians were acknowledging that deep structure alone could not specify meaning; that surface structures also make a contribution to meaning; that transformations preserve some but not all meaning; and that deep structure and surface structure are not rigidly distinct. In spite of efforts to suspend it in the name of simplicity, the cycle of investigation intermittently reasserted itself, and with devastating consequences. As it strove for increasing generality of application the model confronted its developers with an unhappy choice between sustaining simplicity at the cost of exactness, or pursuing exactness further by replacing the simple with the increasingly unwieldy. A linguistic model that had launched itself with an enthusiastic embrace of novelty in linguistic systems was increasingly unable to accommodate its apparently inexhaustible demands.

As a generative semantics began to appear on the scene to challenge the priority of formal matters that had first governed the model, Chomsky's initially clear picture of levels and linkages became much less clear and much more controversial. Revisionists like Lakoff and McCawley were soon prepared to challenge almost all of the original and many of the subsequent theoretical commitments. Lakoff rejected Chomsky's restriction of linguistics to the study of competence and argued that language should be studied in all its manifestations; he rejected the distinction between grammaticality and acceptability and thus the belief that a grammar can specify in advance of the linguistic event the nature of the grammatical; he challenged the necessity for generative (production, projection) grammars, the notion that language consists primarily of a formal set of sentences, and the belief that linguistic form could usefully be studied independent of its context and function; he asserted the priority of meaning in setting up systems of linguistic description and objected to the inappropriate imposition of clear order upon fuzzy language systems. McCawley agreed with many of these views and added that the acquisition of language is ultimately related to the acquisition of culture.[14]

In a remarkably brief period the Chomsky revolution and reaction to it recapitulated the events in linguistics that surrounded Saussure's major intervention. The competing claims of necessity and novelty, temporarily resolved, renewed their conflict with disruptive effect. Saussure's intermittent attempts to establish order by excluding disorder disguised rather than resolved the problem, and Chomsky's initial attempt to establish order by absorbing disorder eventually served only to do the same. The major irony of Chomsky's approach to linguistics is the inconsistency between his initial desire to give a central role in linguistics to the problem of accounting for linguistic creativity and his subsequent conviction that linguistic theory should concern itself primarily with "an ideal speaker-listener, in a completely homogeneous speech community" (*Aspects,* p. 3). In such a community with such a speaker what room is there and what need is there for linguistic creativity? To focus linguistics on shared competence rather than diverse performance is to remove from creativity a necessary context of disorder, and, as a consequence, with implications we will explore later, effectively to eliminate creativity.

The irony of this transition from novelty to necessity in the evolution of one of the most remarkable linguistic theories of the twentieth century is evident enough. But it is by no means an isolated event in modern theory, as the transition in the project of deconstruction from displaying the unexpected to producing a predictable version of the unexpected so emphatically confirms. Though Chomsky's model continued to evolve, it continued to be trapped by its excessive investment in formal devices that not only promised more than they were able to deliver but also revealed the insidious capacity of theory's descriptive power to overreach itself. Efforts to achieve generality in theory, when pursued with sufficient rigor, seem inevitably to force the theorist into a choice between a simplicity that is unacceptably reductive and a comprehensiveness that is unacceptably complex. And differing ways in which generality might be achieved seem to offer only the alternatives of premature descriptive closure or persistently deferred descriptive closure, and it is this dilemma that is so clearly revealed when the development of theories is subjected to scrutiny. And it is this same issue that renders problematic the notion that a theory's final form is necessarily its most productive form. There is much about Chomsky's use of transformations that clarifies the relationships between grammatical structures, but in trying to build a comprehensive model upon an illuminating set of descriptive techniques, Chomsky asked more of them than they were able to deliver. By failing to establish their appropriate limitations, he, in effect, cost them a lot of their credibility. As the development of the model makes clear, powerful descriptive techniques that illuminate some aspects of linguistic order seem only to misrepresent other aspects, and the order and disorder of linguistic systems continue to require some more flexible approach, if a persuasive kind of generality is to be achieved.

Reflecting on these issues three decades after the publication of *Aspects of the Theory of Syntax,* Chomsky reviewed in *The Minimalist Program* the arguments in favor of simplicity and elegance in linguistic descriptions:

> Language is a biological system, and biological systems typically are "messy," intricate, the result of evolutionary "tinkering," and shaped by accidental circumstances and by physical conditions that hold of complex systems with varied functions and elements. . . . Language use appears to have the expected properties; as noted, it is a familiar fact that large parts of language are "unusable," and the usable parts appear to form a chaotic and "unprincipled" segment of the full language. Nevertheless, it has been a fruitful working hypothesis that in its basic structure, the language faculty has properties of simplicity and elegance that are not characteristic of complex organic systems, just as its infinite digital character seems biologically rather isolated. Possibly, these conclusions are artifacts reflecting a particular pattern of inquiry; the range of completely unexplained and apparently chaotic phenomena of language lends credibility to such skepticism. Still, the progress that has been made by the contrary stance cannot be overlooked.[15]

Whatever the progress achieved, the order thus clarified finds itself isolated from rather than productively related to the disorder against which it defines itself. What is evidently still needed is some picture of novelty and necessity in language that will allow generality and descriptive closure to achieve some more fruitful relationship.

The most elementary of the various procedures used to achieve theoretical generality and establish descriptive closure is one we have already encountered. It involves arguments to justify what Derrida has described as the procedure of exclusion.[16] This is a reductive procedure by means of which important diversity in the linguistic system which a theory is compelled to consider is distinguished from unimportant diversity which it can thankfully ignore. This can take the form of Chomsky's distinction between linguistic competence and linguistic performance—a distinction with which he seeks to justify his theory's setting aside "such grammatically irrelevant conditions as memory limitations, distractions, shifts of attention and interest, and errors (random or characteristic)" that a speaker might register in everyday speech with its "numerous false starts, deviations from rules, changes of plan in mid-course, and so on" (*Aspects,* pp. 3–4). Such exclusion can also take heuristic form as in, for example, Lyons's argument that "for simplicity of exposition, we shall assume that the language we are describing is uniform (by 'uniform' is meant 'dialectally and stylistically' undifferentiated): this is, of course, an 'idealization' of the facts. . . ."[17] And as we have seen, it can also take the more radical form found in Saussure's exclusion of diachronic change and synchronic variation from the linguistics of language structure (*langue*). Linguistics has at various times and in various ways excluded as marginal several forms of disorder, including such things as apparent noise in the system, the historical changes it undergoes, the social and regional variations it displays, and the unpredictable effects of individuals creatively adapting it. What is left, those who adopt reductive procedures of exclusion tend to hope, is a coherently ordered and thus fully describable system in which disorder has been not so much explained as explained away.

A different procedure for achieving descriptive generality by resolving the order/disorder problem is not one of reductive exclusion but one of homogenizing absorption. This involves either an insistence that order and disorder are not finally opposed, because apparent disorder can eventually be converted into some prevailing form of order, or an insistence that order is simply a privileged kind of disorder and therefore continuous with what it apparently opposes. And it is in these terms that the complicated relationship between structuralists and poststructuralists, the inheritors of Saussure's often inconsistent arguments, sheds some helpful light.[18] As Culler has rightly argued, structuralism and poststructuralism are not "simple opposites" and many writers have produced work of both putative kinds.[19] Though their presuppositions and points of departure may differ, structuralists and poststructuralists often end up exploring closely related issues as they seek some sort of closure for their activities: "Just as the structuralist study of rules and codes may focus on irregularities, so the deconstructive undoing of codes reveals certain regularities."[20] The inevitability of this convergence is not always readily apparent and a clarification of it will provide a clarification of the complexities of the procedures of exclusion and absorption and of theory's self-defeating pursuit of comprehensive generality.

The rise of Saussure's science of signs, the science of semiology, depended both upon the imaginative generality of the theory and upon the descriptive simplicity and exactness of the method, and what both appear not only to promise but also to demand is the achievement of completeness in description. But achieving completeness is itself a difficult task to complete. And to recognize the problem of descriptive closure involved here is to recognize why a major theory's apparent strength, its comprehensive descriptive claims, so often culminate in reductive justifications of procedures of exclusion and/or absorption. Since Saussure developed his notion of linguistic system, there has been a constant pressure upon those engaged in semiotic description not only to describe current data comprehensively but also to extend their descriptive activities into larger and larger domains. Success in one semiological domain seems always to be the prelude to further challenges in another.

We thus find Roman Jakobson describing in structuralist terms local synchronic systems but also going on to envisage a global linguistic description, "a system of systems," that would encompass all that literary language had been or could be.[21] We encounter Roland Barthes diligently describing relatively restricted systems and codes for fashions in garments, accessories, and footwear, and for preferences in furniture and food, but also seeking to establish a universal grammar of narrative and an exhaustive typology of literary genres.[22] Claude Lévi-Strauss provides some illuminating analyses of distinctive social structures but is soon encouraged enough by the explanatory power of the method that he begins to conceive of the mind as a structuring device and of the cultural context of individual lives as an all-encompassing collection of inherited mythemes (systems of myth).[23] And the enticement to comprehensiveness exercised by structuralist method is most conspicuously visible in the work of Umberto Eco, but it is in his work, too, that the problematic nature of appeals to comprehensiveness becomes unmistakably clear.

Eco argues that "in the final analysis . . . semiotics [is] a substitute for cultural anthropology. . . . [which] is not to say that culture is only communication and signification but that it can be understood more thoroughly if it is seen from the semiotic point of view."[24] To diminish somewhat the role of linguistics in structural/cultural analysis, Eco prefers the term semiotics to Saussure's term semiology. But his basic claim that "the laws of signification are the laws of culture" gives ample support to Saussure's originating belief in the descriptive power of the sign system.[25] If anything, Eco's descriptive ambitions are even larger: "A possible global semiotic system (that is, a representation of a culture in its totality) must take into account every possible use value (that is, every possible semantic content or meaning) of a given object."[26] Though the task he sets himself is daunting, Eco's aims seem logical, coherent, and theoretically consistent. They turn out, in practice, however, to be unachievable, and it is important to recognize the theoretical as well as the practical dilemma that Eco eventually finds himself confronting.

Surveying the achievements of structural/cultural description, Eco notes with satisfaction the progress that has been made in the areas of zoosemiotics, olfactory signs, tactile communication, codes of taste, paralinguistics, medical semiotics, kinesics and proxemics, musical codes, formalized languages, written languages, natural languages, visual communication, systems of objects, plot structure, text theory, cultural codes, aesthetic texts, mass communication, and rhetoric.[27] The implication is that the cultural terrain is steadily being covered and that these local achievements will eventually link up to provide a global account. What soon becomes apparent, however, is that these various semiotic categories are not mutually exclusive, they are not exhaustive, they are not based on any systematic principle of classification, and they do not depict by any means the only ways of dividing and relating cultural phenomena. More worrying still, they suggest not so much the gradual completion of the task of description but the possibility of its infinite extension. Without a governing grid to set limits to the task, the procedure of describing all possible cultural categories from all possible points of view seems endless. The pursuit of comprehensive generality in such a context provides no means of achieving closure. And this not only helps us understand the frequent resort to procedures of exclusion and absorption but also invites us to consider further why the apparently commonsense notion that theory should be capable of covering all the data it seeks to address should turn out to be a problematic assumption.

Eco is not unaware of the emerging problems but finds it difficult to move beyond acknowledging them and toward resolving them. He notes the existing disorder in the discipline of semiotics, wonders whether unity should be achieved inductively or deductively, suggests that the notion of complete description may have to serve only as a regulative hypothesis, and eventually argues that the imbalance and instability of semiotic codes makes necessary a related theory of sign production.[28] The latter course of action is, in effect, an abandonment of the goal of absorbing disorder into order and a reversion to the procedure of excluding disorder from the system. Instead of avoiding the problems of exclusion, attempts at absorption simply lead directly back to them. Whatever the complexity of the situation Eco finally finds himself confronting, however, his argument helps clarify the theoretical as well as practical problems involved not only in the apparently unobjectionable goal of comprehensive cultural description, but also in the goal of complete description of anything. For what we are encountering is the theory-laden status of completeness which, in practice, often turns out to be less complete than it first appears. In effect, each form of completeness tends to become a persuasive form of completeness only by disguising its conversion of the sufficiently complete (that is, sufficient to satisfy the demands of the theory) into the fully complete (that is, sufficient to satisfy the demands of any theory). Some more explicit notion of the sufficiently complete is needed to bring the task of description to a satisfactory form of closure. But in its absence closure tends to oscillate between the forced and the fake, and generality seems achievable only on similar terms.

If a structuralist pursuit of order can ultimately achieve closure only by acknowledging rather than absorbing residual disorder, a poststructuralist description of disorder can likewise achieve closure only by acknowledging an order that finally resists further dismantling. Those who flirted with the notion that deconstruction leads to a recognition of the free play of signifiers and thus to endlessly extendable acts of deconstruction found themselves steadily marginalized in the movement as others stopped deconstructing in order to focus on a small and recurring set of issues. Culler describes this cessation in most general terms as the point at which deconstructive procedure "can no longer identify and dismantle the differences that work to dismantle other differences."[29] Is this, we wonder, the point at which disorder becomes unreadable? Or is it the point at which a more basic form of order is revealed?[30]

Deconstructers differ, of course, but their practice seems regularly to cease at the points at which it can illustrate what the theory presupposes—certain ideas about the nature of writing, about the status of the sign, about the nature of representation, about the hierarchies implicit in linguistic distinctions, and about the indeterminacy of meaning. Paradoxically enough, "the deconstructive questioning of categories and assumptions leads back repeatedly to a small group of problems and gives conclusions that function as knowledge."[31] Such a statement would be heretical to those committed to more radical forms of deconstruction, but attempts to find an alternative goal to that of producing infinite amounts of subsequent text responding to prior text have not yet progressed further than the illustration of presupposition.[32] As is so often the case, the complicated relationship between language, belief, and truth is reduced to the alternatives of monism and relativism.

Though the poststructuralist recognition of the importance of heterogeneity and disorder is admirable in itself, practitioners nevertheless find themselves struggling along with the structuralists to find an illuminating means of relating order to disorder in some way that looks less like a theoretical defeat. Attempts to exclude one from the other or to absorb one into the other have thus proved unsatisfactory means of achieving theoretical generality and descriptive closure. The temporarily excluded and the putatively absorbed repeatedly reassert themselves as irremovable and irreducible, and theory oscillates between reductive circularity and inclusive inadequacy. Saussure's retreat from the disciplinary dangers of unconstrained heterogeneity seems justified enough, but his taking intermittent refuge in a domain of uninterrupted homogeneity leaves intact a basic problem that structuralism and poststructuralism in their different ways redescribe, and that transformational-generative grammar was not able to resolve.

The recent linkage between Chomsky's work and computer languages tends to confirm that the power of the descriptive techniques, while appropriate to some areas of syntax and to the operations of machine languages, is both excessive and inappropriate to the operations of many aspects of natural languages. The transformations that once promised to explain our ability to produce and understand new sentences in fact explain only a restricted kind of formal creativity. And as Hasan subsequently argued: "Creativeness does not consist in producing new sentences. The newness of a sentence is a quite unimportant—and unascertainable—property, and 'creativity' in language lies in the speaker's ability to create new meanings: to realize the potentiality of language for the indefinite extension of its resources to new contexts of situation."[33]

To argue that creativity is as much a matter of creating new meanings in new contexts as of producing new combinations of formal items is to reverse the priority between form and meaning in Chomsky's model, just as revisionists like Lakoff and McCawley demanded. But Hasan's remarks emerge not only from the controversies surrounding transformational-generative grammar but also from the linguistic research precipitated by the arguments of J. R. Firth. Long criticized for its commitment to the less easily formalized aspects of language, Firthian linguistics continued to develop its interest in problematic but unavoidable domains of linguistic research, not the least of which was the relationship between novelty and necessity. Firth's rejection of the unitary nature of languages, his insistence that no progress in the discipline was likely to occur until "linguistics recognizes that its principal objective is the study of meaning," and his determination to give technical status to the notion of context all served to place elements of potential disorder at the heart of the ordering activities of linguistics.[34]

Derrida is by no means the first to have argued that if meaning is contextual and context is open-ended, then meaning too is open in problematic ways.[35] But such openness does not, in Firthian linguistics, encourage arguments that the limited constraints provided by contexts are equivalent to a lack of constraint. Indeed, if there is no constraint there is no context, but an appropriate recognition of the role of context requires that it be given a regulative rather than determining role in the construction of meaning. From this point of view, Chomsky's notion of a language as a set of well-formed sentences that can be described in advance of their use seems meretricious, and an alternative argument would be that "In principle, what is well-formed is whatever can be shown to be interpretable as a possible selection within a set of options based on some motivated hypothesis about language behavior."[36] The key phrase here is "language behavior," a return to and revision of Chomsky's initial interest in "actual language" and an extension of it into domains of social interaction rather than into psychological domains of human knowledge. From this point of view someone learning a language is not primarily learning how to produce well-formed sentences, but "learning how to mean" in social contexts.[37] As a consequence, the operational unit of language is not the sentence but the text broadly conceived as a unit of discourse in a process of social exchange.[38]

Firth's polysystemic linguistics evolved through the work of M. A. K. Halliday and others first into a Scale and Category model, then into a Systemic model, and then into a Social Semiotic model. And again there is something to be learned about theory by tracing the trajectory of this theory's development as it seeks to accommodate the intractable demands of linguistic novelty and necessity. Even as his model, like Chomsky's, was driven to achieve increasing generality, Halliday remained true to the nonunitary perspective adopted by Firth and persistently mistrusted the notion of a grand synthetic vision of language.[39] He thus preferred to address the issue of novelty as one not limited in advance by formal restrictions but both enabled and constrained by the irreducible disorder of linguistic systems and by the contextual diversity within which they function. The site of engagement with language remains as Firth described it, one in which dialogue, context, and meaning are intricately interwoven and unlikely to yield a unified picture for generality to encompass. As Halliday puts it:

> I am often asked by teachers if it is possible to give a succinct account of the essential nature of language in terms that are truly relevant to the educational process. It is not easy to do this, because it means departing very radically from the images of language that are presented in our schoolbooks and in the classroom: not only from the older image, which was focussed on the marginalia of language and gave about as good a picture of what language is really like as a book of etiquette would give of what life is really like, but also from the newer one, which is focused on the mechanisms of language and reduces it to a set of formal operations. We have to build up an image of language which enables us to look at how people actually do communicate with one another, and how they are all the time exchanging meanings and interacting in meaningful ways. (*Social Semiotic*, p. 207)[40]

This reluctance to establish a simple governing picture and the preference for providing a site of social engagement registers the importance to Firth and

Halliday of a linguistic point of departure which involves dialogue being exchanged rather than one in which an ideal speaker talks to himself or herself. It is this concern for language in action that accounts for the persisting interest in the role of disorder in Firth and Halliday's linguistics. Even when Halliday contemplates a "fuller picture" it is one characterized by "a high degree of indeterminacy . . . representing the indeterminacy that is present throughout language, in its categories and its relations, its types and its tokens" (*Explorations,* p. 108).[41] This indeterminacy is accompanied by heterogeneity, creativity, and change that make it impossible, in a sociological context, to separate language as a formal system from language as a social institution in such a way as to incorporate only order into the former and both order and heterogeneity in the latter.[42] Here there is no room for distinctions between *langue* and *parole,* or competence and performance, or ideal and actual languages, and no place for gestures of exclusion that would remove recalcitrant disorder from the space cleared for order. Indeed, efforts to locate productive pictures of the relationship between order and disorder are a persistent feature of the evolving theory.

As Halliday's model develops, and the initial appeal of formal order diminishes, "even the concept of rules is . . . threatened" and Halliday is eventually inclined to view rules as flexible resources that promote creativity rather than as unbreakable laws that prevent it (*Social Semiotic,* pp. 4, 192). Playing with the rules and not just by them is a characteristic feature of linguistic and social behavior, and it must somehow be included in the realm of recognizable novelty. Rules thus become, in Saussurean terms, means of limiting arbitrariness rather than of merely replicating inherited forms of order. Instead of retreating to ideal languages in ideal worlds, Halliday insists that linguists confront the realities of sociological contexts, contexts in which "we have, in fact, to 'come closer to what is actually said'; partly because the solution to problems may depend on studying what is actually said, but also because even when this is not the case the features that are behaviorally relevant may be just those that the idealizing process most readily irons out" (*Explorations,* p. 54).

This commitment to confronting disorder as well as order persists throughout the various revisions the model undergoes, though the kinds of novelty accommodated and the techniques for relating order to disorder are steadily extended. Like Chomsky, Halliday is determined to accommodate diversity and novelty in the linguistic system, but like Chomsky again, he feels the imperative to generalize further, leading him inexorably toward the point at which descriptive generality and descriptive circularity intersect. And in Halliday's case, given the measure of his commitment to accommodating unavoidable diversity and accepting irreducible disorder, it is fascinating to observe both his journey toward the same destination and his resolute refusal to arrive there. And as is the case with Chomsky's theorizing, it is by no means evident that the final form that the theory attains will necessarily be its most productive form.

Firth's acknowledgment of multiple order in polysystemic languages made up of many registers and many dialects is recapitulated and extended by Halliday who seeks to take the full measure of the problems they present. Like Chomsky before him, Halliday has insisted upon the importance of reconciling linguistic necessity and novelty. As he puts it: "The linguistic system . . . is a system of variation. . . . [It is] not . . . a system of invariants, the way the layman (or the philosopher of language) tends to see it, but . . . a system with a great deal of flexibility in it. There is no evidence that the man in the city street has some overall integrated speech system lurking somewhere at the back of his mind. Rather, he has internalized a pattern that is extraordinarily heterogeneous" (*Social Semiotic,* p. 155). In the face of such heterogeneity the task of the linguist is to help us deal with it, not help us exclude it from or absorb it into related forms of order: "Language, unlike mathematics, is not clearcut or precise. It is a natural human creation, and, like many other natural human creations, it is inherently messy. Anyone who formalizes natural language does so at the cost of idealizing it to such an extent that it is hardly recognizable as language any more, and bears little likeness to the way people actually interact with one another by talking" (*Social Semiotic,* p. 203). The responsibility of the linguist is to limit such idealization and "instead of rejecting what is messy . . . accept the mess and build it into the theory" (*Social Semiotic,* p. 38).

These are, of course, brave words and the problems presented by fuzziness, messiness, and novelty are not to be resolved simply by acknowledging their presence. As description is subject, as we have seen, to demands that it be simple, exact, and general, Halliday, too, confronts the twin dangers that his model will be judged wanting if it cannot cover all linguistic data and dismissed as inflexibly circular if it does.[43] His efforts to reconcile the generalizing demands of order and the particularizing demands of disorder provide a tension that persists throughout the various revisions that his theory undergoes, but what intermittently emerges among the attempts to describe recalcitrant data is a recognition of the reciprocal nature of the relationships between data and theory on the one hand and theorist and theory on the other.

Like Chomsky, Halliday seeks to establish and relate a series of linguistic levels and distribute among them the responsibility for describing the complexities of linguistic patterns. Like Chomsky, too, he has to decide at some point whether to treat his model as heuristic or ontological. And in both cases he has to pursue generality without being taken over by it.

The initial Scale and Category stage of Halliday's theory attempts to account for linguistic events in terms of three levels of abstraction: substance, form, and context, levels which indicate the scope of the theory and the major role that meaning plays in it. "The substance is the material of language: 'phonic' (audible noises) or 'graphic' (visible marks). The form is the organization of the substance into meaningful events: 'meaning' is a concept, and a technical term, of the theory. The context is the relation of the form to non-linguistic features of the situations in which language operates, and to linguistic features other than those of the item under attention: these being together 'extratextual' features" ("Categories," p. 53).[44]

Although meaning and context are of major importance, the level of form has a central place in the initial picture and incorporates both grammatical and lexical patterns. The shift from one to the other occurs when increasingly refined patterns of grammatical typification have to give way to patterns that depend on words as individual lexical items rather than as generalizable types. Although form might seem instrumental when described as "the organization of substance into meaningful events," it appears to govern rather than be governed by meaning. Indeed formal meaning is distinguished from contextual meaning with the latter described as "logically dependent" on the former. Furthermore, in the process of linguistic description "formal criteria are crucial, taking precedence over contextual criteria" ("Categories," p. 53).[45] Domains of order and domains of disorder are both included at this stage of the theory, but it is clear that formal order is being established as the means of explaining linguistic function. Though various attempts are to be made to prevent the formal patterns from governing the whole model, it is clear, at this stage, that Halliday is expecting of the formal system a generality of application that is as likely to give him trouble as Chomsky's "all and only" ambitions gave him.

In this first stage, Halliday is seeking to establish the value of his theory by contrasting its formal descriptive power with the impressionistic and *ad hoc* categories of grammars in use in the world of English education. There is an instrumental imperative as well as a descriptive imperative in place at the outset, but the relationship between them is not yet clear.[46] Though he was later to contrast the messiness of language with the tidiness of mathematics, Halliday, at this point, characterizes his descriptive apparatus as a "calculus" and was clearly seeking to give formal order maximum scope ("Categories," p. 52). Even at this most formal stage, however, the theory included efforts to accommodate the fluidity of linguistic form, and this is where we encounter the first of Halliday's attempts to give formal status to the relationship between order and disorder—at this point by introducing the variable scale of delicacy. But the efforts to give formal and flexible status to the relationship between order and disorder lead to increasing concern for the relationship between theory and theorist.

Grammatical form is given flexibility as well as coherence by being described in terms of system/structure relations which allow grammatical categories to be more and more precisely differentiated. Structural description is not just to be mechanically applied but to be creatively deployed. It first provides primary structures which account for the most general level of categorization, then secondary structures which make differentiations within primary categories, then tertiary structures which make differentiations within secondary structures, and so on, there being no theoretically imposed limit to this process. Instead of treating categorization in terms of fixed alternatives, the theory deals with structural relations in terms of "a continuum carrying potentially infinite gradation" ("Categories," p. 56). This approach to categorization in terms of clines accommodates both a speaker's ability to use language to make more or less refined distinctions and the linguist's need to focus upon more general or more precise distinctions according to the task at hand. Thus "the range of variation that is being treated as *significant* will itself be variable, with either grosser or finer distinctions being drawn according to the type of problem that is being investigated" (*Explorations,* p. 54).[47]

The scale of delicacy represents an early attempt to build the fuzziness of language into both theory and description and to acknowledge that most linguistic categories "are distinct enough at the centre but shade into one another at the edges."[48] The mechanism of delicacy not only promotes a variable "fit" between generality, simplicity, and exactness but also increases the flexibility the descriptive device provides linguists in exploring language patterns. A recognition of the fuzziness of categorization is not so much accommodated with difficulty as assimilated and put to productive use, in ways that increasingly rely on the interpretive rather than mechanical skills of the describer. For what Halliday quickly realizes is that variations in the relationship between theory and data have immediate implications for the relationship between theory and those who seek to deploy it. Here there is much work for the describer to do, and in effect the balance between sufficient and excessive use of systematization is adjustable by the person using the system. "As the description increases in delicacy the network of grammatical relations becomes more complex. The interaction of criteria makes the relation between categories, and between category and exponent, increasingly one of 'more/less' rather than 'either/or.' It becomes necessary to weight criteria and to make statements in terms of probabilities . . . the 'more/less' relation itself, far from being an unexpected complication in grammar, is in fact a basic feature of language and is treated as such by the theory"("Categories," p. 63).[49] Instead of opposing generalized order to particularized disorder, Halliday thus established an open-ended descriptive gradation that steadily lowers the level of generalization and the degree of order until an appropriately precise description is arrived at. Here order and disorder themselves are treated as locations on a continuum rather than as opposed alternatives, and differing degrees of simplicity, exactness, and generality are available to the theorist wishing to respond to their claims but to avoid being taken over by the imperatives, particularly the generalizing imperative, that they express.

Such a descriptive apparatus depends heavily on the abilities of the describer, who in seeking to deploy theory is, in effect, compelled to continue developing it. And this dependence increased steadily as Halliday's theory shifted from an assumption of the first stage in which it shared with Chomsky a commitment, though more flexibly applied, to the centrality of generalized form, to the second stage at which it began to explore the centrality of generalized function. As linguistic theories of various kinds were developing rapidly, Halliday recognized the dangers of excessive formalization, even if flexibly applied, and its unhappy tendency in Chomsky's work to produce mechanical descriptions that excluded from the linguistic system all those imponderable forms of disorder that made linguistic creativity possible. The pole of comparison at the model's second stage was no longer that of the unsystematic variety in impressionistic schoolroom grammars but that of the highly formalized, excessively systematized, and incipiently mechanistic grammar provided by Chomsky. The impracticality of distinguishing language as a formal system from language as a social institution became even more clear as Halliday's model evolved. The notion of linguistic function achieved increasing importance and the link between excessive formalization and the reductive imposition of order became increasingly clear. A linguistic theory committed to accommodating novelty had to be a theory committed to accommodating the persistent and not necessarily regular change that linguistic systems undergo. And the switch to regarding linguistic rules as resources to be functionally exploited rather than as laws to be formally obeyed is one that leads logically to a further shift in the relationship between theory and data by redistributing the priority between linguistic form and linguistic function.

Posing to himself the question "what is language" Halliday moves away from his initially formal model, which makes theory responsible chiefly to linguistic data, and argues that it must be even more responsive to those wishing to put theory to use. "The only satisfactory response" to the question of what constitutes language is, he argues, "why do you want to know?" (*Explorations,* p. 9). In choosing among theories we want not just simplicity, generality, and exactness, but "to understand, and to highlight, those facets of language which bear on the investigation or the task at hand" (*Explorations,* p. 9). As Halliday's own theory undergoes a radical modification, the switch in the status of theories from formal adequacy to functional instrumentality accompanied a new picture of the linguistic terrain he wished to explore. In his introduction to *Explorations in the Functions of Language,* Halliday justified his switch from formal to functional linguistic description on the basis of tasks he himself wished to undertake, and he extrapolated from this a notion of language structure and linguistic theory that begins with heuristics and moves through instrumentality toward an unexpected reconsideration of the claims of ontology.

> The five papers that make up this book are linked by a common theme. They are all concerned with exploring a functional approach to the study of language.
> A functional approach to language means, first of all, investigating how language is used: trying to find out what are the purposes that language serves for us, and how we are able to achieve these purposes through speaking and listening, reading and writing. But it is also more than this. It means seeking to explain the nature of language in functional terms: seeing whether language itself has been shaped by use, and if so, in what ways—how the form of language has been determined by the functions it has evolved to serve.[50] (*Explorations,* p. 7)

If his first model sought to extend the claims of form, this reshaped model now seeks to functionalize linguistic form. But to give function priority over form is to give the diversity of contextual meaning priority over the more regular order of linguistic form (no matter how fuzzy either may turn out to be). Halliday's insistence on the priority of linguistic function is an important one, for it is in the context of language as a social institution enabling the exchange of meaning, rather than in the more restricted context of language as a formal system for producing grammatical sentences, that he plans to account extensively for the coexistence in language of order and variety, convention and invention, necessity and novelty, persistence and change. Like Chomsky, he recognizes the importance of accommodating creativity and of finding a way to make more complex, more flexible, and more precise Saussure's notion of sign system and of the relational status of the sign. Instead of Chomsky's notion of a transformational grammar, however, Halliday offers a function-based systemic grammar, one in which Saussure's notion of a unitary sign system is adapted, via Firth's revisions, into a complex polyvalent network of systems.

What the notion of a system network enables Halliday to address is Saussure's inconsistent claims that, on the one hand, a sign is the focus of an indefinite number of contrasts and, on the other, something that is defined by being what the others with which it contrasts are not. Instead of having an indefinite number of unclear systemic choices realized by a single element of structure, Halliday organizes systems into networks and networks into realizations of functions, so that system networks can incorporate an indefinite series of clearly finite choices that again invoke the concept of delicacy.

> Considering language in its social context . . . we can describe it in broad terms as behavior potential; and more specifically as meaning potential. . . . This leads to the notion of representing language in the form of options. . . . Each option is available in a stated environment, and this is where Firth's category of system comes in. A system is an abstract representation of a paradigm; and this . . . can be interpreted as a set of options with an entry condition—a number of possibilities out of which choice has to be made if the stated conditions of entry to the choice are satisfied. . . . That is to say, for every choice it is to be specified where, under what conditions that choice is made. The "where," in Firth's use of the concept of a system, was "at what point in the structure"; but we interpret it here as "where in the total network of options." Each choice takes place in the environment of other choices. This is what makes it possible to vary the "delicacy" of the description: we can stop wherever the choices are no longer significant for what we are interested in. (*Explorations,* p. 55)

This notion of instrumental closure is Halliday's alternative to the generalizing imperative that forces formal systems to try to extend their reach to the point at which they cover all the data. And as we have seen, efforts to achieve descriptive closure by pushing generality to its most comprehensive lead either to endlessly deferred closure or to the kind of imposed closure whose descriptive circularity removes from the data their responsiveness to novelty and change. Halliday seeks to avoid this problem by linking ordered systems to variable contextual functions. Though the complexity of these system networks is considerable, individual systemic choices are limited in scope and fairly simple both in conception and in exemplification. A system network includes a great many choices, but they are described in sequence and involve only a few alternatives at a time. In these terms a picture of language function emerges which provides more extensive and more sophisticated ways of reciprocally relating order and disorder.

The concept of linguistic function cannot, however, enter the model as a merely impressionistic description of individual action in a particular context. The notion of linguistic function is to achieve technical status by being typified without being standardized, and Halliday's efforts to establish this lead him inexorably toward a collision between his earlier insistence upon the heuristic and instrumental status of linguistic descriptions and his emerging conviction of the ontological status of linguistic functions. And what is thereby set in opposition is the flexible generality of instrumental inquiry and the fixed generality of ontological discovery. For lurking behind the demands for comprehensive generality is the hope that inquiry might eventually reveal some form of final truth.

A child learning language, Halliday argues, begins not just by learning grammatical rules and vocabulary but by mastering some basic language functions. These elementary functions include the instrumental "I want" function, the heuristic "tell me why" function, the imaginative "let's pretend" function and a few others (*Explorations,* p. 17). Children are learning as much how to do things as how to say things. They begin with a notion of linguistic function that is a very limited generalization from particular uses and operate with only one linguistic function at a time. In the later stages of childhood, however, they begin to adopt the adult practice of subordinating the proliferating uses of language to a few abstract function types and to use linguistic form in a polyphonic manner so that several different functions can be served simultaneously by a single sequence of words. Halliday thus distinguishes between microfunctions that indicate the local work done by certain kinds of grammatical items (e.g., subject and object functioning grammatically as actor or goal) and macrofunctions that characterize certain general kinds of task we expect language to perform for us. It is these abstract macrofunctions that provide the key means of relating formal and semantic patterns and of relating order to disorder via multiple order, and it is these abstract macrofunctions that provide a focus for the emerging conflict between the model's heuristic and ontological claims. For what accompanies the emerging ontological claims is yet another form of theoretical circularity, one of functional generality, that threatens Halliday's ability to accommodate novelty and change as strongly as the imperatives of formal generality threatened Chomsky's.

Halliday's model envisages three major macrofunctions: the ideational, the interpersonal, and the textual. Collectively, they provide the functional basis for a grammatical form that supplies three related sets of resources to the speaker:

> The ideational component is that part of the grammar concerned with the expression of experience, including both the processes within and beyond the self—the phenomena of the external world and those of consciousness—and the logical relations deducible from them. The ideational component thus has two sub-components, the experiential and the logical. The interpersonal component is the grammar of personal participation; it expresses the speaker's role in the speech situation, his personal commitment and his interaction with others. The textual component is concerned with the creation of text; it expresses the structure of information, and the relation of each part of the discourse to the whole and to the setting. (*Explorations,* p. 99)

Others before Halliday have sought to establish function-orientated linguistic theories, but Halliday goes on to justify his selection by arguing that these macrofunctions are not just heuristically imposed but can, in fact, be recognized in the nature of the grammatical systems.[51] If a grammar has a functional basis, the choices it offers, like those earlier envisaged by Firth when he dispersed meaning throughout the various levels of language, are simultaneously choices of meaning and form. A grammar so conceived is one of "content form" with a "stratal form of organization" that enables it to channel "complex meaning selections into single integrated structures. The way it does this is by sorting out the many very specific uses of language into a small number of highly general functions which underlie them all" (*Explorations,* p. 98). Instead of having a separate set of formal items for each specific or general function, language utilizes a polyvalent structure governed by these macrofunctions which not only enables but requires single elements to contribute simultaneously to several structural patterns and functional goals.

In these terms, Halliday is able to describe not a single order which precipitates a residual disorder, but multiple forms of order which operate simultaneously, each of which can function with differing degrees of emphasis and precision. Though each macrofunction generates formal patterns that are internally highly organized, the relationships between functions are highly flexible and offer another means of accommodating variety into systematization. Within each functional component there is "a high degree of interdependence" among operating choices, but among the components there is little mutual constraint, so necessity and novelty can not only coexist but be creatively related (*Social Semiotic,* p. 187). With such a functional model, order and disorder can be productively linked and ontological considerations serve only as exploratory hypotheses.

In a grammar so conceived, some familiar formal terms acquire specific functional status. The transitivity system for example describes the organization of a clause in terms of its ideational (experiential) function; the mood system describes its organization in terms of its interpersonal function; and the theme system describes its organization in terms of its textual function. Each system gives a detailed account of the various systemic choices realized by individual formal elements and by groups of formal elements, so that a complex picture emerges of polyphonic multifunctioning structures. Viewed in the context of each of these system/function networks, a single word sequence displays a variety of structures that register different kinds of organization of different kinds of information serving different kinds of purposes. In effect, a single sequence of words carries several kinds of information in a variety of different ways by exploiting a series of systemic networks.

The transitivity network thus addresses the speaker's role as observer and organizer of general experience, the mood network deals with the speaker as an organizer of a social exchange, and the theme network accounts for the speaker's choices as an organizer of a text.[52] The transitivity network treats transitivity as a feature of a clause, and not just of a verb, and it accounts for the choices among processes, participants, and circumstances that a speaker introduces into a clause. For example, it distinguishes among action process, mental process, and relation process; among three participant, two participant, and one participant processes; among participants in terms of actor, beneficiary, or attribute; and among a variety of accompanying circumstances. The mood network addresses interactional types of speech function that characterize the nature of social exchange; whether a clause is to serve as a statement, a question, or a command; how the speaker assesses the authority of what is being said; whether it is regarded as self-evident, highly probable, or merely possible. The speaker here is not just a producer of sentences but an organizer of a social situation, taking up a certain role and assigning others certain roles. The theme network addresses the organization of language as an operational text designed to function in specific kinds of contexts. It deals with whether certain elements are to be regarded as given or new, known or unknown, emphasized or not emphasized.[53] And the potential overlap between given/new and known/unknown registers the ability of these system networks to trace systemic choices from those indicating radical alternatives to those indicating subtle and partial differentiation.

The earlier scale of delicacy among categories is now built into the system network which includes both specific choices from which single selections must be made and, at a further degree of differentiation, options which may or may not be selected, and at an even further degree of differentiation, potential options that the system network, being open-ended, has not yet codified. This functional/structural system network moving from well-defined order toward the increasing disorder of partial differentiation and fuzzy distinctions is informatively exemplified in an image Halliday earlier used simply to describe a more restricted form of delicacy, but which now also registers the diverse but related sets of choices exhibited in a system network. Descriptive closure, Halliday suggests, can be instrumentally pursued "to that undefined but theoretically crucial point (probably statistically definable) where distinctions are so fine that they cease to be distinctions at all, like a river followed up from the mouth, each of whose tributaries ends in a moorland bog" ("Categories," p. 62).

This image of multiple paths of descriptive delicacy from Halliday's early work would now have to be complicated by the recognition that the various tributaries have varying relations to each other and disappear into differently located bogs with differing rapidity. The early Halliday whose efforts to establish the formal adequacy of a grammar that could still incorporate the fuzziness of language has by now given way to a Halliday who wishes to establish the functional adequacy of a grammar designed not to limit the role of linguistic disorder but to emphasize it and clarify its relationship to flexible modes of order. One of the things the formal/functional transitivity network clarifies, for example, is the acute instability of transitivity in English which Halliday describes as being "in a state of considerable flux" (*Social Semiotic,* p. 116).[54] Such formal instability is now, however, not just an isolated instance of disorder but a contextualized disorder clarified by (though not converted to order by) a recognition of its relationship to more stable patterns that operate at a certain point in a grammar and serve a particular function.

This capacity of system networks to relate order illuminatingly to disorder is a significant extension of what was achieved by the earlier descriptive features of delicacy and clines. An analysis that conceives of choices not only in terms of fixed alternatives but also in terms of increasingly refined gradations on a variety of related continua is one able to reconcile Saussure's conflicting recognitions of closed and open systemic choices. It is also one that can accommodate the recognition that while one end of a continuum may be significantly different from the other, there is not necessarily a clear point at which a decisive change occurs. What makes a change decisive, indeed, is not its formal manifestation but its contextual significance. Thus Halliday, unlike Chomsky, regards grammaticality as a cline and would resist attempts to distinguish it from contextual acceptability.

The macrofunction/microfunction model up to this point retains a productive balance between necessity and novelty and between the demands of heuristics and ontology. But the question of context has been steadily begged since its inclusion as a formal level in Halliday's first model. Though it has been steadily complicated by the developing model, it is not until the next stage of the theory, the social semiotic stage, that Halliday gives central attention to it and to the potential it offers for combining linguistic theory with sociological theory, thereby achieving even greater generality for linguistic theory and description. But the imperatives of generality lead Halliday, as they have led others, to an unexpected encounter with hermeneutic circularity.

As we have noted, context is a particularly difficult notion to control, and to give it technical status is to confront problems of disorder even greater than those considered in giving technical status to the concept of linguistic function. And once again Halliday's tactic is first to typify the concept and then to seek to give that typification an ontological basis by relating it both to the formal patterns exhibited in language and to the patterns of activity exhibited by speakers in social life. Halliday's approach to the conflict between order and disorder in language and linguistics has been, as we have seen, to adopt neither the procedure of exclusion nor the procedure of absorption but to rely instrumentally on a procedure of mutual accommodation that involves multiple and variable differentiation. Order and disorder themselves have been treated as opposing ends of a continuum, in fact of several continua, rather than as radical alternatives and irreducible opposites. This is neither to abandon a distinction nor to deconstruct it but to clarify the work it can do for us by giving it both technical and variable status. Halliday has sought to do the same with the apparent opposition between form and meaning, and the same procedure is now applied to the apparent opposition between verbal language and social context.

A functional grammar has built into it the recognition that form and context are reciprocally related, and as his model moves into its third stage, Halliday makes the implicit both more explicit and more formal. Indeed, if the first stage of the model was primarily formal and the second stage set out to functionalize form, the third stage is, in effect, an attempt to formalize function by formalizing context. The context in which linguistic choices are made is social as well as verbal, and to provide context with a suitable technical status, it must be typified. Otherwise the particularity of context would be endlessly pursued. The attempt to retain a level of complexity while refining a term sufficiently to enable it to do useful work is a characteristic strategy of Halliday's, and it is striking to see what happens when the balance is temporarily lost and order suddenly reverts from the regulative to the authoritative.

Meaning potential is now described as "the range of options characteristic of a specific situation type" and the context is conceived of as "a semiotic construct, having a form (deriving from the culture) that enables the participants to predict features of the prevailing register—and hence to understand one another as they go along" (*Social Semiotic,* pp. 109, 2). This formalization of context reemphasizes the importance of treating every national language as an aggregate of sublanguages rather than pursuing some underlying norm or common core. But this step toward the further accommodation of diversity is accompanied by a sudden reimposition of uniformity that reminds us once more of the ways in which the imperatives of generality reduce the very variety they compel us to accommodate. Although Halliday eventually regards text and context as codetermining, the procedure of formalizing function leads him temporarily to overstate the power of context and move it beyond the merely regulative to the necessary and determining. To see Halliday, however temporarily, fall into this trap, is not only to recognize once again the capacity of theory to undermine itself by overstating its claims for descriptive generality but also to encounter an informative response to the quickly recognized problem. And the reemergence of the problem and the nature of the response have implications for both theory and theory development beyond the realms of linguistics.

Halliday had, in fact, raised the possibility at the first stage of his model that "one could set up a unit of contextual statement features of which would determine grammatical features"; but the theory had since become increasingly flexible and open-ended.[55] It is surprising therefore to see the word "determine," rather narrowly conceived, reappear in the social semiotic stage of the model, which seeks to relate the disciplines of linguistics and sociology. Here, one feels, there is little room for programmatic rules, as Kress has pointed out. Until recently, he notes,

> neither linguists nor sociologists were attempting to connect the two disciplines in a sufficiently serious fashion to lead to the establishment of the necessary categories. One of the problems is size: the micro-level of linguistics does not readily match the macro-level of sociology. It had also been felt by many linguists (and changes in this view are extremely recent—where there are changes) that while linguistic behavior

rests on the shared knowledge by speakers of a finite set of abstract rules, which could be enumerated and described, the same was not true of social behavior, which was seen as infinitely variable and not rule governed. This is not and was not the view of sociologists; the concept of role, for instance, depends on the assumption of a community's sharing a set of rules of social behavior. Neither sociologists nor linguists had asked the question: what are the appropriate categories for the statement of the context of the largest linguistic units.[56]

Halliday, however, set out to address precisely these issues. As we have noted, the operational unit of linguistics was to be not the sentence, but the text; the site of description is not one of the language sample in isolation but of speakers interacting in social contexts; learning language is not just a matter of learning how to produce well-formed sentences but of learning how to put them to use in social situations.[57] It is this perspective that generates Halliday's apparently odd formulations that "learning a language is learning how to mean" and that "language development is . . . the development of a meaning potential" (*Explorations,* p. 24). Instead of drawing a distinction, as Chomsky does, between competence and performance on the basis of what a speaker knows versus what a speaker does, Halliday distinguishes between what a speaker can do and what a speaker actually does, and this involves understanding what a speaker *does mean* in the context of what the speaker *can mean.* It is in this way that Halliday seeks to develop the implications of Firth's remark, subsequently elaborated by Wittgenstein, that language is best viewed not just as a verbal mechanism but as a way/form of life.

Halliday's implicit critique of Chomsky's favored distinction is persuasive enough. The problem with a dichotomy between knowing and doing is that it is based on two different kinds of abstraction requiring different kinds of description, and this effectively prevents us from explaining what a speaker does in terms of what the speaker knows: "what he does will appear merely as a random selection from within what he knows" (*Explorations,* p. 67). But the converse danger of trying to explain what speakers do in the context of what they can do is the familiar one of formalizing "can do" in rigidly systematic terms that preclude variety and change. And Halliday, in formalizing a social semiotic, threatens to do precisely that. He argues that "in a social perspective we need both to pay attention to what is said and at the same time to relate it systematically to what might have been said but was not" (*Explorations,* p. 67).

Everything hinges, of course, upon how the word "systematically" is used. In the second stage of his model, Halliday regularly relied on the notion that form is a realization of function and stressed that the form/function match was complex, open-ended, and changing. As the notion of language as social semiotic takes shape, the word "determines" increasingly replaces the word "realizes," and the always appealing but always dangerous notion of descriptive generality begins to push to one side the notions of multiplicity and open-endedness: "Language is itself a potential: it is the totality of what the speaker can do. . . . We are considering, as it were, the dynamics of the semantic strategies that are available to him" (*Explorations*, p. 110). Such comprehensive generality, in by now familiar ways, instantly encourages necessity to overcome novelty. The linguistic system now becomes "the product of the social system," and "the social structure determines the various familial patterns of communication . . . [and] through the intermediary of language, the forms taken by the socialization of the child" (*Social Semiotic,* pp. 190, 113).[58] Halliday invites us to investigate "*which* kinds of situational factor determine *which* kinds of selection in the linguistic system" (*Social Semiotic*, p. 32). The typification of contexts now encourages Halliday to explain how certain kinds of context determine certain kinds of language use, for "'the [semantic] system' is an abstract conceptualization of the totality of the user's potential in actually occurring situation types" (*Social Semiotic,* p. 85).[59] A semantic system so conceived will help us understand "how it is that ordinary everyday language transmits the essential patterns of the culture: systems of knowledge, value systems, the social structure and much else besides" (*Social Semiotic,* p. 52).

This is, of course, to see social structure in rather rigid terms, reminiscent of Medvedev and Vološinov, and to see social beings largely in the role of passive receivers of the social and linguistic systems they inherit. In familiar ways, such attempts to achieve generality of description lead to reductive pictures of what is being described, and this conception of social semiotic leaves out both the variety of the social environment and the speaker's capacity for creative response to it. To try to conceive of linguistic potential in terms of the totality of what a speaker can do is to replicate even while revising Chomsky's efforts to characterize all and only the sentences of the language.

Halliday's excursion into the field of sociology thus returns him somewhat inadvertently to the semiological terminology of complete comprehensiveness and closed systems that his own work had managed to transcend in the field of linguistics. The image of language as an open-ended multiple structure analogous to a river and its tributaries gives way to an image of language as "an elaborate piece of circuitry made up of two or three complex blocks of wiring with fairly simple interconnections," and the contextual environment, like the verbal environment, becomes one of rigid and limited systemic choice (*Explorations*, p. 110).

It is in these terms that the social system appears to determine the linguistic system, for "a social reality (or a 'culture') is itself an edifice of meanings—a semiotic construct" and "meanings are created by the social system and are exchanged by the members in the form of text" (*Social Semiotic*, pp. 2, 141). There seems as little room here for linguistic novelty as there was in Chomsky's invocation of an ideal speaker/hearer in a homogeneous speech community.

There are two important implications of this temporary lapse into the terminology of totalities, closed systems, and determining factors. One is, of course, the difficulty of maintaining an appropriate balance between order and disorder in theory and description, which is made even more difficult by the imperatives of generality, and which repeatedly leads to procedures of absorption or exclusion. The other is the status, heuristic or ontological, of statements made in theory and description and their consequences for the issues Halliday has intermittently raised about the relationship between theory and data on the one hand and theory and theorist on the other. Though, in correcting his overinvestment in ontological claims, Halliday quickly returns to reaffirming the productive relationship between order and disorder in linguistic systems, it is evident that his efforts to produce better pictures of that relationship register an uncertainty about the appropriate scale and necessary clarity of informative pictures.

As far as the order and disorder issue is concerned, even as Halliday lapsed into the vocabulary of comprehensive and closed semiology, he continued to pursue the implications of linguistic disorder, novelty, and change. He was, for example, intermittently reminding himself that "the normal condition of the semantic system is one of change." He also argues that "the 'fuzziness' of language is in part an expression of the dynamics and the tensions of the social system [which also exhibits] ambiguity, antagonism, imperfection, inequality and change"; that text and context are mutually determining; and that what a child encounters in learning language "is not something fixed and harmonious but something shifting, fluid and full of indeterminacies" (*Social Semiotic*, pp. 78, 114, 3, 116). Halliday had not at this point forgotten the disorder that accompanies order in language, but under the imperatives of generality he lapsed into a terminology that sets them in opposition to rather than in relation to each other. Though the readjustment is left until the final page of his chapter on "language as social semiotic," the lapse enabled Halliday to offer a retrospective revision of his deterministic picture, one which includes yet another means, that of reciprocal feedback, for reconciling necessity and novelty in both the linguistic system and the social system:

The social system is not something static, regular and harmonious, nor are its elements held poised in some perfect pattern of functional relationships.

A "sociosemiotic" perspective implies an interpretation of the shifts, the irregularities, the disharmonies and the tensions that characterize human interaction and social processes. It attempts to explain the semiotic of the social structure, in its aspects both of persistence and of change, including the semantics of social class, of the power system, of hierarchy and of social conflict. It attempts also to explain the linguistic processes whereby the members construct the social semiotic, whereby social reality is shaped, constrained and modified—processes which, far from tending towards an ideal construction, admit and even institutionalize myopia, prejudice and misunderstanding.

The components of the sociolinguistic universe themselves provide the sources and conditions of disorder and change. These may be seen in the text, in the situation, and in the semantic system, as well as in the dynamics of cultural transmission and social learning. All the lines of determination are *ipso facto* also lines of tension, not only through indeterminacy in the transmission but also through feedback. The meaning of the text, for example, is fed back into the situation, and becomes part of it, changing it in the process; it is also fed back, through the register, into the semantic system, which it likewise affects and modifies. The code, the form in which we conceptualize the injection of the social structure into the semantic process, is itself a two-way relation, embodying feedback from the semantic configurations of social interaction into the role relationships of the family and other social groups. . . . In the light of the role of language in social processes, a sociolinguistic perspective does not readily accommodate strong boundaries. The "sociolinguistic order" is neither an ideal order nor a reality that has no order at all; it is a human artefact having some of the properties of both. (*Social Semiotic,* p. 126)

It is this recurring attempt to readjust the relationship between theory and data so that it can accommodate both order and disorder that is most characteristic of Halliday's work in linguistics. And it is not some final model that he achieves, but an evolving set of strategies for coping with theory's tendency to overreach itself that point the way forward for theorists in general. For Halliday, as for Chomsky, there is finally no big picture of which all their informative little pictures form a productive part, and it is in this sense that tracing something of the trajectory of a theory's development can be more informative than attempts to locate its final or most fundamental form. Seeking to make room for regularity, variety, indeterminacy, creativity, novelty, and change, Halliday approaches language not in terms of a set of rules that prescribe what can be said, but in terms of an inherited resource that is constantly being developed and modified, not in terms of social features determining linguistic features, but in terms of social and linguistic patterns that enable us to make informed predictions about each other's behavior, not in terms of a fixed range of options from which speakers must choose, but in terms of a range of options characteristic of recognizable situation types in the context of which speakers characteristically make and develop choices (*Social Semiotic*, pp. 192, 32, 109). And in a striking further image, he captures something of the reciprocity of order and disorder that clarifies not only the evolving and precarious nature of both, but also the evolving nature of any theory that seeks to accommodate the intractable demands of linguistic necessity and linguistic novelty. Social order and linguistic order can best be approached, he argues, in terms of "a continuing conversation" in which "a world is not only built, but . . . is kept in a state of repair and ongoingly refurbished" (*Social Semiotic*, p. 81).[60] The building and rebuilding continue together, as multiple and changing forms of order lend each other mutual support.

Theory, in such a context, can only be productively deployed if it is persistently developed, if it, too, is somehow in motion. The site of theoretical engagement with language is, for Halliday, one that must make room for more than misleading claims to comprehensiveness. It must provide the theorist with productive access to the multiple local orders of "innumerable microsemiotic encounters" which invoke "all the various semantic subsystems" of a language and society on the move. Here multiple and moving order is an indispensable feature of any more general picture we establish either of language or of society, and theory which evaluates itself solely on the basis of its simplicity, exactness, and generality is doomed to oscillate between inadequacy and excess. Some other criteria must thus be invoked, criteria that govern the kinds and degrees of simplicity, exactness, and generality that will serve, and also the relationships between their competing claims in the context of social and linguistic diversity and change. And this leads Halliday, as it leads us, to consider further both the evolving relationship between theory and theorist and the uncertain scale and scope of any informative picture we invoke of the relationship between order and disorder in language. "It is perhaps not too farfetched to put it in these terms: reality consists of meanings, and the fact that meanings are essentially indeterminate and unbounded is what gives rise to that strand in human thought—philosophical, religious, scientific—in which the emphasis is on the dynamic, wavelike aspect of reality, its constant restructuring, its periodicity without recurrence, its continuity in time and space" (*Social Semiotic*, p. 139).

In invoking the disciplines of philosophy, religion, and science, Halliday invites reconsideration of what he was initially unprepared to offer—the kind of big, inclusive pictures that such disciplines have traditionally sought to supply. But Halliday's emphasis is less on comprehensive unity than on the kinds of continuity that can accommodate both persistence and change. In effect, Halliday invites us to ponder, in realms of multiple and changing order, what the appropriate relationship is between locally illuminating pictures with little general applicability and those of larger and more durable consequence. For what is ultimately at issue for the linguistic theorist is some means of establishing a more flexible relationship between the general typifications upon which linguistic methodology relies and the idiosyncratic particular cases upon which the life of a language depends. And it is in just such terms that literary theory, too, requires an adjustment of its modes of linguistic conceptualization, as they have direct implications in the discipline of literary studies for appropriate contextualization and control.

Theory, as it emerges from these linguistic contexts, must somehow provide not just descriptive categories and techniques to be judged primarily in terms of their tidiness and generality, but also guidelines for their use, for relating theory to data, that do not exhaust their potential for further use. In an important sense, theory, so conceived, must somehow avoid occupying all the conceptual space it opens up. There is thus, as Halliday belatedly recognized, a problematic relationship between the heuristic generality of an investigative theory and the ontological generality of theory-based conclusions. And the evolution of Halliday's theories returns us to the vexed problem of the relationship between theory, theorist, and belief.

Theories in the terms that Halliday predominantly employs are not sets of rules governed by founding beliefs, but resources guided by initial and evolving beliefs, assumptions, and predispositions. Their guidelines may take various forms, as we will see in the next chapter, and not being inclusive in their scope, they cannot be exclusive in their function. And the gap that must always remain open between the generalities of theory and the particularities of data is one that can only be bridged by a theorist who has learned how to use theory as an instrument of discovery, by someone who has, in effect, recognized that deploying a theory involves further developing that theory.[61]

Such considerations return us inexorably to the pluralist dilemma of how to establish relationships between competing theories in a manner that cannot itself be fully theorized. For what is emerging from a "linguistic turn" toward more sophisticated linguistic theory is a more complex relationship not only between theory and data but also between theory and theorist. And what the theorist of more flexible theory must be able to do is to distinguish in an evolving theory those techniques of description and interpretation that serve primarily the generalizing imperative of a theory from those techniques of description and interpretation that are susceptible to adaptation and thus convertible from one vocabulary to another and from one local context to another. For in a world of variety and change, inquiry shifts from locating unity to tracing continuity, and this requires us ultimately to consider whether the role of belief in theoretical inquiry is to guide rather than govern the choices that make further and other belief possible. The recurring tension between the claims of a theory to heuristic or ontological status has thus significant implications for the theorist who seeks to use theory as a means of traveling beyond it.

Chapter 4 Wittgenstein: Facticity, Instrumentality, and Theory

Of the many issues that emerge from a review of post-Saussurean linguistics, few are as important as the precarious attempts to reconcile linguistic theory with linguistic variety and linguistic change. In spite of the considerable interest in linguistic creativity expressed by Chomsky and Halliday, both found themselves, at key points in the development of their theories, adopting positions which effectively exclude it. Both made subsequent efforts to include it again, but their lapses into unforeseen rigidity register the difficulties involved in requiring theory to be both comprehensive and open-ended. The possibility of locating comprehensive order strongly attracts linguistic theorists of the most diverse kinds, no matter how explicit their initial commitment to linguistic variety, linguistic creativity, or linguistic change. Sustained pursuit of comprehensive order, however, impels advocates and opponents alike toward a structural determinism that is embraced by the former with enthusiastic recognition and encountered by the latter with sudden surprise.

Though the pursuit of comprehensive monosystemic order in realms of multiple order requires the construction of increasingly complex descriptive devices, repeated efforts have been made by linguists to reconcile the competing claims of simplicity, generality, and exactness by pursuing ever larger external coverage and ever greater internal coherence. In the background is a constantly reemerging monistic conviction that to be persuasive, to be seen to work, a theory needs to demonstrate its ability to deal predictably with as many facets of language as possible, leaving the theorist with little subsequent work to do. The pursuit of this goal leads linguists, as we have seen, to try to convert multiple order into comprehensive order by excluding some modes of order as irrelevant disorder or by reducing apparent variety to harmless variation. Through such procedures of exclusion and absorption a theory establishes a putatively comprehensive unity to replace pervasive disunity, with the implication, such linguists apparently believe, that the theory has enhanced its claims to authority by improving our understanding of language, revealing its hidden coherence, and increasing our control of our social and psychological environments.

It is by now widely recognized, however, that what we do not necessarily gain by invoking comprehensive systems that govern our cultural, social, and linguistic environments is control. As Halliday belatedly reminded himself, if it should prove possible to claim that we have described comprehensively the structural codes that establish the total conditions in which individuals live their social lives, control seems to pass not to the individuals but to the cultural context. It becomes arguable and has indeed been argued, that the sum of social conditions not only characterizes the nature of social life but actually establishes the possibility of there being such a thing as social life. In such circumstances individuals, being unable to change the structure of their inherited cultural environment, become subject to it, and, in effect, live by playing out the possibilities prescribed by preexisting social codes. Particular individuals may come and go upon the cultural scene, but the social codes that govern their social lives precede their appearance and persist after their departure. As a consequence, the subjected individual simply becomes the site upon which various semiotic codes, each in itself unchanging, converge. Language, in such a context, appears less like something spoken by unique individuals trying to get idiosyncratic things done than like something that speaks through the voices of homogenized subjects whose freedom does not extend beyond the right to select and combine lines from an inherited script. Far from increasing individual control, the imposition of unified order in realms of multiple order threatens to decrease it to the point at which it effectively disappears.

Such reduction of individual control provides, however, a picture of the state of human affairs that seems to some both enlightening and persuasive. There are those who rejoice in the image of the decentered subject, of the individual agent dissolved into the codes, political or otherwise, that were formerly assumed to be under individual control. But to others, as we noted earlier, such a picture is both unpersuasive and unwelcome, for it fails to account for elements of human creativity, individual responsibility, and social change that experience has suggested to be otherwise constituted. To the latter there is some puzzlement at the emergence of determinism in the work of those supposedly promoting individual control through comprehensive description. Oddly enough, it seems, the case for individual freedom and control depends not upon the replacement of disorder by order but upon the perpetuation of disorder. Or, to put it another way, upon the recognition that attempts to picture social data in comprehensive and unified terms register the mistaken ambitions of theorists who have not come to terms with the problematics of deploying theory in a world of variety and change. What we have thus been examining is the tendency of deterministic pictures to reestablish themselves in the work of sophisticated theorists who are aware of the impending problems and set out initially to avoid them. Only when we understand the processes by which these large deterministic pictures reemerge and eradicate more diversified local pictures will we be able to recognize the potential of an alternative approach to theory that can accommodate a persisting but productive disorder.

We must thus extend discussion of the appropriate relationship between order and disorder into further discussion of the control allowed individuals in theory-defined domains, the control assigned to theorists of the theories they create, and the control exerted by theory on the data it confronts. These points bear directly on the tendency of modern literary theory to promote an aggregate of local monisms, each of which is based upon unyielding presupposition and settled belief. But the role of the theorist, we must begin to recognize, is not merely to set a theoretical apparatus in motion, nor merely to adjust it where needed, but, in some more complex manner, to exhibit and attest to its worth.

What is needed, it seems, is some basis for theory justification that removes or revises the role of simplicity, generality, and exactness and provides, as Halliday's instrumental criterion was designed to provide, some other or some further ground for judging adequacy. As a point of departure, we might return to the notion that there appears to be a radical inconsistency between widespread demands that a theory explain all the facts of a field or a discipline and an equally widespread acknowledgment that all modes of description are necessarily partial and selective.

Any serious description of any range of facts is, it is generally recognized, theory laden in ways that affect what the description selects for attention and how it combines the data it selects. One has only to consider, as Austin does, the different kinds of description of a presidential assassination that might be produced by, say, a bystander, the Federal Bureau of Investigation, a physician, a sociologist, an economist, and a politician.[1] The event might be described, in turn, as a terrifying shock, a major crime, a terminal injury, a reaction to injustice, a result of financial instability, and an act of revenge. Each respondent would describe the event in a certain way, each might be right in a certain way, but all would regard the others' descriptions as inadequate substitutes for their own. The various local descriptions register larger presuppositions about the nature of the data to be described and about the possible functions which the description might serve. Fundamental to theory-laden description is thus the motivated selection of certain aspects of an event to focus on and of certain other classes of event to which to relate them.

Notions of comprehensiveness and facticity become complicated in such a context, and it is not easy to find an accounting of the merits of multiplicity that can remedy the apparent loss of empirical certitude. But it is precisely here that the responsibility of the theorist/practitioner becomes most visible. Such, indeed, is the weight of this responsibility that even those who argue for an instrumental grounding of theory and for heuristic facticity often find themselves inadvertently returning to ontological claims to give their theories greater authority. And these claims to external foundations soon lead to renewed demands for comprehensiveness and coherence, which precipitate, in turn, renewed confrontation with reductive determinism.

The characteristic evolution of this general problematic is visible in the work of Saussure, Chomsky, and Halliday alike. When Saussure had to consider what might control a nonfoundational, nonempirical sign system, he quickly found himself confronting the question of the relationship between theory and fact, but his initial sophistication in dealing with the matter did not preclude a reemergence of the naive empiricism that he had apparently rejected.[2] As we have noted, Saussure set out to challenge the notion that signs acquire their meanings from objects to which they refer. His alternative theory of the sign was that it consisted of a relationally established and systemically sustained entity made up of an abstract and conventional signal and an abstract and conventional signification. The system of signs rather than individual material objects then provided the means of controlling and explaining various modes of signifying, and it is, of course, this transition from atomic to structural explanation that gave rise to the notion of structuralism. But once we accept that systems define and control signs, we must then consider what controls the abstract system.

For someone as opposed as Saussure was to a discipline of bits and pieces based on *ad hoc* abstractions, an answer in terms of something comprehensive and concrete is logical enough. Ironically, however, such an answer impelled him to relate his abstract system to something as solid and sharable as the empiricism it replaced. The newly conceived abstract system of linguistic structure (*langue*) was quickly assigned a social and historical reality that provided it with a firm, comprehensive, and unchanging foundation: "Linguistic structure is no less real than speech, and no less amenable to study. Linguistic signs, although essentially psychological, are not abstractions. The associations, ratified by collective agreement, which go to make up the language are realities localised in the brain. . . . A language, as a collective phenomenon, takes the form of a totality of imprints in everyone's brain, rather like a dictionary of which each individual has an identical copy."[3] Though Saussure recognizes the possible heuristic value of theories, he is simply not prepared to rest his case on the explanatory power of his own theory. He wants to be able to justify the claim that his theory locates and doesn't simply create the facts it confronts, so he assigns them an ontological status which, along with claims to comprehensiveness, inexorably produce deterministic consequences.

Although the motives that led Saussure down this track are evident enough, it is interesting to see both Chomsky and Halliday, in spite of their awareness of the dangers to which Saussurean structuralism had proved vulnerable, take very similar steps to solidify the status of their own theories. When Chomsky describes, illuminatingly enough, the process of level creation in linguistic theory, he registers his awareness of the necessarily selective nature of linguistic description. And when he insists on the centrality to linguistics of accounting for the native speaker's ability to construct and understand new sentences, he seems to be giving his theory an instrumental status. But when he begins to apply the word "natural" with increasing frequency to his techniques of description, it becomes apparent that ontological and not just heuristic and instrumental claims are to be made for the theory and its facts. Discussing the relationships between sentences as his model depicts them, Chomsky is soon arguing that "we are led to a picture of grammars as possessing a natural tripartite arrangement" (the one he characterizes as consisting of phrase structure, transformations, and morphophonemics).[4] He also refers from time to time to a natural algebra of transformations, a natural definition of linguistic level, a natural way of accounting for relations between sentences, and a natural order discoverable in linguistic data.[5]

As this trend continues to develop in Chomsky's work, the claims to ontological status begin to extend, just as Saussure's began to extend, beyond the local domain of linguistics and into larger and larger spheres of implication. An apparently incautious claim that, in generating an infinite set of grammatical utterances from a finite set of data, a grammar "mirrors the behavior of the speaker" is soon qualified, but it is subsequently revised and extended.[6] If a language is a set of sentences and a grammar is a device that generates that set of sentences, Chomsky argues, then a grammar of a particular language is effectively a theory of that language, and such a grammar/theory can be attributed to the native speaker who displays the linguistic abilities described in the model.[7] The putatively heuristic device is thus assigned a psychological reality, and this gives rise to sweeping philosophical claims about its implications for the nature of mind.

> Clearly, a child who has learned a language has developed an internal representation of a system of rules that determine how sentences are to be formed, used, and understood. Using the term "grammar" with a systematic ambiguity (to refer, first, to the native speaker's internally represented "theory of his language" and, second, to the linguist's account of this), we can say that the child has developed and internally represented a generative grammar, in the sense described. . . . As a precondition for language learning, [the child] must possess, first, a linguistic theory that specifies the form of the grammar of a possible human language, and, second, a strategy for selecting a grammar of the appropriate form that is compatible with the primary linguistic data [which it has encountered]. . . .
>
> On the basis of the best information now available, it seems reasonable to suppose that a child cannot help constructing a particular sort of transformational grammar to account for the data presented to him, any more than he can control his perception of solid objects or his attention to line and angle. Thus it may well be that the general features of language structure reflect, not so much the course of one's experience, but rather the general character of one's capacity to acquire knowledge—in the traditional sense, one's innate ideas and innate principles. . . . By pursuing this investigation [of general linguistic theory], one may hope to give some real substance to the traditional belief that "the principles of grammar form an important, and very curious, part of the philosophy of the human mind" (Beattie, 1788).[8]

This attempt to locate "a mental reality underlying actual behavior" such that "a child cannot help [but construct] a . . . transformational grammar" is directly analogous to Saussure's claim that his theory has uncovered a social and psychological reality.[9] And it is instructive to see Halliday, who is even more explicitly committed to the notions of creativity in language, instrumentality in theory, and selectivity in description, eventually end up making ontological claims of similar scope.

As we noted earlier, one of Halliday's responses to the question "what is language," was "why do you want to know?"[10] In doing so, he explicitly acknowledges that pragmatic concerns will have a direct bearing on the aspects of language we expect a theory to highlight and explain. He also makes quite clear his recognition that there could be no such thing as a complete linguistic description or even a neutral linguistic description, that is, one that gives equal attention to every element of language. Early in his career Halliday and coauthors argued that: "It is not true that only one model can represent the nature of language; language is much too complex for any one model to highlight all its different aspects equally clearly. The problem in any instance is to select, or devise, the model that will be most suitable for the purpose in view."[11] At a later point, Halliday was still arguing that "there is no such thing as 'all the linguistic features of an utterance' considered apart from some external criteria of significance" and was thus effectively rejecting both ontological claims and criteria of comprehensiveness.[12] But as he made the shift to treating linguistic form as a product of linguistic function, his attempts to give linguistic function a more than instrumental basis and linguistic theory a more than instrumental status led to the sudden reemergence of concerns for the ontological and the comprehensive. And it is instructive to see how directly the two are linked and how quickly their combination produces deterministic consequences.

The first step down this road is taken when Halliday begins to differentiate his own functional approach from that of predecessors by claiming that his set of linguistic functions can be regarded not merely as means of registering external interests, but as means of establishing causal links between the internal patterns of language and external social functions: "A purely extrinsic theory of language functions does fail to take into account one thing, namely the fact that the multiplicity of function, if the idea is valid at all, is likely to be reflected somewhere in the internal organisation of language itself."[13] If this is so, then the linguistic functions that govern linguistic form can be assigned a historical and not just heuristic status and the descriptions of linguistic form can be said to reveal a structural reality that is ultimately a social reality. And Halliday is soon prepared to make a case for such underlying social reality as strongly as Chomsky made his for a psychological reality.

What has happened in the course of the evolution of language—and this is no more than a reasonable assumption, corresponding to what happens in the development of language in the individual—is that the demands made on language have constantly expanded, and the language system has been shaped accordingly. There has been an increase in the complexity of linguistic function, and the complexity of language has increased with it. Most significantly, this has meant the emergence of the stratal form of organisation, with a purely formal level of coding at its core. This performs the function of integrating the very complex meaning selections into single integrated structures. The way it does this is by sorting out the many very specific uses of language into a small number of highly general functions which underlie them all.[14]

With the historical "emergence" rather than the heuristic positing of a stratal form of organization, Halliday is able to claim that his own functional framework (ideational, interpersonal, and textual) is an externally "neutral" description, one "designed to take into account the nature of the internal, semantic and syntactic patterns of language."[15] Almost immediately these ontological claims are linked to claims to completeness and comprehensiveness. The theory provides, we are told, "a general characterization of semantic functions—of the meaning potential of the language system," and the need to explain the significance of what a speaker says by establishing what he might have said but did not takes Halliday inexorably along the path from ontological to comprehensive claims.[16] And as we have seen, it is but a short step from there to a deterministic social semiotic.

Halliday's belief that his tripartite framework "is imposed by the form of internal organization of the linguistic system" thus parallels a similar tendency in the work of Saussure and Chomsky to convert the heuristically posited into the empirically found, and his insistence that it is possible to establish exhaustively the meaning potential of language parallels similar efforts by Saussure and Chomsky to give their theories not only ontological but also comprehensive status.[17] And as an apparently unavoidable consequence, all three theories begin to become foundational rather than instrumental and deterministic rather than heuristic. In effect, they incline toward presupposing what they apparently discover, and both theory and description serve to recover rather than uncover the facts with which they deal.

Given Saussure's determination to replace a discipline of bits and pieces with a discipline focused on and based on homogeneity, it is not too surprising that his work leads inadvertently to an unforeseen determinism. It is more surprising, however, to see Chomsky's theory proceed in this direction, given his evident awareness of the dangers of Saussurean structuralism and his initial interest in explaining what Saussure could not explain, the nature of linguistic novelty and linguistic creativity.[18] It is even more surprising to encounter the same development in Halliday's work, given his insistence on the importance to language and linguistics of creativity, variety, change, indeterminacy, and instrumentality. But what is most important is the implication, emerging intermittently from the work of all three theorists, that the authority of a theory depends less upon the theorist's capacity to deploy it usefully and persuasively than upon its own capacity to uncover tangible realities. As we have noted, however, ontological claims, far from rescuing an abstract theory from the structuralist dilemma of deterministic circularity, tend to reintroduce the problem by renewing the imperative that description be complete and comprehensive. In effect the claims of ontology and comprehensiveness are mutually reinforcing, and they serve together to trap the theorist in the theory rather than provide an instrument of investigation whose worth might be demonstrated by leading the theorist beyond the limits of the theory's apparent capacity.

There is thus something about the triple imperatives of simplicity, generality, and exactness that diminishes the flexibility of the relationship between generality of theory and the particularity of data in such a way that necessity repeatedly reasserts its priority over novelty, and the theorist becomes a monist trapped in a machine. The "linguistic turn" in related disciplines has thus, in general, been, as Rorty earlier suggested, a turn toward necessity. But the nature of this turn has itself been governed by a limiting picture of the role of theory that does less than justice to what theory in general and linguistic theory in particular have to offer. If we want theory to serve as an instrument of inquiry, rather than as a mechanism that reveals what it presupposes, we need not only to change the attitude of theorists, but also to reconceive the relationship between the generalities that constitute theory and the particularities of the data they confront. In effect, we need to develop another picture of theory.

Although this key relationship between the general and the particular in theoretical inquiry has been a subject of debate since classical times, the most radical contribution to the debate in modern times has been made by Ludwig Wittgenstein in the realm, appropriately enough, of philosophy of language. And what Wittgenstein has to offer can advance our understanding on several fronts. Pondering "our craving for generality" and our tendency to slight "the particular case," Wittgenstein saw the need for some more productive relationship between them that would allow us to take appropriate account of linguistic complexity.[19] This led him steadily to engage several of the issues that we have traced in linguistic and literary theory, notably those involving necessity and novelty, fixity and change, theory and data, theory and theorist, belief and doubt, and conviction and discovery.

Signaled very early in his preface to *Philosophical Investigations* is Wittgenstein's wariness both of the tendency of presupposition to convert into conclusion and of the readiness of the method user to disappear into the mechanics of the method: "I should not like my writing to spare other people the trouble of thinking. But, if possible, to stimulate someone to thoughts of his own" (*PI*, p. x).[20] Such, indeed, is his wariness of premature conviction in both himself and others that it could be claimed that Wittgenstein's enigmatic work offers no larger argument, generates no eventual theory, and establishes no governing philosophy. But the counterclaim would be that what he offers is something that might respond to the theoretical dilemmas we have been encountering by suggesting another notion of argument, another understanding of theory, and another kind of philosophy. And to grasp its larger implications we need to bear in mind not only the descriptive and epistemological problems we have encountered in theoretical and descriptive linguistics, but also the arguments of Saussure and Bakhtin that order is a means of limiting, not excluding, disorder.

Among the well-known thinkers whose ideas have achieved prominence in modern theoretical debate, Wittgenstein strikes many as the most problematic. It is often difficult to get any precise sense of what the fuss is about. Theorists with a Wittgensteinian turn of mind seem firmly convinced about their position but betray little of the inclination, so common in other forms of theory today, to noisily advertise or graphically display the origins of their intellectual labors. Direct recourse to Wittgenstein's writings often seems no more satisfying. His major work, *Philosophical Investigations,* is a peculiar aggregate of loosely related paragraphs which offers no detailed statement of intended goals, no sustained elaboration of a narrative thread, and no triumphant summary of achieved conclusions. As theory and philosophy, the work seems oddly structured and open to a variety of uses. Although the author's preface to this enigmatic work registers his awareness of what might appear to be missing, he seems at best to be only semiapologetic about it:

> It was my intention at first to bring all this together in a book whose form I pictured differently at different times. But the essential thing was that the thoughts should proceed from one subject to another in a natural order and without breaks.
>
> After several unsuccessful attempts to weld my results together into such a whole, I realized that I should never succeed. The best that I could write would never be

more than philosophical remarks; my thoughts were soon crippled if I tried to force them on in any single direction against their natural inclination.—And this was, of course, connected with the very nature of the investigation. For this compels us to travel over a wide field of thought criss-cross in every direction.—The philosophical remarks in this book are, as it were, a number of sketches of landscapes which were made in the course of these long and involved journeyings. (*PI*, p. ix)

The absence of a conventional narrative coherence and the absence of inflated claims are thus not accidental. Wittgenstein's concern for finding an appropriate structure is explicitly linked to what he feels are the demands of the ideas he has to offer. The book is finally, he suggests, "only an album," by means of which we can get "a picture of the landscape" which he repeatedly traverses in his intellectual "journeyings" (*PI*, p. ix). Though Wittgenstein is dealing primarily with philosophy of language rather than theory more generally conceived, the implications of his work are evident enough. There seems little danger here that theoretical discourse conceived in these terms will become self-confirming, that conclusions will be implicit in presuppositions, or that theorists will be left with only illustrative work to do.

We should, of course, be alert to the implications of the image of an album for a philosopher whose initial reputation was established by arguments in favor of a picture-theory of meaning. His earlier attempts to establish for every proposition a definitive picture are superseded by later attempts to sketch out "tolerable" pictures whose application extends beyond the sentence and whose value depends on neither their singularity nor their singleness. His declining interest in establishing definitive scenes is accompanied by a growing interest in sketching emerging landscapes, whose complicated contours require repeated journeyings from one imprecise locale to another. Journeying is, indeed, one of the favorite images employed in the text. Language we are told is "a labyrinth of paths" (*PI*, p. 82, par. 203); a philosophical problem has the form "I don't know my way about" (*PI*, p. 49, par. 123); and "a rule stands there like a sign-post" (*PI*, p. 39, par. 85) offering us helpful guidance but not explicit instructions. The journeys seem fraught with danger, the map of the terrain imprecise at best, and the destination not clearly known. And instead of the comprehensive coverage and descriptive closure that others have pursued, Wittgenstein seems content to rely on a series of evocative images. While it appeared problematic for Saussure, Chomsky, and Halliday to be unable to produce a large and consistent picture that could accommodate all the little pictures each successively supplied, Wittgenstein seems determined to convert that apparently disabling acknowledgment into a potentially enabling recognition. The "album" of variously related pictures might well provide perspectives that no single comprehensive picture might be able to supply.

The concern that Wittgenstein exhibits for the structure of his book is quite evidently related to the images used within it and to the nature of the investigations he is conducting. To recognize this is to recognize one of the reasons why the book has seemed philosophically obscure, and why it is nevertheless possible to locate via its obscurities an appropriate mode of participation in what it has to offer. The repeated images of journeying, of failing to get under way, of getting lost when under way, and of arriving at the wrong destination are intriguing enough in themselves, but they invite us to consider which journey Wittgenstein might wish the theorist to take and which destination the theorist might thereby arrive at. Wittgenstein's constant wandering from point to point, from paragraph to paragraph, and from image to image have led many to question whether he actually has a philosophical position to offer us, whether he has indeed a summarizable set of philosophical beliefs, and whether there is or could be a Wittgensteinian approach to things in general.

This is of major consequence, of course, to anyone wishing to use Wittgenstein's work in developing explanatory theory or interpretive practice. If we compare his work to, say, that of Kant, Hegel, Marx, Freud, Lacan, Barthes, or Lévi-Strauss, or to that of many other thinkers whose work has been of major consequence in the modern era, we can get some sense of what the problem is. Wittgenstein offers us no clearly defined system of analysis, no elaborate set of theoretical distinctions, and (apart from a sprinkling of characteristic metaphors) no highly developed technical vocabulary. While a Freudian analysis of a text instantly declares itself to be so, it can be difficult to identify as such a Wittgensteinian analysis. There is no elaborate jargon to give the game away, no set of presuppositions to be posited and illustrated, no characteristic goals that pronounce themselves in advance. Though these might serve to save us from the perils of imperialistic theory, the question inevitably arises whether there is or could be a Wittgensteinian theory of art or of interpretation or, indeed, of anything else. And this question is of the same order as those which register doubts about whether Wittgenstein can, in any conventional sense, be said to have a philosophy.

Wittgenstein himself is keen to offer support to those who might entertain such doubts. Rejecting the ambitions of his youth, Wittgenstein warns us, as he warns himself, that "we may not advance any kind of theory" nor any kind of final "explanation" (*PI,* p. 47, par. 109), nor any definitive "method" (*PI,* p. 51, par. 133). Nor is there to be any attempt to make a breakthrough to some underlying foundation or transcendent goal: "We feel as if we had to *penetrate* phenomena: our investigation, however, is directed not towards phenomena, but, as one might say, towards the '*possibilities*' of phenomena" (*PI*, p. 42, par. 90). His argument is directed less toward final discovery than toward local equanimity, the satisfactory result is regarded less as a matter of resolving an issue than of rendering it harmless: "The real discovery is the one that makes me capable of stopping doing philosophy when I want to.—The one that gives philosophy peace, so that it is no longer tormented by questions which bring *itself* in question" (*PI*, p. 51, par. 133).

The resistance Wittgenstein displays to the temptation to offer any kind of comprehensive, all-embracing theory is indeed a resistance to the troubling consequences repeatedly encountered by those who advance such theories—the gnawing doubts and ultimate frustrations that result from attempts to absorb multiple phenomena into unifying frameworks. At a time when theory is itself riddled with such doubts, at a time when Derridean deconstruction has dramatized what followers of Wittgenstein have long known, at a time when major scholarly journals have highlighted debate about the viability of literary theory,[21] there is reason to reconsider what Wittgenstein had to say that bears upon the nature of theory and what he was able to display as a possible alternative.

The word "display" is carefully chosen. It relates both to Wittgenstein's characterization of his book as an album and to the potential dilemma of those so dismayed by the theory revolution as to adopt the stance of the antitheorist. As many would be quick to point out, to argue for or against theory is to make a theoretical argument, and there is little for people to gain in involving themselves in inadvertent self-contradiction. Wittgenstein's alternative to existing theory is not an antitheory any more than his alternative to existing philosophy is an antiphilosophy. Not unlike Firth in another discipline, Wittgenstein offers instead a philosophical procedure displayed in action, a philosophical technique that can be variously exemplified, a philosophical process that refuses to become a reified product. Though Wittgenstein, as noted above, warns us against our "craving for generality" and our "contemptuous attitude towards the particular case," his aim is not to substitute the particular for the general but to locate a relationship between the two that prevents them or us from coming to final and definitive resting points, which, in the context of novelty and change, must always seem premature. Such refusal of final resting points is not, however, a refusal of all resting points, and grasping the difference is essential to our understanding of the dilemmas of theoretical comprehensiveness and descriptive closure we have been widely encountering.

Indeed, one of the recurring images in Wittgenstein's writing is of philosophy as a form of therapy: "the philosopher's treatment of a question is like the treatment of an illness" (*PI*, p. 91, par. 255). The human mind, like the human body, exhibits recurring weaknesses and is prone to recurring illnesses. Some forms of treatment will correct the problems, but as they will not rule out the possibility of recurrence, we need both to keep the remedies to hand and to try to ward off renewed dangers before they strike. Habits of mind, like habits of the body, are, however, very hard to break, and it takes persistent intellectual effort to prevent ourselves from lapsing into habits we thought we had transcended.

For Wittgenstein, many philosophical problems arise from habits of this kind, and he is prepared to characterize his own philosophical procedure as one of "assembling reminders for a particular purpose" (*PI*, p. 50, par. 127). Such reminders are to be assembled in the light of, are to establish their viability and gain their function from, not some comprehensive and static framework, but some awareness of "the philosophical problems" (*PI*, p. 47, par. 109) that generate philosophical activity. And the philosophical activity about which he is most concerned in *Philosophical Investigations* is that precipitated primarily by problems which emerge when we attempt to explain to ourselves the nature of language and its relationship to knowledge, belief, and truth.

As we have already seen, there are few areas of concern more central to theoretical activity in a variety of fields than inherited assumptions about the nature of language, and few issues are more likely to activate the illnesses that Wittgenstein's therapeutic techniques are designed to treat. To rehearse some of Wittgenstein's arguments on these issues is to cover well-trodden ground, but also to remind ourselves of reminders that modern theory seems often to have forgotten. More important, however, is that in doing so, we will encounter in action aspects of Wittgenstein's thinking that can only be encountered in action. Knowing, in Wittgenstein's later philosophy, is not easily separated from doing, and skepticism is not easily separated from belief. As a consequence, theory and practice acquire a relationship that avoids the determinism that follows so quickly upon modern theory construction, and theorists soon find themselves acquiring larger responsibilities.

The first voice we encounter in *Philosophical Investigations* is not that of Wittgenstein, but that of Augustine. The second is that of Wittgenstein offering clarifications and corrections to the views of Augustine. In this process of interaction between competing perspectives Wittgenstein more often plays both roles, alternately offering the view that inherited habits of mind encourage and the view that a more enlightened mind might offer instead. Cavell describes these as the voice of temptation and the voice of correctness, but, as others have remarked, it would be more accurate to call the second voice the voice of correction.[22] Indeed, Cavell himself points out that it is not easy to abstract from the conflicting voices a summary of what is wrong or right about either position.[23]

Wittgenstein's is not a philosophy of correct positions but of corrections to positions that might most readily be adopted. By exposing the unsatisfactoriness of particular philosophical stances, Wittgenstein absolves us from the need to answer the unanswerable questions repeatedly generated by misconceived notions of simplicity, generality, exactness, ontology, heuristics, and related concerns. Thus Wittgenstein responds to Augustine's description of how we learn a language (through elders pointing out objects and naming them) not by arguing that the description is right or wrong but by summarizing it, indicating its limitations, and then illustrating its shortcomings:

> These words, it seems to me, give us a particular picture of the essence of human language. It is this: the individual words in language name objects—sentences are combinations of such names.—In this picture of language we find the roots of the following idea: Every word has a meaning. This meaning is correlated with the word. It is the object for which the word stands.
>
> Augustine does not speak of there being any difference between kinds of word. If you describe the learning of language in this way you are, I believe, thinking primarily of nouns like "table," "chair," "bread," and of people's names, and only secondarily of the names of certain actions and properties; and of the remaining kinds of word as something that will take care of itself.
>
> Now think of the following use of language. . . . (*PI*, p. 2, par. 1)

Wittgenstein opposes Augustine's illustration of language acquisition with an illustration of language use, an illustration designed to demonstrate that we use the words "five," "red," and "apple" in different ways, and that any attempt to base a theory of language acquisition or linguistic meaning on any one of them is to fail to do justice to the others and to the fact that there are many "kinds of word" that function in many different ways. Like Firth, Wittgenstein insists upon considering language in the context of social exchange and this leads him, as it led Firth, to an insistence upon the multiplicity of linguistic form and function. Just as important is his readiness to use a local example (sending someone shopping) to oppose the example Augustine uses to cover language in general. Wittgenstein opposes Augustine's big picture with a small picture whose consequences are disruptive but whose implications seem, initially at least, much more local. Here, at the outset, we see the beginnings of the assembling of Wittgenstein's album, of his set of philosophical reminders that function as corrections to misleading habits of mind and as guidelines for further thought. And what we need to consider are the implications of Wittgenstein's collection of pictures for our understanding of language and linguistic theory, and not least for the ways in which local awareness can achieve larger consequence without aspiring to comprehensive applicability.

The particular habit of mind Wittgenstein initially addresses is, of course, carefully chosen. The quotation from Augustine is not the only possible example but it is one with far-reaching implications. The conviction that the meaning of a word is the object for which it stands is one we have encountered before and it is a conviction that dies hard. Indeed, one of the reasons for its persistence is its entanglement in a pattern of assumptions about the nature of language and the nature of knowledge that have a direct bearing on what we assume to be the nature of theories and the nature of the facts they confront. Wittgenstein points out, again by example, that our tendency to confuse the bearer of a name with the meaning of a name is a tendency that presents us with insurmountable problems: "When Mr. N.N. dies one says that the bearer of the name dies, not that the meaning dies. And it would be nonsensical to say that, for if the name ceased to have meaning it would make no sense to say 'Mr. N.N. is dead'" (*PI*, p. 20, par. 40). But he is well aware that this is not simply a theoretical commitment on our part. After years of having it pointed out to us that the same word can be used to refer to different objects (e.g., I, that, it), that the same object can be referred to by various words (e.g., John F. Kennedy, the first husband of Jacqueline Bouvier, the president assassinated in Dallas), and that many words do not refer to objects (e.g., afterward, hello, exciting), even the most advanced forms of contemporary theory continue to be tempted by the most primitive forms of signifier/signified vocabulary.[24]

Augustine's words, Wittgenstein argues, provide a particular picture of language; they are embedded in and inseparable from a way of thinking whose consequences are much more widely dispersed. Wittgenstein's concern is not so much with the theoretical correctness of an alternative theory of meaning but with the intractability of certain presuppositions about the ways in which our language functions. To correct such habits of mind we need therapy, and not just theory, for theory without therapy can simply transfer us from one set of disabling presuppositions to another. What is at issue is not just the difference between enabling and disabling presuppositions but also our disposition to use theory or philosophy in ways that reduce the potentially enabling into the inadvertently disabling. Therapy must thus address the many facets of the problem and not just its most visible manifestation.

As we noted earlier, what is primarily at issue in the reference theory of meaning is that it offers a comforting and apparently commonsense explanation of the principles of control that enable our language to function. And assumptions about that mode of functioning persist, even among those most aware of the problematic status of reference. Though there are many variations on the theme, Wittgenstein is less concerned with addressing any particular variant than with correcting an intractable and misleading habit of mind with implications, as we noted earlier, far greater than we might at first suspect. Characteristic of that habit of mind are the assumptions that a unified object-world provides language with a firm external foundation, important rules of use, a major privileged function, and an obvious preeminent form. It is these larger implications as well as the local issue of meaning that Wittgenstein is seeking to confront.

The foundation, of course, has long been regarded as empirical: "the individual words in language name objects . . . [the] meaning is . . . the object for which the word stands" (*PI*, p. 2, par. 1). The important rules have been those of logic, the kind of logic established by analytic philosophers. The privileged function (to cite Bertrand Russell) has been regarded as follows: "The essential business of language is to assert or deny facts" (the primary function, coincidentally enough, of philosophical propositions).[25] And the preeminent form has been, of course, the form of the statement, the assertion, the philosopher's true/false proposition.[26] Wittgenstein had, at one time, shared many of these convictions and, early in his career, had recorded in a notebook that "my *whole* task consists in explaining the nature of the proposition."[27] But a key strategy of his later work is to dismantle the whole conceptual apparatus that had arranged this set of assumptions about language, knowledge, and truth in such a way that they seemed to provide each other with mutual support. And his recurring strategy is to restore multiplicity at every level of theory and description, but at the same time to suggest how that multiplicity is limited and controlled.

As far as the proposition is concerned, he is now prepared to reconsider its status and its importance: "Why," he asks, "do we say a proposition is something remarkable?" (*PI*, p. 43, par. 93). Well, he answers, partly because of the enormous importance philosophers have habitually attached to it, and partly because "a misunderstanding of the logic of language seduces us into thinking that something extraordinary, something unique, must be achieved by propositions" (*PI*, pp. 43–44, par. 93). Wittgenstein's response is to query this tendency to privilege any one form of utterance by upgrading various other forms of language. He asks us to imagine languages without propositions, such as a language consisting only of orders and reports in battle, or of questions designed simply to elicit the answers "yes" and "no" (*PI*, p. 8, par. 19). And he once suggested "that a serious and good philosophical work could be written that would consist entirely of *jokes* (without being facetious). Another time he said that a philosophical treatise might contain nothing but questions (without answers). In his own writing he made wide use of both."[28]

Having queried the status of the supposedly preeminent form of language, Wittgenstein moves steadily along to question whether language is primarily devoted to the truth and knowledge business of asserting and denying facts and to suggest instead that it has a multitude of equally important functions embedded in a multitude of language-games that we regularly play (*PI*, pp. 11–12, par. 23). And this leads logically enough to his efforts to dismantle once and for all the empirical foundation of language by contrasting meaning as the single process of reference with meaning as variable use in various language-games.

Though it is important to recognize the habits of mind Wittgenstein is opposing, it is just as important to note the techniques of correction he adopts. Wittgenstein is not interested in substituting another set of privileged elements for those he is now trying to dismantle. His aim is not just to revalue one mistakenly privileged form of language, but to remove the notion that there is or should be a single privileged form. He likewise wishes to do away with the notion that there is or should be a single primary function for language; he resists the temptation to replace one set of comprehensive rules for language use with another set; and he displays no interest in offering a new foundation for language to replace the one he is dismantling. "Philosophy," he argues, "may in no way interfere with the actual use of language; it can in the end only describe it. For it cannot give it any foundation either. It leaves everything as it is" (*PI*, p. 49, par. 124). Philosophical problems are solved "not by giving new information, but by arranging what we have always known" (*PI*, p. 47, par. 109).

It is this concern for a certain kind of rearrangement of what we have always known that leads Wittgenstein to rely less on conventional philosophical argument, which might substitute one privileged picture for another, and more on illuminating reminders that both individually and collectively exhibit irreducible but not random multiplicity.[29] Rhetorical presentation and philosophical procedure thus merge in the focus on exemplary instances. And it is for this reason that Wittgenstein relies less on philosophical assertion than on illuminating examples. If we are inclined to think, for instance, that all words function in the same way, he asks us to imagine a text in which punctuation marks are typed out as words (comma, period, etc.) (*PI,* p. 3, par. 4). The possible confusion between ordinary words and punctuation marks would be, he suggests, a confusion no less significant than the one that occurs because our various word types (noun, adjective, etc.) are not always distinctively marked, with the result that we regard their typographical similarity as registering a functional similarity (*PI,* p. 6, par. 11). He asks us to think of the diversity of tools in a tool box, and offers this as a reminder that they cannot all be equated just because they are all tools. He asks us to think of the control handles in a steam locomotive which all look more or less alike (because they are all meant to be handled): "But one is the handle of a crank which can be moved continuously (it regulates the opening of a valve); another is the handle of a switch, which has only two effective positions, it is either off or on; a third is the handle of a brake-lever, the harder one pulls on it, the harder it brakes; a fourth, the handle of a pump: it has an effect only so long as it is moved to and fro" (*PI,* p. 7, par. 12). The images multiply and we can add our own. Today we might conceive of a control panel at a space exploration center, where pressing one button activates a television screen, pressing another sets off a fire alarm, another opens a door, another launches a rocket, and so on.

It is, of course, open to us to construct our own examples, for Wittgenstein's use of multiple examples registers a clear refusal to establish a single definitive example. He does not try out several and then recommend the best one, nor does he circumscribe the task and the examples needed to complete it. Each example sheds one kind of light on an issue, and that is then supplemented by others. None covers all aspects of an issue and none achieves a uniquely privileged status; and this is, of course, in keeping with the antifoundational thrust of Wittgenstein's ongoing therapeutic activities, and with his interest in promoting further thinking rather than precipitating its false closure. There is an evident resistance displayed in these activities to a premature reliance upon the empirically given or to a premature assertion of comprehensive applicability.

Wittgenstein's album of examples is designed to replace any privileged picture (like Augustine's) that we might allow not only to guide but to govern our thinking about language. And the relationship between his refusal to offer a countertheory and the reluctance of Firth and Halliday to establish a comprehensive theory that traps the theorist in a theory machine becomes increasingly clear. Examples as Wittgenstein wishes to employ them cannot constitute a closed set or a privileged series. Their function is designedly therapeutic, they address our persisting ills and contribute to our continuing health by promoting our continuing intellectual mobility. And one of the key ways in which they do so is the very multiplicity the examples exhibit. Many of the philosophical problems that we encounter, he argues, arise because of our tendency to nourish our imaginations with only one kind of example (*PI*, p. 155, par. 593). Wittgenstein's technique is to offer us examples of many kinds so that we can see by the light of their variety and thus resist the tendency to absorb the multiplicity of language into some reductive explanatory schema. For one of the key reminders that he is trying to accommodate and to share is the reminder of what we have encountered elsewhere: that the multiplicity of language is not the multiplicity of a fixed state but the multiplicity of an evolving organism, in which the uses of words, sentences, and modes of discourse are constantly open to extension and revision whose novelty will constantly elude our generalizing attempts to unify them: "How many kinds of sentence are there? Say assertion, question, and command?—There are *countless* kinds: countless different kinds of use of what we call 'symbols,' 'words,' 'sentences.' And this multiplicity is not something fixed, given once for all; but new types of language, new language-games, as we may say, come into existence, and others become obsolete and get forgotten" (*PI*, p. 11, par. 23).

This emphasis on existing and emerging multiplicity is characteristic of Wittgenstein's depiction of language. It dictates the structure of his text, explains the function of multiple examples in his chosen mode of discourse, and clarifies the role that example-making plays in the philosophical discourse he illustrates and incites. And it is important to trace the large implications for theory construction and theory use that follow directly from this insistence upon linguistic multiplicity and linguistic change, for the procedure his work exemplifies is one that invites emulation rather than replication. It is a procedure that redirects thinking, rather than one that compels thinking to travel in any particular direction or to arrive at any particular goal. Wittgenstein's work is designed to guide rather than govern the investigative mind, and it thus exhibits a more complex relationship between theory and data and theory and theorist than those we have been exploring hitherto.

Exemplary instances rather than comprehensive philosophy or achieved conclusions play a key role in Wittgenstein's argument, and they function, as does much of Firth's theoretical work, not by offering comprehensive coverage but by supplying local correction and larger guidelines. Cumulatively they register not a philosophical position but a philosophical process of positioning. And to recognize that is to recognize that Wittgenstein's interest in assembling reminders for particular purposes is something more than a diverting variant on in-house skirmishing between professional philosophers. To ask whether Wittgenstein has a philosophy or not, or whether he has a theory of language or not, is to register presuppositions about the possibilities of philosophy and theory that he does not share. Wittgenstein's aim is to reconceive the nature and use of philosophy and of theory. And like Firth and Halliday, he recognizes that influencing the use of philosophy is an important means of influencing the forms that philosophy takes.

Wittgenstein's interest is in philosophizing as a form of philosophy, in learning how to move around rather than in how to arrive, in showing how to continue an intellectual journey rather than how to end it prematurely. As a result, his philosophizing becomes of interest and consequence to anyone with any kind of personal, social, or professional concern for understanding how language works and how we might use theory to clarify how it works. In a narrow sense, it is true, he does not have a "philosophy" to offer at all: there is little in his later work that is reducible to a systematic array of beliefs or rules of procedure. But it is just such narrow conceptions of theory that lead us repeatedly toward circularity and determinism by reducing the flexibility of the relationship between theoretical generality and the particularity of the data confronted and by restricting the role of the theorist to that of minder of a machine. What Wittgenstein offers is a philosophical technique displayed in action. What he is able to demonstrate is less a philosophy, or a theory, or a position, than a technique of philosophizing, theorizing, positioning—a technique based not upon postulates and propositions but upon images, examples, models, and multiple voices. Here there is no question of a fixed and unchanging set of beliefs to which followers must assent, because the interacting voices rarely reduce to a single voice.[30] And this is a technique that we are invited not just to learn, but to develop. Such, indeed, is the larger implication of Wittgenstein's remark that: "I should not like my writing to spare other people the trouble of thinking. But, if possible, to stimulate someone to thoughts of his own" (*PI*, p. x).

The thoughts that Wittgenstein is keen to stimulate are the kind that might emerge from those who, released from disabling presuppositions about the relationships among language, reference, truth, and knowledge, among theory, unity, ontology, and belief, and among method, generality, exactness, and simplicity, seek to explore the new terrain. In a manner of considerable usefulness to the potential pluralist, Wittgenstein demonstrates the means by which prospective theories can open up more space than they can occupy and by which aspiring theorists can command the terrain at which contrasting theories intersect. The dialogic nature of his mode of exploration invites other voices to join the conversation, continue it, redirect it, and, just as important, take responsibility for it.

These emphases upon multiplicity and creativity have, however, served for some to locate Wittgenstein in the camp of the philosophical skeptics rather than in the camp of the system-building believers. Indeed, so brilliantly has Wittgenstein displayed the multiplicity and contingency of language that followers of the more recent strategist of skepticism, Jacques Derrida, seemed uncertain whether to regard him as an ally or as an adversary. Seduced by the siren-song of continuous contingency, deconstructionists often had a great deal of difficulty locating any clear goal beyond it.[31] But Wittgenstein's exploration of contingency is designedly therapeutic—it refuses us one kind of closure while opening up access to others, it refuses us final belief without excluding firm belief. To argue that "the method that Wittgenstein is teaching is precisely the method of destabilization"[32] is to recognize the anticredulity strain in Wittgenstein's work but to overlook the strain that is, as Altieri points out, just as strongly antiskeptical.[33] Wittgenstein seeks to avoid the false alternatives posed by those whose work suggests, on the one hand, that if theoretical procedures are to define anything they must govern everything, and, on the other, that if theoretical procedures do not govern everything they define nothing. Such monistic and relativistic imperatives serve only to keep the traditional seesaw swinging up and down.

Wittgenstein's technique of complex positioning does not imply the endless deferral of locating a position. Indeed his interest in closure is explicit in his remark in *Philosophical Investigations* that "The real discovery is the one that makes me capable of stopping doing philosophy when I want to.—The one that gives philosophy peace, so that it is no longer tormented by questions which bring *itself* into question" (*PI*, p. 51, par. 133). Such closure is, of course, a far cry from that provided by the final imposition of comprehensive theory and unyielding belief. It is more of a resting point than a destination, but it does not seem to be without an earned justification. Indeed, the very fact that Wittgenstein went on to write a manuscript on the viability of "certainty" is indicative of his interest not just in dismantling premature belief but also in dismantling premature doubt. Philosophers who wish to describe and not simply prescribe must not only expose the premature but also find a place for both conviction and doubt in language-games, including their own. Wittgenstein's images are thus characteristically double-edged; they respect the unity and variety of concepts, the repetition and revision of language-games, the control and creativity of language use, the replication and renovation of meaning. And these concerns bear directly upon the relationships between theory and data and between theory and theorist.

If it seems difficult to conceive of entities that are both single and multiple, Wittgenstein's most famous images display those features repeatedly and register the vital importance of both. Indeed, his two most characteristic voices diverge on precisely this point of the viability of attempts to reconcile unity and variety. But it is important to recognize the direct connection between his attempts to reconcile unity with variety in his examination of concepts and his attempts to mediate between belief and doubt in our use of them. For Wittgenstein is repeatedly concerned to avoid the inadvertent slide into monistic or relativistic thinking. What is very much at issue in this conflict of voices is whether Wittgenstein's concept of language-game (or form of life) inadvertently supplies what he has been seeking to avoid: a new foundation as enabling and disabling as the one he has so determinedly dismantled, a new theory whose aspirations to comprehensiveness lead inexorably toward deterministic inclusion and exclusion.

> Here we come up against the great question that lies behind all these considerations.—For someone might object against me: "You take the easy way out! You talk about all sorts of language-games, but have nowhere said what the essence of a language-game, and hence of language, is: what is common to all these activities, and what makes them into language or parts of language. So you let yourself off the very part of the investigation that once gave you yourself most headache, the part about the *general form of propositions* and of language."
>
> And this is true.—Instead of producing something common to all that we call language, I am saying that these phenomena have no one thing in common which makes us use the same word for all,—but that they are *related* to one another in many different ways. And it is because of this relationship, or these relationships, that we call them all "language." (*PI,* p. 31, par. 65)

Far from attributing to language a common core and a fixed boundary, Wittgenstein seeks to conceive of language as both one thing and many. It is in this context of linguistic unity and variety that the most famous of Wittgenstein's images emerge, but what is also at stake here is a concerted effort to accommodate the competing claims we have encountered elsewhere of novelty and necessity, skepticism and foundationalism, contingency and control.

As is well known, Wittgenstein's description of the variety of games we play with the word "game" generates an image of "family resemblance" to indicate the way in which various similarities serve to unify this otherwise disparate grouping. It is not necessary that specific similarities run across the whole group or that the various similarities form a closed set. The continuities serve to supply, as they later did for Halliday, what other conceptual approaches cannot—due observance of the unity and variety of the concept. And it is important to note how quickly Wittgenstein moves on from this image to another in which *continuity* is the most visible feature: "Why do we call something a 'number'? Well, perhaps because it has a—direct—relationship with several things that have hitherto been called number; and this can be said to give it an indirect relationship to other things we call the same name. And we extend our concept of number as in spinning a thread we twist fibre on fibre. And the strength of the thread does not reside in the fact that some one fibre runs through its whole length, but in the overlapping of many fibres" (*PI*, p. 32, par. 67). At another point Wittgenstein uses the image of language "as an ancient city" (*PI*, p. 8, par. 18) whose multiform organization provides an evolutionary record of the various forms of architecture, transportation, and community living that have created it. In one image after another it becomes apparent that continuity is Wittgenstein's key to reconciling the competing claims of unity versus variety, fixity versus change, foundationalism versus skepticism, necessity versus novelty, and certainty versus doubt. We repeatedly encounter images of unity, continuity, and multiplicity, each of which Wittgenstein is at pains to incorporate into his album of reminders, and it is this fascination with the possibilities of continuity that open up, for Wittgenstein, another means of relating the general to the particular, and, for us, another means of relating theory to data and theorist to theory.

What is important is that we recognize that the stability invoked in these images of contingency is a stability that is neither feeble nor foundational but provisional and historical. Wittgenstein's examples repeatedly display patterns of similarities that invoke chains of similarities. Concepts don't just have a use, they have a history of use, and though we are free to revise it, we are not free to ignore it. There is a principle of control as well as a principle of contingency exemplified in these various images: the variety exemplifies the contingency and the continuities the control. The much abbreviated slogan about meaning that Wittgenstein almost casually offers: "the meaning of a word is its use in the language" (*PI*, p. 20, par. 43) is a phrase that invokes not just use, but, in terms that Firth would approve, "use in the language." As Wittgenstein's examples repeatedly indicate, as his insistence upon offering reminders repeatedly exemplifies, language is a historical phenomenon and signs are "souvenirs."[34] To use them is not to encounter separately either their unity or their diversity but to engage with their evolving history of use in the language—a history of combining with and contrasting with other words in language-games made up of words, things, events, processes, and actions which constitute, in another of Wittgenstein's famous phrases: "forms of life" (*PI*, p. 11, par. 23, p. 226).

Though Staten finds the latter term either metaphysical if applied strongly or misleading if applied weakly,[35] it is in their differing estimates of the power, importance, and diversity of historical constraint that Derrida and Wittgenstein most strongly diverge. It is helpful in this respect to bear in mind a comment made by philosopher William James when defending his philosophy of pragmatism and pluralism against charges that it offered no principles of control beyond situational expediency. In matters involving change of belief we are in general, he argues, "extreme conservatives." Acceptable novelty, he goes on, "preserves the older stock of truths with a minimum of modification, stretching them just enough to make them admit the novelty, but conceiving that in ways as familiar as the case leaves possible. An *outrée* explanation, violating all our preconceptions, would never pass for a true account of a novelty. We should scratch round industriously till we found something less excentric. . . . New truth is always a go-between, a smoother-over of transitions."[36] The past as a series of forms of life, as a set of residues of earlier community activity, is alive in us and in our language. It provides us with regulative principles and also with points of departure, and to fail to do justice to both, however we balance their claims, is to fail in general to establish "a clear view of the use of our words" (*PI*, p. 49, par. 122).

To lose contact with the regulative principles, to see only the multiplicity that characterizes language at every level, is to fall prey to the very philosophical skepticism Wittgenstein is at pains to avoid. Such skepticism sets out to undermine all belief and opens up everything to the challenge of doubt. To adopt such a stance is, to Wittgenstein, to fail to command a clear view of the role that doubting plays in our discourses of assertion and belief. To lose touch with regulative principles, to fail to establish an adequate account of them, is to give ourselves, as Wittgenstein so unexpectedly puts it, "a false picture of doubt" (*OC*, p. 33, par. 249).[37] Paradoxically enough, the false picture of doubt must be adjusted not just to rescue the viability of certainty, but to lend credibility to the process of doubting itself. And it is in just this context of reciprocity between certainty and doubt that theory, as a means of discovering the unexpected, must confront the vexed relationships between theory and belief and its implications for the relationships between theory and data and theory and theorist. For what is at stake here is neither an unquestioning reliance upon inherited belief nor a skeptical suspicion of all belief, but a mobilization of current belief as something that makes further and other belief possible. And it is characteristic of Wittgenstein's procedure of repicturing the landscape that he seeks to establish the nature and role of settled belief by examining the nature and function of doubt.

Recognizing that his activity of explaining by example is never complete, never definitive, and therefore always subject to doubt, Wittgenstein seeks to redraw our picture of doubt and its role in language-games. When skeptical philosophers deal with doubt, he notes, they tend to convert it into an unending process, one that destabilizes everything. Yet, he argues, in ordinary use no explanation "stands in need of another—unless *we* require it to prevent a misunderstanding. One might say: an explanation serves to remove or to avert a misunderstanding—one, that is, that would occur but for the explanation; not every one that I can imagine" (*PI*, p. 41, par. 87). He argues against the notion that "secure understanding is only possible if we first doubt everything that *can* be doubted, and then remove all these doubts" (*PI*, p. 41, par. 87). Furthermore, he notes, it is folly for us to say that "we are in doubt because it is possible for us to *imagine* a doubt" (*PI*, p. 39, par. 84). These remarks and others which register the antiskepticism stance of *Philosophical Investigations* are subsequently picked up and extended in *On Certainty*, a text which goes on to pose the key questions about philosophical skepticism: How is doubt introduced into language-games and consequently how is it controlled? (*OC*, p. 60, par. 458).

Once again Wittgenstein employs his recurring tactic of showing that philosophers tend to ask words (in this case, doubt and certainty) to perform tasks that are inconsistent with their characteristic uses. To say we "know" something is, for Wittgenstein, to be "familiar with it as a certainty" (*OC*, p. 35, par. 272). But certainty about such knowledge does not necessarily reside either in our having investigated the issue or in our having had the issue proved to us or in our having had all imaginable doubts about it addressed and discounted. Many things count as certain to us because specific kinds of continuity have emerged in the forms of life we have experienced. And such forms of life are necessarily historically based:

> There are countless general empirical propositions that count as certain for us.
> One such is that if someone's arm is cut off it will not grow again. Another, if someone's head is cut off he is dead and will never live again.
> Experience can be said to teach us these propositions. However, it does not teach us them in isolation: rather, it teaches us a host of interdependent propositions. . . .
> If experience is the ground of our certainty, then naturally it is past experience.

And it isn't for example just *my* experience, but other people's, that I get knowledge from. (*OC,* pp. 35–36, pars. 273–75)

For someone to come along and imagine ways in which we might doubt such certainty is to disturb our quiet but not to disturb our conviction. And it is just such a role that radical skepticism has come to play in literary theory. Once again Wittgenstein resorts to an example to embody the point at issue. We are asked to imagine a pupil who will not accept anything explained in class and who constantly interrupts the teacher with doubts about the existence of things, the meanings of words, the uniformity of nature, and other such issues. The teacher eventually insists the pupil stop interrupting because "your doubts don't make sense at all" (*OC,* p. 40, par. 310). The pupil, Wittgenstein argues, has not learned how to ask appropriate questions and has not learned the range and role that doubt has earned in this language-game. These illustrative doubts are deliberately extreme, but they serve to force radical skeptics to come to terms with the difference exhibited not just in our practice, but in their own practice between doubts that are reasonable and doubts that are unreasonable and also to consider how, in a world of linguistic multiplicity, they and we differentiate between the two.[38]

The impracticality of doubting everything is obvious enough, but Wittgenstein's point is stronger. There is built into every language-game a role for doubt and a role for certainty and we learn what they are as we learn the language-game. But if this is so, are language-games, whose evolution Wittgenstein had earlier insisted upon, suddenly locked once more in place? Does every language-game have, after all, a fixed and unchallengeable foundation? Was Armstrong right to argue that theory and belief are mutually determining? Worse again, has Wittgenstein, in his efforts to restrict doubt, done so only by reintroducing the very unmoving foundation that he had sought to dismantle in *Philosophical Investigations?* Wittgenstein is quick to address this problem. If there are such things as reasonable doubt and reasonable certainty, we must nevertheless take into account the fact that "what men consider reasonable or unreasonable alters" (*OC,* p. 43, par. 336). Wittgenstein thus seeks to maintain the distinction between reasonable and unreasonable doubt, to accommodate the fact that the contrast can change, and nevertheless retain it as a form of control that prevents contingency from sliding into chaos.

Wittgenstein's solution to this problem is a subtle one, but a vital one for the issues of theory and belief that emerged in our earlier discussion of the relationship between theory and theorist. Instead of linking unity with fixity and variety with change, he reverts once more to the possibilities of continuity that had been implicit in his earlier image of extending a concept as if we were weaving a thread. But now the image of continuity switches from that of a thread to that of a river—a river which exhibits not the opposed alternatives of unity and variety but two related features differentiated by contrasting speeds of change. The two contrasting speeds of change register two differing kinds of continuity that characterize two separable but not separate components.

> I did not get my picture of the world by satisfying myself of its correctness; nor do I have it because I am satisfied of its correctness. No: it is the inherited background against which I distinguish between true and false.
>
> The propositions describing this world-picture might be part of a kind of mythology. And their role is like that of rules of a game; and the game can be learned purely practically, without learning any explicit rules.
>
> It might be imagined that some propositions, of the form of empirical propositions, were hardened and functioned as channels for such empirical propositions as were not hardened but fluid; and that this relation altered with time, in that fluid propositions hardened, and hard ones became fluid.
>
> The mythology may change back into a state of flux, the river-bed of thoughts may shift. But I distinguish between the movement of the waters on the river-bed and the shift of the bed itself; though there is not a sharp division of the one from the other. (*OC*, p. 15, pars. 94–97)

This image of two different speeds of change, of the riverbed moving more slowly than the river waters, registers Wittgenstein's ability to accommodate our competing convictions about unity and variety without allowing either to substantiate claims about foundationalism or skepticism. The possibility of further variety leaves room for doubt to function, the actuality of inherited stability prevents doubt from having unlimited play. Things stand fast for us without needing to stand permanently. What is certain and what is doubtable are separable without being separate. We are not in doubt just because we can imagine a doubt; a doubt needs to impress us as a useful doubt, and to do so it must reveal its own certainties so that we can indeed regard it as a doubt worth taking seriously. As Wittgenstein puts it, "If I wanted to doubt the existence of the earth long before my birth, I should have to doubt all sorts of things that stand fast for me. And that something stands fast for me is not grounded in my stupidity or my credulity. . . . A doubt that doubted everything would not be a doubt. . . . Doubt itself rests only on what is beyond doubt" (*OC*, pp. 31, 59, 68, pars. 234, 235, 450, 519).

The process of locating the appropriate role of doubt in a language-game thus serves to clarify both the role of doubt and the role of certainty without making the former unlicensed and the latter unchallengeable. Things stand fast for us because we learn with particular language-games the slowly evolving relationship between reasonable and unreasonable doubt. And it is in this sense that knowledge in a world of linguistic multiplicity can be firm without being final, and that belief can serve as an evolving resource rather than as a premature destination.

It is tempting, of course, to ask for the criteria that enable us to distinguish reasonable from unreasonable doubt, but this is once again to ask in general terms more of the local stabilities in our language than they can be expected to deliver. And Wittgenstein is determined to do justice to both the stability and contingency of belief. "Our talk," says Wittgenstein, "gets its meaning from the rest of our proceedings" (*OC,* p. 30, par. 229), and we cannot look for final grounds: "As if giving grounds did not come to an end sometime. But the end is not an ungrounded presupposition: it is an ungrounded way of acting" (*OC,* p. 17, par. 110). If it is not possible to give our actions final grounds, it is nevertheless possible to characterize the constraints that guide action without governing it. Things stand fast for us not because of external grounds but because of conventional history of use, because of established forms of life, because of inherited characteristics of discourse, because of recognizable generic constraints, because of certain things we decide to exempt from doubt in order to investigate things it seems more fruitful to doubt. Since the riverbed of thought does change, it is possible to imagine situations in which anything can be doubted. But this does not make everything equally worth doubting at all times and it does not remove from doubt the necessity of leaving something exempt from doubt if the word doubt is to function at all.

To the skeptical mind, this may still prove too likely to leave us trapped in inadequate systems of belief. But it also forces the skeptical mind to acknowledge and account for the certainties that circumscribe its own doubts. Wittgenstein's insistence on the stability and continuity of language and knowledge, as well as on their contingency and multiplicity, leaves us free to make a variety of cases for reasonable doubt and also free to offer a variety of defenses against unreasonable doubt. More important, it reminds skeptics and believers alike that they have to find ways of accommodating both fixity and change. If some certainties are presupposed in particular language-games, it makes no sense to doubt them prematurely for one is not then engaging the language-game in play. But it also makes no sense to rely on them unquestioningly for the language game would then cease to evolve. "I really want to say that a language-game is only possible if one trusts something. . . . It may be for example that *all enquiry on our part* is set so as to exempt certain propositions from doubt, if they are ever formulated. They lie apart from the route travelled by enquiry" (*OC,* pp. 66, 13, pars. 509, 88).[39] The caveat about formulating such propositions is, of course, an important one, for there is much that guides our actions that cannot be summarized but only displayed. This is one of the reasons why an inability to describe definitively the typical case is not to be equated with an inability to recognize untypical ones (*OC,* p. 6, par. 27). And Wittgenstein's concern for what can only be displayed is registered in his insistence upon actions, events, journeys, and multiple images. As a consequence of these concerns, he brings forward to *On Certainty* several of the techniques he employed in *Philosophical Investigations.* The latter is, however, a more finished work, while the former is an assemblage from notebooks, so it is difficult to assess its overall form.[40] But the concern for multiple images and the concern for what can only be shown take us back to the form of *Philosophical Investigations* and to the consequences of both books for the status and function of literary theory.

What sort of procedure, we might ask, will enable us to make the key distinction between reasonable and unreasonable doubt if the language-game in question, if the very concept of language-game itself, is neither clearly defined nor firmly bounded? How are we guided in our playing of games that involve multivalued pieces and lack complete and exhaustive rules? Well, says Wittgenstein, putting this question to himself, "How should we explain to someone what a game is? I imagine that we should describe *games* to him, and we might add: 'This *and similar things* are called "games."'" And do we know any more about it ourselves?" (*PI,* p. 33, par. 69). The answer, of course, is that we do not. This is not, however, an indication that we are inadequately informed, but a reminder designed to restore some flexibility to our use of abstract forms of discourse. Wittgenstein's elaboration of this point is also an elaboration on both the technique of positioning his philosophizing exemplifies and the structure of the book he writes to exemplify it.

> One gives examples and intends them to be taken in a particular way.—I do not, however, mean by this that he is supposed to see in those examples that common thing which I—for some reason—was unable to express; but that he is now to *employ* those examples in a particular way. Here giving examples is not an *indirect* means of explaining—in default of a better. . . .
>
> Isn't my knowledge, my concept of a game, completely expressed in the explanations that I could give? That is, in my describing examples of various kinds of game; showing how all sorts of other games can be constructed on the analogy of these; say-

ing that I should scarcely include this or this among games; and so on. (*PI,* pp. 34, 35, pars. 71, 75)

The mode of definition may well be inexact, but, in another of Wittgenstein's famous phrases: "'inexact' . . . does not mean 'unusable'" (*PI,* p. 41, par. 88). Indeed, such inexactness is a necessity for usability. There is no point in trying to establish exact definitions or final theories for linguistic concepts and linguistic processes whose history of use exemplifies their multiplicity and open-endedness. It is like asking which shade of green is the real green; or precisely how old is someone who is middle-aged; or trying to decide how sharply defined we wish to make a photograph of a speeding car. We offer examples as modes of orientation, recognizing that any other mode of orientation can be misunderstood, too. Working against "our craving for generality" and our neglect of "the particular case," Wittgenstein searches for particular cases in the light of which we can characterize sets of particular cases. The exemplary instance, in effect, achieves a largeness that takes it beyond the local without reaching prematurely toward the comprehensive. And it is in just such contexts that judgments about reasonable and unreasonable doubt are made. But it is important to recognize that the exemplary instance can only characterize and not prescribe the possibilities of a language-game, and this reminds us once again of the need for several such instances, and not just one.

To recognize this is to recognize the importance of one further implication of Wittgenstein's use of examples that bears directly upon his concerns for multiplicity, for reminders, for provoking further thought, and for provoking others to thoughts of their own. And it is an implication with large consequences for those interested in linking Wittgenstein's techniques to literary theory and to the problematic relationships between theory and theorist and theory and data.

Discussing the various examples he has invoked, Wittgenstein makes clear that they are neither irredeemably particular nor authoritatively general. And as they do not seek to encompass everything about the material they address, they do not lead Wittgenstein, as the metaphors of Saussure, Chomsky, and Halliday led them, to misplaced ontological claims. One of the reasons these examples are neither deterministic nor foundational is that they are meant to function as an array of orientating images that clarify rather than define the data they confront. The examples of language-games he has employed serve not to conclude investigation but to help it continue.

> Our clear and simple language-games are not preparatory studies for a future regularization of language—as it were first approximations, ignoring friction and air-

resistance. The language-games are rather set up as *objects of comparison* which are meant to throw light on the facts of our language by way not only of similarities, but also of dissimilarities.

For we can avoid ineptness or emptiness in our assertions only by presenting the model as what it is, as an object of comparison—as, so to speak, a measuring-rod; not as a preconceived idea to which reality *must* correspond. (*PI*, pp. 50, 51, pars. 130, 131)

This refusal of premature ontological claims and premature investigative closure is a refusal of a deterministic picture of intellectual inquiry that seems to reassert itself so readily even among theorists strongly disposed to resist it. Wittgenstein's album of exemplary pictures, of characterizing reminders, thus helps us mediate between the generality of theory and the particularity of data by deploying an array of measuring rods, a series of investigative instances in the light of which we can locate, by way of similarity *and* difference, the key characteristics of particular cases. And it is in the context of this shift in the relationship between theory and data that we can perceive the larger implications of Wittgenstein's philosophizing for what we might now wish to conceive of as literary theorizing rather than literary theory.

Wittgenstein's reliance upon the evocative example relates his work to a major modern tradition, but it is important to recognize how his conception of the model as measuring rod addresses the dilemma of discovery with which it is often confronted. Theorists in many disciplines have been seeking in recent years to come to grips with the increasing recognition that our activities of speaking, thinking, and knowing are grounded less in empirical data and more in figurative concepts that open up areas of conceptual space. Yet the premature reliance upon master tropes always threatens to transform the figurative back into the ontological and the contingent into the comprehensive, just as it did in the linguistic work of Chomsky and Halliday. As we have noted, one of the widely recognized consequences of such activities is that any framework of inquiry, whether it is psychological, sociological, anthropological, or (otherwise) figurative, is that it tends to become both departure point and destination. The same is also true of literary inquiry. As we noted earlier, if, in literary criticism, critics invoke psychological neuroses as a point of departure, they often end up discovering what they began by positing. If they rely on archetypes as their point of departure, they usually end up discovering yet another exemplification of an archetype. Mythic patterns, dream structures, hermeneutics of desire, new critical ironies and paradoxes, structuralist binary oppositions, deconstructive chasms and abysses, and cultural exposés of imperialism, sexism, and other forms of oppression, constantly remind us, in the achieved conclusions, of a critic's privileged presuppositions.

As everyone recognizes, figurative language as a ground for interpretive activity has the capacity to serve as a mode of orientation, a method of situating the particular, a means of mobilizing stable belief. But does it also have, as we asked earlier, the capacity to serve as a means of investigation, as a means not just of mobilizing belief but of changing it, as something that offers not just a ground upon which to stand but a point of departure from which to proceed? Can the figurative mode of orientation also function as a means of discovery; can it help us locate the unexpected and not just uncover what figuration presumes to be there?

What so often happens when we apply our investigative metaphors is that "seeing something in terms of X" degenerates into "seeing something as X" and then finally into simply "seeing X." The initially heuristic becomes the prematurely ontological, and the figurative mode of orientation becomes not the means of discovery but the thing to be (re)discovered. What we need to establish is that there is a possibility of discovery even when what we see is constantly encountered in the context of presuppositions about what we are likely to see. Even if it is true that facts are always theory laden, we have to understand the process by which theory can nevertheless make possible the discovery of the unexpected. What we need and what Wittgenstein is able to clarify is the means by which we can use initial belief to guide rather than govern the choices that make further and other belief possible. The theorist in such a context is not merely adopting a theory but also taking responsibility for its creative adaptation.

The question that faces us is how our figurative means of knowing can provide access to knowledge that is neither given in some ontologically prior form nor fully codified by us in advance of our encounter with it. To recognize the function of Wittgenstein's album of orientating examples is to recognize what such theorizing may be able to offer that theory in its more global forms cannot. The choice we often force upon ourselves of discovering either what we presuppose or the real facts out there independent of presupposition is an unnecessary one, and it emerges from a recurring erroneous assumption—that our mode of inquiry should consist of a single, unified, harmonious set of procedures of the kind that might be adequately judged by criteria of simplicity, generality, and exactness. It is this assumption that is intermittently challenged by the linguists who seek to place order and disorder in reciprocal relationship, and it is this assumption that Wittgenstein's variously constituted philosophical album so visibly opposes.

Wittgenstein's insistence upon the model as measuring rod, on the example as an object of comparison, and on the importance of multiple measuring rods and multiple perspectives has direct implications for the role of the theorist. For they are all means of insisting not only that general and particular be more flexibly related but also that the mode of measuring itself be measured. And only if the mode of measuring is itself subject to measure can it function as an instrument of discovery. Wittgenstein's concern for similarities *and* differences prevents us from converting the investigative example into "a preconceived idea to which reality *must* correspond (The dogmatism into which we fall so easily in doing philosophy)" (*PI*, p. 51, par. 131). Such dogmatism is not restricted to philosophers. Literary theorists and theorists in other domains are also prone to the error of "[predicating] of the thing what lies in the method of representing it. Impressed by the possibility of a comparison, we think we are perceiving a state of affairs of the highest generality" (*PI*, p. 46, par. 104). The difficulty here lies in allowing the theorist to maintain control of the instrument of investigation, the mode of inquiry, the means of understanding, so that they do not convert into something that controls the theorist. And that exertion of control depends upon the theorist's readiness to deploy resources diverse enough to generate questions rather than homogeneous enough to dictate answers. But if complex questions always arise about the relationship between any theory and the facts it purportedly isolates and organizes, such questions become even more complex if some of the theorist's discoveries seem likely to emerge at the site of intersection of several theories. It is, however, in just this context that we can begin to recognize how the apparent dilemma of the uncertainly situated pluralist might become an enabling rather than disabling condition.

When we ask ourselves what is being measured by the theoretical model and whether it is simply the things the model posits or the things in themselves beyond the model, we force ourselves to choose between two unpalatable options. What is being perceived beyond what a particular model posits is related data seen from a related point of view. The measured data are neither completely inside the model nor completely outside it. What the model measures and what measures the model is something seen in terms of another model or another component of the same model. This is neither to be trapped in a hermeneutic circle nor to be free of hermeneutic circles, but to participate in a polysystemic process of discovery in which the various modes of orientation function as a polysystemic means of discovery. Unified comprehensive theory is always likely to end up imposing reductive order, and our means of investigation needs to be more variable internally and more receptive externally if it is to enable rather than disable the theorist. Wittgenstein's album of exemplary reminders is itself both an example of and a reminder of our need to establish, whatever our field of inquiry, an armory of investigative instruments rather than a comprehensive and incipiently reductive theory.

Such a shift in the relationship between theories and between theories and data helps clarify the implications of Bakhtin's more general observation that "languages do not *exclude* each other, but rather intersect with each other in many different ways," and it also suggests the larger responsibilities theorists must assume in deploying theoretical resources.[41] Theorists, it seems, must provide not just descriptive categories and techniques to be judged primarily in terms of their simplicity, generality, and exactness, but also guidelines for their use, for relating theory to data, that do not exhaust their potential for further use. The theorist is needed not just to construct and apply theory but to situate theory in the context of other theory and demonstrate how it can be adapted as it is deployed. Theories in such terms are not sets of rules governed by founding beliefs, but resources guided by initial and evolving beliefs, assumptions, and predispositions that cannot be explicitly theorized and must be exhibited in various ways. It is thus the theorist's responsibility not only to construct and deploy theories but also to demonstrate that the efficacy of any theory depends, paradoxically enough, not upon its claims to comprehensiveness but upon its not occupying all of the conceptual space it opens up. This involves, as the next chapter will suggest, a realignment of history, theory, and criticism and a reconsideration of the nature and function of interpretation. And as we will see, this serves to reinforce the strength of Graff's argument that disciplinary inquiry registers the "curious accretion of historical conflicts that it has systematically forgotten."[42] Wittgensteinian reminders are thus repeatedly required, not just to clarify disciplinary conflicts, but also to clarify the status of a discipline's best and most hard won ideas. For those for whom renewal of a discipline is of the first importance, recognizing the further viability of the resources of the past is a more promising procedure than the premature rejection of the partly understood.

Though it would be possible to abstract many principles from Wittgenstein's philosophizing, few are more important to modern literary theory than those that relate to our capacity to control our own investigative procedures. Wittgenstein's aggregate of philosophical reminders reactivates our awareness of the problematic status of our investigative instruments and of their constant tendency to oscillate between inadequacy and excess. If we overemphasize their inexactness, we become convinced that all possible doubts are necessary doubts. If we ignore their necessary inexactness, we become prematurely certain of results that overlook counterevidence. Two principles might therefore guide our use of investigative theory and interpretive practice: no interpretive practice or investigative theory is persuasive if it offers no general principles or procedures for constraining doubt, for preventing possible doubt from converting into necessary doubt. No interpretive practice or investigative theory is persuasive if it succeeds only in rediscovering in the data its own origins in figurative language, if it displays no general procedures for preventing possible certainty from converting into premature certainty.[43] In both cases the model as measuring rod is misused and the means of discovery dissolves into the problematics of the mode of investigation.

It thus becomes apparent why the relativistic and monistic impulses in literary theory are closely related, for the premature doubts of interpretive procedure are part of the same problem as those of premature certainty. In both cases the mode of orientation fails to function as a means of discovery and is judged by that failure. Only to the misguided metaphysician is the loose and multiple structure of languages and texts endlessly worth rediscovering, and only to their alter egos does interpretation require a precision and finality to which it can never aspire. As Wittgenstein's album of illustrative reminders and exemplary measuring rods repeatedly displays, appropriate therapy consists of guidelines to action not guarantees to certainty. No matter which collection of theoretical instruments we adopt, the user's deployment of them must be guided by an awareness of the schematic nature and function of theory and its most productive relationship to data and to other theory.

When we rely, as we must, on images, examples, metaphors, models, case studies, instances, and so on, as the figurative basis of our hermeneutic activities, we rely on their status as multiple approximations; it is folly to lament their individual inexactness and folly to rely unjustifiably on their individual precision. What we need is an acknowledgment of and repeated reminders of their status as various and mutually measuring approximations—approximations that help us confront the mobility of signs and their complex but controllable modes of signifying. In the context of convention-based language-games we confront reasonable and unreasonable doubt, reasonable and unreasonable certainty, and seek to distinguish between them by locating them in the variedly moving riverbed of historical continuity and historical change. Though such pictures of the linguistic landscape remain considerably complex, we can, as a consequence of Wittgensteinian philosophizing and literary theorizing, view such complexities with equanimity, for the models we use to measure can also be measured, and the historically grounded instruments of investigation can indeed function as means of discovery. Furthermore, because multiple models can also be measured, the pluralist theorist is not simply affirming all theories as equally useful, but adopting and adapting selected theoretical instruments and thereby suggesting means of traveling beyond them.[44] The gaps that thus open between theory and theorist and between theory and data are necessary gaps that make discovery of the unexpected possible.

Though there is, of course, no fixed set of rules for distinguishing valuable from valueless discovery, any more than there are final rules for distinguishing reasonable from unreasonable doubt, the investigator using examples to investigate some body of data is personally providing an example of what it is like to use examples in a productive way. The theorist using theories to discover both the expected and unexpected displays the process of informed inquiry in action and demonstrates the ways in which initial belief can make further and other belief possible. For the pluralist theorist, the informed and informing voice is not the solipsistic voice of the mechanical imagination but the exploratory voice of the improvisational imagination, adapting new and inherited forms of expertise to new and inherited circumstances. Our decision to model our activity upon that theorist's has no higher court of appeal than the forms of life, forms of discourse, forms of discovery, and forms of community that are invoked by it and follow from it. Wittgenstein's album of exemplary reminders provides a set of signposts that guides us through the "labyrinth of paths" that constitutes our language, and it does so without diminishing the labyrinth or disguising the paths. To follow, as a theorist, Wittgenstein's example is not to be constrained by an inherited picture but to be educated into a process of picturing—one that invites us to find our way toward the future by judiciously representing to ourselves characteristic examples of the sharable past (*PI,* p. 49, par. 122). And to enter into that process of picturing is to understand why Bertolt Brecht, surveying similar terrain, was once prompted to conclude that "anyone with [only] one theory is lost."[45]

Chapter 5 Literary and Cultural Studies: Theory, History, and Criticism

LITERARY THEORY

It is evident that there are strong points of contact between the strategies of Wittgenstein seeking to develop new pictures of linguistic terrain, the theorizing of linguists who have sought to relate order to disorder in linguistic systems, and the efforts of pluralists to navigate between monism and relativism in literary studies. The use of theoretical discourse as an instrument for investigating creativity, for linking continuity to change, and for providing access to the unexpected requires in each case that theories be deployed in such a way that they do not occupy all the conceptual space they open up. Theories so conceived display a degree of internal multiplicity and a capacity for productive interaction both with other theories and with the data they confront. And pluralism in such a context achieves both a clearer definition and a clearer set of responsibilities. Although some of the theories deployed in literary studies might well have emerged from attempts within the discipline or without to provide a big inclusive picture, a key role of the pluralist theorist is to demonstrate how each can not only work, but work well, as one small picture among others.

This has direct implications for the way in which we conceive, in literary studies, both of the nature of theory and of the nature of pluralistic disciplinary inquiry.

When Booth characterized the pluralist's dilemma in seeking to deploy a variety of theories as that of having to affirm both the "*irreducible* variety of critical languages" and their capacity to interact productively, he did not recognize the extent to which the apparent dilemma derives from our readiness to treat the different languages as if they were internally homogenous and therefore mutually exclusive.[1] There is, we should recognize, a reciprocal relationship between the internal multiplicity of any mode of discourse and its capacity for external exchange. And it is in this sense that the character of theory and the character of pluralism become mutually illuminating. To highlight the internal diversity of critical languages is both to preserve for each its characteristic treatment of order and disorder and to provide for each a complex potential for interaction with others.

It is in this pluralistic sense that several of the linguists we have discussed conceive of a national language as an aggregate of its subsets (regional dialects, social registers, and individual idiolects), and that Bakhtin is able to argue that "languages do not *exclude* each other, but rather intersect with each other in many different ways."[2] The adoption of pluralistic perspectives in such contexts constitutes not so much a theoretical commitment of the kind that leads Mitchell to conceive of "pluralism as dogmatism"[3] but a strategic awareness of a characteristic linguistic situation with direct implications for the ways in which we contemplate the relationships among the theoretical, historical, and critical voices in literary studies.

As Wittgenstein points out, it is always possible to tidy up linguistic processes by providing stipulative definitions of terms and establishing comparatively unified technical languages.[4] But we would mislead ourselves if we conceived of this as a necessary procedure to enable modes of discourse to function properly and if we believed that a technical language would ultimately prove resistant to the unevenly distributed internal changes that Saussure so persuasively describes.[5] A pluralistic perspective is one that treats the variety of modes of discourse, their internal multiplicity, and their capacity for external interaction as enabling rather than disabling linguistic conditions. If these benefits are to be recognized, realized, and sustained however, rather than removed by misplaced forms of linguistic idealism, they need to be carefully situated in the context of disciplinary practice. For the tendency of modes of theoretical discourse to degenerate into a relativism of competing monisms is, we should recognize, as much a consequence of the limitations of those deploying the theories as of the limitations of the particular modes of discourse. In this respect, a misleading picture of the linguistic terrain encourages defenders and opponents of a frequently politicized status quo to allow particular languages, as Genet puts it, "to congeal" into reality.[6]

A major difficulty here, however, is that of enabling theorists to recognize this as everyone's problem, not just everyone else's. To point it out in a particular case is not yet to have adopted an adversarial stance toward the concerns that inform any particular theory. Washington clarifies, in this regard, the typically contested contemporary situation when he discusses the tendency of today's politicized theorists to take pride in going beyond the monistic readings provided by humanists, the bourgeoisie, the imperialists, the patriarchy, the ruling class, and so forth who, the argument goes: "Stop reading when the text stops saying what it ought to have said."[7] As Washington points out, there is simply no difference, in this respect, between the procedures assigned to the putative villains in this argument and those followed by the supposedly more enlightened heroes. In spite of competing claims to more sophisticated reading strategies, both sides are equally vulnerable to the charge that they stop reading when presupposition has been converted into conclusion. What is at stake is simply competing versions of what a text "ought to have said." This is, of course, the inevitable consequence of conceiving of criticism and theory in fixed ideological terms and of critical activity in terms of deploying rather than investigating a set of beliefs.[8] And it is just such limited and limiting use of theories that lends credence to the argument that theories generate the facts that apparently serve to confirm them.

Although a pluralistic perspective is not inconsistent with durable belief, a productive use of the insights of Freud, Marx, Saussure, Foucault and other major thinkers would require us to resist the temptation to extrapolate monistic systems from their work. We would seek instead to assemble investigatory principles, exploratory generalizations, and informative examples that register both a degree of conviction and a degree of doubt, so that informed theoretical inquiry could incorporate interaction with other theories dealing with closely or more distantly related aspects of human experience. Even when an influential writer seems most inclined to offer the big picture that explains everything, we need to restore it to its status as one picture among many, one means of abstracting from complex human situations, one more perspective whose own internal multiplicity keeps it open to other perspectives and to mutual contestation and accommodation. It is not just a coincidence that a common criticism of major theorists is their inconsistency—a criticism regularly made of Marx, Freud, Saussure, Stanislavski, Brecht, Lévi-Strauss, and almost any other thinker who has made sustained efforts in a major field of inquiry in the humanities and social sciences. As their inquiries continue, their theories evolve, and as they are employed in practice, they change. This is precisely what happened in the case of major linguists like Chomsky and Halliday. Our recurring mistake is to assume that such theories are moving toward some firm and final order or that underlying their variations is a unified system that we need to excavate.

To attribute to Freud, for example, a fixed system of analytic convictions, or to Marx a fixed theory of socioeconomic structure, or to Saussure a fixed picture of linguistic terrain is in these and other cases an evident misappropriation of what is actually available from them in particular and from theorists in other disciplines in general. Though major theorists move back and forth between supplying large pictures and struggling with the complexities of local and recalcitrant ones, Freud (and psychologists in general) are interested in minds and not just in particular systems of analysis; Marx (and sociologists in general) are interested in social continuity and change, not just in single systems for representing it; and Saussure (and linguists in general) are interested in language, not just in one current system for investigating it. To reduce these disciplines and their complex activities to systems abstracted from the work of one or two practitioners is to fail to accommodate their internal multiplicity, their evolving goals, and their instrumental adoption of investigative techniques (however determinedly these are sometimes defended). The general dismissal of vulgar Marxists and vulgar Freudians is a dismissal of a doctrinaire appropriation of otherwise varied insights, and it is no coincidence that strong contemporary feminist concerns quickly generated an anthology entitled *Feminisms*.[9]

An illuminating case in point is provided by Michel Foucault, whose extensive writings have been widely invoked by contemporary critics, theorists, and historians. Reviewing in 1976 the evolution of his own work, Foucault noted that, although his various projects had been "closely related to each other, they have failed to develop into any continuous or coherent whole."[10] Wondering whether he ought to be apologetic about this state of affairs or to promise more coherence in a while, Foucault remarks instead upon "something that perhaps was not initially foreseen, something one might describe as precisely the inhibiting effect of global, *totalitarian theories*."[11] To Foucault, it matters little whether such theories are advanced by establishment or antiestablishment thinkers, for the strategic problems presented for both by the premature cessation of exploration are directly parallel: "Which theoretical-political *avant garde*," he asks, "do you want to enthrone in order to isolate it from all the discontinuous forms of knowledge that circulate about it?"[12]

This emphasis upon the discontinuous forms of knowledge generated by different forms of discourse does not lead Foucault toward what he describes as the relativism of a "soggy eclecticism . . . that laps up any and every kind of theoretical approach," but toward a belief in "the *local* character of criticism" whose authority is based, as the authority of his own ideas is based, upon what author and reader "can make of them."[13] Though Foucault goes on to make characteristically sweeping generalizations about the ways in which power is exercised "in a society such as ours, but basically in any society,"[14] he situates alongside such homogenizing generalities the localizing and diversifying possibilities that he recognizes must somehow accompany them.

In a manner reminiscent of the struggles of Chomsky and Halliday to reconcile explanatory generality and current belief with recalcitrant data and emerging novelty, Foucault argues on the one hand that "we are forced to produce the truth of power that our society demands, of which it has need, in order to function" and, on the other hand, that this apparently fixed and general state of affairs is neither quite so fixed nor quite so general: "Power never ceases its interrogation, its inquisition, its registration of truth."[15] In the space between the words "interrogation" and "registration," the local and the global, the particular and the general, the multiple and the single, and the changing and the fixed seek some form of complex accommodation. Such accommodation invokes the recurring concerns of a pluralism which neither compels people to move on to new belief, nor grants them the comfort of final belief. And it is precisely here that we need to establish some clearer pictures of the role that the internal multiplicity of an evolving theory plays in facilitating both its continuing viability and its capacity for external exchange.

If it is difficult to overlook the imperative to generalize in Foucault's work that has encouraged his followers to indulge in much formulaic discussion of power struggles between establishment and antiestablishment voices, it is also evident that the claim that criticism is best regarded as "local" sits uneasily alongside attempts to describe the basic power structures, struggles, and strategies of societies in general. But Foucault himself, like many another influential thinker, tends to be more flexible in his thinking and more provisional in his conclusions, particularly his most general conclusions, than is the case with many of the followers his work has attracted. But generality, we must recognize, like durability, is not in itself a mistaken goal. When Foucault argues that all criticism is necessarily local, the contrast he is inviting is with a generality that is pursued to the level of the universal, a generality that produces, in effect, the "global, *totalitarian theories*" he warns himself and us against. But generality, as Wittgenstein has shown, can be otherwise conceived.

It is, of course, obvious enough that if influential thinkers in their various disciplines had relied upon fixed and unyielding beliefs in developing their theories or their methodologies, they would themselves have been incapable of discovery, for only local multiplicity, strategic uncertainty, and a readiness to change make discovery (however temporary) possible. But it remains equally true that without a considerable degree of conviction and a determined effort at generalization, their theories would not have become anything like as influential. Indeed, the effort to generalize, when productively pursued, does, of course, facilitate inquiry, for it can lead directly to an awareness that larger contexts might yet be usefully invoked and that the investigative terrain might yet be usefully restructured and reconceived. A strictly local perspective on a single issue, a single commitment, or a single concern, however, is less likely to promote further inquiry. Ironically enough, the zealot's fierce commitment to a single concern narrowly conceived is likely to prove inadequate not just to the more general concerns of criticism but also to the clarification and resolution of that single concern.

Single or specialized factor analysis is always likely to be inadequate if the challenge of generality is not adequately met, if the investigative context is prematurely and narrowly defined, if the character of criticism remains primarily local, and if the theoretical instruments are derived from a single theory. As Ellis has pointed out: "When it comes to literary analysis . . . the nature of literature itself almost guarantees that single-factor analysis will be disastrous. The diversity of literary texts has no limit: they are written by all kinds of people and about every conceivable aspect of human life and experience."[16] Indeed they are, and the linguistic theories we have been considering also suggest that textuality itself, as Derrideans never tire of demonstrating, is always likely to be internally multiple. But the larger issue emerging from these various sources is not whether irreducible disorder must always undermine the ordering principles of a text, but whether we can conceive of some other way in which order and disorder and generality and particularity might illuminatingly interact. For pluralists this would make internal multiplicity an enabling rather than disabling condition, provide generality with some other role than that of pursuing the self-imprisoning universal, and involve some productive linkage between provisional belief and pragmatic purposiveness.

When Halliday sought to deal with his conviction that language patterns are much more fuzzy and much less precise than we commonly tend to assume, the governing procedure was not to abandon general claims in favor of merely local observations but to "accept the mess and build it into the theory" of how language works.[17] The pictures provided by polysystemic linguistics are thus of a series of related systems, each of which exhibits internally a continuum of order that runs from either/or choices to more/less choices, but each of which also connects externally to the others in a highly flexible manner. These flexible connections, restricted neither to hierarchical nor transformational relationships, enable the systems to function internally with differing kinds of emphases and differing degrees of precision. They can also interact externally in a manner that allows for unpredictable but not unaccountable creativity. Order of sufficient generality is established to allow related disorder to function as a resource rather than as a disabling disruption.[18] The local thereby achieves a degree of largeness without claiming to be global, and creativity, while rule oriented, is not rule bound. The sufficiency relationship between generalizing order and localized disorder is not one to be settled once and for all, but something to be settled provisionally by engaged voices contemplating both what degree of largeness will serve to get something satisfactory done and what degree of generality will suggest to relevant others that it has been done well. This double demand, transferred to the domain of literary inquiry, requires us to establish some equivalent reconciliation between global and local claims in literary theory and between the global and local persuasiveness of pluralism as a strategy that relates, but does not equate, theory, history, and criticism.

These are difficult issues, and they have emerged in a variety of ways in contemporary debate about the nature and function of pluralism in literary studies. In her critique of pluralist discourse, Rooney argues that it is in its pursuit of the global that pluralism becomes, in effect, self contradictory. The "problematic of general persuasion,"[19] she argues, is the rock upon which pluralism must ultimately founder, for pluralism, as she conceives it, has less to do with a resistance to dogmatism or a tolerance of diversity than with a conviction that conversation will lead to consensus:

> Pluralistic forms of discourse first imagine a universal community in which every individual (reader) is a potential convert, vulnerable to persuasion, and then require that each critical utterance aim at the successful persuasion of this community in general, that is, in its entirety. This demand ensures a conversation in which every critic must address a general or universal audience. This theoretical generality marks the limit of the pluralist's humanism, and it is the only absolute pluralism requires to sustain its practice.[20]

This is evidently a problematic picture for pluralism, as it suggests either a built-in limit to its scope or, in its anticipation of ultimate uniformity, a built-in limit to its durability. This is doubly troublesome because it suggests either the unacknowledged exclusion of some participants from the pluralist conversation or the likelihood that pluralism, in repeatedly crossing bridgeable gaps, will use itself up, for there will eventually be nothing left to be pluralistic about. And this is, of course, the reason for Booth's insistence, in his characterization of pluralism, upon both the irreducible variety of critical languages and their capacity for productive interaction.

Rooney is quite right to introduce the concepts of conversation and persuasion into the functioning picture of pluralistic inquiry. But in light of the issues she raises, it is evident that pluralistic interaction between critical languages cannot be conceived in terms of universal persuasion and final conclusion. But neither can it be conceived as a series of merely local exchanges. In effect, this dilemma is precisely the one that Chomsky and Halliday struggled with, that Wittgenstein so strenuously sought to resolve, and that Foucault so clearly encountered when he attempted to reconcile his global statements about power struggles in all societies with his emerging conviction that critical analysis based on his work can only be local in its implications. Pluralist claims to having reconciled the local with the global can thus be couched neither in terms of the relativistically local simply satisfying itself nor of the universally large producing complete consensus.

The scene of productive pluralist engagement is better conceived, like the alternative dialogical scene of linguistic engagement that has emerged from our review of modern linguistic theory, not as one in which the local is projected into the global and persuasion serves to unite all concerned, but as one in which the local achieves a degree of largeness that serves to satisfy a group of diverse speakers to a certain extent for a while. As William James noted in attempting to define pluralism, for pluralists there is always for every context an outside—but not one established in advance and for all time.[21] What is not now included is not forever excluded, but there is no way of ultimately including everything. Generality is a necessary pursuit but a provisional achievement, in a world of diverse social and cultural material and competing individual and group interests. Sufficient order is conversationally established and reestablished to keep disabling disorder temporarily at bay.

With the "commonsense" implications of reference theories of meaning and monological pictures of language constantly reasserting themselves, we are, of course, always likely to mislead ourselves about what will suffice. It is difficult to be constantly alert to the implications of a reconceived linguistic terrain in which ordering language and ordering the world through language are activities that stop not when we have established the truth but when we are satisfied that, for the moment, we have included enough and we know enough. The "we" is a variable group, and satisfaction is based not solely upon prior criteria but upon a mode of interaction that evolves in practice and guides without governing further interaction. Saussure's illuminating description of the collective process by which we connect and distinguish linguistic features is one that established the priority of the system over the sign, but it is not one that results in fixed signs being placed in fixed systems so that the reference theory is simply supplemented by an earlier process of differentiation.[22] The flexible systemic relationship between word and world is not a means of rejecting connections between word and world, as Ellis so clearly illustrates in his English/German comparison of the use of the words "warm" and "hot," but a means of incorporating speakers into the process of making and remaking satisfactory distinctions and connections.[23] What Saussure's nonrelativist and nonmonist picture of language suggests is that the double linguistic movement of grouping and distinguishing is a matter of differentiation by variable degree that invokes a pragmatic and contextual principle of determination by degree. And arguments about who should be included in the conversation will not change that situation however widely the net is cast. Persuasion is partial, provisional, and nonuniversal, partly because that is the way language in a conversational context often seems to work and partly because theory runs up against its own limits when it pursues generality beyond a productive point and seeks to become uniform and universal in its applicability.

There is, however, a more vital point that follows upon these observations about the internal multiplicity of a theory and the necessary limitations of its powers of generalization. What Rooney describes as the limits of pluralism, in its inability to be both universally applicable and permanently pluralistic, is not in fact a recognition of the limits of pluralism but, in ways the pluralist must carefully clarify, a recognition of the limits of theory. That order in linguistic systems is always related to some form of residual disorder is a complex but enabling linguistic condition that linguistic theory cannot remove, any more than literary theory can remove it in literary studies. The notions of sufficient order and related disorder continue to beg further questions to be taken up in the context Rooney rightly advocates, that of clarifying the nature of pluralistic conversations and the status of consensus and conviction. But what such conversations bring rapidly into the foreground is the necessity of recognizing the points at which we encounter the limits of literary theory, particularly when it confronts, as it must, the internal multiplicity of literary textuality. And that internal multiplicity is widely insisted upon.

We noted in an earlier chapter the ways in which the works and remarks of Yeats, Joyce, Eliot, Forster, and others focused intermittently upon a productive relationship between order and disorder in cultural contexts, and it is helpful at this point to note some further examples. For the larger implications of these literary instances begin to emerge when we link the issue of reconciling order with disorder to the complex contemporary problem of reconciling a theory with the putative facts it purports to isolate and confront.

The New Critics' fetishizing of tension, irony, and paradox, for example, emerges from attempts to relate rather than simply contrast textual order and disorder. In similar vein, Wellek and Warren, in their groundbreaking *Theory of Literature,* assign literature a "stratal" mode of organization in which differing modes of order coexist.[24] And Ralph Cohen has argued persuasively that literary genres are characteristically mixed modes whose conventions consist of differing kinds of regularities borrowed from a variety of other genres.[25] In another domain, Arthur Miller, reflecting on his own procedures as a writer, has remarked: "I was brought up—in the theatre—thinking that life is messy (most people don't know what the hell they're doing from one minute to the next, including me), that the function of the play is to arrive at a moment of intense, burning clarity about this mess—but you've got to deliver the mess. And this contradiction makes the drama. That's what it's all about."[26] In a related but different context, Bertolt Brecht, in his arguments in favor of an Epic theatre, insists upon a "separation of the elements" of the theatrical event so that the various components of lighting, costume, gesture, plot, etc., can compete rather than converge and order and disorder can coexist.[27] And it is in the writings of Brecht that some of the larger implications of troublesome attempts to link order and disorder to theory and practice become more clear, for they lead directly to a different notion of pluralistic conversation than the one that Rooney invokes.

For Brecht, the procedure of foregrounding the multiple forms of order in the drama has a triple function: it reminds the audience of the Wagnerian observation that the theatre is the site of intersection of several different art forms; it displays something of Brecht's conception of the characteristically heterogeneous nature of human experience; and, most important of all, for our purposes, it demands of the audience a particular mode of attention. Brecht described this as "complex seeing,"[28] a mode of attention that is neither uniform for an individual nor unified for a group: "As we cannot invite the audience to fling itself into the story as if it were a river and let itself be carried vaguely hither and thither, the individual episodes have to be knotted together in such a way that the knots are easily noticed. The episodes must not succeed one another indistinguishably but must give us a chance to interpose our judgement. . . . The parts of the story have to be carefully set off one against another by giving each its own structure as a play within the play."[29]

Though Brecht's insistence upon the relationship between the internal multiplicity of a play and the audience's varied perspective of "complex seeing" emerges from the work of a dramatist, it is not a perspective restricted to the theatre. When Bakhtin, who conceived of the social linguistic scene as one "teeming with actual and possible languages," turned to literary and cultural issues, he focused his attention on the novel because of the evidence it provides of the interaction of differing languages and differing principles of order. More recently, Henderson has developed this point further by arguing that the "emancipatory impulse" of black women novelists leads them to exploit their capacity to "speak/write in multiple voices," though this literary multivocality seems both more widely valid and of more general applicability.[30] In this context, the cultural/linguistic hybridity of such central concern to postcolonial theorists is one of many kinds of hybridity that inhabit creative and critical modes of discourse. And as far as poetry is concerned, Cleanth Brooks, for related reasons, which will be developed further in due course, was inclined to argue a generation ago that "the least confusing way in which to approach a poem is to think of it as a drama" in which the poet's voice is subsumed in the speaker's voice and competing elements are put in play.[31] For Brooks, the creation of poetry is an ordering activity that retains the residue of its ordering in its final mode of order, and there is something about that procedure that makes the dramatic monologue become for him an exemplary instance of poetry in action.

There are, perhaps, good reasons for considering whether literary studies, which has tended to marginalize the drama, particularly the drama conceived as a performance text, would have been better served by attempts to derive its disciplinary practices from drama studies rather than from studies of poetry and fiction, not the least of which would be a better understanding of the relationship between order and disorder in mixed art forms and the theorizing of language in the context of the competing voices of dialogue rather than in the context of a dominant author, speaker, narrator, or character (whose reliability or otherwise can then be debated).[32] But that would be the subject of another book on theoretical activity from Plato to Wilde. Suffice it to say that we will return shortly, as Brecht himself did, to the image of conversation to clarify the larger implications of a contested textuality that promotes and requires, not as Rooney envisaged, the emergence of consensus, but some form of complex contextualizing and complex seeing.

For the moment, it is simply necessary to note the range of literary contexts within which attempts to relate linguistic order and disorder have been made, the possibility they collectively raise that language in general and literature in particular function by establishing sufficient order to keep disabling disorder at bay, and the potentially illuminating linkage between Brecht's notion of complex seeing and the pluralist's armory of investigative instruments. For what is ultimately at issue here is whether it is the function of literary theory, any more than of linguistic theory, to settle in advance the complex relationship between order and disorder in every text, and thus project its generality into universality, or whether we should treat order and disorder like any other general features of literature, and assume that they are open to a variety of kinds of deployment. And it is then the role of the critic rather than the theorist to demonstrate the ways in which order and disorder are or are not reconciled in particular texts.

To follow this line of argument is, however, to recognize that what follows upon the pluralist's interest in getting beyond the confines of any single theory is, in effect, the problem of getting beyond theory itself. For the notion that theory provides a discipline's outer circle, by dictating the nature of all the activity within it and all the facts that can emerge from it, is one more of the unhappy consequences of the monistic imperative to link too directly language, belief, knowledge, and truth. If we are to reconceive linguistic and literary terrain in terms of a characteristic multiplicity of discourses and voices, the pluralist, rather than seeking to promote final consensus, must seek to situate the voice of the theorist in the conversational context of other voices, as, in effect, one voice among many. And if the relationship between linguistic order and disorder is not conceived as a fixed theoretical principle but as a variable literary resource, what then follows for the vexed relationship between theory and the data it confronts, or to put it another way, the relationship between theory and fact?

To those who have been inclined to argue that because facts are, as Goethe pointed out, always theory laden, they are therefore theory produced, there is no way of getting outside theory.[33] But to those who conceive of theories as repositories of investigative instruments that function as measuring rods, the general is not a way of subsuming the particular but of providing access to it. A theory serves us best if it is deployed in such a way that it does not attempt to occupy all the conceptual space it opens up, and if it leaves the theorist and others informed by theory with subsequent work to do. For what lies beyond what theory addresses are other procedures for generating and handling certain kinds of facticity. In the literary discipline, it is also the role of the literary historian and literary critic to deal with whatever facticity the discipline can locate. But the difficult issue is the relationship between these data and the theoretical, historical, and critical voices that impinge upon them.

It can, of course, always be argued that the facticity handled by literary history and literary criticism cannot consist of established facts because everything is subject to theoretical doubt. But we have encountered that problem before, along with Wittgenstein's insistence that a doubt about facticity must convince us that it is a reasonable doubt. And part of the process of convincing us that the doubt is a reasonable one is a confirmation from the doubter of the kinds of facticity that are being treated as exempt from doubt in order to enable this doubt to function as a productive doubt. And the larger implication of this is that we are no longer questioning the general status of facticity, but weighing in both theoretical and evidentiary terms the claims of one kind of facticity versus another. And at whatever point that argument is sufficiently settled for a group of practitioners (in ways outlined at the end of the preceding chapter), certain kinds of facticity function for a while as shareable data. But the settling of facticity is not simply an issue for theory to confront. Literary history, literary criticism, and literary theory can indeed function as complementary rather than contrasting or combined concerns, because theory is not necessarily the means of establishing the outer circle that contains in advance everything they can collectively produce. If theory is treated not only as a means of measuring but also as something to be measured, it cannot so readily be misused as the primary source of the facts it appears to confront. And in a sense that needs careful elaboration, pluralist approaches to facticity thus open up access to the unexpected and unanticipatable novelty that has provided literary theory with such intractable problems. The issue of getting beyond theory is thus inextricably intertwined with the issue of relating theory appropriately to fact and to other dimensions of disciplinary practice.

As the status of facticity and its relationship to theory is a complex and hotly contested issue, both in literary studies and elsewhere, it is useful to note at this point the intermittent arrival of Thomas Kuhn at similar conclusions about the limits of theory in his much discussed *The Structure of Scientific Revolutions*. Kuhn's book has remained a focus of sustained attention over many years, not least because the relationship between changeable fact and changeable theory has itself received extensive attention in a variety of contexts in recent decades. It is implicated in the philosophical work of Charles Sanders Peirce; it has been invoked by Frederick Nietzsche in his remarks on metaphor and truth; it has been much discussed in philosophy of science, notably by Karl Popper as well as Thomas Kuhn; and it has received radical epistemological formulation both in Feyerabend's challenge to generalized method and in Fish's challenge to all interpreted facts (on the grounds that facts are created by the interpretive techniques that locate them).[34]

It is, however, of particular pertinence that the problematic relationship between theory and fact should emerge in the empirical sciences, in the field in which the empirical foundation of fact might seem most secure. Kuhn's interest in the issue of contingent facticity followed upon his recognition that the development of knowledge in various scientific fields tends to be one of ill-explained discontinuity rather than, as we might at first assume, one of slowly evolving continuity. He provides numerous examples to demonstrate the point that the things that scientists once accepted but no longer accept as facts are often no more or less justifiable than things they currently accept as facts. He thus seeks to develop another image of the history of science, one that portrays it as a series of discrete periods in which scientific communities commit themselves first to one set of theories and related facts and then to another. As the theories which hold sway for a while are superseded, many of their putative facts seem to disappear with them. The history of science, as Kuhn describes it, thus consists of periods of stability interrupted by intermittent epistemological revolutions, and this leads him to argue that "scientific fact and theory are not categorically separable" (*Revolutions,* p. 7).[35] Consequently, when a scientific revolution occurs and a new period of stability is established, the scientists who have made the transition from one epistemology to another find themselves dealing with a change so radical that Kuhn compares it to living in a different world with a different set of facts to explain.

This part of the argument, which subsumes facticity within a temporarily dominant theory, gives Kuhn some serious difficulties when he attempts to relate change to continuity in scientific endeavors, not the least of which is one of formulation:

Though the world does not change with a change of paradigm, the scientist afterward works in a different world. . . . What occurs during a scientific revolution is not fully reducible to a reinterpretation of individual and stable data [for] the data are not unequivocally stable. . . . But is sensory experience fixed and neutral? Are theories simply man-made interpretations of given data? The epistemological viewpoint that has most often guided Western philosophy for three centuries dictates an immediate and unequivocal, Yes! In the absence of a developed alternative, I find it impossible to relinquish entirely that viewpoint. Yet it no longer functions effectively. . . . Two groups of scientists see different things when they look from the same point in the same direction. Again, that is not to say that they can see anything they please. Both are looking at the world, and what they look at has not changed. But in some areas they see different things, and they see them in different relations one to the other. . . . In a sense that I am unable to explicate further, the proponents of competing paradigms practice their trades in different worlds. (*Revolutions*, pp. 121, 126, 150)

Though the difficulties of formulation are evident enough, they register not Kuhn's readiness to give ontological status to theories instead of to empirical data, but his recognition that some third option is needed that prevents facts from being either simply given by the natural world or simply created by the theories that appear to confront them. It is evident to Kuhn that the facts produced by various historical theories constitute a facticity that serves for a while as knowledge. The language-game of truth and falsity thus, for Kuhn, exists largely within the realm of normal science and has little to do with Popper's concern for falsifying theory on the basis of an appeal to raw fact. But this image of tidy packages of theory/fact/knowledge/belief/truth succeeding each other through the centuries continues to trouble Kuhn. On the one hand, he recognizes that there is some kind of complex continuity to scientific knowledge even as theories rise and fall, and on the other, he feels that there is something not quite right about conceiving of theory as the ultimate basis of consideration for anyone investigating professional activity in the sciences. And it is this notion of the limits of theory that relates most directly to our current concerns.

Though he is never able to explain, even to his own satisfaction, precisely why it matters that something larger than theory and theory replacement is at issue when "normal science" and revolutionary science collide, he is convinced that shared professional activity depends on something other than agreements and disagreements over theory: "Scientists themselves would say that they share a theory or set of theories, and I shall be glad if the term can ultimately be recaptured for this use. As currently used in philosophy of science, however, 'theory' connotes a structure far more limited in nature and scope than the one required here" (*Revolutions,* p. 182). What is at issue, it seems, in the development of scientific knowledge is not just theory but some contextualization of theory among other elements of scientific practice and disciplinary procedure. And the parallels with the disciplinary roles of literary theory, literary history, and literary criticism are evident enough.

During periods of stability, Kuhn argues, communities of scientists establish order in their fields by basing their normal science activities not upon shared theories that circumscribe their every move but upon exemplary scientific achievements that provide them with both a shared point of departure and a degree of recalcitrant disorder. Such achievements combine empirical and theoretical features by displaying "law, theory, application, and instrumentation" in persuasive interaction (*Revolutions,* p. 10). In this part of the argument, theory is not the outer circle that controls all claims to facticity, but one of several ways of generating facticity. Kuhn refers to both the exemplary achievements and the research traditions they foster as paradigms, paradigms which dictate the nature and the range of problems scientists think it worth investigating and the nature and range of solutions they think it worth accepting. But Kuhn's readiness to use the term paradigm in one part of the argument for the initial exemplary achievement, and in the other part of the argument for the presumably unified research tradition that follows from it, helped confuse the key distinction he draws between work based primarily on an exemplary achievement and work based primarily on a shared theory. The former, unlike the latter, is, he feels, characteristically open and multiple, for scientists can "agree in their *identification* of a paradigm without agreeing on, or even attempting to produce, a full *interpretation* or *rationalization* of it" (*Revolutions,* p. 44). A paradigmatic scientific achievement has theoretical implications but is not fully reducible to an instance of or an illustration of any particular theory. Indeed, the theoretical guidelines derived from it evolve in the practice of following it as an example.

By displaying law, theory, application, and instrumentation in illuminating interaction, a particular scientific achievement persuades groups of scientists not that they should share a single theory or adopt a set of common beliefs but that they might productively model their own work upon it in a variety of different and related ways. In this context theory neither precedes nor subsumes practice, and scientific training in such terms consists of learning "by doing science rather than by acquiring rules for doing it" (*Revolutions,* p. 191). Consequently, there is no comprehensive theory or method whose generality circumscribes all the related research activity or entirely precludes the unexpected. And as modeling activity can be of many kinds for many purposes, the research paradigm, in the multiple-modeling sense of the word, that develops from the exemplary achievement is, Kuhn intermittently recognizes, more likely to be heterogeneous than homogeneous, to display the coherence of relatedness without achieving the coherence of consensus. As a consequence, particular research paradigms can develop in different directions from a single paradigmatic achievement, enabling "several traditions of normal science [to] overlap without being coextensive" (*Revolutions*, p. 50). In a manner we have encountered before, multiplicity within facilitates exchange without, and what matters in community activity is not uniform belief but informative exchange across differences that may or may not be reduced by the exchange.

What the paradigm as exemplary instance thus generates is not a uniform research field circumscribed by unified theory but a variously ordered research field in which variety plays an important role, one that would be eliminated if a paradigmatic theory were given foundational status in the field. Normal science seen from the inside is thus not as uniform as Kuhn describes it when he looks at it from the outside in the context of a scientific revolution.[36] At that point Kuhn stops noting the variety inside each field and talks of competing kinds of variety as if they were competing kinds of sameness—in effect, competing monisms, competing worldviews. And this is, of course, a homogenizing move we have encountered before, both within fields of inquiry and without. It also has the consequences we have encountered before, and whenever Kuhn makes it he finds himself struggling to get beyond it again.

Though Kuhn never resolves, even to his own satisfaction, the issues that he persistently confronts, his arguments help us recognize in scientific fields what Wittgenstein would have us recognize in philosophy of language: complex and illuminating relationships between order and disorder, between belief and doubt, between originating activity and evolving theory, between generality and provisionality, between coherence and diversity, between continuity and change, and between theorizing and facticity. What Kuhn does clearly recognize, however, is that theory is not necessarily equivalent to a static, self-enclosed, self-justifying, logical circle in which presuppositions masquerade as discoveries and inherited or earned belief serves only to generate and justify struggles for authority and power.

Though only intermittently aware of its implications, Kuhn provides an illuminating contextualization of theory and a reconception of its role in disciplinary practice. When a paradigmatic scientific achievement displays "law, theory, application, and instrumentation" in promising but multiple interaction, formal theory becomes one of several components in the investigative process (*Revolutions,* p. 10). It is no longer deterministic because it is no longer the comprehensive sum of all components and it cannot serve as the outer circle that somehow governs or includes them all. But it is also not disablingly particularistic. Instrumental and heuristic it may be, but it moves beyond the merely local to achieve the largeness and durability of a variously constituted disciplinary matrix that changes slowly. And when sudden periods of rapid change occur, they are made possible by and guided by what slower change has problematized and ratified. Evolutionary and revolutionary change are not so much alternative procedures as successive and renewable stages of inquiry.

If theory is thus regarded as one (limited) way of exemplifying issues that are exemplified in several ways at once, we can begin to grasp what is involved for the pluralist in Kuhn's arguments that knowledge can be exhibited operationally as well as conceptually, that scientists can learn "by doing science rather than by acquiring rules for doing it," and that embryonic facts can be encountered by scientists who do not yet have a theory in which to include them (*Revolutions,* pp. 191, 52–65). Though such scientists do have historical, theoretical, and methodological commitments, they are not locked inside their theories, completely subject to them, or unable to see beyond them. Those scientists who cultivate their ability to "see" the world in multiple terms can allow both theory and method an enabling degree of largeness without granting them a comprehensiveness that becomes deterministic. An evolving history of disciplinary practices intermittently reconfigured by exemplary events is every bit as important as any theoretical apparatus abstracted from such events. As we recognized in our survey of the work of Chomsky and Halliday, there are perspectives that emerge from studying the development of major theories that are obscured by efforts to establish their final or fundamental form. And as the theorizing of Brecht suggests, complex seeing, collective enterprise, and individual discovery are all reciprocally related.

What holds disciplinary knowledge together, for Kuhn, is thus not given facts, nor shared theories, but research communities that maintain coherence without establishing uniformity. What gives a group coherence is not that all members have common beliefs, share a common theory or recognize a common set of facts, or that they are creating and sustaining a common worldview. What gives them their coherence is their capacity to share enough in terms of history, theory, and practice to make differences intermittently surmountable and exchange of various kinds possible. Kuhn's "disciplinary matrix"[37] serves not as a monistic means of eliminating disorder but, to return to a phrase used earlier, as a dialogic means of limiting arbitrariness.[38] In their reading, their publications, their correspondence and their conferences scientists, like practitioners of other disciplines, confront a potentially coherent diversity in which various kinds and degrees of continuity supply both problems and potential that unity could never provide. Productive activity in scientific fields and elsewhere consists not of attempts to eliminate disciplinary differences but of learning how to bridge them so it is possible to move around among them. It is as much a mistake to exaggerate that diversity into chaos as to misconstrue the coherence as common belief.

It is, of course, always open to "young turks" or to the avant-garde in any discipline to claim that established diversity is effective homogeneity, but various avant-gardes have intermittently flourished and promoted rapid change because it becomes repeatedly apparent that existing diversity is not the disciplinary uniformity it sometimes appears. Though individual attitudes differ, if scientists and theorists in other fields can resist the monistic urges toward unity, comprehensiveness, and final truth, they might well concede that internal disciplinary diversity is usually limited enough to exclude chaos and flexible enough to accommodate (often with difficulty) radical change. But to resist the monistic urges that elevate differences into ideological divisions, they need some other picture of a productive relationship between theory, practice, and facticity.

Kuhn's complex and sometimes inconsistent arguments thus suggest that this is no simple matter, for what is at stake in the problematic relationship between theory and fact includes the coherence of disciplines, the status of investigative instruments, the nature of change, the evolution of facticity, the situatedness of theories, the limitations of methods, the role of the theory user, the nature of productive exchange in disciplinary communities, and the diversity and durability of community beliefs. In a variety of ways, these concerns converge on those of the various other theorists we have encountered struggling to reconcile disciplinary order with disorder, but Kuhn's efforts to situate theory in the context of other modes of disciplinary activity return us to the vexed question of how best to relate literary theorizing to other forms of disciplinary practice, notably those of literary history and literary criticism.

What emerges from consideration of disciplinary facticity in Kuhn's work is a clearer sense in literary and cultural studies of the conversational context in which literary theory functions. A literary theory serves us best when conceived not as an internally homogeneous self-enclosed circle, but as an internally pluralistic and externally open form of discourse engaged in frequent exchange with other theories, with literary texts, with the related discourses of literary history and literary criticism, and with relatable forms of discourse in other fields. Literary theory can thereby help the literary historian and literary critic not only to multiply but also to refine the armory of methodological instruments. It can invite us to appropriate the most advanced forms of thinking in related fields such as psychology, sociology, philosophy, linguistics, and anthropology, but it must resist the urge to elevate any one of these to a privileged and independent status or to try to synthesize them into a single all-embracing model. It must also resist the urge to convert *those* recognitions into an acceptance of a pluralism of relativistic monisms or into a metaphysics of multiplicity, irreducibility, and iterability. When theory has had its say, there remains a great deal of other practical work to be done, but if theorizing has done its work appropriately, that work is neither excessively untidy nor depressingly unlimited, for a range of contingent facticity is made available for historical and critical discussion that is addressed by the interacting voices of the theorist, historian, and critic, but not necessarily circumscribed by any of them. And what therefore needs to be clarified is their complex mode of disciplinary exchange.

LITERARY HISTORY

If it is, by now, apparent that the "linguistic turn" toward necessity has had unfortunate implications for the development and deployment of literary theories, it is also the case that it has had an unfortunate impact on the way in which the literary discipline has come to conceive of the relationship between its various activities and its primary cultural documents. The misconceived pursuit of a single privileged perspective has seemed the only alternative to the chaos of unlimited multiplicity. But the option of a limited and exploratory multiplicity is what a pluralism of interacting voices seeks to characterize and exemplify. When Wittgenstein tried to clarify the general difference between those who wish to establish a large governing picture of linguistic terrain and those who wish to rely upon an open set of little pictures, he suggested that: "We feel as if we had to *penetrate* phenomena: our investigation, however, is directed not towards phenomena, but, as one might say, towards the '*possibilities*' of phenomena" (*PI*, p. 42, par. 90). It is this sense of opening up rather than closing down that characterizes the pluralist's preference for multiple perspectives. But the pluralist's sense of possibility is, like Wittgenstein's, more restricted than that invoked by relativists and more attuned to other restrictions than those inadvertently encountered by deterministic Derrideans, for it involves an instrumental awareness of the historical conventions, earned convictions, and inherited beliefs that enable and constrain whatever possibilities theorists, historians, and critics put in play.

As there would be no point in renewing the literary discipline's oscillations between monism and relativism by advocating a linguistic turn toward unlimited possibility as an alternative to the discipline's misguided linguistic turn toward necessity, the pluralist needs to clarify the roles of and relationships among literary history, literary criticism, and literary theory when literary theory is regarded as functioning most productively in terms of constrained generality, irremovable multiplicity, and sustained awareness of its own limits. Though a monistic approach to theory would force us to treat literary history and literary criticism as subordinate activities and a relativistic approach to treat them as autonomous concerns, there are good pluralist reasons for treating all three as complementary, nonhierarchical perspectives to be deployed in related but different ways. For if trouble emerges for theory when it fails to recognize the nature of its own limits, it is likely enough that history and criticism will prove vulnerable to the same problems.

To conceive of the procedures of literary history and literary criticism in the same pluralistic way that we have considered those of literary theory would initially be to emphasize their provisional and investigative status. Their presuppositions, protocols, and procedures would, like those of literary theory, be situated in the context of Wittgenstein's comparison between rules and signposts. This would simultaneously clarify their provisional status and help us recognize how the general principles they embody serve us by providing access both to what precedes our current work and to what lies beyond whatever currently encompasses it. But what would then be at issue is not just the provisional nature of critical, historical, and theoretical perspectives, but their modes of intersection and interaction and the status of the data that emerges from their collective exchange. And it is the responsibility of pluralists both to characterize that conversation and to clarify the nature and function of the interpretive data that emerge from it.

Wittgenstein's description of the relationship between linguistic rules and linguistic data helps clarify the status not only of any theoretical apparatus we might adopt, but also of any historical or critical methodology we might wish to deploy:

A rule stands there like a sign-post.—Does the sign-post leave no doubt open about the way I have to go? Does it shew which direction I am to take when I have passed it; whether along the road or the footpath or cross-country? But where is it said which way I am to follow it; whether in the direction of its finger or (e.g.) in the opposite one?—And if there were, not a single sign-post, but a chain of adjacent ones or of chalk marks on the ground—is there only *one* way of interpreting them?—So I can say, the sign-post does after all leave no room for doubt. Or rather: it sometimes leaves room for doubt and sometimes not. And now this is no longer a philosophical proposition, but an empirical one. (*PI,* pp. 39–40, par. 85)

Though this clarification of the limitations of rules, systems, theories, and philosophies and this insistence upon their instrumental and pragmatic status is characteristic of Wittgenstein, what is of importance here is the indication that after a certain point, investigative issues must move beyond philosophical, theoretical, and procedural generalities to the evidentiary and practical particulars of the data that the discipline confronts. And in literary studies, the data to be confronted are assembled in large part, but in different ways, by literary historians and literary critics.

A literary theory engaged in ongoing dialogue with literary history and literary criticism will, in the first instance, need to find its way back to the aggregate of constraints supplied by the past, to the continuities that provide novelties with a persuasive historical context and cultural significance. Though deconstruction, for example, rightly drew attention to the disorder lurking within the order of any text, it converted a useful insight into a less useful truism by elevating a normal feature of language, capable of serving a variety of functions, into a repeatedly rediscovered revelation about particular texts. If we take it that linguistic systematization always involves contested forms of order keeping disabling disorder at bay, we need historical evidence to help us distinguish a possible fissure in a text from one with a persuasive historical provenance. Otherwise, from an ahistorical point of view, all texts become the same text, all revealing the same linguistic tensions. Order may always be contestable but, as the speed of geological change would suggest, an impending crisis is not always an imminent one. Order is what is carved out of chaos for a while, but it has its historical duration, and anachronistically imposed crises remain no more than that. The issue is, of course, analogous to that raised by Wittgenstein when he argued that we are not in doubt just because it is possible for us to imagine a doubt (*PI,* p. 39, par. 84). Literary texts, we must always bear in mind, are as ordered and chaotic as any other forms of linguistic data and as any other products of social practice. They thus require techniques of description and interpretation that neither understate nor overstate the claims of both order and disorder, and, as we must eventually consider, they may also require a conception of the status of interpretation rather different than that to which we have become accustomed.

To reassert the claims of history is not, however, to reassert the claim that history, rather than theory, might provide the outer circle that circumscribes all disciplinary activity and therefore dictates the discipline's facticity. To move in that direction would be to return to the historicism whose excessive desire for authority and generality led it to make the same erroneous arguments for self-sufficiency, comprehensiveness, and systematization that subsequently distorted theory into a mode of reductive determinism. Nor is it to resort to those aspects of the New Historicism which, as Pechter has persuasively argued, change the basis for deterministic activity without always changing the procedure of deterministic engagement.[39] Literary history, like literary theory, has had a great deal of trouble mediating between its opposing interests in local particularities and comprehensive generalities, and a pluralistically situated historical voice needs to establish a productive balance among them. A theoretically informed literary historian would need to recognize from the outset the importance of treating historical conventions and historical data as part of the repertoire of measuring rods at the discipline's disposal. But this has not, so far, become a characteristic means of deploying them.

On the one hand we are often told in footnotes that a particular character in a novel is really a historically specific person, like the author's cousin or the third son of a little known duke, and, on the other, we are asked to adopt a uniform picture of a period in which all texts reproduce the characteristics of a single worldview. In the former case we are offered the name of someone about whom we know little or nothing as a means of helping us understand something about which we feel we do not know enough. In the latter case we are offered answers that preclude and make putatively anachronistic a great many of our questions. The former inappropriately reduces generality and the latter inappropriately reduces particularity in ways that suggest the need for Wittgenstein's more flexible linking of the particular and the general. The voice of the literary historian can engage productively with the voice of the literary theorist only if it, too, can locate an illuminating relationship between the historical particularity and cultural generality of literary texts. And the appeal of the New Historicism in recent years has been based in large part on its putative ability to do precisely that.

When New Historicism appeared on the disciplinary scene, it sought from the outset to mediate between relativistic and monistic historical generality by insisting upon the inherent multiplicity of the literary periods that [Old] Historicism had tended to treat as both internally unified and hierarchically arranged. As Hillis Miller described the new terrain: "Periods differ from one another because there are different forms of heterogeneity, not because each period held a single coherent 'view of the world.'"[40] Instead of being a unified cultural/historical context in which authoritative voices could function as one person speaking for all, the historical terrain envisioned by New Historicists is a contested terrain which provides the site of engagement of a variety of social voices expressing a variety of competing interests. The role of historical scholarship is then to reveal and relate the contrasting voices of contested historical moments that exhibit differing kinds and degrees of order and disorder. From a pluralistic perspective this is all promising enough, provided that the competing voices are not pictured as carrying equal weight. But in trying to give the various voices appropriate weight, New Historicism ran quickly not just into trouble, but into familiar trouble or, at least, trouble familiar to anyone who has attended closely to the dilemmas of literary theory.

If historical periods are pictured displaying uncritically the relative weight then assigned to competing voices, historical investigation is likely to reinforce by repetition imbalances between social groups that few would now regard as appropriate. But if they are pictured in ways that begin to correct the imbalance, historical contexts are misrepresented. The issue of appropriate historicity intersects here with the familiar issue of relating complex particularity to coherent generality. However it is approached, this is a complicated problem, but the unfortunate way in which New Historicism handled the problem quickly returned it to procedures it had rejected in the hands of [Old] Historicists. Instead of exploring a local dialogical picture of social multiplicity in which many voices speak out in many ways of many things, New Historicists have often tended to pursue generality of methodological application by portraying cultural conversation as being devoted to one major topic: the uneven playing field; having one primary goal: the negotiation of power; and exhibiting one privileged kind of contestation: that involved in reinforcing or resisting the hierarchical status quo. Consequently, the characteristic methodological reliance of the New Historicists upon the unexpectedly illuminating anecdote and their otherwise promising "broad shift from political, military, and diplomatic history to economic, social, and cultural history, and ... the history of private life" serve not so much to reveal the complex particularity of new historical vistas as to consolidate the general applicability of today's political concerns.[41]

This is doubly unfortunate, as an impoverished notion of the nature of the conversation between our era and earlier eras effectively circumscribes for New Historicism the range and function of conversation in earlier eras. And both limitations serve to clarify the impoverished nature of historical inquiry if it does not sustain a productive conversation with theorists and critics. As Cantor puts it, New Historicism is by and large "an attempt to rewrite history in order to champion the marginal, the outcast, the long suppressed figures, such as Caliban in *The Tempest*. At the same time, it tries to show how major cultural figures we have long admired were actually implicated in historical forms of oppression, usually along lines of race, class, and gender. As a form of cultural history, the New Historicism is always countercultural. . . . The New Historicism represents the egalitarianism of the contemporary world set loose to rewrite the cultural history of the past."[42] In history so configured, participants are primarily pictured as complicit with or opposed to the posited status quo, and the open-ended inquiry into other eras degenerates into a familiar process of rediscovering what has been presupposed. Though the initial impulses of New Historicism are promisingly related to the pluralistic perspectives emerging in the linguistic contexts outlined earlier, the practice of New Historicism has lacked a theoretical context sophisticated enough to enable it to make the most of its early promise, particularly the promise to provide a more complex site of interaction between past and present concerns.

Cantor, like Pechter, finds unsatisfactory the reduction of historical debate to issues of power and the limitation of strategies of conversation to subversion and containment, not least because they do less than justice to the very diversity of interest that New Historicism at first emphasized. The initial promise to convert a monological cultural scene into a polyvocal one is vitiated when the many potential voices are reduced to two and the two to the simple alternatives of containment and subversion. Odd though it may seem, however, this reductive move has become a characteristic one among those seeking to open realms of discourse to historically marginalized or conceptually new voices. And what is at issue here is a limited and limiting contemporary perspective that effectively constrains both the revisionary nature and subversive potential that New Historicism might otherwise justly claim. The inadequate historicity of New Historicism thus often registers rather than resolves a familiar problem of historical analysis, and the reemergence in New Historicism of the characteristic problems of Old Historicism helps clarify the limits of historical inquiry and the potential for more productive exchange among historians, theorists, and critics.

It is, for example, something of an oddity that modern narratives of social, psychological, and epistemological liberation repeatedly characterize the conflict of containment in ways that make liberation seem both more urgent and more unlikely than it might otherwise appear. Such is the power assigned to historically established authority by those demanding attention to new voices that the new voices often have no room for maneuver and little new to say. Characterized as marginalized voices, they are not only reduced to simply opposing, but robbed of any other interest. They become, in effect, not dialogical voices promoting new conversations, but monological mouthpieces for protests that do not lead beyond themselves.[43]

Whatever the historical justification from case to case for picturing the terrain this way, it registers a pattern widespread enough to raise questions about why so many different kinds of historical problems are pictured in much the same form. Marxists, for example, seek to liberate us from the constraints of capitalist class consciousness, but paradoxically end up questioning the historical role of human agency. Freud seeks to liberate us from neuroses generated by repressed concerns but releases us only into ordinary human unhappiness. Derrida wants to help us evade the clutches of historical logocentrism but concedes at the outset that deconstruction can only function if there is something logocentric to deconstruct. Feminists regularly seek to liberate women from the oppression of patriarchal culture but sometimes have difficulty locating nonpatriarchal terrain that might provide women with anything but the role of victim, the resistance of silence, or the resort to familiar female stereotypes. And most surprising of all, Bakhtin, while making such an eloquent case for multiple languages and competing voices, incautiously reduces these options, at one point, to those of centralizing "official" forces and decentralizing unofficial forces that serve respectively to strengthen or subvert historically established cultural conventions.[44] What appears to happen with some regularity is that the establishment enemy of freedom is characterized as an abstract rather than individual (or even human) agent who, while initially displaying a degree of complexity, is then homogenized and demonized in ways that contribute both a compelling urgency to the narrative of liberation and an obstacle of insurmountable proportions to those aspiring to be liberated.[45] And the homology among these narratives is, of course, taken to its logical conclusion by Foucault when he extends the Marxist attack on the viability of bourgeois individualism into an argument that the whole notion of individuality is an illusory one in a world dominated by social codes.[46]

Though Foucault eventually goes in a quite different direction and Bakhtin soon puts such dualistic thinking behind him, the three characteristic components of narratives of liberation (picturing the enemy as abstract, homogenous, and demonic) inevitably make liberation from oppression very difficult, not least because problems that emerge from beyond human agency cannot readily be addressed in human or historical forums. As a consequence, the liberating potential of dialogized voices both within and across eras is vitiated in advance. Indeed, the possibility that the abstract enemy speaks not with one voice but with many is treated not as a welcome sign of limited social exchange leading to larger social exchange, but of internal contradictions in choric establishment discourse that betokens its ultimate, but not imminent, ruin. In a manner we have encountered before, the putatively liberating voice of theoretical/historical/social inquiry, lacking an adequate mode of feedback from the data, imposes rather than explores an explanatory picture, even upon a context intermittently pictured as polyvocal. That imposed picture is not finally one of enabling historical exchange among multiple voices, but one of static and endlessly repeated conflict between two opposed perspectives.

New Historicism is thus a movement of considerable importance both because it registers so clearly a major problematic of historical inquiry and because it intermittently clarifies the nature of its resolution. The widespread and ironic tendency of historical analysis to freeze the flow of time, rather than to respond adequately to the unpredictability of some of its movement, reveals something of the tendency of historical analysis, like theoretical analysis, to overreach itself, to base its claims for authority on unsustainable generality, to impose a monological picture even on supposedly dialogical cultural terrain. There is thus good reason to consider whether sustained inquiry into the dialogical status of historical eras depends in part upon what the pluralist must advocate: a recognition of the limits of historical inquiry and a sustained commitment to the dialogical status of disciplinary inquiry. The promise of New Historicism is often vitiated by an older historicist impulse that needs to be tempered by voices of other kinds offering the other perspectives of theorists and critics.

Ironically enough, the route to this alternative is implicit in some of the pluralist procedures invoked by the New Historicists. If we insist, for example, that New Historicism follow through on its initial impulses, it takes but a moment's thought about the precariousness of leadership ("uneasy lies the head that wears a crown") to remind us that historical power has always been contested at many levels. And it takes but a moment's further thought about the shifting contexts of daily life to remind us that, for most putative victims, there is a constant movement between centers and margins, between positions of relative authority and relative subservience (not to mention other topics and strategies of conversation). Someone moving today between conversations with partners, children, teachers, policemen, religious figures, bank managers, bus drivers, colleagues, and lovers will oscillate between positions of relative ascendance and relative subservience. A world with many centers offers participants a variety of kinds of power and status and a variety of other kinds of interest.

In effect, one of the problems with New Historicism is not that its practical or theoretical pictures of heterogeneous and contested historical terrain are too complicated, but that neither is complicated enough to clarify the nature of either historical change or historical inquiry. Uneven playing fields do not so much preclude the possibility of diverse social exchange as provide one of its characteristic conditions.[47] And for anyone inclined to argue that all conversation is therefore suspect, it is worth considering why authors of narratives of liberation are so inclined to restrict social exchange to strategies of subverting and sustaining the status quo. Their reluctance to characterize the nature of historical liberation in positive rather than negative terms, in a vocabulary of "free to" rather than "free from," is a reluctance that registers not just limited political perspectives, but an unwillingness to deal with an inescapable problematic of historical inquiry.

The implied alternatives for change emerging from narratives of liberation are the restoration of the uneven playing field with players' positions at center and margin reversed, the imposition on all players of someone's version of equality, or the unpredictable consequences of liberated players speaking for themselves. The first option reinstates the initial problem in different terms. The second is unlikely to last for long, for, as Peter Weiss has so cogently remarked, people will bang their heads against equality of achievement as readily as they will against any other externally imposed constraint.[48] The third and unpredictable option then remains the only one that could convincingly exemplify historical liberation. The point would not be that total freedom has then been achieved, but that, in the context of persisting social, economic, and biological constraints, sufficient degrees of freedom have emerged to make behavior not fully predictable. And that very unpredictability has problematic implications both for narratives of historical liberation and for historians in general. For the question that then emerges is whether we have reached, in the historically unpredictable, something that, in being unpredictable, lies beyond the reach of historical characterization.[49] And if, at this point, we do indeed recognize an apparent limit to strictly historical analysis, we nevertheless encounter within the literary discipline the need for a further level of investigation that is, in effect, more true to New Historicism's initial principles than to much of its actual practice. But the limits reached by such practice are, in fact, theoretically informative in ways that clarify the disciplinary relationship between the voices of theorist and historian, for history, like theory, begins to undermine itself when it loses its sense of its own limitations, when it tries to function as a monological voice of assured conviction instead of a dialogical voice of collaborative inquiry.

The uneven playing field characterized by New Historicists is a static and intolerable state of affairs if there is only one field and one game, but it is in precisely those terms that such historicism tends to mislead us, overlooking both the variety of ways we participate in discourses of power and the variety of other forms of discourse in which we engage. The pluralist's similar interest in engaging with voices hitherto unheard is by no means so restricted, and it encourages us to consider the pluralistic consequences of the New Historicist reminder that the world has always been a heterogeneous place occupied by heterogeneous voices speaking heterogeneous languages. With that as the site of theoretical/historical engagement, we would need not only to create a conversational scene more complex than that of subversion and containment but also to situate the voice of the historian more carefully in the context of the voices of the theorist and the critic. For what becomes apparent is that historical explanation cannot alone suffice to deal with historically emerging problems. And to clarify what is at stake here we need to recognize the limits of historical inquiry as clearly as we recognize the limits of theoretical inquiry, for only then can we characterize the nature of productive exchange among theorists, historians, and critics in a dialogical mode of disciplinary inquiry.

In seeking to characterize historically pertinent conversations (a) within historical eras, (b) across historical eras, and (c) within the literary discipline, we need to do what New Historicism largely tended not to do: situate the historian's voice in a dialogical context with those of the theorist and critic. And it is in that context that we need to reexamine the issue that realigned New Historicism with Old Historicism, even as it sought to transcend the earlier approach: the relationship between the historical particularity and cultural generality of literary texts, which somehow function as cultural documents for readers both in their own and in subsequent eras.

Here again the particularity and generality of concepts as Wittgenstein analyzes them and the local ordering of languages as recent linguists envisage them suggest helpful ways forward. If we take each of the three kinds of conversation in turn, we can recognize something of the complex dialogical status of historical inquiry. Within a particular historical era, we can explore the general significance and the individual particularity of textual voices by locating them in the context of a partially ordered but unsynthesizable set of historical generalities characteristic of that era. These can consist of particular cases of convention use, character typology, plot pattern, and so on that have achieved exemplary status, or they can consist of schematic summaries of a number of such cases to guide us in our investigation. But what we are investigating is the evolving heterogeneity of an era, not its underlying or emerging uniformity. Functioning as measuring rods, these historical generalities guide but do not govern our access to particular cases, for they inevitably register not only the interests of the era we are exploring but also the interests of our own era. In seeking to do some justice to both eras, we will also need to turn our attention to the second kind of conversation and develop further the image of historical inquiry as one of conversation between eras. This involves distinguishing and connecting conversations going on within each era, as well as giving some sustained thought to the nature of conversation itself.

If we adopt a pluralistic perspective and recognize that other eras were no more likely to be homogeneous than our own and that their populations were no less interested in ways of living other than their own, we can see that the problem of exploring differences between eras is no more (and no less) conceptually or practically problematic than that of exploring the diversity of our own era. In one sense this simplifies historical matters, for an initial recognition of the pluralistic nature of our own experience in a pluralistic world renders less problematic historicist concerns about the difficulties of access across eras. Such difficulties can seem insurmountable when they proceed from a historicist version of periodicity that, by intermittently freezing the flow of time, conceives of successive eras in terms of a relativism of mutually exclusive monisms. But they seem less problematic, though still difficult, when we recognize that moving across diversified contemporary cultural space is not significantly different from moving across diverse cultural times. The interplay of similarities and differences suffices to make exchange between eras possible and historical exploration viable. Historically informed and pragmatically deployed aggregations of exemplary instances, characterizing samples, and schematic poles of comparison supply typifications of a constantly but unevenly moving past that, through similarities and differences, provide access simultaneously to historical convention and to textual idiosyncrasy. In terms of the question posed earlier by Wellek and Warren, we are interested not just in the conventional and innovative aspects of Shakespeare's work but also in how each can illuminatingly be related to the other. But, here again, however, in moving from the conventional to the unconventional, we move eventually from the historically predictable to the historically unpredictable. And as before, when confronting the unpredictable, we find ourselves moving beyond what literary history, however conceived, can persuasively claim to encompass. And it is at that point that we need to move on to the third kind of conversation that involves not just historical voices interacting within an era, or historical inquiry reaching across eras, but historians engaging with theorists and critics in a manner that achieves a level of generality beyond that of strictly historical facticity.

To follow the path that leads us beyond the expertise of the literary historian is not to reduce the status of historical analysis but to situate it in the context in which it is best able to balance historical generality and particularity with textual generality and particularity. As Ellis has argued in another context, "It is not an antihistorical view of literature to insist that we not pursue historical localization and explanation, but only a determination to preserve the sense of history in the experience of literary texts in the appropriate way."[50] History, in this sense, is not of the local and particular that has remained local and particular, nor of the general that has incorporated all particularity—rather it is of the local and particular that has earned, or might earn, exemplary status in our culture.[51] To adopt the vocabulary of an earlier stage in the argument, it is a matter of invoking historically the local that has become culturally larger without becoming a unified or universal type. Such typifications can be regarded as models for literary creation and/or as investigative instruments for literary reception, but in either case we need to use them with care. If we press historical typifications too far, we freeze the flow of time, understate the heterogeneity of historical eras, and undervalue their literary diversity; if we insist too much on the priority of local historical information, we divert attention from the generality of implication idiosyncratic texts must acquire if they are to become cultural and not just personal and private documents.

In these complex historical conversations, useful historical information is that whose generality is large without being comprehensive and whose local particularity contributes to without exhausting its cultural generality. Whether we use actual instances of literature as exemplars or whether we use descriptive summaries of texts, recurring textual features, social customs, cultural conventions, significant events, and so forth, the theoretical status, provisional nature, and investigative function of the exemplary models remains the same. Such exemplars serve to characterize the continuities that make the form of a text recognizable and thereby provide access to the discontinuities that make it individual and unusual. But it is in characterizing the individual and unusual nature of a literary text that the voice of the literary historian intersects with and is supplemented by that of the literary critic. And in seeking to construct a flexible literary history with a repertoire of investigative instruments, it intersects with the voice of the literary theorist.

A literary history conceived in terms of the above is not an assembly of true historical facts or a systematization of all pertinent historical facts or a picture projected backward of our contemporary social and political obsessions. Rather, it consists of an array of variously related and relatable typologies that serve not to exhaust what texts can mean but to facilitate access to literary texts for readers confronted with the diversity both of their own era and of those that have preceded it.

Literary history that is theoretically informed because theoretically engaged will thus exclude less on the basis of limited historical concerns and include more on the basis of irreducible historical diversity, diversity which neither earlier eras nor our own are likely to exhaust. A theoretically informed literary history will situate itself in the realm of the exemplar rather than in the realm of the ungeneralizable particular or the inflexible generality, and the literary historian, acknowledging that literature deals with possible worlds as well as actual worlds, will seek to deploy historical evidence in a way that opens access to what lies beyond what can be accounted for by historical evidence.[52] For it is precisely the historically unanticipatable novelty that provides historians with data that lie beyond historical explanation, and which underlines the importance of recognizing that history, like theory, must resist the temptation to occupy all the conceptual space it opens up. Indeed, literary history often finds itself awash in historical evidence and it is only through its interaction with literary theory and literary criticism that it can decide what its evidence is worth and what it is evidence of. The feedback between theory and history in disciplinary activity thus has an analogous feedback in the mutually informing relationship between history and criticism, and it is to that third voice that we next must turn.

LITERARY CRITICISM

As Howard has rightly suggested, New Historicism effectively launched itself as an undertheorized movement in which "neither the rationale for the method nor the status of the knowledge produced" were subjected to sufficiently sustained reflection.[53] This continues to be the case, in spite of some of the illuminating work that has subsequently appeared. As a consequence, New Historicism's image of multiple historical voices within particular eras is not yet productively situated either in the context of exchange between historical eras or in the context of dialogical disciplinary inquiry. There is therefore a significant irony in the fact that in initially defining itself not only against Old Historicism but also against formalist criticism, with its heavy emphasis upon the priority of internal textual evidence, New Historicism closed off a dialogue with a form of criticism that it might well have sought to engage.[54] Such a conversation between historian and critic would not be restricted, as debate between historian and critic has often been restricted, to disagreements over the relative merits of extrinsic and intrinsic evidence, but would broaden inquiry about the ways in which historical and critical analyses diverge and intersect. And a useful point of departure would be the role of critical protocols in the work of the literary historian. For the very procedures by which Pechter, Cantor, Montrose, Howard, and others critique the New Historicism have built into them a reliance upon critical and even formalist protocols that require, for example, that a descriptive interpretation meet, among others, criteria of adequacy, consistency, inclusiveness, and nonreductive larger applicability.

A historical analysis that fails to do justice to textual complexity, that contradicts itself in interpreting the text, that applies to some parts but not to others, or whose procedures seem not to be applicable beyond this particular text is likely to find itself vulnerable to the kind of charge invoked by Pechter when he faults New Historicism for demonstrating more clearly its power over the text than the power of the text.[55] For many critics, an exemplified openness to the unexpected novelty of the text is a prerequisite for judging the adequacy, consistency, and generalizability of any descriptive interpretation. And it is precisely here that the historian's use of evidence, however ingenious its historical trajectory, is ultimately limited to the historically explainable and therefore anticipatable novelty. And this is both its strength and its weakness. For what is at issue here is not the conflict between extrinsic and intrinsic modes of analysis and evidence, but the relationship between historical and critical voices of inquiry.

It is no accident that, having often reduced dialogue to the alternatives of subversion and containment, New Historicists have tended to overstate the power of the latter. In an important sense, the truly subversive move, the paralogical and unexpected novelty, lies beyond the reach of solely historical analysis which is characteristically in pursuit of the typical or typifying. To move beyond that and, in effect, to continue the project of deploying historical information, we need to employ some of the very formalist critical procedures against which New Historicism has tended to define itself. At some point the historical project needs to be supplemented by a critical project. But it is also the case that formalist procedures require some historical contextualization if their densely argued versions of the unexpected are to be persuasive. If these two projects cannot usefully be reduced to a conflict between extrinsic and intrinsic pictures of the terrain, or to an exchange between historians testifying to a single unified moment in the past and critics adopting a selective perspective in the present, the pluralist will need to supply a more sophisticated picture of illuminating exchange between historian and critic. And, as we shall see, that will ultimately involve not only a clarification of the nature of productive disciplinary conversation, but some sustained reflection upon the nature of conversation itself.

To clarify the role of the critic in disciplinary conversation, we will need to examine more closely the impulse to separate historical from critical work on the basis of a contrast between extrinsic and intrinsic inquiry. The difficulty of maintaining a distinction between the two is evident enough. As Ellis argues, "Common to almost all critical positions is the use of information from outside the text to interpret the text, and the crucial question is that of the characterization of that information, not of whether we are entertaining any information at all—for clearly we are."[56] And as others have pointed out, what might seem intrinsic, and therefore critical, for one reader, because it invokes knowledge the reader shares, might seem extrinsic, and therefore historical, for another who does not share that knowledge.[57] Distinguishing between what is ontologically inside and outside a text is not a promising line of inquiry, and insofar as it has been pursued, it has tended to be on the basis of a critical methodology blind to the sources of its own insights.

Just as misleading is the appeal to the intrinsic to justify a current critical concern for getting back to the text, after decades of increasingly complex attention to theoretical, historical, and cultural contexts. Conceived as a necessary restoration of balance in a conversation, such a move seems quite appropriate. Conceived as an exclusionary move that would establish literary criticism, in the name of the intrinsic, as the outer circle of the discipline would, however, recapitulate the very moves that have confronted theory and history with intractable problems. Just as theory and history cannot usefully provide the outer circle that accommodates all disciplinary activity, neither can criticism, and when it seeks to do so by invoking the principle of the intrinsic, it tends to rely upon methods that promote the kind of self-imprisoning generalities that have characterized similar efforts by theorists and historians. And in every case the potential for locating persuasively the unexpected novelty is one of the first casualties of a misplaced desire for order, authority, and control—a desire that inevitably provokes a renewed commitment to its radical opposite, and this, in turn, reinstates the unexpected as an arbitrary, rather than more generally illuminating, event.

To recognize that criticism, like history and theory, cannot usefully occupy all the conceptual space it opens up, is to consider what is at stake for the critic, as well as for the theorist and historian, when a shift is contemplated from a monological to a dialogical mode of disciplinary inquiry. And one of the most important issues is the status of a critical interpretation. As is the case with theory and history, a shift in our understanding of the nature of disciplinary inquiry has consequences for the status of evidence and the role of argument, and in the case of criticism, it has major consequences for the way in which we conceive of the nature and function of interpretive activity. One of the ways, for example, in which overlooked implications of the reference theory of meaning have persisted even after its widespread rejection is the continuing readiness of critics to conceive of texts as monological statements, statements either by authors or by the texts themselves. And this conception underlies even those deconstructive arguments, recently so fashionable, that a text always denies at one level what it asserts at another. To conceive of language in terms of such a picture is, we noted earlier, to assume that language is primarily in the business of making statements, transmitting information, establishing propositions, and transferring messages. In every case such assumptions invoke a passive rather than active receiver and, as is the case with "intrinsic" criticism, make monologue rather than dialogue the characteristic site of linguistic engagement. What is then invited and has, at times, been supplied is an equally weak counterargument that establishes the voice of the reader/critic, rather than that of the author, as the monological voice of authority.

It is also the monological tendency to reduce complex textual inquiry to simplistic ideological assertion that is the most obvious contemporary weakness of both politicized theory and politicized criticism. In such static contexts, what little action occurs is limited to the transfer of prepackaged textual information, however variously it is exemplified. But even before political imperatives both adjusted and reinforced its appeal, this always misleading picture of the "intrinsic" led literary criticism in the past to conceive of its activity as a primarily internal attempt to locate precisely that prepackaged information, to ascertain the intent of the writer, to establish whether it is unified or self contradictory, and in effect to find out what the text really means. As always, such implicit expectation of definitive answers precipitates, once it is recognized that no right answer can be established, the argument that there are an infinite number of answers, all of which are equally right. And this in turn promotes the proliferation of relativistic monisms in which critics make equally valid claims for the intrinsic nature of their interpretations, and that constantly invoked false picture renews the oscillation between demands for imposed authority on the one hand and insistence upon the acceptability of anarchy on the other. If, however, we are both to follow and travel beyond the various versions of interactive reading developed by reception theorists and give reader and text the status of voices in a dialogue, a rather different picture emerges of the nature and status of the critical activities of interpretation and evaluation, one that provides yet another indication of the potential for productive dialogue between critics, historians, and theorists.

As has often been argued, one of the key rules in any set of rules governing a sophisticated game is the rule that says "these are not all of the rules." The trouble for many with a dialogic mode of criticism is that it seems not to lead us to what a text-based interpretation by a passive/receptive reader seemed always to promise—the valid and singular meaning of the text established by the text's rules. And, in effect, what the debate between formalists and historians over intrinsic and extrinsic criticism has ultimately been about is the legitimacy and viability of that requirement.

The status of an act of interpretation has, however, from time to time been reconceived, in ways that bear directly upon the intrinsic/extrinsic issue and upon the complex ways in which we need to picture the disciplinary relationships among critical, historical, and theoretical voices. For Brooks, in 1947, the whole notion of interpretation as critical restatement, as a process of converting the text's language into some other language, continued to seem as highly problematic as it had seemed to Montaigne in the sixteenth century. In an argument against the heresy of paraphrase, Brooks argued that interpretive activity must surely be doing something other than restating in different terms what the text had already said.[58] The point of interpretation so conceived is not, he argues, immediately apparent, and it invites either the argument that the interpretation, as it uses different words, must be saying something other than the text says, or the argument that an interpretation, as yet another statement, must surely stand as much in need of interpretation as the text whose meaning it was supposed to have appropriated. Brooks thus set out to reexamine the nature and function of interpretation by reconceiving the nature and function of a poem.

Having argued first, that poetry does not, in fact, make "statements," second, that the meaning of a poem is not to be confused with a paraphrase, and third, that the goal of interpretation is not and could not usefully be to say in a different way what the poem has said already, Brooks turned to explanatory pictures to suggest other ways of conceiving of the structure of poetry, the nature of meaning, and the function of interpretation. And as the pictures succeed each other, the role of interpretation becomes increasingly problematic:

> The essential structure of a poem . . . resembles that of architecture or painting: it is a pattern of resolved stresses. Or, to move closer still to poetry by considering the temporal arts, the structure of a poem resembles that of a ballet or musical composition. It is a pattern of resolutions and balances and harmonisations, developed through a temporal scheme. Or, to move still closer to poetry, the structure of a poem resembles that of a play . . . something which arrives at its conclusion through conflict—something which builds conflict into its very being. The dynamic nature of drama . . . allows us to regard it as *an action* rather than as a formula for action or as a statement about action. For this reason, therefore, perhaps the most helpful analogy by which to suggest the structure of poetry is that of the drama, and for many readers at least, the least confusing way in which to approach a poem is to think of it as a drama.[59]

There are problems with this, of course, as many will want to know how, once we conceive of a poem as a drama, we are to take account of their evident differences. Though Brooks's point of comparison was the dramatic monologue, his evolving images, moving from architecture to music to drama, give greater and greater scope to the notion that a text is best considered as a stored event with temporal dimensions rather than as a unified object with spatial dimensions, and that what it offers is not, as "intrinsic" criticism often suggests, an embroidered message but a complex experience without clearly defined boundaries. And if we have post-Wagnerian perspectives to guide us, we will extend Brooks's image of dramatic action in the direction of dramatic interaction.

To think of a poem as "an action" involving "conflict" is thus, in by now familiar ways, to move from considering order and disorder as opposed states of affairs and to conceive of individually contested and collectively competing forms of order achieving sufficient equilibrium to promote our renewed and renewable attention. What Brooks's images lead him toward is the recognition that ordering, like speaking and theorizing, is an activity for which the shorthand of nouns, statements, and states of affairs is often misleading. The eventfulness of a text provides a more informative context for characterizing acts of interpretation than the limited and limiting notion that what an author has to say is somehow equivalent to some kind of statement, and that same notion of eventfulness renders precarious the resort to such spatial metaphors as the intrinsic and the extrinsic.

Brooks's succession of comparisons registers his struggle to find images that will enable him to affirm simultaneously the structural integrity of the text we interpret and the active nature of the reader's engagement with the text in the process of reading and interpreting. To neglect the reader's active engagement is to invite spurious claims for validity and finality in acts of interpretation; to neglect the text's integrity is to precipitate a babel of critical voices and open the way to the deconstructive processes that followed in their wake. The key difficulty for Brooks, however, is that of reconciling the static spatial implications of textual structure and the active temporal implications of interpretive activity. And the direction in which his comparisons take him is toward an understanding of the eventfulness of a structured text that will allow a structured text and unfolding experience of it to meet on the same plane of interaction. His most illuminating suggestion in this regard is that an interpretation functions not just as a summary of textual statement but as a set of guidelines for textual engagement. His alternative to thinking of interpretation as a restatement of an earlier statement is to think of it, as Firth thought of linguistic description—as a means of access to what lies beyond what it can fully encompass.[60]

At this point we can begin to recognize the consequences for critical interpretation of the acknowledgment that literary criticism, like literary theory and literary history, cannot productively seek to provide the outer circle that governs disciplinary activity. For the key point of critical activity so conceived is that it provide access to the text through a history of engagement between texts and readers that the current reader is invited to continue. As Iser was subsequently to argue, a role for the reader is built into the text whose words thus function more dialogically than monologically.[61] The reader, having identified the assigned role, can, of course, respond to it and revise it, for the initial historically situated dialogue between reader and text generates further and other dialogue as history unfolds. In a larger sense, therefore, disciplinary inquiry involves critical and historical exchange. Interaction between reader and text of the kind that recognizes that the rules deployed in engagement "are not all of the rules" must consequently produce interpretations whose claims to authority cannot rest upon claims to finality. And it is in this sense and others that criticism, like theory and history, cannot productively occupy all the conceptual space it opens up.

It is interesting to note that Brooks uses the same image of erecting "scaffolding" to describe critical activity that Firth uses to describe the linguist's activity, and for him, too, it provides a means of access to, and not an alternative version of, the texts it confronts.[62] The image of scaffolding that allows us to clamber around, move in and out of, and explore inside an unfolding text by means of an externally erected and adjustable grid is thus illuminating in a variety of ways, not the least of which are the flexible relationships between inside and outside so conceived, their implications for the relationship between intrinsic and extrinsic criticism, and their consequences for the ways in which we picture both the interaction between text and reader and the interactions among theorists, historians, and critics.

The notion that a major function of criticism is to provide access to an experience by facilitating further exchange, rather than to provide an alternative formulation by summarizing a text's final meaning, will appear problematic only if it has been assumed either that the latter is equivalent to the former or that the latter is the only way to achieve the former. Once we recognize, however, the different pictures of language from which these alternatives emerge, we will realize that they are not convertible into each other.

Characteristic of the linguistic, cultural, and disciplinary pictures that we have been examining is the notion of a community or disciplinary language consisting of an open set of interacting language-games rather than of a unified central core with minor variations. Such a picture serves to make the notion of a single national or disciplinary language problematic, for each lacks both a fixed core and a final boundary. In a linguistic environment thus made up of a historically evolving but open set of language-games, a literary text is, in some sense, as Hirsch remarks, a language-game that is played only once.[63] It is both like and unlike what the national language has contained before, and like and unlike in different degrees other literary texts that precede and succeed it.

It is thus no coincidence that Wellek and Warren framed one of the standard conundrums of disciplinary inquiry by focusing upon the balance between similarity and difference among various texts. Do we study Shakespeare because he is the archetypal Elizabethan or because he is markedly different from all other Elizabethans? We can, of course, resolve this conundrum by arguing that we need to locate the similarities among writers in order to situate appropriately their differences. But that is not, in fact, to imply that a new mode of saying emerges from each writer who produces a new kind of statement in a game that is played only once. For it is the recurring image of singular textual statement that generates a misleading image of interpretation as restatement of the singular message. If we switch, however, from a monological to a dialogical picture of the cultural activity promoted by any text, we will argue not that it is a game played only once but that it is played many times and in many related but different ways as history unfolds. And in relating ourselves productively to that process, we need to adopt and adapt critical, historical, and theoretical perspectives.

To consider interpretation in this light, as, in effect, a means of access to the experiences a text offers, we need not so much a final summary of its meaning or a conversion of its whole meaning into some other terms, but an enabling clarification of its principles of organization, its conventions, its innovations, the models it follows and initiates, the social customs it invokes, the contexts it assembles, the modes of experiencing and knowing it explores, the strategies and goals of its major speakers, and much else that historians and theorists must help supply. To refer to these as aspects of its meaning would not be wrong, but to picture our use of them in interpretation as summarizing meaning rather than clarifying the processes of meaning-making is seriously misleading. An interpretation that clarifies processes of meaning-making, that promotes access to the experiences the text offers, engages the reader in an activity that does not invoke misleading expectations of completeness, comprehensiveness, validity, and finality. Such a critical project serves not to summarize meaning but to promote productive reader/text exchange, by facilitating access to the processes of meaning and modes of experience enacted in partly familiar and partly unfamiliar language-games. In such realms of pluralistic literary and critical discourse, what is at issue in acts of interpretation is their historical instrumentality, not their ultimate rightness or their complete comprehensiveness or their capacity to achieve universal persuasion. Their mode of comprehensiveness is not to summarize all meaning, but to provide illuminating access to extensive structural and textural detail and to suggest or imply provisional modes of access to further detail. The latter requires creative work on the part of the reader in terms of extrapolation and supplementation that may or may not precipitate some subsequent reconfiguration of the process. But the facticity generated by this process is not only instrumental; in the context of disciplinary cultural conversation it has to earn a certain disciplinary authority and achieve some cultural duration. And what earns interpretations their authority is, among other things, their capacity to resist claims of arbitrariness, reductiveness, and anachronism. In terms of this picture of critical activity, criticism, too, finds, as do literary history and literary theory, its historical contingency, its instrumental status, and its need for constant interaction with the related modes of discourse generated by other disciplinary voices.

If, in effect, we make the same argument about critical method that we have made about theoretical and historical inquiry, we will begin to recognize the force of a pluralistic argument that conceives of the three disciplinary activities as three different ways of abstracting from, organizing, and contextualizing literary data. These three voices may be internalized by a single individual or they may be distributed among individuals, but each functions as a necessary though not sufficient mode of access to literature, and their pluralistic mode of interaction has illuminating consequences for the ways in which we conceive of the status of a text, the nature and function of interpretation, and the role of the reader in cultural conversation. For what is emerging in this pluralistic picture of disciplinary dialogue is the recognition that a literary text ultimately lies beyond the reach not only of theoretical, historical, and critical presupposition, but also beyond their collective conclusions. This is not to endow literature with a romantic mysteriousness and ineffability but to locate a productive pluralistic picture that leaves the reader, as theory left the theorist, history the historian, and methodology the critic, with subsequent work to do. The destination is not implicit in the point of departure, and methodologies, creatively combined, provide access to the unexpected that lies beyond them.

Literary criticism thus requires what literary theory and literary history can help supply: an armory of investigative instruments that include exemplary instances or characterizing models of conventions, genres, periods, and methodologies whose multiplicity requires of the method user creative combination and sensitive deployment. Generalizations from theory and history serve to provide points of departure for criticism which, in turn, provides points of departure for the experiences enacted in the text. These are, however, necessary points of departure that promote access to the particular experience a text enacts by locating the text in the context of a pragmatic set of related and evolving but unsynthesizable generalities. Whether we use actual instances of other literature or other social documents as exemplars or whether we use local or large descriptive summaries, the provisional nature and investigative function of the models as measuring rods—both measuring and being measured—remain the same. Such exemplars serve to characterize the continuities that make the principles of textual organization recognizable and at the same time they provide access to the discontinuities that make it individual and unusual. If we thus resist the anachronistic resort to excessive claims for authority and anarchy and recognize the regulative power of exemplary guidelines, we can clarify the implications for the reader of this pluralistic picture of productive exchange among theorists, historians, and critics that transcends the limitations of the intrinsic/extrinsic distinction and the various assumptions about the nature of interpretation upon which it is based.

DIALOGICAL DISCIPLINARY INQUIRY

To situate disciplinary inquiry in the complex context of exchange both among authors and readers and among critics, historians, and theorists will require us to give the notion of conversation itself a somewhat more sophisticated status. With conversations of various kinds not only informing but characterizing theoretical, historical, and critical inquiry, it is necessary to consider more carefully the whole notion of conversation as an instrument of investigation. To whatever extent it is true, as Bakhtin argues, that "a reified model of the world is now being replaced by a dialogic model," it remains important to characterize conversation not just as an informing scene of linguistic and cultural engagement, but as an instrument of disciplinary inquiry whose investigative nature is emerging from a variety of perspectives and contexts.[64]

Plato's early concern in *Phaedrus* about the displacement of writing from the context of dialogical community exchange has its contemporary analogues in the theoretical arguments of Saussure, Bakhtin, Firth, Halliday, and others for whom the scene of conversation provides a much more informative site of engagement with language and linguistic function than the recently prevalent one of studying sentences as decontextualized statements.[65] In a conversational context, utterances function as instruments of social exchange and register the order and disorder of collective, collaborative, and contested activity. If we invoke, instead, a monological picture, critical interpretations become a succession of critical statements that interact productively neither with the text nor with each other. And that danger was evident long before Derrida noted the endless proliferation of acts of interpretation, a process only intensified by poststructuralist versions of intertextuality. As Montaigne described the situation four hundred years earlier:

> Who would not say that glosses augment doubt and ignorance, since there is no book to be found, whether human or divine . . . whereof the difficulties are cleared by interpretation? The hundredth commentator passes it on to his successor in a thornier and knottier form than it had been found by the first one. When did we ever

agree to say: "This book has enough comment, there is now no more to be said about it?" . . . There is more ado to interpret the interpretations than to interpret the things, and there are more books upon books than upon any other subject. We do nothing but write glosses upon one another.[66]

Waswo, contemplating this unhappy scene, directs us to an alternative interpretive picture derived from Montaigne's characterization of speech in general as purposive, interactive, social exchange. Montaigne both anticipates and extends the contested dialogic context that Bakhtin was subsequently to invoke, for he stresses the role of the listener, as much as that of the speaker, and just as important is the reciprocity of the relationship he describes between them: "A speech belongs half to him who speaks and half to him who hears. The latter ought to prepare himself to receive it according to the movement with which it is delivered. As with tennis-players, he who receives the ball shifts about and takes his position according to the movements of the one who is hitting the ball to him, and according to the kind of stroke."[67] By extension, Waswo argues, as the ball moves back and forth, each adjusts to the moves of the other, and in the cultural conversation between critics and texts that emerges from Montaigne's picture of interactive dialogue, Montaigne, in effect, "postulates the crucial role of the hearer, the interpreter, the audience—all of us—in the communal manufacture of meaning."[68] Montaigne could thus characterize contested dialogue as sensitive to conventions and protocols without reducing it, as Iser was subsequently reluctant to reduce it, to a mere struggle for mastery.

For Montaigne, as for Wittgenstein, linguistic exchange is a social transaction with both a social history and a contemporary implication, but the notion that meaning-making is a matter of social transaction does not imply, as Waswo rightly points out, that meaning is therefore indeterminate: "On the contrary, a game or a hunt, in order to be performed at all, has both rules and constraining circumstances: we 'must' play it according to these. As social process, the language-game changes with time, at any moment of which the scope for able exercise of both will and skill is . . . great but not infinite."[69] And what prevents it from being infinite is the recognition, implicit in Montaigne's tennis image, of the reciprocal relationship between server and receiver and thus between speaker and listener. We might also wish to extend the image in the contemporary world of professional sports and public events by invoking the role of an audience in regulating that reciprocity. In a conversational context the capacity of any speaker to gain a public hearing and earn some public authority is dependent not just upon an inventive capacity to speak but also upon a demonstrable capacity to listen.

In the communal manufacture of meaning, the right to be listened to is closely related to the responsibility to listen with care, sympathy, and appropriately informed sensitivity. And in the context of disciplinary inquiry, though the text cannot speak back for itself, it is up to the interpreter and the reader of interpretations to occupy alternately the position of textual speaker(s)/listener(s) and interpretive speaker/listener and to make historically, theoretically, and critically informed judgments about how well any speaker has listened to others. The persuasiveness of an interpretation in a dialogical context thus becomes a rather different matter, as we have seen, than is the case with monological restatement. We therefore need to consider further the nature and status of interpretation so conceived, as it has direct implications for the ways in which we picture the dialogical relationships among critics, historians, and theorists, and the cultural functions of literary inquiry.

It is, of course, always possible, when receiving service in tennis, to hit the same shot back no matter which service is received; it is also possible to catch the ball and throw it back, to kick it into a nearby gutter, or to head it ingeniously into a nearby basketball net. In the first case, an audience would judge that the receiver had limited abilities no matter how impressive the single shot; in the other three cases an audience is likely to judge either that the receiver's will exceeds that person's skill, or that the skill being demonstrated is not of the kind appropriate to the game the server initiates. While either or both of these two judgments will seem justifiable in some circumstances, they will usually suggest that the receiver, whatever the other abilities displayed, has not mastered the game the audience turned up to watch—even though what the audience hopes to see involves a good deal of creativity on both sides. A paralogical move, for example, that has the potential to change the nature of the game, is not precluded in advance, though it may generate initial controversy.

The parallel argument for acts of interpretation will suggest that the persuasive power of the voice of the interpreter emerges from an empowerment by the voice(s) of the text, which have demonstrably been heard and responded to. And that empowerment, in literary studies, also involves the regulatory perspectives of theorists, historians, and critics whose intersecting interests inform but do not exhaust the procedures for playing the appropriate game. But to recognize the intersecting nature of these regulatory but differing interests is to begin to recognize one of its major implications. The triangulation of sophisticated but limited interests not only consolidates convention, clarifies innovation, and provides access to the unexpected but also suggests the mutual reciprocity of these procedures.

This reciprocity is important, for it has major implications for our understanding of the cultural context within which disciplinary inquiry functions. And this has particular significance at a time when some have sought to set literary studies and cultural studies in necessary opposition to each other. The three-way dialogue among the voices of theorists, historians, and critics provides a notion of limited disciplinary order that will suffice for many to reactivate the linguistic conflict between authority and anarchy that has persisted for more than two thousand years. It is always possible to renew the urges we have encountered so often—either the urge to insist that a game must be fully governed by rules if it is to be a coherent game or the urge to argue that because games leave room for creative moves, they are ultimately unstable, so no moves can definitively be judged as either appropriate or inappropriate. Once again we must have recourse to Wittgenstein's reminders that inexact does not mean unusable and that our systems of conceptual, social, and linguistic order are as much based on guiding examples from which rules are extrapolated as upon rules from which examples are extrapolated.[70] And it is in this sense that disciplinary listening involves awareness not just of textual nuance but also of the cultural reciprocity of renovation and innovation. For it is in the historicity of the reciprocity between order and disorder that a dialogical mode of literary inquiry links cultural creativity to cultural continuity. To clarify the nature and importance of that reciprocity, we should consider carefully Booth's reconfiguration of the intrinsic/extrinsic issue and its implications for a pluralism of disciplinary and textual voices.

For Booth, as for Montaigne, the image of conversation is an informative one, as is the interactive context and reciprocal responsibilities it implies. For him, the putative contrast between intrinsic and extrinsic criticism emerges not from an ontological difference requiring spatial metaphors but from a strategic difference that is clarified by temporal metaphors distinguishing between different moments in the playing of the game: one, the moment when the historically informed reader registers a recognition of the boundary conditions generated by the order and disorder of a historically situated text, and another when that reader indicates the degree to which those boundary conditions are to be accepted or rejected. And these two distinguishable moments of listening carefully and responding in kind have an impact on the authority any critical voice achieves in the larger community to which textual and critical voices are addressed.

Situating his argument, like Montaigne's, in the context of the protocols of everyday conversation, Booth argues that "the violations we respect most will be based on a preliminary act of justice and understanding: I know what *you* want, you words there on the page (and now in my mind), implying as you do a community of norms and a sharing of goals. I have attended to you, I *understand* you—*and* I hereby repudiate, or correct, or deplore, or explain, or attack you in terms that you had either ignored or had hoped to repress."[71] Booth refers to these two moments as those of understanding and overstanding, and it is not, of course, necessary that the two moments be presented sequentially. They are more a matter of alternating directions attention takes than of mutually excluding modes of attention. But such overstanding needs to be socially, historically, and theoretically informed if it is not to replicate deconstruction's often ahistorical treatment of the relationship between linguistic order and disorder. Appropriately situated, however, the elucidation of this process provides an illuminating picture of cultural exchange among critics, historians, and theorists, although, like any other picture, this one serves to clarify a distinction without settling all of its implications.

Montaigne's image of speech as a tennis game between speaker and listener, Booth's image of a contested conversation between reader and text, Brooks's image of erecting a scaffolding to promote reader/text interaction, and Iser's image of a rejectable role provided for the reader by the text—all demonstrate the importance of exemplary images in guiding critical practice. They help characterize critical practice in pluralistic and interactive terms, and they clarify in differing ways the status of disciplinary conversation among several voices. But the conversations they characterize in such different ways are not reducible to any single governing picture of textual, disciplinary, or cultural exchange. Like Wittgenstein's pictures, they guide but do not govern our cultural inquiry, and like Halliday's rules, they regulate activity that they do not completely define. If criticism, history, and theory neither individually nor collectively establish the outer circle that governs everything that occurs within the discipline, the reader who uses them for guidance is not impelled to assent to all of their implied beliefs, or to look to them for guarantees, or to assume that destinations are given in their points of departure.

We cannot, we should recognize, ask theory, history, or criticism to establish in advance all the rules of critical engagement and, as the repeatedly emerging problematic of comprehensive generality has illustrated, we place ourselves at a disadvantage when we try to do so. Rather, as Montaigne's tennis image illuminatingly indicates, we need to put our theoretical, historical, and critical resources to creative use by responding in a variety of ways to the servers/authors, not by informing them in advance of all that they can and cannot do. As

Wittgenstein persuasively argues, at certain points philosophical and theoretical engagement must hand over to practical matters of evidentiary and historical engagement and thus to the creative and mutually regulated capacities of the theorist/historian/critic/reader.[72] The sense of surprise we often derive from texts, and the experiences of uncertainty, puzzlement, obscurity, and anomaly are all symptoms of our pluralistic engagement with a text's linguistic and experiential otherness. Once we abandon hopes for, expectations of, and premature reliance upon linguistic, theoretical, historical, and critical monisms of various kinds and adopt the presuppositions of a purposive pluralism, we recognize the normality of engagement with such otherness in a world whose literary component is no more nor less pluralistic than its other linguistic and social components.

Booth's interactive image thus intersects with Montaigne's tennis image by reinforcing the recognition that pluralistic theory, history, and criticism cannot codify in advance what a reader's engagement with a text's otherness will precipitate or require. But appropriately and severally deployed, they can provide persuasive access to that otherness. The question of the intrinsic and the extrinsic in criticism is thus replaced by the recognition of revealing or misleading strategies of response, whose adequacy is a matter of complementary historical, theoretical, and critical judgments.

> We have thus bypassed . . . the dispute about whether texts have a single determinate meaning. We have substituted the rather different double claim: different texts come alive in us in different ways and thus insist on different boundary conditions for our "appropriate" questions or responses. Some texts will try to set a single direction of questioning, and some will not. But *all* texts try to present boundary conditions which all experienced readers will recognize. Whether the readers choose to *honor* the boundaries is an entirely different question.[73]

It is, indeed, and it is at this point no longer a philosophical issue to be settled by theoretical disputation alone but an evidentiary and pragmatic issue to be decided by the contingencies of historical situatedness, community diversity, and critical exchange. What is not possible is some adaptation of the intrinsic/extrinsic contrast into one of a text's meaning versus its significance, as the distinction between them will vary from reader to reader and from era to era.[74] And it will also change as we, as readers, interacting with voices in and around cultural documents, steadily or not so steadily change and become other than we have so far been by participating in textual worlds other than those we have so far known. But distinguishing among our various responsibilities as readers in the context of our responsibilities to other readers is a more compelling version of the issues involved.

Conversation so conceived between text and reader and among critics, theorists, and historians leads directly to a picture of cultural conversation in which the authority of a voice depends not so much upon political power as upon a demonstrated capacity to listen and respond to the diversity of voices that constitute a text, a discipline, and a culture. To listen is not necessarily to agree, for the contested nature of eras, cultures, and conversations is one of the key recognitions of a dialogical mode of disciplinary inquiry. The mode of listening that gives an individual voice a degree of authority is, however, its capacity to address rather than to repress the positions it opposes, to link disagreement to agreement, change to continuity, novelty to conventionality, and, in ways that have been variously exemplified in earlier parts of this argument, disorder to order, and freedom to necessity.

It is in these several senses that this century's linguistic turn toward necessity has served so badly a literary discipline inclined for other reasons to settle for an institutional pattern of relativistic monisms that preclude rather than promote exchange. The alternative pictures that have been emerging in a variety of different contexts recognize a reciprocal relationship between order and disorder in every form of discourse, in every historical era, and in every cultural construct. These pictures suggest change in the status of disciplinary inquiry not only by reconfiguring the relationships among the voices of critics, historians, and theorists but also by reconstituting the status of the very cultural contexts subjected to that inquiry. For what has followed with an unhappy logic from the basing of cultural inquiry upon modes of discourse constructed as a relativistic series of monological monisms is the construction of cultural contexts and eras themselves as a relativistic series of monological monisms (with or without potentially subversive components or unstable hybrids). The so-called "culture wars" in contemporary social and institutional contexts are directly related to the logic of choric (re)statement, monological uniformity, and external opacity and exclusion that have characterized the misuse of theory, history, and criticism in the process of cultural inquiry.

The difficulty of constructing a productive picture of intercultural exchange is directly related to the misleading picture of monological linguistic necessity, which is transferred so easily from general notions of the nature of language to homogenizing assumptions about the structure of forms of discourse, historical eras, national enterprises, cultural contexts, theoretical and critical methodologies, patterns of individual and community belief, and categories of race, class, or gender. For cultural, like linguistic, exchange depends upon our awareness of the status in every culture of order and disorder, of internal variety, and of ongoing change, and also upon our capacity to locate the continuities that enable us to make sense of the changes, relate differences to similarities, and achieve degrees of coherence in the absence of consensus. And the potential for misunderstanding involved here has proved particularly acute for those most committed to remedying the social consequences of historical power inequities.

In order to make the case for relief from historical modes of oppression related to race, ethnicity, class, gender, and nationality, advocates have appropriately relied upon a commonality of interest in the issue among those in each oppressed group, as an initial means of redressing the historical wrong. Though this is an essential first step, if exclusively attended to, it can generate the misleading impression that such commonality of interest is the only common interest of the group and, indeed, the group's only interest. A heterogeneous social grouping is thus potentially misrepresented as a homogeneous one whose own self-perception is reduced to that of historical victimization and whose primary agenda is simply to attest to that victimization. Advocates of relief from historical oppression who rely initially on this common identity to make their case can subsequently find themselves trapped in their own rhetoric when the strategic stereotyping is eventually resisted both by the group being so reductively pictured and by opponents who, while ready to acknowledge the history of discrimination or oppression, insist that transcendence of victim-victimizer stereotypes is an essential prerequisite to liberation from the historical oppression.

The important issue is not who is right or who is wrong here, but where to position the various kinds of rightness involved in these arguments. The homogenizing of an otherwise diverse group around a common political interest is strategically an essential first stage for clarifying, dramatizing, and mobilizing a group claim against historical social injustice. And this is particularly necessary when the complex nature and historical durability of an injustice has rendered it initially less than fully visible and still insufficiently attended to, even when made clearly visible. In such circumstances nothing will change if attention is not polemically gained. There can even be some temporary advantage in stereotyping others not included in the group as being collectively responsible for the group's unjust treatment, as this, too, is likely to mobilize thinking about the issues involved. But the challenge on all sides is when and how to move beyond the initial polemics to restore attention to the implicit heterogeneity of all the groups involved.

As far as the historical victims are concerned, a reemphasis on their heterogeneity as a group and on the multifaceted nature of each individual's identity is essential if the narrative of historical entrapment and thwarted liberation is not to become, for them, another kind of trap. And the heterogeneity of all groups with which the oppressed group might advantageously re-engage needs also to be reemphasized at some point, along with the multifaceted nature of all those people's identities, too. Otherwise the narrative of entrapment and liberation is unable to move beyond the initial phase of dramatizing the problem toward clarifying its resolution. Unless all involved move on to the second phase, the latent pluralist potential of diversity within individuals, within social groups and across social groups is vitiated and the possibility of social exchange more productive than that of the past is prohibited by the widespread power of prejudicial presupposition.

It is, of course, in just such a context that the possibility of pluralism degenerating into dogmatism can so readily be contemplated. In the absence of a mutual understanding of the issues involved, the potential of pluralist perspectives can be undermined by political polarization, and pluralism can slide inadvertently into either monism or relativism, as preceding parts of this argument have repeatedly shown. Booth has indicated that pluralism has many forms, and the need for regulatory pictures to maximize its potential has thus been extensively demonstrated above. To make the most of what pluralism has to offer we require, as Wittgenstein would suggest, both the therapy of multiple picturing and the guidelines of related theorizing. At some stage in the narratives of social liberation, such enabling pluralist strategies need to be effectively invoked. Indeed, at the point when the arguments progress, as they must, beyond the "free from" stage of adversarial polemics to the "free to" stage of collaborative engagement, those unfolding narratives need to move beyond strategic stereotyping to incorporate a recognition of the heterogeneity of self, social structure, historical era, and cultural situatedness. The narratives can then attempt to generate awareness of opportunities for, and not just obstacles to, the self-realization they seek to promote. Such self-realization is only possible if individuals on all sides recognize and activate the many potential identities of self and other that make new social groupings possible, on the basis of ever-evolving group interests and an ever-extending social mobility for all concerned. Recognition of the benefits of such social mobility does not preclude the possibility of enduring participation in some forms of group identity, nor does it ignore the possibility that persisting prejudice may constrain the behavior of some participants.

In sum, we should not underestimate the need, at an early stage of movements to remedy social injustice, for advocates to position and mobilize their arguments by overemphasizing group homogeneity at the expense of group heterogeneity. But we should also not underestimate the need, at a later stage of such movements, for a renewed emphasis on group heterogeneity over group homogeneity. Unfortunately the "culture wars" have tended to bog down on both sides when the two components of the argument have been positioned as two opposing perspectives, rather than as two different stages in the same argument. Those most in need of redress from historical injustice have often been ill-served by prolonged polemical characterization of the cultural issues involved, when more varied perspectives are needed to help remedy historical injustices related to race, ethnicity, class, nationality, and gender.

It is thus interesting to note that what emerges from a recent review article of several books on cultural construction and cultural conflict is not the now-dated notions of overall cultural consistency or rigid cultural division, but the notion of "culture as muddle," for cultures, we are told, "are not singular things: they are bundles of characteristics. The trouble is that such characteristics are highly ambiguous. Some push one way, some another." Furthermore, "cultures never operate in isolation. When affecting how people behave, they are always part of a wider mix. That mix includes government policies, personal leadership, technological or economic change and so on. For any one effect, there are always multiple causes," and what the writer thus feels forced to conclude is that "culture is so imprecise and changeable a phenomenon that it explains less than most people realize."[75] This is undoubtedly true, but without adequate instruments of inquiry or even an adequate picture of the appropriate nature of inquiry, we lack the capacity to be responsive to the diverse patterns of a culture, to its contested forms of continuity, and to its consequent capacity to derive new forms of continuity from productive exchange among peoples, regions, eras, and nations.

To listen well is thus not to impose our monologue upon others, to force what we already know and understand upon what we do not yet know or understand, but to deploy our knowledge and beliefs in such a way that they make other knowledge and belief always possible, though not always necessary. For the forces of continuity and change in cultural exchange are as reciprocally related as those that Saussure, Firth, Bakhtin, Halliday, Wittgenstein, and others envisage in linguistic exchange. Indeed, it should also come as no surprise to discover that the category of culture itself is every bit as complex as the various categories that constitute or position a culture. The social, economic, political, technological, legal, historical, geographical, and linguistic coordinates of a culture tend to raise as many questions as they answer for those engaged in cultural explanation. Should we, for example, "lump together all European countries into one culture, though they speak different languages, while separating Spain and Mexico, which speak the same one? Is the Catholic Philippines western or Asian?" and so on.[76]

It soon becomes evident that a culture is not a uniform structure grounding common beliefs and fixed rules of behavior, but an evolving set of resources that have historically been characterized by diversity and change as well as by durability and continuity. The recent tendency in some circles to treat Western culture as a homogeneous category reflecting the shared views of dead white males is one more instance of the unthinking imposition of a monological picture on a dialogical tradition. A moment's reflection serves to remind us of the radical disagreements among major Western thinkers, of the fact that what earns someone a place in Western traditions is having something new, often radically or disturbingly new, to say, and of the constant exchange between ideas rather roughly characterized as Western and others just as roughly characterized as non-Western. These observations do not, of course, serve to resolve concerns about power inequities in the construction of a culture, but they do provide a more promising point of departure for addressing them and for considering the future role of historically diminished voices.

Cultural history of the kind that facilitates cultural inquiry and cultural exchange is thus not a monolithic version of a uniform and unified cultural heritage of common customs, beliefs, and practices. It does not inadvertently reinforce homogenizing stereotypes or invite monological summary, or make cultures or cultural categories seem mutually exclusive, or make members of a particular culture or category seem mutually interchangeable, or leave them with no cultural responsibilities beyond those of chorically repeating views that have been chorically repeated before. Nor does it reduce the strategies of cultural change to those of either reinforcing or subverting the status quo. Rather, it provides an aggregate of variously related typologies and emblematic instances which characterize, without rigidly defining, genre types, social, cultural, and literary conventions, established modes of value, and inherited kinds of discourse that collectively constitute the contested and precarious continuities of each culture, and, just as important, it clarifies the responsibility we all have for their preservation and renewal, as well as for their revision.[77] For these continuities will be assembled differently and contested differently as history itself unfolds. And therein lies the reciprocity of cultural continuity and cultural change and the collective responsibility that every community must take for continually reconciling the two. For what we ultimately encounter in tracing the trajectory of a pluralistic and dialogical mode of cultural inquiry is the reciprocal relationship between a collective responsibility to the past and a collective responsibility for the present and future.

Cultural conservation is thus not to be confused with cultural conservatism. An understanding of any culture's past that cannot cope with debate about canonicity, about abuse of political power, about social diversity and hierarchy, about the roles of popular and established culture, about gender bias, about cultural exchange, and so forth is a sense of the past that lacks confidence in the best of the past, however contested, to answer questions put to it. The questions themselves, of course, need to be put in a sophisticated manner so that we do not simply witness a monism uselessly projecting itself backward. A formulaic diagnosis and denunciation of earlier orthodoxies, for example, leads us only to where we began, but a well-informed cultural inquiry will investigate the contested past not just as a source of inadequate answers to contemporary questions but as a source of, among other things, better questions. Because of the importance of contemporary cultural and political causes, it is important to recognize that they are not well served by proponents seeking to fight old wars with even older weapons or today's campaigns with the strategies of yesterday. For a sophisticated challenge of the present to the past is, in fact, what keeps the best of the past alive as a communal resource. And this is as true of dominant as of less dominant cultures.

Rather than being that which is rejected with difficulty, a cultural past, with all its contested complexity and precarious coherence, is, we should recognize, only sustainable with difficulty. As with patterns of language and patterns of behavior, if we do not renew them they gradually disappear, like the piano-playing skills of one of Chekhov's protagonists who cannot remember when she forgot how to play.[78] But a renewal that relies solely upon repetition removes tradition from the context of social exchange, which is the only context within which it can have a cultural life. A revalued past is thus not a replication of its initial status nor a modern reinvention of its nature, but an exploratory resituating of complex and contested ways of inherited knowing and valuing, that can survive in no other way. Each cultural past needs constantly to be renewed if it is, in fact, to be conserved as a communal resource, if it is effectively to constitute a community's past, and such renewal includes the possibility of changing awareness of what the past, carefully attended to, might fruitfully provide.

Halliday's adopted image of this process, we recall, is of "a continuing conversation" in which a world is not only built, "but . . . is kept in a state of repair and ongoingly refurnished."[79] A past reinvented would not, of course, be the past at all but simply the present projected backward. And a past simply replicated would no longer be alive. An ongoing conversation between text and reader and between past and present constitutes, instead, a mode of inquiry into cultural continuity, variety, and change that can do full justice to the claims of the canonical and the contested and to the historicity and reciprocity of order and disorder in linguistic, textual, and cultural domains. And it is in this dialogical and pluralistic context that an evolving literary history must, for every literary culture, come to terms with similarly evolving literary theory and literary criticism.

In a related argument about cultural community and cultural change, Ellis has warned against the dangers both of attributing a text primarily to the local context of its composition and of attributing it solely to the more general context of the community alive at the time of its writing.[80] The cultural community that keeps a text alive as a cultural document transcends particular historical eras and regions and is partly constituted by the very texts it preserves. Literary texts, he argues, are thus characteristically modern archaic texts whose conventions are neither simply old nor anachronistically new but repeatedly renewable. Literary history, in such terms, is a means of generalizing about literature that at times does and at times does not rely on linear chains of chronology.[81] As literature does not necessarily progress, as the evolution of conventions is multilinear rather than linear, the process of historical comparison needs to be informed by chronology but not limited to it, for the movement of cultural history is affected by, though not restricted to, the new voices that enter the cultural conversation and promote new forms of continuity with the voices of the past.

Those who would change a culture's canon because they have learned its lessons well recognize the complementary relationship between novelty and conventionality and our need for continuity to inform change.[82] But those who would sustain or change it because they imagine it to be monolithic, ideological, and uniform have not yet learned, first, that coherence and continuity do not necessarily exclude diversity and novelty and, second, that a category that does not yet include something is not necessarily committed to excluding it. To assign to any canon a single status and a uniform point of view that reflects a uniform ideology is to display an ignorance of the variety of history, language, and culture. It is also to project one more time the instinctively univocal picture that, as Wittgenstein so clearly demonstrates, diverts us into misleading encounters with putative authority and putative anarchy. To project such authority or to attack the assumed uniformity of a canon or of individual texts by revealing a diversity that must imply relativistic abysses and chasms is to reactivate the seesaw between extremes of authority and anarchy that the same misleading picture generates. The middle ground of a pluralistic culture, pluralistic canon, pluralistic textuality, pluralistic language, and pluralistic methodology is ours to occupy when we take off the glasses that project the misleading picture onto all of the above. The removal of those glasses will not serve to correct historical inequities, but it will alter the shape of the perceived problems and facilitate better strategies for addressing them.

The complex seeing that succeeds such uniform seeing is very much dependent upon the recognition that the illuminating scene of linguistic/cultural engagement is not a monological one of imposed authority, nor a dialogical one in which languages rather than individuals intersect, but a dialogical one in which the conversations of an era are continued and extended in the conversations in a text, in the conversations between texts and readers, and in the conversations between readers and other readers ranging widely across time and space. In this dialogical cultural context there is ample room for literary history, literary theory, and literary criticism to interact, but no room for any one of them to flourish without coming constantly to terms with the diversity generated by the others. In such contexts, conversations among multiple voices within eras and across eras are renewed by readers who weave and reweave our cultural webs as they interact with cultural documents and with the dialogically related voices of theorists, historians, and critics. In doing so, they continue the conversations that characterize our cultures, and continuing those conversations by demonstrably listening well means not just repeating them, but extending them with the new voices and new ideas of each successive era. Tradition in such a context serves simultaneously as an instrument of cultural continuity and as an engine of cultural change.

In the context of dialogical disciplinary inquiry, the voices of literary theorizing, historicizing, and criticizing can thus serve collectively to provide complex access to texts whose cultural durability attests to the importance of our reviewing and renewing them by continuing to engage dialogically with them. And, as we have noted, it is only because we review and renew them that they can serve as cultural documents at all. Acts of interpretation are part of the process of reviewing and renewing our cultural past, and they rightly address new as well as old questions to evolving canons that must always be reconsidered in order to be renewed. This procedure of continuous renovation can flourish only if we can link continuity with change, order with disorder, and generality with particularity in ways that are precluded by any linguistic turn toward monological necessity rather than toward dialogical multiplicity, change, and exchange. The alternative linguistic turn suggested by much of the work of Saussure, Firth, Bakhtin, Halliday, Wittgenstein, and others offers a more flexible mode of linguistic conceptualization that links contextualization both to creativity and to control. And the pluralistic picture that emerges for literary theory is one in which theory can avoid merely ratifying its own presuppositions and provide instead, through its interaction with history and criticism, illuminating access to the unexpected.

Literary theorizing, we have thus come to recognize, goes sadly astray when it seeks to govern rather than guide acts of literary interpretation, when it tries to replace rather than regulate the kinds of evidence that historical and critical activities provide. The role of theory is not to replace or dismantle historical and critical evidence but to guide our use of it, to help us sort out issues of relevance, priority, and persuasiveness. As Graff has argued in another context, theory should function "not as a set of systematic principles . . . or a founding philosophy, but simply as an inquiry into assumptions, premises, and legitimating principles and concepts," and this is, to some extent, correct.[83]

We clearly need to be conceiving of a more humble role for theory and theorists than that envisaged by those who find transhistorical descriptions appealing, or by those who wish to deploy theory to advance contemporary political causes, or by those who find novelty diverting no matter what its relationship to history. Too often such comprehensiveness on the one hand and such novelty on the other turn out to be persuasive only to those whose knowledge of cultural history, cultural variety, and cultural change is rather limited. But theory is also a means of defining and resolving practical problems, particularly when theorizing invokes the resources of several theories and not just one. When theory is not prematurely focused upon system building or on field defining, it can still serve to provide durable instruments whose durability is testimony to the recurrence of certain kinds of problems rather than to the viability of certain kinds of solutions. The ongoing resolution of local investigations feeds back into the armory of investigative instruments, adding to them or refining them as need be, but the serviceability of durable reminders is not something that holds out the promise that complete systems or definitive procedures will eventually emerge from theoretical activity.

This more humble role for literary theory is not necessarily an unacceptable diminution at a time in which the authority of theory has been brought widely into question by those making excessive claims for its ability to reveal definitive forms of order or disorder. It has long been apparent that if we ever found a grand schema of order that incorporated all of literature and which guaranteed that interpretation would have predictable results, we would soon lose interest in literature. A grandiose supertext of a culture that could mean only one thing is about as interesting as the notion of a pitiful multitext that can mean anything, and in both cases the obligation to keep a culture alive by renewing it is not met.

From a pluralist's point of view, there is thus much work for a theorist, historian, and critic to do besides that of deploying a single theory, period construct, or critical method. And the appeal of reader-response criticism in recent years has grown from its emphasis on the constitutive role of the reader in the cultural and dialogical process of creating meaning. Though this can be a disabling insight if relativistically rather than pluralistically contextualized, it can become, as it often does in the hands of Iser, an enabling recognition of the reader's role in the transactions that continually occur between text and reader, past and present, convention and invention, culture and creativity, presupposition and discovery, certainty and doubt, and continuity and change.[84] The element of movement that Brooks sought to introduce into critical metaphors is an element which, when extended from textual action to cultural interaction, reminds us of the importance of the process of interpreting, and not just of the production of interpretations; it reminds us that cultural conversation is a matter of renewing and not just of rediscovering, of inquiring and not just of receiving, of reconfiguring and not just of decoding.

Literary theory, literary history, and literary criticism are, thus, in pluralistic terms, complementary rather than alternative forms of discourse whose productive modes of interaction can be variously exemplified but not restrictively defined. Though each may suggest big inclusive pictures or remind us of big pictures from the past, each can flourish only by encouraging local pictures to interact in ways that make larger discovery possible. When Firth argued in linguistics for a distinction between "*a general linguistic theory* applicable to *particular linguistic descriptions*" and "*a theory of universals* for *general linguistic description*," he recognized the dangers of misleading demands for uniform and comprehensive order in pluralistic domains that are severally, variously, and partially ordered.[85] What Firth suggested was what Wittgenstein also recommended, the use of generalities of sufficient largeness to provide useful points of departure rather than generalities of such comprehensiveness that they define the destination in the point of departure.

What Firth recognized, too, was the necessity of acknowledging the multiplicity of language and method if we are to accommodate change and promote discovery, and if we are to relate diverse cultural continuity to the similar diversity of contemporary culture. A linguistic turn toward such recognitions would acknowledge the centrality of conversation to linguistic theory and clarify the importance of a polysystemic linguistics that relies on generalities of sufficient largeness to allow order to engage with disorder, past to engage with present, continuity to engage with change, and convention to engage with creativity.[86] And if we return to the vocabulary of Brecht, the complex seeing of a pluralistic literary discipline would serve a similar function. Such complex seeing would provide informed points of departure, facilitating the kinds of access to texts, canons, and cultures that would enable a reader of literary criticism, history, and theory to claim not that he has been told what he must initially believe or that she has been shown where she must eventually arrive, but that disciplinary conversation has taken the reader to the point at which he or she can say, in Wittgenstein's phrase, now I can go on by myself.[87]

Literary theorizing, literary historicizing, and literary criticizing are thus not necessarily the substitutes they sometimes threaten to be for the process of individual engagement with idiosyncratic texts, but complementary means of providing guidelines and instruments that enhance the reader's personal ability to participate in the complex process of cultural inquiry. They thus provide for the reader not certainty, as opposed to doubt, but putative certainties and prospective doubts whose persuasiveness or otherwise is weighed in the light of the conventionality and novelty of language-games that accommodate the various continuities of a varied culture. Such language-games record each evolving culture's capacity, through productive social exchange, not only to ratify belief, but also to accommodate change, generate novelty, and promote unexpected discovery.

Notes

PREFACE

1. Frank Lentricchia, "Last Will and Testament of an Ex-Literary Critic," *Lingua Franca,* 6 (6), September/October 1996, p. 64.
2. Ibid.
3. René Wellek and Austin Warren, *Theory of Literature* (New York, 1956), pp. 16, 19.
4. Ibid., pp. 17–18.
5. Ibid., p. 19.
6. Ibid.
7. Ibid., p. 8.
8. Wayne C. Booth, *Critical Understanding: The Powers and Limits of Pluralism* (Chicago, 1979), p. 40.
9. As McClintock has cogently argued, the valorization of the term "post-colonialism" threatens to reduce all of history and all other cultural trajectories to their relationship with colonialism: "Other cultures share only a chronological, prepositional relation to a Euro-centered epoch that is over (post-), or not yet begun (pre-)." The consequent danger is that "colonialism returns at the moment of its disappearance"(Anne McClintock, "The Angel of Progress: Pitfalls of the Term 'Post-Colonialism,'" *Social Text,* 31/32, 1992, p. 86).
10. Gerald Graff, *Professing Literature: An Institutional History* (Chicago, 1987), p. 227.

11. Ibid., p. 243.
12. John Henry Newman, *The Idea of a University*, ed. Frank M. Turner (New Haven, 1996), p. 107.
13. Ibid., p. 105.
14. Ibid., pp. 97–99.
15. Ronald S. Crane, *The Languages of Criticism and the Structure of Poetry* (Chicago, 1986), p. 13.
16. Ibid., pp. 27, 31.
17. Ibid., p. 32.
18. Booth, *Critical Understanding*, p. 33. On the emergence and deployment of the term "pluralism" at the University of Chicago, see Richard McKeon, "Criticism and the Liberal Arts: The Chicago School of Criticism," *Profession*, 82, 1982, pp. 1–18.
19. Ibid., p. 26.
20. Gustav Bergmann, cited by Richard Rorty, *Consequences of Pragmatism* (Minneapolis, 1982), p. xxi.
21. Booth, *Critical Understanding*, p. 40.
22. Carl Woodring, *Literature: An Embattled Profession* (New York, 1999), p. 182.
23. Ibid., pp. 185, 183.
24. Paul A. Cantor, "The Primacy of the Literary Imagination, *or* Which Came First: The Critic or the Author?" *Literary Imagination*, 1 (1), Spring 1999, p. 151.
25. Ferdinand de Saussure, *Course in General Linguistics*, ed. Charles Bally and Albert Sechehaye, trans. Roy Harris (London, 1990), p. 1.
26. Virginia Woolf, *To the Lighthouse* (Middlesex, 1964), p. 237.
27. Ibid., p. 229.
28. Michel Foucault, *Power/Knowledge: Selected Interviews and Other Writings, 1972–77*, ed. Colin Gordon (New York, 1980), p. 80.
29. Woodring, *An Embattled Profession*, p. 183.
30. George Eliot, *Middlemarch* (Middlesex, 1965), p. 314.
31. Wellek and Warren, *Theory of Literature*, pp. 268–69.

INTRODUCTION

1. Gustav Bergmann, cited by Richard Rorty, *Consequences of Pragmatism* (Minneapolis, 1982), p. xxi.
2. The reasons for the restricted nature of these presuppositions, for the repeated investments in "recurring thematics" (p. 302), are laid out in detail by Edward Pechter, "The New Historicism and Its Discontents: Politicizing Renaissance Drama," *PMLA*, 102 (3), 1987, pp. 292–303.
3. Frank Lentricchia, "Last Will and Testament of an Ex-Literary Critic," *Lingua Franca*, 6 (6), September/October 1996, p. 64.
4. For similar reasons, Brian Vickers, in *Appropriating Shakespeare: Contemporary Critical Quarrels* (New Haven, 1993), traces the recent evolution of theory-based criticism of Shakespeare as a prelude to trying to redirect it. He also recognizes the importance of returning to Saussure and to a variety of linguistic theorists to provide an enabling context

for renewing Shakespeare criticism. As I will argue, however, the issues involved are of even larger scope, and what is ultimately at issue for literary studies is the complex relationships among critical, historical, and theoretical modes of discourse.
5. Gerald Graff, *Professing Literature: An Institutional History* (Chicago, 1987), p. 184.
6. Pechter, "The New Historicism," pp. 292–303.
7. Stanley Edgar Hyman, *The Armed Vision* (New York, 1955), p. 3.
8. Graff, *Professing Literature*, p. 241.
9. Jonathan Culler, *On Deconstruction: Theory and Criticism after Structuralism* (Ithaca, 1982), p. 9.
10. If literary theory and literary criticism were to serve, as Rorty suggests, "as a source of youth's self-description of its own difference from the past," we might wonder whether that is the end of their activity or the beginning. Will they prefer a sense of discontinuity that excludes continuity, and if so, what will they seek to do with that sense of difference that will not involve establishing something on the basis of it? And will the function of that be primarily to give the youth of the following year something from the past to define themselves against? (Richard Rorty, *Philosophy and the Mirror of Nature* [Princeton, 1979], p. 168).
11. Peter Washington, *Fraud: Literary Theory and the End of English* (London, 1989), p. 11. Though Washington's views on these intellectual activities are largely unsympathetic, this by no means diminishes the importance of current movements to improve the social status of those whose opportunities are restricted by inherited attitudes toward race, class, and gender. It is because those movements are so important that it is unfortunate to have their progress impeded by conceptual problems also inherited from others.
12. Lionel Trilling, *The Liberal Imagination* (New York, 1950), p. 272.
13. Leela Gandhi, *Postcolonial Theory* (New York, 1998), p. 167. See also her comment that the challenge for the field is to promote "the seemingly impossible collusion of poststructuralist scepticism with Marxist historicism" (p. 74).
14. Wayne C. Booth, *Critical Understanding: The Powers and Limits of Pluralism* (Chicago, 1979), p. 232.
15. Richard Rorty, *Contingency, Irony, and Solidarity* (Cambridge, U.K., 1989). "My defense turns on making a firm distinction between the private and the public. . . . The social glue holding together the ideal liberal society . . . consists in little more than a consensus that the point of social organization is to let everybody have a chance at self-creation to the best of his or her abilities" (pp. 83–84). Though Rorty seeks to provide a counterbalance to the "Nietzchean attitude" that "the point of human society is not the general happiness but the provision of an opportunity for the especially gifted—those fitted to become autonomous—to achieve their goal" (p. 142), the claims of "irony" and "solidarity" in the argument seem heavily weighted toward the former rather than the latter, not least, perhaps, because "the ironist is the typical modern intellectual" (p. 89). For further discussion see Michael Fischer, "Perspectivism and Literary Theory Today," *American Literary History*, 2 (3), Fall 1990, pp. 528–49.
16. As Pavel puts it, "the philosophical contribution of structuralism and poststructuralism is flawed in its core: the selection of language as the main concern of human sciences and philosophy." While acknowledging the historical importance of the linguistic turn,

Pavel argues that current cultural debate in France confirms that "the study of language has ceased to provide the key to philosophy and to the humanities." Whatever the virtues of this argument for the French intellectual scene, there is reason to consider whether the basic problem was the turn toward linguistics or toward a particular kind of linguistics. As Pavel subsequently asks: "why . . , once language had been chosen as the locus for theoretical change, was there no debate on its nature and functions?" (Thomas G. Pavel, *The Feud of Language: A History of Structuralist Thought,* trans. Linda Jordan and Thomas G. Pavel [Oxford, 1989], pp. vii, 2, 126).

17. Richard Rorty, *Consequences of Pragmatism,* p. 27. In the later *Contingency, Irony, and Solidarity,* Rorty is inclined to talk of redescriptions rather than of new theories.

18. Edward Sapir, "The Status of Linguistics as a Science," *Selected Writings of Edward Sapir* (Berkeley, 1949), p. 162.

19. Ludwig Wittgenstein, *Tractatus Logico-Philosophicus,* trans. D. F. Pears and B. F. McGuinness (London, 1969), p. 115.

20. "For the function of language is not merely to *repeat* definitions and distinctions which are already present in the mind, but to formulate them and make them intelligible as such. . . . Myth and art, language and science, are in this sense configurations *towards* being: they are not simple copies of an existing reality . . . but a diversity of forms which are ultimately held together by a unity of meaning" (Ernst Cassirer, *The Philosophy of Symbolic Forms,* vol. 1, trans. Ralph Manheim [New Haven, 1953], p. 107).

21. See Antoine Meillet, *The Comparative Method in Historical Linguistics,* trans. Gordon B. Ford (Paris, 1966), pp. 25–26: "each linguistic fact is part of a system where everything holds together." In the physical sciences, the challenge to the priority of order over disorder is registered most strongly in the implications of the second law of thermodynamics.

22. Claude Lévi-Strauss, *Tristes Tropiques,* trans. John Weightman and Doreen Weightman (New York, 1981), p. 178.

23. From the 1960s on, Vickers argues, "Theory was elevated to the status of a separate, self-contained literary activity, and Vincent Descombes recalls 'the weighty and rather arrogant tone adopted in the sixties to talk about theory. . . . Thirty years later the arrogance seems even less justified, and it becomes increasingly important to resist the notion of theory as a self-fulfilling enterprise'" (Vickers, *Appropriating Shakespeare,* p. xiii). See also Frank Lentricchia's recent repudiation of his earlier commitment to theory: "With no regrets, I tell you that I have nothing new to offer to the field of literary theory" (*"Last Will,"* p. 63). As Vickers puts it: "Each of the groups involved in this struggle for attention is attempting to appropriate Shakespeare for its own ideology or critical theory" (p. x).

24. John Dennis, in *Before the Romantics: An Anthology of the Enlightenment,* ed. Geoffrey Grigson (Edinburgh, 1984), p. 141.

25. James Joyce, *A Portrait of the Artist as a Young Man* (New York, 1983), pp. 149–50.

26. T. S. Eliot, "The Waste Land," in *The Complete Poems and Plays: 1909–1950* (New York, 1980), p. 39.

27. W. B. Yeats, "The Second Coming," in *Selected Poetry,* ed. A. Norman Jeffares (London, 1968), p. 99.

28. T. S. Eliot, "The Waste Land," p. 46.
29. Joyce, *Portrait*, p. 162.
30. For further discussion of this distinction see C. K. Ogden's *Opposition: A Linguistic and Psychological Analysis* (Bloomington, 1967). Waswo clarifies one of the key points as follows: "There are opposites that are mutually exclusive (i.e., genuinely contradictory, like open-shut, black-white), and there are opposites that are mutually implicative (like two sides of a coin, or a street). The relation between the opposites of the first class, though it may exhibit degrees, is such that they cannot exist at the same time in respect to the same object; the relation between those of the second class is that they must: we cannot have one without simultaneously having the other. When relations of the second sort are mistaken for the first, enemies are made of complementarities whose necessarily mutual presence is thus misconstrued as hostility and erroneously generalized as contradiction" (Richard Waswo, *Language and Meaning in the Renaissance* [Princeton, 1987], p. 299).
31. E. M. Forster, "Art for Art's Sake," in *Two Cheers for Democracy* (London, 1972), p. 88.
32. Tom Stoppard, *Arcadia* (London, 1993), pp. 5, 48.
33. Lévi-Strauss, *Tristes Tropiques*, p. 53.
34. My aim is not, of course, to provide an exhaustive reading of Saussure or a comprehensive survey of modern linguistics, but to provide sufficient analysis of both to indicate ways beyond current perspectives and to encourage others to explore further. Note also that I am not inclined to draw a strong line between linguistic theory and philosophy of language, as that line often registers the tendency of some linguists to explore phonology and syntax at the expense of semantics, as well as the tendency of some philosophers to explore the vexed problem of meaning independent of issues arising in phonology and syntax. Sampson has also made the case that the disciplinary divisions between "Linguistic Semantics" and "Philosophical Semantics" has not served linguistics well: "When linguists first began to think about semantics, it is quite likely that many of them had only a dim awareness that the issues they faced had been discussed intensively by philosophers for many years (indeed, centuries) before them" (Geoffrey Sampson, *Making Sense* [Oxford, 1980], p. 73).

CHAPTER 1: LITERARY THEORY AND LINGUISTIC THEORY

1. Wayne C. Booth, *Critical Understanding: The Powers and Limits of Pluralism* (Chicago, 1979); Robert Scholes, *Textual Power: Literary Theory and the Teaching of English* (New Haven, 1985); Gerald Graff, *Professing Literature: An Institutional History* (Chicago, 1987); John M. Ellis, *Against Deconstruction* (Princeton, 1989) and *Literature Lost: Social Agendas and the Corruption of the Humanities* (New Haven, 1997); Paul B. Armstrong, *Conflicting Readings: Variety and Validity in Interpretation* (Chapel Hill, 1990); David Damrosch, *We Scholars: Changing the Culture of the University* (Cambridge, Mass., 1995); Carl Woodring, *Literature: An Embattled Profession* (New York, 1999). As it turned out, the weakly constrained creativity of deconstruction was something of an illusion.
2. Booth, *Critical Understanding*, p. 228.
3. Immanuel Kant, *Critique of Pure Reason*, quoted by Booth, *Critical Understanding*, p. 232.

4. Graff, *Professing Literature*, pp. 241–42.
5. Such is the disenchantment with what literary theorists made of deconstruction that Norris can only begin to defend Derrida against John Ellis's critique (*Against Deconstruction*) by dismissing a whole generation of American theorists as the "US-domesticated variant" of deconstruction. Citing a passage from *Of Grammatology*, Norris emphasizes how "it specifically disowns the attitude of free-for-all hermeneutic license—or the downright anti-intentionalist stance—that Ellis so persistently attributes to Derrida. And of course it must also create problems for those among the deconstructionist adepts who likewise take him to have broken altogether with values of truth and falsehood, right reading, intentionality, authorial 'presence' and so forth" (Christopher Norris, *What's Wrong with Postmodernism: Critical Theory and the Ends of Philosophy* [Hemel Hempstead, 1990], pp. 139, 162).
6. Booth, *Critical Understanding*, p. 198.
7. Ibid., p. 211. The case for "Pluralism as Dogmatism" is made by W. J. T. Mitchell in *Critical Inquiry*, 12 (3), Spring 1986, pp. 494–502. See also Ellen Rooney, *Seductive Reasoning: Pluralism as the Problematic of Contemporary Literary Theory* (Ithaca, 1989).
8. The many problems Ellis points out include the incoherent (and hastily revised) argument for the priority of writing over speech; the cultivation of terminological obscurity for theoretical commonplaces; the claim that misreading is a good thing when applied to other people's texts but a sign of unfairness when applied to your own; the competing claims about linguistic stability and instability emerging from different components of the argument; the trivializing predilection for putting one extreme formulation against another; the peculiar inconsistency between skeptical theory and dogmatic practice; and ignorance of the work of those who had already taken discussion of many of the key issues to a level of sophistication that deconstruction by and large does not match (Ellis, *Against Deconstruction*).
9. Ibid., p. 157.
10. Graff, *Professing Literature*, pp. 5–6.
11. As Graff puts it: "Although the turn of the century saw the imposition of a uniform canon of English literature, traditionalists complained that the curriculum had all but dissipated the civic potential of the canon by breaking it up into such disconnected fragments that students could get no clear sense of its unity. Far from being organized on a centralized logocentric model, the American university is itself something of a deconstructionist, proliferating a variety of disciplinary vocabularies that nobody can reduce to the common measure of any metalanguage" (Graff, *Professing Literature*, pp. 12–13).
12. Ibid., pp. 249–50.
13. Ibid., pp. 252, 258.
14. Booth, *Critical Understanding*, pp. 40, 6.
15. The case for a more collaborative approach to scholarship and teaching is admirably developed by David Damrosch in *We Scholars*.
16. John Lyons, *Introduction to Theoretical Linguistics* (Cambridge, U.K., 1969), p. 4.
17. Ludwig Wittgenstein, *Philosophical Investigations*, trans. G. E. M. Anscombe (New York, 1969), p. 2.
18. Scholes, *Textual Power*, pp. 86–110.

19. Wittgenstein, *Philosophical Investigations,* pp. 48, 44, pars. 115, 96.
20. Richard Waswo, *Language and Meaning in the Renaissance* (Princeton, 1987), pp. 25–35.
21. Ibid., p. 300.
22. Ibid., p. 266.
23. Waswo's version is suitably emphatic: "Cultural change, to insist on the obvious, is a sloppy business; its accurate description is not likely to be tidy. Ideas and literary works are not people; the history of their life cycle is not that of a predictable biological continuum. They appear, are hailed or ignored, imitated and misconstrued, used for often contradictory purposes, are enshrined, attacked or forgotten, perhaps to reemerge sooner or later, intact or fragmented, in similar or remote contexts, with the same or with quite different emotional resonance. Such, in brief compass, was the fate of the simple observation of vernacular change as made from Dante to Waller" (ibid., pp. 63–64).
24. Ibid., p. 271. These observations also raise a theoretical dilemma about the relationship between theory and practice: "if we pay most attention to what Renaissance writers say about language, we are likely to dismiss it as jejune and simplistic cliché. If, on the other hand, we pay most attention to what they do with language, we may attribute to them theoretical positions they had not in fact attained" (ibid., p. 80). Waswo's argument is, however, directed at the more complex issue of the relationships among actual practice, available theory, and acceptable conclusions.
25. Ibid., p. 103. One of the interesting extensions of referential thinking is that words rather than language in general were the chief focus of linguistic attention. Waswo points out that the term "language" is absent from indices of the period's scholarly works, and that the period's vocabulary of discourse about discourse "includes no single term for what we today automatically understand by 'language'—that is, a unitary, all-inclusive concept of any systematic means of communication." Indeed, the earliest metaphorical extension of the term language to another context is Shakespearean (pp. 85–86).
26. Ibid., p. 132. To acknowledge this is not necessarily to accept all of Waswo's controversial arguments and evidence, as he himself has noted some mistranslations in his work. But these errors rarely affect his overall argument and the force of counterarguments is often diminished by a historicist tendency to offer presupposition as evidence. As Sampson points out, that same tendency is apparent in many aspects of the work of Chomsky and his followers when they argue for a "limited view" of mind rather than a "creative view" (Geoffrey Sampson, *Making Sense* [Oxford, 1980], pp. 1–19).
27. Derrida argues that "There is no sense in doing without the concepts of metaphysics in order to shake metaphysics. We have no language—no syntax and no lexicon—which is foreign to this history; we can pronounce not a single destructive proposition which has not already had to slip into the form, the logic, and the implicit postulations of precisely what it seeks to contest. . . . As soon as one seeks to demonstrate . . . that there is no transcendental or privileged signified and that the domain or play of signification henceforth has no limit, one must reject even the concept and word 'sign' itself—which is precisely what cannot be done. For the signification 'sign' has always been understood and determined, in its meaning, as sign-of, a signifier referring to a signified. . . . We cannot do without the concept of the sign, for we cannot give up this metaphysical complicity without also giving up the critique we are directing against this complicity" (Jacques

Derrida, *Writing and Difference,* trans. Alan Bass [Chicago, 1978], pp. 280–81). On another occasion Derrida argues that "The movements of deconstruction do not destroy structures from the outside. They are not possible and effective, nor can they take accurate aim, except by inhabiting those structures. . . . Operating necessarily from the inside, borrowing all the strategic and economic resources of subversion from the old structure . . . the enterprise of deconstruction always in a certain way falls prey to its own work" (*Of Grammatology,* trans. Gayatri Chakravorty Spivak [Baltimore, 1976], p. 24). For further discussion of this point, see also chapter 4, note 31.

28. Booth, *Critical Understanding,* p. 211.
29. Ibid., pp. 198, 219–32.
30. An understanding of the postcolonial manifestations of hybridity would thus require the comparison of differing kinds of hybridization seen from a variety of points of view and in terms of a variety of modes of critical discourses.
31. Paul B. Armstrong, *Conflicting Readings: Variety and Validity in Interpretation* (Chapel Hill, 1990). All page references are to this edition. I explore the limitations of single issue/single context analyses in more detail and from differing angles in chapters 3, 4, and 5.
32. Paul Bové, quoted by Graff, *Professing Literature,* p. 176.
33. As Graff puts it: "there is something patronizing about assuming a priori that coherence is always achieved or—as in deconstructionist readings—always undone" (ibid., pp. 230–31).
34. The issues here are complex. Fish tends to position the reader in an "interpretive community" whose shared beliefs lead directly to the conclusions the beliefs generate. In interpretive debate, he argues, "one is always and already proceeding within a structure of beliefs. . . . We try to persuade others to our beliefs because if they believe what we believe, they will, as a consequence of those beliefs, see what we see; and the facts to which we point in order to support our interpretations will be as obvious to them as they are to us. Indeed, this is the whole of critical activity, an attempt on the part of one party to alter the beliefs of another so that the evidence cited by the first will be seen *as* evidence by the second" (Stanley Fish, *Is There a Text in This Class? The Authority of Interpretive Communities* [Cambridge, Mass., 1980], p. 365). The familiar error of homogenizing our beliefs, interests, or assumptions is apparent here, as Scholes was quick to point out: "the notion of a single, monolithic *set* of assumptions makes the same totalitarian error that Fish makes in other places. Different, even conflicting, assumptions may preside over any reading of a single text by a single person. It is in fact these very differences—differences *within* the reader, who is never a member of a single unified group—it is these very differences that create the space in which the reader exercises a measure of interpretive freedom" (*Textual Power,* p. 154).

Armstrong, in somewhat different terms, refers us to Peirce's essay "The Fixation of Belief" (*Collected Papers of Charles Sanders Peirce,* volumes 5 and 6, ed. Charles Hartshorne and Paul Weiss [Cambridge, Mass., 1965], pp. 223–47) and argues that "The inability to know something with certainty is what makes it possible and even necessary to choose one or another set of beliefs about it. Belief does not exclude choice; quite to the contrary, it requires it" (*Conflicting Readings,* pp. 181–82). The difficulty here is one of situating and mobilizing the contingency of belief, whether it is within, or just between,

sets of beliefs. For, as Ellis puts it: "Peirce saw the crucial point . . . that new knowledge may profoundly change our understanding of old knowledge rather than simply build on it" (John M. Ellis, *Language, Thought, and Logic* [Evanston, 1993], p. 22).
35. Armstrong, *Conflicting Readings,* pp. 79, 96, 151, 181. See in particular p. 79: "the hypotheses we generate to make sense of a text necessarily reflect our fundamental convictions about the world." Contrast Sampson's argument: "Not all our thought is deductive; we all commonly acquire new beliefs by induction from our observations. New beliefs formed by induction are general statements; they are not mere reports of individual observations or conjunctions of observations, and they do not deductively follow from observation statements although observation statements follow deductively from them. In Popperian terms, beliefs formed by induction are unpredictable *guesses*" (Sampson, *Making Sense,* p. 98).
36. Graff, *Professing Literature,* p. 227.
37. Booth, *Critical Understanding,* p. 40.
38. Wittgenstein, *Philosophical Investigations,* p. 48, par. 115. As Waswo puts it: "What Saussure was attempting to eliminate from his careful redefinition of the composite 'sign' [was] the whole dualistic picture of the world that lies in the Western vocabulary of discourse. . . . Saussure found 'sign' defective in two ways: (1) by its presumption of standing for or corresponding to preextant entities in the world; (2) by its presumption of independent status as *the* semantic unit" (*Language and Meaning,* p. 17). The difficulty of eradicating the picture is, he notes, widely apparent, for "The inability even of theories that revel in iconoclasm and delight in the free play of signifiers to jettison the very notion of 'standing for' recalls Saussure's inability to scrap 'sign' even after he had defined it to the vanishing point" (p. 304). Seeking to clarify the same issue, Haas argues that "A language, one might say, requires at least two words. Language and meaning take their origin from difference of meaning" (W. Haas, "The Theory of Translation," *Philosophy,* 37, July 1962, p. 221). To question a referential relationship between words and what lies beyond them is not, for Haas, to argue that there is no relationship, but to begin to reformulate it.
39. Wittgenstein, *Philosophical Investigations,* p. 49, par. 122.
40. Ibid., p. 45, par. 103. What we subsequently "see" is, of course, anything but self-evident. Sampson offers us alternative forms of picture construction whose limitations he, too, seeks to transcend: "I have argued that there is in the world a real phenomenon, namely human intellectual activity, which is not a mere myth like witchcraft or spiritualism but about which no scientific theory can be constructed. We can describe how humans have thought in the past, but we cannot make true predictions about how they will think in the future. . . . Now many people hold that if mental activity is real it *must* be treatable by the scientific method. After all, the mind must be some sort of machine, even if a highly complex one (they argue), and in principle the workings of any machine can be specified. . . . The notion that some subjects can in principle be discussed only in the historical style of the humanities rather than the predictive style of the sciences seems to such people mere mysticism" (*Making Sense,* p. 91). The important issue is the vexed relationship between methodological techniques on the one hand and creativity and change on the other.

CHAPTER 2: SAUSSURE, FIRTH, AND BAKHTIN

1. Editor's Preface to the First Edition, Ferdinand de Saussure, *Course in General Linguistics*, ed. Charles Bally and Albert Sechehaye, trans. Roy Harris (London, 1990), pp. xviii–xix.
2. Ibid., pp. xix, xx.
3. Anticipating possible objections, the editors offer the following defense: "We may be told that this 'unity' is not complete. Saussure in his teaching never claimed to cover the whole of linguistics, or to throw equal light on every aspect of the subject. In practical terms this would have been an impossibility, and in any case his interests lay elsewhere. His main concern was with the fundamentals of the subject, to which he applied certain basic principles of his own. They are present throughout his work, running through it like the warp of a well woven cloth of varied texture. He does not attempt to cover wide areas of linguistics, but chooses topics where he can either provide his principles with particularly striking applications, or else test them against some rival theory. This is why certain disciplines are scarcely mentioned—semantics, for example. But we do not feel that such gaps weaken the architecture of the whole. The absence of a 'linguistics of speech' is more serious. This had been promised to those who attended the third course of lectures, and it would doubtless have occupied a prominent place in later series. The reason why that promise was never kept is only too well known. Here, we confined ourselves to collecting together Saussure's elusive hints concerning this barely outlined project, and putting them in their natural place in the scheme" (ibid., p. xix).
4. Saussure, *Course*. All page references are to the Harris edition.
5. Two classic cases here are Grimm's Law and Verner's Law governing the First Germanic Consonant Shift. Strang describes this process concisely and notes in passing that "linguists now feel some squeamishness about the use of the term *law* in linguistics, though in the 19c it had a considerable vogue." (Barbara M. H. Strang, *A History of English* [London, 1970], p. 411).
6. The complexities of semiotic systems and their relationships are explored in chapter 3 with particular reference to the work of Umberto Eco.
7. John M. Ellis, *Language, Thought, and Logic* (Evanston, 1993), pp. 62–63.
8. Saussure's elaboration of the point constitutes an early warning to those who would later adopt his vocabulary but miss the point: "Any linguistic entity exists only in virtue of the association between signal and signification. It disappears the moment we concentrate exclusively on just one or the other" (*Course*, p. 101). Those who envisage, in recent jargon, the existence of free-floating signifiers would have, in Saussure's terms, the problem of having nothing to float.
9. See also Saussure's comment: "In a language, as in every other semiological system, what distinguishes a sign is what constitutes it" (ibid., p. 119).
10. "In linguistic structure everything in the end comes down to differences, and also to groups" (ibid., p. 127). The uncertain transmission of Saussure's ideas is evident in the mixed emphases of such sentences, and in this case it has encouraged a tendency to focus on signs making distinctions rather than on systems establishing groups. A similar mixed emphasis recurs on the issue of positive and negative terms in language with similarly un-

fortunate results. At one point Saussure notes that "in a language there are only differences, *and no positive terms,*" but he soon qualifies this blunt assertion: "to say that in a language everything is negative holds only for signification and signal considered separately. The moment we consider the sign as a whole, we encounter something which is positive in its own domain. . . . The moment we compare one sign with another as positive combinations, the term *difference* should be dropped. It is no longer appropriate. It is a term which is suitable only for comparisons between sound patterns (e.g., *père* vs. *mère*), or between ideas (e.g., 'father' vs. 'mother'). Two signs, each comprising a signification and a signal, are not different from each other, but only distinct. They are simply in *opposition* to each other" (ibid., pp. 118–19). Many who have adopted Saussure's terminology appear to have heard of the terms *signifiant* (signal or signifier), *signifié* (signification or signified), along with difference, and negative value, but have somehow overlooked the terms sign (as he uses it), opposition, and positive value.

11. This comparison is somewhat confusing as it employs a vertical image to illustrate a horizontal principle of linearity. More important, however, is Saussure's failure to supply a closed set of contrasts and his use of the term "etc." This has important consequences, as we will see later, for attempts to describe the value of a sign in a system as "being whatever the others are not" (ibid., p. 115).

12. As Saussure puts it: "Where syntagmas are concerned . . . one must recognise the fact that there is no clear boundary separating the language, as confirmed by communal usage, from speech, marked by freedom of the individual. In many cases it is difficult to assign a combination of units to one or the other. Many combinations are the product of both, in proportions which cannot be accurately measured" (ibid., p. 123).

13. On the problematics of deploying the term "ideology," see Raymond Geuss, *The Idea of a Critical Theory* (Cambridge, U.K., 1981), pp. 4–26. Focusing eventually upon ideology as "false consciousness" among agents who "are deluded about their own true interests," Geuss, amalgamating the work of several social theorists, argues that the inherent aim of a "critical theory" is to establish itself as "the self-consciousness of a successful process of enlightenment and emancipation" through which agents become aware of "how they ought rationally to act to realize their own best interests" (pp. 45, 58, 77). Such a critique of ideology is possible, he argues, "only if we can extract the very instruments of criticism from the agents' own form of consciousness—from their views about the good life, from the notions of freedom, truth, and rationality embedded in their normative epistemology. It is the particular insidiousness of ideology that it turns human desires and aspirations against themselves and uses them to fuel repression. . . . The positive task of the critical theory is to . . . 'separate' the underlying genuine human wants, values, needs, and aspirations from their ideological mode of expression; only then can agents hope to attain correct perception of their wants and needs, and form correct views about their real interests" (pp. 87–88). The one problem, of course, is that the evaluative words invoked here, such as "false," "best," and "correct," are difficult to deploy across a variety of ideological terrains. As Rorty puts it: "the problem of how to overcome authority without claiming authority" is "*the* problem of ironist theory" (Richard Rorty, *Contingency, Irony, and Solidarity* [Cambridge, U.K., 1989], p. 105).

14. James Joyce, *A Portrait of the Artist as a Young Man* (New York, 1983), p. 150.

15. Richard Rorty, *Consequences of Pragmatism* (Minneapolis, 1982), p. 27.
16. J. R. Firth, *Papers in Linguistics, 1934–51* (London, 1969). All page references are to this edition.
17. Firth, *Selected Papers of J. R. Firth, 1952–1959,* ed. F. R. Palmer (Bloomington, 1968), p. 18. See also Firth's comment: "the contextual technique I advocate . . . allows discontinuity and change of measure and value from context to context. . . . A term is to be considered first in relation to its context and secondly to the relevant linked alternance. What relations it may have to the language as a whole is difficult to guess. To treat language as a sort of unity does not mean that every element is to be regarded as in equal relation to every other element" (*Papers,* p. 74).
18. Firth's notion of the individual's continuity and change is directly parallel with that of language, and he makes every effort to link conformity with creativity, conventionality with idiosyncrasy, and the past with the present and future. The multiplicity of the social self is directly linked to the multiplicity of local modes of discourse that have been mastered: "Every social person is a bundle of *personae,* a bundle of parts, each part having its lines. If you do not know your lines you are no use in the play. It is very good for you and society if you are cast for your parts and remember your lines. . . . we must consider language, like personality, as a systematic linking of the past with the present and with the future. . . . There is the element of habit, custom, tradition, the element of the past, and the element of innovation, of the moment in which the future is being born. When you speak you fuse these elements in verbal creation, the outcome of your language and of your personality. What you say may be said to have a style, and in this connexion a vast field of research in stylistics awaits investigation in literature and speech. The continuity of the person, the development of personality, are paralleled by the continuity and development of language in a variety of forms" (*Papers,* p. 184). As we shall see in subsequent chapters, the notion of continuity rather than unity is a valuable means of discussing domains characterized by both fixity and change, but Firth's hopes for a stylistics that might accommodate such a notion have yet to be fully realized.
19. Vološinov, for example, shares Bakhtin's belief in the importance of studying instances of verbal interaction in concrete situations, but he is then inclined, as Bakhtin is not, to go on to argue that "The immediate social situation and the broader social milieu wholly determine—and determine from within, so to speak—the structure of an utterance" (V. N. Vološinov, *Marxism and the Philosophy of Language,* trans. Ladislav Matejka and I. R. Titunik [New York, 1973], p. 86). Vološinov can, however, be more ambivalent about the relationship between local ideological idiosyncrasy and general social conformity, as also can Medvedev: What is lacking, he argues, "is precisely a developed sociological doctrine of the distinctive features of the material, forms, and purposes of each area of ideological creation. . . . Of course, each area has its own language, its own forms and devices for that language, and its own specific laws for the ideological refraction of a common reality. It is absolutely not the way of Marxism to level these differences or to ignore the essential plurality of the languages of ideology. The specificity of art, science, ethics, or religion naturally should not obscure their ideological unity as superstructures of a common base, or the fact that they follow the same sociological laws of development. But this specificity should not be effaced by the general formulas of these laws" (P. N.

Medvedev, *The Formal Method in Literary Scholarship: A Critical Introduction to Sociological Poetics,* trans. Albert J. Wehrle [Cambridge, Mass., 1978], pp. 3–4). There is much in the work ascribed to Vološinov and Medvedev to raise suspicions that the theories elaborated are worded in ways designed to diminish the political dangers of writing in that era.

20. Mikhail M. Bakhtin, *The Dialogic Imagination,* ed. Michael Holquist, trans. Caryl Emerson and Michael Holquist (Austin, 1981). All page references are to this edition.

21. Ladislav Matejka traces Russian interest in the theoretical implications of dialogue to one of Badouin de Courtenay's students, Lev Ščerba, in 1915 (Appendix to Vološinov, *Marxism and the Philosophy of Language,* p. 171). Roman Jakobson, in his 1921 essay, "On Realism in Art," clarifies the status of "realism" in terms of author/reader interaction (*Readings in Russian Poetics: Formalist and Structuralist Views,* ed. Ladislav Matejka and Krystyna Pomorska [Ann Arbor, 1978], pp. 38–46). Montaigne had also offered an informative image somewhat earlier: "A speech belongs half to him who speaks and half to him who hears. The latter ought to prepare himself to receive it according to the movement with which it is delivered. As with tennis players, he who receives the ball shifts about and takes his position according to the movements of the one who is hitting the ball to him, and according to the kind of stroke" ("Of Experience," Michel de Montaigne, *The Essays of Michel de Montaigne,* vol. 3, trans. Jacob Zeitlin [New York, 1936], p. 289).

22. Vološinov, *Marxism and the Philosophy of Language,* p. 81.

23. As Morson and Emerson put it, for Bakhtin, "Language . . . is always language*s*." Gary Saul Morson and Caryl Emerson, *Mikhail Bakhtin: Creation of a Prosaics* (Stanford, 1990), p. 140.

24. Bakhtin regards literary language as the site upon which consciousness of the need to choose among local languages is particularly acute, for the speaker/reader is not necessarily at home in any one of them.

25. Bakhtin also addresses in this context the issue of whether the word "language" loses its capacity to make useful distinctions when it is applied to local variants. It is the capacity of such local variants to offer different and competing "points of view on the world" that, he feels, justifies this use of the term (*Dialogic Imagination,* pp. 291–92). See also his comment: "A social language . . . is a concrete socio-linguistic belief system that defines a distinct identity for itself within the boundaries of a language that is unitary only in the abstract" (p. 356). Bakhtin here registers symptoms of Armstrong's tendency to overstate the coherence of individual languages, but his recognition of the importance of local ordering is compelling.

26. Compare Firth's related views which shift the emphasis from the dominator to the dominated: "Conversation is much more of a roughly prescribed ritual than most people think. Once someone speaks to you, you are in a relatively determined context and you are not free just to say what you please. . . . The moment a conversation is started, whatever is said is a determining condition for what, in any reasonable expectation, may follow. What you say raises the threshold against most of the language of your companion, and leaves only a limited opening for a certain likely range of responses. This sort of thing is an aspect of what I have called contextual elimination. There is a positive force in

what you say in a given situation, and there is also the negative force of elimination both in the events and circumstances of the situation and in the words employed, which are of course events in the situation. Neither linguists nor psychologists have begun the study of conversation; but it is here we shall find the key to a better understanding of what language really is and how it works" (Firth, *Papers*, pp. 28, 31–32).

27. Roman Jakobson and Jurij Tynjanov, "Problems in the Study of Literature and Language," in Matejka and Pomorska, *Readings in Russian Poetics*, p. 80.
28. Ibid., p. 81.
29. Note, in particular, Homi K. Bhabha's exploration of hybridization in discourse and culture in *The Location of Culture* (London, 1994). The appeal of the notion of hybrids to postcolonial theory in general is immediately evident, though it leaves a great deal of further theoretical and practical work to be done.
30. The voice is, of course, that of Saussure, *Course*, p. 189.
31. See also the comment: "The object of synchronic study does not comprise everything which is simultaneous, but only the set of facts corresponding to any particular language. In this, it will take into account where necessary a division into dialects and sub-dialects. The term *synchronic*, in fact, is not sufficiently precise. *Idiosynchronic* would be a better term, even though it is somewhat cumbersome" (*Course*, pp. 89–90).
32. "It is difficult to say what the difference is between a language and a dialect. Often a dialect is called a language because it has a literature" (*Course*, p. 202).
33. Where we do encounter radical breaks between contiguous language communities, it is "because the intermediate dialects have disappeared" as a consequence of (usually political) forces that "obliterate transitions" (*Course*, p. 203). There is much in Saussure's work, as well as Bakhtin's, that bears upon the issue of hybridization in discourse and culture.
34. Saussure's ideas on this matter parallel Firth's on "contextual elimination" and seem to introduce into his linguistics of *langue* a need for consideration of contexts most appropriately located in a linguistics of *parole*. He suggests a process "which involves eliminating mentally everything which does not lead to the desired differentiation at the point required" (*Course*, p. 129).
35. "In linguistic structure everything in the end comes down to differences, and also to groups" (*Course*, p. 127). The instrumental status of groups leads Ellis to argue that the word "equivalence" is preferable to the word "similarity" in describing the basis for group composition (*Language, Thought, and Logic*, pp. 27–44).
36. "It is because the linguistic sign is arbitrary that it knows no other law than that of tradition, and because it is founded upon tradition that it can be arbitrary" (*Course*, p. 74).

CHAPTER 3: CHOMSKY AND HALLIDAY

1. Philip W. Davis, *Modern Theories of Language* (Englewood Cliffs, 1973), p. 3.
2. Ibid., p. 7.
3. Ibid.
4. E. D. Hirsch, *Validity in Interpretation* (New Haven, 1967), p. 70. Hirsch goes on to indicate why this is a misleading picture of the challenge interpreters confront.

5. Noam Chomsky, *Syntactic Structures* (The Hague, 1957). All page references are to this edition.
6. Noam Chomsky, *Aspects of the Theory of Syntax* (Cambridge, Mass., 1965). All page references are to this edition.
7. The phrase "infinite use of finite means" is borrowed from Wilhelm von Humboldt.
8. J. T. Grinder and S. H. Elgin, *Guide to Transformational Grammar: History, Theory, Practice* (New York, 1973), p. 174.
9. Chomsky includes grammaticality in the study of competence but assigns acceptability to the separate study of performance. For further discussion see *Aspects*, pp. 11–12.
10. Jerrold J. Katz, *Semantic Theory* (New York, 1972), p. 40. The earlier coauthored essay by Katz and Jerry A. Fodor was "The Structure of a Semantic Theory," *Language*, 39 (2), 1963, pp. 170–210.
11. Ibid.
12. Bernard Harrison, "Review of J. J. Katz, *Semantic Theory*," *Mind*, 83, October 1974, p. 603.
13. Ibid., p. 605. Harrison also expresses his puzzlement that Katz should believe that the investigation of meaning "is somehow structurally or methodologically analogous to the elucidation offered by physical science of the question 'What is matter?'" (p. 600).
14. See George Lakoff and James McCawley in *Discussing Language,* ed. H. Parret (The Hague, 1974), pp. 151–78, 249–77.
15. Chomsky, *The Minimalist Program* (Cambridge, Mass., 1995), p. 29. From the early 1980s Chomsky has increasingly sought to characterize the human "language faculty" in general and to restate claims for a "universal grammar." The locus of variable order is the "cognitive system" of the language faculty while the vexed problems of recalcitrant disorder are located in the "performance system." The relationship between the two continues to be uncertain, but the new point of departure is radical enough. "The P & P [principles and parameters] approach maintains that the basic ideas of the [linguistic] tradition, incorporated without great change in early generative grammar, are misguided in principle—in particular, the idea that a language consists of rules for forming grammatical constructions (relative clauses, passives, etc.). The P & P approach held that languages have no rules in anything like the familiar sense, and no theoretically significant grammatical constructions except as taxonomic artifacts. There are universal principles and a finite array of options as to how they apply (parameters), but no language-particular rules and no grammatical constructions of the traditional sort within or across languages" (pp. 5–6). Not surprisingly, this leads Chomsky down a familiar path: "My personal feeling is that much more substantial idealization is required if we hope to understand the properties of the language faculty, but misunderstandings and confusion engendered even by limited idealization are so pervasive that it may not be useful to pursue the matter today. *Idealization,* it should be noted, is a misleading term for the only reasonable way to approach a grasp of reality" (p. 7).
16. Jacques Derrida, *Of Grammatology,* trans. Gayatri Chakravorty Spivak (Baltimore, 1976), p. 39. See also *Glas,* trans. John P. Leavey and Richard Rand (Lincoln, 1986), pp. 91–93. Derrida's example in each case is the work of Saussure.
17. John Lyons, *Introduction to Theoretical Linguistics* (Cambridge, U.K., 1969), p. 141.

18. In literary criticism Miller distinguishes the two approaches as those of canny and uncanny critics but notes that both "would . . . be impossible without modern linguistics." J. Hillis Miller, "Stevens' Rock and Criticism as Cure, Part 2," *Georgia Review,* 30, 1976, p. 336.
19. Jonathan Culler, *On Deconstruction: Theory and Criticism after Structuralism* (Ithaca, 1982), pp. 24–26.
20. Ibid., p. 223.
21. Roman Jakobson and Jurij Tynjanov, "Problems in the Study of Literature and Language," in *Readings in Russian Poetics: Formalist and Structuralist Views,* ed. Ladislav Matejka and Krystyna Pomorska (Ann Arbor, 1978), pp. 79–81.
22. Roland Barthes, *Elements of Semiology,* trans. Annette Lavers and Colin Smith (New York, 1967); *The Fashion System,* trans. Matthew Ward and Richard Howard (Berkeley, 1990); "Introduction to the Structural Analysis of Narratives," *Image, Music, Text,* trans. Stephen Heath (New York, 1977), pp. 79–124; *S/Z,* trans. Richard Miller (New York, 1974).
23. Claude Lévi-Strauss, *Tristes Tropiques,* trans. John Weightman and Doreen Weightman (New York, 1981); *Structural Anthropology,* trans. Claire Jacobson and Brooke Grundfest Schoepf (London, 1968); *The Raw and the Cooked: Introduction to a Science of Mythology,* vol. 1, trans. John Weightman and Doreen Weightman (London, 1970); *From Honey to Ashes: Introduction to a Science of Mythology,* vol. 2, trans. John Weightman and Doreen Weightman (London, 1973).
24. Umberto Eco, *A Theory of Semiotics* (Bloomington, 1976), p. 27.
25. Ibid., p. 28.
26. Ibid., p. 26.
27. Ibid., pp. 9–13.
28. Ibid., pp. 9, 128–29, 4. See also his comment that "properly speaking there are not signs, but only *sign-functions*" (p. 49).
29. Culler, *On Deconstruction,* p. 242.
30. On this issue, Miller points out that although de Man and Derrida are rational, patient, and rigorous in their interpretive activities, "nevertheless, the thread of logic leads in both cases into regions which are alogical, absurd. . . . Sooner or later there is the encounter with an 'aporia' or impasse. The bottom drops out, or there is an 'abyssing', an insight one can almost grasp or recognize as part of the familiar landscape of the mind, but not quite, as though the mental eye could not quite bring the material into lucid focus. . . . In fact the moment when logic fails in their work is the moment of their deepest penetration into the actual nature of literary language, or of language as such" (Miller, "Stevens' Rock," pp. 336, 338).
31. Culler, *On Deconstruction,* p. 223.
32. Miller rightly expresses a concern that the recent turn toward history, as a retreat from theory, involves, as a consequence, an unquestioned reliance upon unexamined presuppositions, in particular on "an unexamined ideology of the material base, that is, to a notion that is metaphysical through and through, as much a part of Western metaphysics as the idealism [that most cultural materialists] would contest" ("The Triumph of Theory, the Resistance to Reading, and the Question of the Material Base," *PMLA,* 102, 1987,

pp. 281–91). Some years earlier, Miller noted that "the question of the kind of literary history which would result from the application of a deconstructive rhetoric to the study of literature has hardly yet begun to be answered" ("Deconstructing the Deconstructers," *Diacritics,* 5 [2], Summer 1975, pp. 24–31). The question still awaits a satisfactory answer.

33. Ruquaiya Hasan, cited by Michael Halliday, *Explorations in the Functions of Language* (London, 1973), p. 50.
34. J. R. Firth, *Selected Papers of J. R. Firth, 1952–59,* ed. F. R. Palmer (Bloomington, 1968), pp. 168–205.
35. Derrida argues that "no meaning can be determined out of context, but no context permits saturation" and he goes on to question both the firmness of a text's borders ("the text overruns all the limits assigned to it") and the reader's capacity to delimit contexts ("Living On: Border Lines," *Deconstruction and Criticism,* ed. Harold Bloom et al. [New York, 1979], pp. 81, 84). Culler suggests that "meaning is context-bound, but context is boundless," and before going on to refine the issue, he notes the temptation to "identify deconstruction with the twin principles of the contextual determination of meaning and the infinite extendibility of context" (*On Deconstruction,* pp. 123, 215).
36. Halliday, *Explorations,* p. 69. It should be noted that there is no necessary connection here with behaviorist theories of meaning. As Halliday puts it elsewhere: "It has always seemed to me, and again here I am simply following Firth, that behaviorist models will not account for linguistic interaction or for language development. There is a very curious notion that if you are assigning a significant role to the cultural environment in language learning you are a behaviorist. There is no logical connection here at all" (*Discussing Language,* ed. H. Parret, pp. 109–10). Simplistic notions of situational stimulus/response analysis have no place in any of the theories being discussed.
37. M. A. K. Halliday, *Language as Social Semiotic: The Social Interpretation of Language and Meaning* (London, 1978), p. 121.
38. As Halliday puts it: "Language does not consist of sentences; it consists of text, or discourse—the exchange of meanings in interpersonal contexts of one kind or another" (ibid., p. 2).
39. Halliday criticizes such large pictures in the following terms: "The philosopher's approach to language is always marked by a very high degree of idealization. In its extreme form, this approach idealizes out *all* natural language as irrelevant and unsystematic and treats only constructed logical languages; a less extreme version is one which accepts sentences of natural language but reduces them all to a 'deep structure' in terms of certain fundamental logical relations. Competence, as defined by Chomsky, involves . . . a lower degree of idealization than this. But it is still very high from other points of view, particularly that of anyone interested in language as behavior. Many behaviorally significant variations in language are simply ironed out, and reduced to the same level as stutterings, false starts, clearings of the throat and the like. . . . There is always some idealization, where linguistic generalizations are made; but in a sociological context this has to be, on the whole, at a much lower level" (*Explorations,* pp. 53–54). It is interesting to note, in this respect, the recent tendency of some of Chomsky's followers to focus upon computer languages and their logical structure.

40. Halliday, *Language as Social Semiotic: The Social Interpretation of Language and Meaning* (London, 1978). All page references are to this edition.
41. Halliday, *Explorations in the Functions of Language* (London, 1973). All page references are to this edition.
42. As Halliday puts it: "Some linguists . . . would explain all variation institutionally. Others (myself among them) would argue that this is to make too rigid a distinction between the system and the institution" (*Social Semiotic*, p. 190).
43. An earlier example of the mingling of similarity and difference is provided by Montaigne: "If there were no similarity in our faces, we could not distinguish man from beast; if there were no dissimilarity, we could not distinguish one man from another. All things hold together by some similarity" (Michel de Montaigne, "Of Experience," *The Essays of Michel de Montaigne, vol. 3,* trans. Jacob Zeitlin [New York, 1936], p. 270).
44. Halliday, "Categories of the Theory of Grammar," (1961), reprinted in *Halliday: System and Function in Language,* ed. Gunther Kress (London, 1976). All page references are to this edition.
45. There are hints of both exclusion and absorption in Halliday's early attempts to reconcile grammar and meaning; see "Categories," p. 69.
46. It is no accident that one of the earliest books on the evolving theory was a collaborative venture and that its title linked theory to a particular kind of theory use. See M. A. K. Halliday, Angus McIntosh, and Peter Strevens, *The Linguistic Sciences and Language Teaching* (London, 1964).
47. When Halliday's theory became more functional than formal, he also described meaning potential in terms of delicacy: "The meaning potential is the range of *significant* variation that is at the disposal of the speaker" (*Explorations,* p. 54).
48. Halliday, "Types of Process" (1969), in Kress, *Halliday,* p. 161.
49. For Halliday, such a recognition of the "improbability of certainty" is a means of strengthening and not weakening both theory and description. The scale of delicacy "frees the rest of the theory from what would otherwise be the weakening effect of this feature of language. The category of structure, for example, is the more powerful because it can be used to state the patterns of a given unit comprehensively at the primary degree without the assumption that it has accounted for all the facts" ("Categories," p. 63).
50. The word "determines" in this context introduces potential problems that are briefly realized in the third, social semiotic, stage of model development.
51. Halliday distinguishes his technical deployment of the term "function" from that of other linguists in *Social Semiotic,* pp. 46–52.
52. For Halliday, a text is "a polyphonic composition in which different semantic melodies are interwoven, to be realized as integrated lexicogrammatical structures. Each functional component contributes a band of structure to the whole" (*Social Semiotic,* p. 112). Each functional component provides the speaker/writer with a range of options affecting the organization of experience, the organization of social exchange, and the organization of text.
53. Halliday provides a brief account of the system networks of transitivity, modality, and theme in Kress, *Halliday,* pp. 159–213. See also the diagrams on pp. 104–12.
54. See also Kress, *Halliday,* p. 162.

55. Halliday, "Grammatical Categories in Modern Chinese," in Kress, *Halliday*, p. 37. Kress cites this remark in his interesting discussion of the development of Halliday's theory and of his apparently having "performed a switch of theories" (pp. vii, xvii).
56. Introduction, Kress, *Halliday*, p. xii.
57. Text is increasingly identified as a unit of social dialogue, though it includes many other forms of text: "It is natural to conceive of text first and foremost as conversation: as the spontaneous interchange of meanings in ordinary everyday interaction. It is in such contexts that reality is constructed, in the microsemiotic encounters of daily life. The reason why this is so, why the culture is transmitted to, or recreated by, the individual in the first instance through conversation rather than through other acts of meaning, is that conversation typically relates to the environment in a way that is perceptible and concrete, whereas other genres tend to depend on intermediate levels of symbolic interpretation" (*Social Semiotic*, p. 140).
58. Halliday draws extensively upon the sociolinguistic work of both Basil Bernstein and William Labov in his efforts to situate language in a social context.
59. For further discussion of context, including the descriptive features of field, tenor, and mode and the shifting relation between text and context, see *Social Semiotic*, pp. 139, 141, 143, 114.
60. Halliday is here adapting a quotation from Berger and Kellner's article on "Marriage and the construction of reality" in *Recent Sociology, No. 2: Patterns of Communicative Behavior*, ed. Hans Peter Dreitzel (New York, 1970). Richard Rorty was later to redescribe the discipline of philosophy in similar terms. See his *Philosophy and the Mirror of Nature* (Princeton, 1979).
61. As we will see more clearly in chapter 5, it is no coincidence that, as Morson and Emerson trace the development of Bakhtin's attempts to locate a productive relationship between order and disorder in both linguistic and cultural domains, they encounter radical shifts of perspective that they find difficult to evaluate. Bakhtin, they note, at times seems to favor a simple contrast between the inevitable centripetal ["official"] forces of order and the equally inevitable centrifugal ["unofficial"] forces of disorder (pp. 30, 43, 140). At other times he is ready to celebrate the ludic potential of the forces of carnivalesque disorder (p. 67). And at others he struggles to characterize the complex interaction of the various forces of order and disorder. Pointing toward some of the larger implications of the issue, Morson and Emerson warn from the outset that "Books about thinkers require a kind of unity that their thought may not possess. This cautionary statement is especially applicable to Mikhail Bakhtin, whose intellectual development displays a diversity of insights that cannot be easily integrated or accurately described in terms of a single overriding concern" (Gary Saul Morson and Caryl Emerson, *Mikhail Bakhtin: Creation of a Prosaics* [Stanford, 1990], p. 1). This raises questions, of course, about the responsibility felt by Saussure's editors to produce from his series of lectures a "synthesis" that presents his ideas as "an organic whole." (Editors' Preface to the First Edition, *Course in General Linguistics*, ed. Charles Bally and Albert Sechehaye, trans. Roy Harris, London, 1990, p. xix). It is also interesting to note that the editor of Firth's later essays is inclined to blame "the fact that [Firth] was both during his lifetime and afterwards so misunderstood" upon his readiness to settle for publishing essays seriatim, rather than

publishing something that demonstrated more clearly the scope, application, and underlying pattern of his theoretical activities: "It was believed in his years of retirement that he was busy preparing a book entitled *Principles of Linguistics* which was already advertised in the booksellers' catalogues and that he was also thinking about a grammar of English. But among the papers left at his death there was not one sheet that belonged to either of these projects" (Firth, *Selected Papers,* p. 2). In chapters 4 and 5, I address more directly the issues raised by theory evolution and theory presentation.

CHAPTER 4: WITTGENSTEIN

1. J. L. Austin, *How to Do Things with Words* (Cambridge, Mass., 1962). For a perceptive study of Austin's work, see Keith Graham, *J. L. Austin: A Critique of Ordinary Language Philosophy* (Sussex, 1977).
2. Saussure's basic question "What is the actual object of study?" clearly presupposes a certain kind of answer when he ponders the peculiar status of linguistic data: "Other sciences are provided with objects of study given in advance, which are then examined from different points of view. Nothing like that is the case in linguistics. Suppose someone pronounces the French word *nu* ('naked'). At first sight, one might think this would be an example of an independently given linguistic object. But more careful consideration reveals a series of three or four quite different things, depending on the viewpoint adopted. There is a sound, there is the expression of an idea, there is a derivative of Latin *nūdum,* and so on. The object is not given in advance of the viewpoint: far from it. Rather, one might say that it is the viewpoint adopted which creates the object. Furthermore, there is nothing to tell us in advance whether one of these ways of looking at it is prior to or superior to any of the others" (*Course in General Linguistics,* trans. Roy Harris [London, 1990], p. 8).
3. Saussure, *Course in General Linguistics,* pp. 15, 19.
4. Noam Chomsky, *Syntactic Structures* (The Hague, 1957), p. 45.
5. Ibid., pp. 44, 47, 6, 68.
6. Ibid., p. 15.
7. Ibid., pp. 13, 49, and *Aspects of the Theory of Syntax* (Cambridge, Mass., 1965), p. 8.
8. Chomsky, *Aspects,* pp. 25, 59.
9. Ibid., pp. 4, 59.
10. M. A. K. Halliday, *Explorations in the Functions of Language* (London, 1973), p. 9.
11. M. A. K. Halliday, Angus McIntosh, and Peter Strevens, *The Linguistic Sciences and Language Teaching* (London, 1964), pp. 17–18.
12. Halliday, *Explorations,* p. 62.
13. Ibid., p. 105.
14. Ibid., p. 98.
15. Ibid., p. 105.
16. Ibid.
17. M. A. K. Halliday, *Language as Social Semiotic: The Social Interpretation of Language and Meaning* (London, 1978), p. 149.
18. In this respect Chomsky refers to the "fundamental descriptive inadequacy of structural-

ist grammars" and to the need to establish "an explicit formulation of the 'creative' processes of language" (*Aspects,* pp. 4–8).
19. Ludwig Wittgenstein, *The Blue and Brown Books* (New York, 1965), p. 18. An earlier version of the Wittgenstein section of this chapter, "Wittgenstein's Philosophizing and Literary Theorizing," was published in *New Literary History,* 19, Winter 1988, pp. 209–37.
20. Ludwig Wittgenstein, *Philosophical Investigations,* trans. G. E. M. Anscombe (New York, 1969). Subsequent quotations from this text are indicated *PI* with accompanying page and paragraph references.
21. An early example is the collection of essays from *Critical Inquiry* in *Against Theory,* ed. W. J. T. Mitchell (Chicago, 1985).
22. Stanley Cavell, *Must We Mean What We Say?* (Cambridge, U.K., 1976), p. 71. These are the characteristic voices in Wittgenstein's improvised dialogues, but they by no means exhaust the voices of the text.
23. Ibid., p. 70, n. 13.
24. In spite of Saussure's insistence that both signal and signification are included within the sign, there is still a widespread tendency to think of meaning in terms of names and objects. More recently, recognition of the lack of such obliging objects has led to much loose discussion about free-floating signifiers (signals) and to a peculiar readiness to elevate the absence of appropriate objects to a mystical status. To convert a mistaken presupposition into a lost possibility is very misleading, and nothing but confusion can follow from attempts to speak of the absence of something which has no potential for presence. To go further and conceive of signifiers (signals) which have lost their accompanying signifieds (significations) is even more confusing, for a signifier without a signified would not be recognizable as a signifier. We also need to recognize that a signified that lacks visible presence is not usefully characterized as absent. What is at issue is one kind of presence versus another, as Haas clearly established many years ago: W. Haas, "The Theory of Translation," *Philosophy,* 37, July 1962, pp. 208–28. Something of the troublesome history of debate about reference can be gleaned from P. F. Strawson's 1956 essay, "On Referring," reprinted in *The Philosophy of Language,* ed. A. P. Martinich (New York, 1985), pp. 220–35. The recurringly problematic nature of referring even in apparently unproblematic circumstances is exemplified in John Ellis's discussion of the word "weed" (*The Theory of Literary Criticism: A Logical Analysis* [Berkeley, 1974], pp. 36–41) and in Richard Waswo's discussion of the word "tree" (*Language and Meaning in the Renaissance* [Princeton, 1987], pp. 11–13).
25. Bertrand Russell, Introduction to Wittgenstein's *Tractatus Logico-Philosophicus* (London, 1969), p. x.
26. This has seemed self-evident to many, and Noam Chomsky takes it for granted in his transformational-generative grammar which has dominated recent American linguistics. Transformations convert the statement form into such derived forms as questions and commands. The possibility of another basic form or of several basic forms has rarely been elevated to the level of discussion.
27. Reported by Georg Henrik von Wright, in Norman Malcolm's *Ludwig Wittgenstein: A Memoir* (Oxford, 1970), p. 7.
28. Ibid., p. 29.

29. It is often the case that Wittgenstein reminds us of what we have so far known only operationally rather than conceptually, that is, he can help us recognize what we have been doing with language, even if we had never conceptualized it before. This is not unlike the process by which children can recognize, years after they have learned to talk, the accuracy of a grammatical description of what they have been doing when speaking.

30. In an impressive study of Wittgenstein's mode of writing, Binkley describes Wittgenstein's philosophizing as "thinking as it happens, not the results ordered, packaged, and neatly labelled" (Timothy Binkley, *Wittgenstein's Language* [The Hague, 1973], p. 201). In terms of Wittgenstein's procedure of composition this is not, of course, an accurate description, but it is a useful indication of the importance of action rather than result in Wittgenstein's thinking, and also of the priority of process over product. Binkley also offers valuable clarifications of the relationship between "use" and "usage" and of the status of the notion of "ordinary language" in Wittgenstein's philosophizing (pp. 94–102). Though there are many commentaries on *Philosophical Investigations,* Binkley's views on Wittgenstein's style of writing seem most steadily consistent with the techniques of the original, and his ideas parallel my own in several important respects.

31. This is not to say that there was no urge to do so. Derrida and the more persuasive of his followers often, at one stage of their work, read texts very carefully indeed (in terms that the authors might well approve). But that was only one stage of the process, and it was rarely clear that the constraints upon subsequent deconstruction registered anything of more general implication than the limited ingenuity of the deconstructer.

From the outset, there was, however, some inconsistency on the issue of generalizable controls in the otherwise happily heterogeneous field of deconstruction. J. Hillis Miller used the forum of the 1986 Presidential Address at the MLA Convention to offer a strong critique of those who failed to do justice to the intentions of the authors of deconstructive critical texts: "The misrepresentation of what Derrida or de Man says about history, politics, and the positive role of the humanities would be incredible if it did not so patently derive from the anxiety of the accusers." This rhetoric of grievance continues with accusations of a "blind refusal to read" and a "blatant and consistent violation of [a] basic ethical obligation." This is scathing commentary on the reading habits of others, but there is little awareness of possible inconsistency when Miller, in the very same paragraph, accompanies his attack on those who would misread the key texts of deconstruction with a reminder of something characteristic of all good reading but fundamental to deconstructive reading strategies—that careful, patient, and scrupulous reading must surely include "the elementary assumption that the text being read may say something different from what one wants or expects it to say or from what received opinion says it says." This is in turn followed by a (yet another) definition of deconstruction which confirms that what is regarded as indefensible when addressed to approved-of texts is still regarded as essential when addressed to others: "'Deconstruction' is the current name for the multiple and heterogeneous strategies of overturning and displacement that will liberate your own enterprise from what disables it" ("The Triumph of Theory, the Resistance to Reading, and the Question of the Material Base," *PMLA,* 102, May 1987, pp. 281–91). Elsewhere, Miller had remarked that "Deconstruction is not a dismantling of the structure of a text but a demonstration that it has already dismantled itself. Its apparently solid ground is no rock but thin air" ("Stevens' Rock and Criticism as Cure, Part 2," *Georgia Review,* 30, 1976, p. 341). To anyone conversant with the complexities of deconstruction, it is evident enough how these seeming inconsistencies might be relatable. Christopher Norris, for example, in his efforts to distinguish Derrida's real views from those of his American followers ("the US-domesticated variant"), emphasizes passages where Derrida focuses upon philosophical and interpretive controls (*What's Wrong with Postmodernism: Critical Theory and the Ends of Philosophy* [Hemel Hempstead, 1990], pp. 134–63). But deconstructers have not been, by and large, as committed to making visible and public what stands fast for them as they have been to make visible and public what does not. For his part, Wittgenstein had, of course, already done so.

32. Henry Staten, *Wittgenstein and Derrida* (Lincoln, 1984), p. 75. Wittgenstein would, of course, be reluctant to be regarded as the teacher of a method.
33. Charles Altieri, "Wittgenstein on Consciousness and Language: A Challenge to Derridean Literary Theory," *Modern Language Notes,* 91, December 1976, pp. 1397–1423. The general line of Altieri's argument is persuasive, but his attempt to convert the residue of ongoing action into an "irreducible ontological base" (p. 1409) involves an unfortunate turn of phrase, as does the argument that "the irreducible bases for human certainty are a variety of ways of acting" (p. 1418). Though one recognizes the Wittgenstein remarks from which Altieri is extrapolating, such formulations invite the kind of riposte that Staten is quick to supply: "Is there any more thoroughly *metaphysical* concept than this?" (Staten, *Wittgenstein and Derrida,* p. 75). Unless there is an ongoing interplay between action and the history of action such that the history of action continues to evolve, action becomes as static as empiricism.
34. Haas, "The Theory of Translation," p. 223.
35. Staten, *Wittgenstein and Derrida,* pp. 75–79.
36. William James, *Pragmatism: A New Name for Some Old Ways of Thinking,* in *"Pragmatism" and "The Meaning of Truth"* (Cambridge, Mass., 1978), p. 35. Though recent work in the history of science and elsewhere confirms that there are, nevertheless, moments of radical change in our thinking, it remains the case that these moments occur in spite of, rather than because of, characteristic attitudes toward radical novelty. Even after seemingly radical change, efforts often continue to rehabilitate some of the problematic past. Indeed, the history of interest in James and others with similar philosophical views illustrates the point. In *The Metaphysical Club* (New York, 2001), Louis Menand provides a magisterial study of the trajectory of pluralism and pragmatism in American thought from the Civil War through the Cold War to the present. Contrasting this intellectual climate after the Civil War with that during the Cold War, he argues: "The value at the bottom of the thought of Holmes, James, Peirce, and Dewey is tolerance. . . . The various offshoots of the pragmatist way of thinking—the educational philosophy, the pluralist conception of culture, the argument for expanded freedoms of expression—were, in a sense, translations of [the] individualist, Protestant ethic into social and secular terms. . . . Pragmatism was designed to make it harder for people to be driven to violence by their beliefs. . . . The Cold War [however] was a war over principles. . . . The notion that the values of the free society for which the Cold War was waged were contingent, relative, fallible constructions, good for some purposes and not so good for others, was not

a notion compatible with the moral imperatives of the age.... And once the Cold War ended, the ideas of Holmes, James, Peirce, and Dewey reemerged as suddenly as they had been eclipsed. Those writers began to be studied and debated with a seriousness and intensity, both in the United States and in other countries, that they had not attracted for forty years. For in the post-Cold War world, where there are many competing belief systems, not just two, skepticism about the finality of any particular set of beliefs has begun to seem to some people an important value again" (pp. 439–41).

37. Ludwig Wittgenstein, *On Certainty*, trans. Denis Paul and G. E. M. Anscombe (New York, 1969). All subsequent references to this text are indicated *OC* with accompanying page and paragraph numbers.

38. This is, of course, the only way that authors of the texts of deconstruction could themselves make claims about being appropriately or inappropriately read.

39. Wittgenstein's renewed concern for propositions in *On Certainty* arises from his interest in grappling with G. E. Moore's arguments about "Proof of an External World," *Proceedings of the British Academy*, 25, 1939, and "A Defence of Common Sense," *Contemporary British Philosophy*, ed. J. H. Muirhead (London, 1925). Note that Wittgenstein is not arguing that all modes of inquiry share the same common ground or that propositions ground all language-games. In some language-games presupposed propositions play a role "like that of rules of a game," while in those games and others there may also be other kinds of rules that provide the stability of the game. Note also Wittgenstein's comment that "the same proposition may get treated at one time as something to test by experience, at another as a rule of testing" (*OC*, p. 15, par. 95 and 98).

40. For a useful study of the evolution of *Philosophical Investigations* and for some stimulating ideas about the relationships between Part 1, Part 2, and *Zettel*, see Georg Henrik von Wright, "The Origin and Composition of Wittgenstein's *Investigations*," in *Wittgenstein: Sources and Perspectives*, ed. C. G. Luckhardt (Sussex, 1979), pp. 138–60.

41. Mikhail M. Bakhtin, *The Dialogic Imagination*, ed. Michael Holquist, trans. Caryl Emerson and Michael Holquist (Austin, 1981), p. 291.

42. Gerald Graff, *Professing Literature: An Institutional History* (Chicago, 1987), p. 257.

43. I have discussed these points in more detail in "Taking the Measure of Theoretical Models," *University of Hartford Studies in Literature*, 17, 1985, pp. 1–12. In his essay on "Human Understanding," Locke emphasizes the importance of the particular exemplar functioning as a mode of measuring the viability of more general principle, and of not allowing the latter simply to impose itself on the former. His cautionary tale in Book 4 ("Of Knowledge and Probability") describes the problematic migration of the rough generalization from an instrument of inquiry into an arbiter of reality and is thus of continuing consequence, whatever its other merits, for reasons immediately perceived by Sir James Mackintosh: "An amendment of the general habits of thought is ... an object as important as even the discovery of new truths.... In the mental and moral world, which scarcely admits of anything which can be called discovery, the correction of the intellectual habits is probably the greatest service which can be rendered to science. In this respect the merit of Locke is unrivalled" (p. 403n). Locke's key observations include the following: that "we take care that the name of *principles* deceive us not, nor impose on us, by making us receive that for an unquestionable truth, which is really at best but a very

doubtful conjecture"; that "rightly considered, the immediate object of all our reasoning and knowledge, is nothing but particulars"; that "in *particulars* our knowledge begins, and so spreads itself, by degrees, to *generals.* Though afterwards the mind takes the quite contrary course, and having drawn its knowledge into as general propositions as it can, makes those familiar to its thoughts, and accustoms itself to have recourse to them, as to the standards of truth and falsehood. By which familiar use of them, as rules to measure the truth of other propositions, it comes in time to be thought, that more particular propositions have their truth and evidence from their conformity to these more general ones, which, in discourse and argumentation, are so frequently urged, and constantly admitted"; and that, as a consequence, "Nothing can be so dangerous as *principles* thus *taken up without questioning or examination;* especially if they be such as concern morality, which influence men's lives, and give a bias to all their actions" (John Locke, *An Essay Concerning Human Understanding,* ed. Alexander Campbell Fraser [New York, 1959], Book 4, pp. 354, 404, 285, 344–45).

44. Citing several times my 1988 essay, "Wittgenstein's Philosophizing and Literary Theorizing," Susan B. Brill extends the notion of traveling beyond particular theories into a technique of "descriptive investigations" that she defines and exemplifies in ways that sometimes reintroduce some of the methodological problems outlined above. See, for example, her suggestion that "a reliance upon the philosophy of Ludwig Wittgenstein provides the literary critic with a descriptive methodology by means of which she will differentiate the diverse language games of a particular text" (*Wittgenstein and Critical Theory: Beyond Postmodernism and Toward Descriptive Investigations* [Athens, Ohio, 1995], pp. 30–32).

45. Bertolt Brecht, *Diaries, 1920–22,* ed. Herta Ramthun, trans. John Willett (New York, 1979), p. 42. "A man with one theory is lost. He needs several of them, four, lots!... You can live well surrounded by them, there are comfortable lodgings to be found between the theories. If you are to get on you need to know that there are a lot of theories...." (September 9, 1920).

CHAPTER 5: LITERARY AND CULTURAL STUDIES

1. Wayne C. Booth, *Critical Understanding: The Powers and Limits of Pluralism* (Chicago, 1979), pp. 211, 25–34.
2. Mikhail M. Bakhtin, *The Dialogic Imagination,* ed. Michael Holquist, trans. Caryl Emerson and Michael Holquist (Austin, 1981), p. 291. It is in this sense that Bakhtin can argue that "the language of a novel is the system of its 'languages'" (p. 262).
3. W. J. T. Mitchell, "Pluralism as Dogmatism," *Critical Inquiry,* Spring 1986, p. 494.
4. Ludwig Wittgenstein, *Philosophical Investigations,* trans. G. E. M. Anscombe (New York, 1969), pp. 32–33, par. 68. All subsequent quotations are from this edition and are indicated by *PI,* with accompanying page and paragraph references.
5. Ferdinand de Saussure, *Course in General Linguistics,* ed. Charles Bally and Albert Sechehaye, trans. Roy Harris (London, 1990), pp. 192–203.
6. Jean Genet, *The Balcony* (rev. ed. 1962), trans. Bernard Frechtman (New York, 1966), p. 96.

7. Barbara Johnson, "Teaching Deconstructively," *Writing and Reading Differently*, ed. G. Douglas Atkins and Michael L. Johnson (Lawrence, 1985), p. 140 (cited by Peter Washington, *Fraud: Literary Theory and the End of English* [London, 1989], p. 111). At her best, Johnson is an excellent close reader, but much of her best practice would fit comfortably within the enterprise of the New Critics, as would her recommendation that we "take indecision, frustration, and ambivalence, not as mere obstacles and incapacities, but as the very richness and instructiveness of the reading process" ("Teaching Deconstructively," p. 145).
8. Washington argues that "Both have their virtues, but on the debit side there is no difference between dogmatic positivism and dogmatic skepticism" (*Fraud*, p. 111).
9. Robyn R. Warhol and Diane Price Herndl, eds., *Feminisms: An Anthology of Literary Theory and Criticism* (New Brunswick, 1991). As the editors put it: "We've used the plural form 'feminisms,' rather than 'feminism,' to acknowledge the diversity of motivation, method, and experience among feminist academics. From the outside, 'feminism' may appear monolithic, unified, or singularly definable. The more intimately one becomes acquainted with feminist criticism, however, the more one sees the multiplicity of approaches and assumptions inside the movement" (p. x).
10. Michel Foucault, *Power/Knowledge: Selected Interviews and Other Writings, 1972–77*, ed. Colin Gordon (New York, 1980), p. 78.
11. Ibid., p. 80. See also his comment: "The attempt to think in terms of a totality has in fact proved a hindrance to research" (p. 81). Jean-François Lyotard generalizes the issue to "the nostalgia of the whole and the one" and exhorts us to "wage a war on totality" (*The Postmodern Condition: A Report on Knowledge* [Minneapolis, 1984], pp. 81–82).
12. Foucault, *Power/Knowledge*, p. 85.
13. Ibid., pp. 81, 79.
14. Ibid., p. 93.
15. Ibid.
16. John M. Ellis, "Radical Literary Theory," *London Review of Books*, 8 February 1990, p. 8.
17. M. A. K. Halliday, *Language as Social Semiotic: The Social Interpretation of Language and Meaning* (London, 1978), p. 38.
18. Ibid., p. 187.
19. Ellen Rooney, *Seductive Reasoning: Pluralism as the Problematic of Contemporary Literary Theory* (Ithaca, 1989), p. 2.
20. Ibid., pp. 1–2.
21. "Everything you can think of, however vast or inclusive, has on the pluralist view a *genuinely 'external' environment of some sort* or amount. Things are 'with' one another in many ways, but nothing includes everything, or dominates over everything. . . . If a thing were once disconnected, it could never be connected again, according to monism. The pragmatic difference between the two systems is thus a definite one. It is just thus, that if *a* is once out of sight of *b* or out of touch with it, or, more briefly, 'out' of it at all, then, according to monism, it must always remain so, they can never get together; whereas *pluralism admits that on another occasion they may work together, or in some way be connected again*" (emphases mine) (William James, *A Pluralistic Universe* [New York, 1909], pp. 321–24).

22. Saussure, *Course,* p. 112.
23. John M. Ellis, *Language, Thought, and Logic* (Evanston, 1993), pp. 62–63. I quote Ellis on this point at greater length in chapter 2.
24. René Wellek and Austin Warren, *Theory of Literature* (New York, 1956), pp. 151–57.
25. Ralph Cohen, "History and Genre," *New Literary History* 17, 1986, pp. 203–18. For related discussion of the internal multiplicity and evolving historicity of genres, see Alastair Fowler, *Kinds of Literature: An Introduction to the Theory of Genres and Modes* (Cambridge, Mass., 1982).
26. Arthur Miller, quoted by Nigella Lawson, "The Exorcism of Arthur Miller," *The Sunday Times* (London), 3 June 1990, sec. 5, pp. 1, 3. Parentheses added.
27. Bertolt Brecht, *Brecht on Theatre,* ed. and trans. John Willett (New York, 1964), p. 37.
28. Ibid., p. 44.
29. Ibid., p. 201.
30. Mae Gwendolyn Henderson, "Speaking in Tongues: Dialogics, Dialectics, and the Black Woman Writer's Literary Tradition," in *Reading Black, Reading Feminist: A Critical Anthology,* ed. Henry Louis Gates (New York, 1990), pp. 137–38.
31. Cleanth Brooks, *The Well Wrought Urn: Studies in the Structure of Poetry* (New York, 1947), p. 204.
32. A compatible consequence would be more of the illuminating kind of work exemplified in Morson's study of the temporality and contingency of novelistic form. His enthusiasm for a conceptual pluralism is informed by Isaiah Berlin's famous essay "The Hedgehog and the Fox," which Morson cogently summarizes and situates (Gary Saul Morson, *Narrative and Freedom: The Shadows of Time* [New Haven, 1994], pp. 269–73).
33. At the head of a major article surveying his own linguistic work, "A Synopsis of Linguistic Theory, 1930–55," J. R. Firth placed a famous remark by Goethe: "*Das Höchste wäre zu begreifen, das alles Faktische schon Theorie ist*" (*Selected Papers of J. R. Firth, 1952–59,* ed. F. R. Palmer [Bloomington, 1968], p. 168).
34. As Fish puts it: "It is interpretive communities, rather than either the text or the reader, that produce meanings and are responsible for the emergence of formal features" (Stanley Fish, *Is There a Text in This Class? The Authority of Interpretive Communities* [Cambridge, Mass., 1980], p. 14). Charles Sanders Peirce, "Pragmatism and Pragmaticism," *Collected Papers of Charles Sanders Peirce, vols. 5 and 6,* ed. Charles Hartshorne and Paul Weiss (Cambridge, Mass., 1965). Friedrich Nietzsche, "On Truth and Falsity in their Ultramoral Sense," *The Complete Works of Friedrich Nietzsche,* ed. Oscar Levy (New York, 1964), vol. 2, pp. 171–92. Karl R. Popper, *Objective Knowledge: An Evolutionary Approach* (Oxford, 1972). Paul Feyerabend, *Against Method* (London, 1978).
35. Thomas S. Kuhn, *The Structure of Scientific Revolutions* (Chicago, 1970). All page references are to this edition.
36. "Often, viewing all fields together, [science] seems . . . a rather ramshackle structure with little coherence among its various parts. Nothing said to this point should . . . conflict with that very familiar observation. On the contrary, substituting paradigms for rules should make the diversity of scientific fields and specialties easier to understand. . . . And even men who, being in the same or closely related fields, begin by studying many of the same books and achievements may acquire rather different paradigms in the course of

professional specialization.... In short, though quantum mechanics (or Newtonian dynamics, or electromagnetic theory) is a paradigm for many scientific groups, it is not the same paradigm for them all" (ibid., pp. 49–50).

37. "All or most of the objects of group commitment that my original text makes paradigms, parts of paradigms, or paradigmatic are constituents of the disciplinary matrix, and as such they form a whole and function together. They are, however, no longer to be discussed as though they were all of a piece" (ibid., p. 182). See again, in this respect, Scholes's counterargument to Fish's notion of the homogeneity and authority of "interpretive communities" (chapter 1, note 34). The key point in literary studies is whether we conceive of each individual's beliefs as a homogeneous and inert set of fixed convictions or as a heterogeneous evolving set of different kinds and degrees of belief that have evolved from a vast array of experiences of many kinds over many years and continue to evolve. An interpretive community of the latter individuals, based on a variety of kinds of similarities and differences among its members, provides a different investigative context than a community of the former, whose comparative unity provides all the problems that Kuhn repeatedly confronts of accounting for change of belief.

38. Saussure, *Course,* p. 131.

39. Edward Pechter, "The New Historicism and Its Discontents: Politicizing Renaissance Drama," *PMLA,* 102 (3), 1987, pp. 292–303. Efforts to develop a new literary history predate by many years, of course, the activities of the New Historicists. The journal *New Literary History,* for example, began publishing in 1969.

40. J. Hillis Miller, "Deconstructing the Deconstructers," *Diacritics,* 5 (2), Summer 1975, p. 31.

41. Paul A. Cantor, "Stephen Greenblatt's New Historicist Vision," *Academic Questions,* Fall 1993, p. 24.

42. Ibid., p. 25.

43. For example, Jane Marcus cites an unpublished paper by Gayatri Spivak that contains the following remark: "To embrace pluralism ... is to espouse the politics of the masculinist establishment. Pluralism is the method employed by the *central* authorities to neutralize opposition by seeming to accept it. The gesture of pluralism on the part of the *marginal* can only mean capitulation to the center" (Jane Marcus, "Storming the Toolshed," in Warhol and Herndl, *Feminisms,* p. 150). It is not yet clear that the voice of resistance or subversion can lead any further, when the presupposed cultural text constrains the creative potential of any literary text written in that era. As Louis Montrose puts it, there is an unresolved debate "between those who emphasize the possibilities for subversion of the dominant ideology and those who emphasize its hegemonic capacity to contain all such attempts" ("Renaissance Literary Studies and the Subject of History," *English Literary Renaissance,* 16 (1), Winter 1986, p. 10).

44. Bakhtin, *The Dialogic Imagination,* pp. 270–75. The equivalent contrast in postcolonial theory is registered in discussion of literatures of "oppression" and "repression" on the one hand, and "resistance" and "subversion" on the other, with various forms of hybridization providing one of the ways forward.

45. As Kastan puts it in reviewing Greenblatt's New Historicist procedures: "The 'particular and local pressures' ... that worked to challenge and disperse power in Renaissance En-

gland get folded into the anonymous operations of a power that is ubiquitous and absolute" (David Scott Kastan, "Demanding History," *Medieval and Renaissance Drama in England*, 5, 1991, p. 347).
46. "The second use of history is the systematic dissociation of identity. This is necessary because this rather weak identity, which we attempt to support and to unify under a mask, is in itself only a parody: it is plural; countless spirits dispute its possession; numerous systems intersect and compete. . . . The purpose of history, guided by genealogy, is not to discover the roots of our identity, but to commit itself to its dissipation" (Michel Foucault, "Nietzsche, Genealogy, History," in *The Foucault Reader*, ed. Paul Rabinow [New York, 1984], pp. 94–95). See also *Power/Knowledge*, p. 117, and "The Subject and Power," afterword in *Michel Foucault: Beyond Structuralism and Hermeneutics,* ed. H. L. Dreyfus and Paul Rabinow (London, 1982).
47. See, for example, Bakhtin's characterization of the contested nature of linguistic exchange: "Language is not a neutral medium that passes freely and easily into the private property of the speaker's intentions; it is populated—overpopulated—with the intentions of others. Expropriating it, forcing it to submit to one's own intentions and accents, is a difficult and complicated process" (*The Dialogic Imagination*, p. 294).
48. Peter Weiss, *Marat/Sade* (New York, 1969), p. 57.
49. It is, of course, interesting to note that, when Montrose ("Renaissance Literary Studies and the Subject of History," p. 9) cites Perry Anderson's remarks that the "'one masterproblem around which *all* contenders have revolved' in the agon of contemporary social theory is 'essentially, the nature of the relationships between structure and subject in human history and society'" (*In the Tracks of Historical Materialism* [Chicago, 1984]), a new vocabulary is being used to revisit the Wellek and Warren question discussed earlier (see preface) about whether we read Shakespeare to learn about his unique individuality or his historical typicality. Montrose recognizes and rejects (as did Wellek and Warren) the invitation such formulations offer for us to choose between conceptions of freedom and necessity so polarized that they promote those oscillations between relativism and monism that are characteristic of recent work in literary studies: "The freely self-creating and world-creating subject of bourgeois humanism is now (at least in theory) defunct. The recent trend in a variety of disciplines has been a perhaps overcompensatory positing of subject as wholly determined by structure. I believe that we should resist the inevitably reductive tendency to think in terms of a subject/structure opposition. Instead, we might entertain the propositions that subject and structure, the processes of subjectification and structuration, are interdependent, and thus intrinsically social and historical; that social systems are produced and reproduced in the interactive social practices of individuals and groups, that collective structures may enable as well as constrain individual agency" (pp. 9–10).

Montrose indicates his indebtedness for these insights to Anthony Giddens, *Central Problems in Social Theory* (Berkeley, 1979) and Teresa de Lauretis, *Alice Doesn't: Feminism, Semiotics, Cinema* (Bloomington, 1984). As the latter puts it: "Subjectivity is an ongoing construction, not a fixed point of departure or arrival from which one then interacts with the world. On the contrary, it is the effect of that interaction . . . and thus it is produced not by external ideas, values, or material causes, but by one's personal, subjective, en-

gagement in the practices, discourses, and institutions that lend significance (value, meaning, and affect) to the events of the world" (*Alice Doesn't*, p. 159).
50. John M. Ellis, *The Theory of Literary Criticism: A Logical Analysis* (Berkeley, 1974), p. 224.
51. For related discussion, see ibid., pp. 121–54.
52. The difficulty of maintaining the appropriate balance between the particular and the general is nicely formulated by Ellis when he argues that historicist period generalizations tend to distort the complex actualities of society and history: "there is more diversity in any group of human beings than they allow, and conversely more continuity in the range of human concerns from one age to the next" (ibid., pp. 226–27).
53. Jean Howard, "The New Historicism in Renaissance Studies," *English Literary Renaissance*, 16, Winter 1986, pp. 42, 39.
54. When Montrose draws attention to the debate "between those who emphasize the possibilities for subversion of the dominant ideology and those who emphasize its hegemonic capacity to contain all such attempts" ("Renaissance Literary Studies and the Subject of History," p. 10), he is approaching from another angle the conflict between the critic's attempt to give the voice(s) of the literary text priority over those of the presupposed cultural text, and the historicist's attempt to reverse that order of priority. It is at the extremes, as Pechter points out, that formalism, on the one hand, becomes a decontextualized free play of interacting signs and historicism, on the other, becomes the crude imposition of a posited cultural text on any literary text written in a particular era. Between these two extremes there are many other kinds of relationships that could be contemplated between the voices of critics and the voices of historians: "We may indeed need [a poetics of Elizabethan power], as we needed and still need [Tillyard's] Elizabethan World Picture, but we need a lot more besides" ("The New Historicism," p. 294).
55. "Acquiring power over the text will seem a costly achievement, since what it sacrifices is the potential power of the text—the power to open up new areas of experience, unfamiliar ways of being in the world. New-historicist procedures are designed to resist any such power, to work around or get beyond immediate textual impressions to arrive at a predetermined point of theoretical understanding, which is the point from which one comes to the text in the first place. . . . New-historicist criticism is a criticism of recognition, of knowing again what one knew before. . . . Putting the text back into history (or better, histories: our histories, its histories) is clearly a valuable project. Maybe it is the only project. In any case, it is far too important to be left to the new historicists" (Pechter, "The New Historicism," pp. 301–2).
56. Ellis, *The Theory of Literary Criticism*, p. 140.
57. For further discussion of this point, see Gerald Graff, *Professing Literature: An Institutional History* (Chicago, 1987), p. 190; and Wayne C. Booth, *Critical Understanding*, p. 241.
58. Cleanth Brooks, *The Well Wrought Urn*, pp. 192–214. See also Michel de Montaigne's remark on the value of interpreters: "Aristotle wrote to be understood. If he did not succeed, still less will another who is not as skilful and is expressing ideas that are not his own" ("Of Experience," *The Essays of Michel de Montaigne*, vol. 3, trans. Jacob Zeitlin [New York, 1936], p. 267).
59. Brooks, *The Well Wrought Urn*, pp. 203–4.

60. "What we may call the systematics of phonetics and phonology, of grammatical categories or of semantics, are ordered schematic constructs, frames of reference, a sort of scaffolding for the handling of [language] events. . . . Our schematic constructs . . . are neither immanent nor transcendent, but just language turned back on itself" (J. R. Firth, *Papers in Linguistics, 1934–51* [London, 1969], p. 181).
61. Wolfgang Iser, *The Act of Reading: A Theory of Aesthetic Response* (Baltimore, 1978).
62. Brooks describes critical formulations in general and summaries of textual statement in particular as "scaffoldings which we may properly for certain purposes throw about the building: we must not mistake them for the internal and essential structure of the building itself" (*The Well Wrought Urn,* p. 199).
63. Hirsch raises this issue to illustrate the appeal and inadequacy of arguments for the existence of unique language-games (E. D. Hirsch, *Validity in Interpretation* [New Haven, 1967], p. 70).
64. Mikhail Bakhtin, *Problems of Dostoevsky's Poetics,* ed. and trans. Caryl Emerson (Minneapolis, 1984), Appendix 2. p. 293. Though the originality and importance of Bakhtin's work in this regard are evident enough, a dialogic mode of disciplinary inquiry needs to find its way beyond both Bakhtin's sometimes directionless emphasis upon the open-endedness of dialogics and his apparent conviction that there is no historical precedent for thinking and inquiring in explicitly dialogical terms, even in the restricted senses in which he uses the word.
65. See the famous passage on the superiority of the spoken word over the written: Plato, *Phaedrus,* trans. R. Hackforth (Cambridge, U.K., 1952), pp. 156–62.
66. Montaigne, "Of Experience," pp. 267–69.
67. Ibid., p. 289. See Vološinov's related remarks: "*Word is a two-sided act.* It is determined equally by *whose* word it is and *for whom* it is meant. As word, it is precisely *the product of the reciprocal relationship between speaker and listener, addresser and addressee. . . .* I give myself verbal shape from another's point of view" (V. N. Vološinov, *Marxism and the Philosophy of Language,* trans. Ladislav Matejka and I. R. Titunik [New York, 1973], p. 86).
68. Richard Waswo, *Language and Meaning in the Renaissance* (Princeton, 1987), pp. 180–81. As Montaigne puts it: "Our opinions are grafted one upon another. The first serves as a stock to the second, the second to the third. Thus step by step we climb the ladder. Thence it comes to pass that he who is mounted the highest has often more honour than merit, for he has only raised himself a grain's height on the shoulders of the last but one" ("Of Experience" p. 269).
69. Waswo, *Language and Meaning,* p. 181.
70. Wittgenstein, *PI,* p. 41, par. 88 (exactness); pp. 26–27, par. 53–54 (rules); p. 34, par. 71 (examples).
71. Booth, *Critical Understanding,* pp. 242–43. Booth's footnote to this remark is also pertinent: "It is perhaps important to make clear that in adopting the language of violation I do not mean to accept the notion, made popular by Barthes, that somehow the pleasures of violation are superior to those of loving surrender, nor the notion that to ask and answer appropriate questions is necessarily a more passive work than imposing one's predetermined questions. It is really romantic tosh to assume that playing 'one's own' games

with Shakespeare or Homer, or even Balzac, is more blissful or more active than the exhilarating task of attempting to meet their demands."
72. Wittgenstein, *PI*, pp. 39–40, par. 85.
73. Booth, *Critical Understanding*, p. 242.
74. Hirsch began to make the case for distinguishing meaning and significance in "Objective Interpretation," *PMLA*, 75, September 1960, pp. 463–79, and developed it further in *The Aims of Interpretation* (Chicago, 1976), pp. 1–13, 74–92.
75. "Cultural Explanations," *The Economist*, 9 November 1996, pp. 23, 25.
76. Ibid., p. 24. The level of generality at which postcolonial theory seeks to function, for example, often involves a homogenizing of "the West" into a single version of its imperialist projects, largely erasing the historical, cultural, and social divisions readily exemplified on a variety of scales in any serious study of differences within and among the various societies so categorized. See, for example, Bernstein's work on the role of elaborated and restricted linguistic codes (Basil Bernstein, "A Socio-linguistic Approach to Social Learning," *Class, Codes, and Control*, vol. 1 [London, 1971]). See also Gandhi's discussion of "non-players" and variously situated players on all sides of imperialist projects (Leela Gandhi, *Postcolonial Theory* [New York, 1998], pp. 167–76).
77. Ellis provides an informative perspective on such issues in *The Theory of Literary Criticism*, pp. 104–54.
78. Irina says of her sister Masha, "She has forgotten how by now. It's three years since she's played. . . . Or four." Irina's ability to speak Italian has similarly slipped gradually away. "I don't remember what in Italian *window* is, or the ceiling there. . . . I'm forgetting everything, every day forgetting," and Tchebutykin has similarly lost touch with his medical training. "They think I'm a doctor, know how to cure any sickness, but I know absolutely nothing. . . . Yes . . . I knew a little something twenty-five years ago, but now I don't remember anything. Nothing" (Anton Chekhov, *The Three Sisters: Best Plays by Chekhov*, trans. Stark Young [New York, 1956], pp. 192, 198, 190).
79. Halliday, *Social Semiotic*, p. 81.
80. Ellis, *The Theory of Literary Criticism*, pp. 147–54, 223–27.
81. As Ellis puts it: "For the most part, technical innovations in literature are new practices from among a range of possibilities that has always been and will continue to be available. One possibility does not supersede the other, and after an innovation by one author, another may return to a previously existing possibility. There is no necessary idea of sequence here" (ibid., pp. 219–20). See also Richard Schechner, *Performance Theory* (New York, 1988), pp. 30–31.
82. The relationship between evolutionary and revolutionary change has precipitated considerable debate over the years. See, for example, Edward Young's famous and not readily consistent remarks on literary creativity: "It is prudence to read, genius to relish, glory to surpass, antient authors," and "rules, like crutches, are a needful aid to the lame, tho' an impediment to the strong" ("Conjectures on Original Composition" [1759], in *The Great Critics: An Anthology of Literary Criticism*, ed. James Harry Smith and Edd Winfield Parks [New York, 1932], pp. 429, 415). See also my discussion of Kuhn's work earlier in this chapter and my remarks on evolutionary and revolutionary change in "Taking the Measure of Theoretical Models," *University of Hartford Studies in Literature*, 17, 1985, pp. 4–8.

83. Graff, *Professing Literature,* p. 252.
84. See Iser, *The Act of Reading.*
85. Firth, *Selected Papers,* p. 190. See also Firth's remark: "Linguistic analysis must be polysystemic. For any given language there is no coherent system (*où tout se tient*) which can handle and state all the facts" (p. 24). An illuminating account of creative thinking on a variety of sites and scales is provided by Alfred North Whitehead, "The Rhythmic Claims of Freedom and Discipline," *The Aims of Education and Other Essays* (New York, 1929), pp. 45–65.
86. Firth regularly insisted upon the importance of the role of the linguist in persuasively relating theoretical principles and descriptive techniques to the evolving complexities of actual utterances: "The linguist must be clearly aware of the levels at which he is making his abstractions and statements and must finally prove his theory by *renewal of connection* with the processes and patterns of life. Without this constant reapplication to the flux of experience, abstract linguistics has no justification" (ibid., p. 19). See also Firth's comment that it is in "the study of conversation . . . [that] we shall find the key to a better understanding of what language really is and how it works" (*Papers,* p. 32).
87. Wittgenstein, *PI,* pp. 59, 72–73, 74, pars. 151, 179, 183.

Bibliography

Altieri, Charles. "Wittgenstein on Consciousness and Language: A Challenge to Derridean Literary Theory." *Modern Language Notes,* 91, December 1976, pp. 1397–1423.
Anderson, Perry. *In the Tracks of Historical Materialism.* Chicago, 1984.
Armstrong, Paul B. *Conflicting Readings: Variety and Validity in Interpretation.* Chapel Hill, 1990.
Atkins, G. Douglas, and Johnson, Michael L., eds. *Writing and Reading Differently.* Lawrence, 1985.
Austin, J. L. *How to Do Things with Words.* Cambridge, Mass., 1962.
Bakhtin, Mikhail M. *The Dialogic Imagination.* Ed. Michael Holquist, trans. Caryl Emerson and Michael Holquist. Austin, 1981.
———. *Problems of Dostoevsky's Poetics.* Ed. and trans. Caryl Emerson. Minneapolis, 1984.
———. *Rabelais and His World.* Trans. Hélène Iswolsky. Cambridge, Mass., 1968.
Barthes, Roland. *Elements of Semiology.* Trans. Annette Lavers and Colin Smith. New York, 1967.
———. *The Fashion System.* Trans. Matthew Ward and Richard Howard. Berkeley, 1990.
———. *Image, Music, Text.* Trans. Stephen Heath. New York, 1977.
———. *S/Z.* Trans. Richard Miller. New York, 1974.

Beattie, James. *The Theory of Language, 1788.* London, 1968.
Berlin, Isaiah. *The Hedgehog and the Fox: An Essay on Tolstoy's View of History.* New York, 1970.
Bernstein, Basil. *Class, Codes, and Control,* vol. 1. London, 1971.
Bhabha, Homi K. *The Location of Culture.* London, 1994.
Binkley, Timothy. *Wittgenstein's Language.* The Hague, 1973.
Bloom, Harold, et al., eds. *Deconstruction and Criticism.* New York, 1979.
Booth, Wayne C. *Critical Understanding: The Powers and Limits of Pluralism.* Chicago, 1979.
Brecht, Bertolt. *Brecht on Theatre.* Ed. and trans. John Willett. New York, 1964.
———. *Diaries, 1920–22.* Ed. Herta Ramthun, trans. John Willett. New York, 1979.
Brill, Susan B. *Wittgenstein and Critical Theory: Beyond Postmodernism and Toward Descriptive Investigations.* Athens, 1995.
Brooks, Cleanth. *The Well Wrought Urn: Studies in the Structure of Poetry.* New York, 1947.
Cantor, Paul A. "The Primacy of the Literary Imagination, *or* Which Came First: The Critic or the Author?" *Literary Imagination,* 1 (1), Spring 1999, pp. 131–51.
———. "Stephen Greenblatt's New Historicist Vision." *Academic Questions,* Fall 1993, pp. 21–36.
Cassirer, Ernst. *The Philosophy of Symbolic Forms,* vol. 1. Trans. Ralph Manheim. New Haven, 1953.
Cavell, Stanley. *Must We Mean What We Say?* Cambridge, U.K., 1976.
Chekhov, Anton. *The Three Sisters: Best Plays by Chekhov.* Trans. Stark Young. New York, 1956.
Chomsky, Noam. *Aspects of the Theory of Syntax.* Cambridge, Mass., 1965.
———. *The Minimalist Program.* Cambridge, Mass., 1995.
———. *Syntactic Structures.* The Hague, 1957.
Cohen, Ralph. "History and Genre." *New Literary History,* 17, 1986, pp. 203–18.
Crane, Ronald S. *The Languages of Criticism and the Structure of Poetry.* Chicago, 1986.
Culler, Jonathan. *On Deconstruction: Theory and Criticism after Structuralism.* Ithaca, 1982.
"Cultural Explanations." *The Economist,* 9 November 1996, pp. 23–26.
Damrosch, David. *We Scholars: Changing the Culture of the University.* Cambridge, Mass., 1995.
Davis, Philip W. *Modern Theories of Language.* Englewood Cliffs, 1973.
Derrida, Jacques. *Glas.* Trans. John P. Leavey and Richard Rand. Lincoln, 1986.
———. *Of Grammatology.* Trans. Gayatri Chakravorty Spivak. Baltimore, 1976.
———. *Writing and Difference.* Trans. Alan Bass. Chicago, 1978.
Dreitzel, Hans Peter, ed. *Recent Sociology, No. 2: Patterns of Communicative Behavior.* New York, 1970.
Dreyfus, H. L., and Paul Rabinow, eds. *Michel Foucault: Beyond Structuralism and Hermeneutics.* London, 1982.
Eco, Umberto. *A Theory of Semiotics.* Bloomington, 1976.
Eliot, George. *Middlemarch.* Middlesex, 1965.
Eliot, T. S. *The Complete Poems and Plays, 1909–1950.* New York, 1980.
Ellis, John M. *Against Deconstruction.* Princeton, 1989.
———. *Language, Thought, and Logic.* Evanston, 1993.

———. *Literature Lost: Social Agendas and the Corruption of the Humanities.* New Haven, 1997.
———. "Radical Literary Theory." *London Review of Books,* 8 February 1990, pp. 7–8.
———. *The Theory of Literary Criticism: A Logical Analysis.* Berkeley, 1974.
Feyerabend, Paul. *Against Method.* London, 1978.
Firth, J. R. *Papers in Linguistics, 1934–51.* London, 1969.
———. *Selected Papers of J. R. Firth, 1952–59.* Ed. F. R. Palmer. Bloomington, 1968.
Fischer, Michael. "Perspectivism and Literary Theory Today." *American Literary History,* 2 (3), Fall 1990, pp. 528–49.
Fish, Stanley. *Is There a Text in This Class? The Authority of Interpretive Communities.* Cambridge, Mass., 1980.
Forster, E. M. *Two Cheers for Democracy.* London, 1972.
———. *A Passage to India.* New York, 1984.
Foucault, Michel. *Power/Knowledge: Selected Interviews and Other Writings, 1972–77.* Ed. Colin Gordon. New York, 1980.
Fowler, Alastair. *Kinds of Literature: An Introduction to the Theory of Genres and Modes.* Cambridge, Mass., 1982.
Gandhi, Leela. *Postcolonial Theory.* New York, 1998.
Gates, Henry Louis, ed. *Reading Black, Reading Feminist: A Critical Anthology.* New York, 1990.
Genet, Jean. *The Balcony,* rev. ed. 1962. Trans. Bernard Frechtman. New York, 1966.
Geuss, Raymond. *The Idea of a Critical Theory.* Cambridge, U.K., 1981.
Giddens, Anthony. *Central Problems in Social Theory.* Berkeley, 1979.
Graff, Gerald. *Professing Literature: An Institutional History.* Chicago, 1987.
Graham, Keith. *J. L. Austin: A Critique of Ordinary Language Philosophy.* Sussex, 1977.
Grigson, Geoffrey, ed. *Before the Romantics: An Anthology of the Enlightenment.* Edinburgh, 1984.
Grinder, J. T., and S. H. Elgin. *Guide to Transformational Grammar: History, Theory, Practice.* New York, 1973.
Haas, W. "The Theory of Translation." *Philosophy,* 37, July 1962, pp. 208–28.
Halliday, M. A. K. *Explorations in the Functions of Language.* London, 1973.
———. *Language as Social Semiotic: The Social Interpretation of Language and Meaning.* London, 1978.
Halliday, M. A. K., Angus McIntosh, Peter Strevens. *The Linguistic Sciences and Language Teaching.* London, 1964.
Harrison, Bernard. "Review of J. J. Katz, *Semantic Theory.*" *Mind,* 83, October 1974, pp. 599–606.
Hirsch, E. D. *The Aims of Interpretation.* Chicago, 1976.
———. "Objective Interpretation." *PMLA,* 75, September 1960, pp. 463–79.
———. *Validity in Interpretation.* New Haven, 1967.
Howard, Jean. "The New Historicism in Renaissance Studies." *English Literary Renaissance,* 16, Winter 1986, pp. 13–43.
Hyman, Stanley Edgar. *The Armed Vision.* New York, 1955.
Iser, Wolfgang. *The Act of Reading: A Theory of Aesthetic Response.* Baltimore, 1978.

James, William. *A Pluralistic Universe.* New York, 1909.

———. *Pragmatism: A New Name for Some Old Ways of Thinking,* in *"Pragmatism" and "The Meaning of Truth."* Cambridge, Mass., 1978.

Joyce, James. *A Portrait of the Artist as a Young Man.* New York, 1983.

Kant, Immanuel. *Critique of Pure Reason.* Trans. Norman Kemp Smith. London, 1950.

Kastan, David Scott. "Demanding History." *Medieval and Renaissance Drama in England,* 5, 1991, pp. 343–53.

Katz, Jerrold J. *Semantic Theory.* New York, 1972.

Katz, Jerrold J., and Jerry A. Fodor. "The Structure of a Semantic Theory." *Language,* 39 (2), 1963, pp. 170–210.

Kress, Gunther, ed. *Halliday: System and Function in Language.* London, 1976.

Kuhn, Thomas S. *The Structure of Scientific Revolutions.* Chicago, 1970.

Labov, William. *The Social Stratification of English in New York City.* Washington, 1966.

Lauretis, Teresa de. *Alice Doesn't: Feminism, Semiotics, Cinema.* Bloomington, 1984.

Lawson, Nigella. "The Exorcism of Arthur Miller." *The Sunday Times* (London), 3 June 1990, sec. 5, pp. 1–3.

Lentricchia, Frank. "Last Will and Testament of an Ex-Literary Critic." *Lingua Franca,* 6 (6), September/October 1996, pp. 59–67.

Lévi-Strauss, Claude. *From Honey to Ashes: Introduction to a Science of Mythology,* vol. 2. Trans. John Weightman and Doreen Weightman. London, 1973.

———. *The Raw and the Cooked: Introduction to a Science of Mythology,* vol. 1. Trans. John Weightman and Doreen Weightman. London, 1970.

———. *Structural Anthropology.* Trans. Claire Jacobson and Brooke Grundfest Schoepf. London, 1968.

———. *Tristes Tropiques.* Trans. John Weightman and Doreen Weightman. New York, 1981.

Locke, John. *An Essay Concerning Human Understanding.* Ed. Alexander Campbell Fraser. New York, 1959.

Luckhardt, C. G. *Wittgenstein: Sources and Perspectives.* Sussex, 1979.

Lyons, John. *Introduction to Theoretical Linguistics.* Cambridge, U.K., 1969.

Lyotard, Jean-François. *The Postmodern Condition: A Report on Knowledge.* Minneapolis, 1984.

Malcolm, Norman. *Ludwig Wittgenstein: A Memoir.* Oxford, 1970.

Martinich, A. P., ed. *The Philosophy of Language.* New York, 1985.

Matejka, Ladislav, and Krystyna Pomorska, eds. *Readings in Russian Poetics: Formalist and Structuralist Views.* Ann Arbor, 1978.

McClintock, Anne. "The Angel of Progress: Pitfalls of the Term 'Post-Colonialism.'" *Social Text,* 31/32, 1992, pp. 84–98.

McKeon, Richard. "Criticism and the Liberal Arts: The Chicago School of Criticism." *Profession,* 82, 1982, pp. 1–18.

Medvedev, P. N. *The Formal Method in Literary Scholarship: A Critical Introduction to Sociological Poetics.* Trans. Albert J. Wehrle. Cambridge, Mass., 1978.

Meillet, Antoine. *The Comparative Method in Historical Linguistics.* Trans. Gordon B. Ford. Paris, 1966.

Menand, Louis. *The Metaphysical Club.* New York, 2001.

Miller, J. Hillis. "Deconstructing the Deconstructers." *Diacritics,* 5 (2), Summer 1975, pp. 24–31.

———. "Stevens' Rock and Criticism as Cure, Part 2." *Georgia Review,* 30, 1976, pp. 330–48.

———. "The Triumph of Theory, the Resistance to Reading, and the Question of the Material Base." *PMLA,* 102, May 1987, pp. 281–91.

Mitchell, W. J. T., ed. *Against Theory.* Chicago, 1985.

———. "Pluralism as Dogmatism." *Critical Inquiry,* Spring 1986, pp. 494–502.

Montaigne, Michel de. *The Essays of Michel de Montaigne,* vol. 3. Trans. Jacob Zeitlin. New York, 1936.

Montrose, Louis. "Renaissance Literary Studies and the Subject of History." *English Literary Renaissance,* 16 (1), Winter 1986, pp. 5–12.

Moore, G. E. "Proof of an External World." *Proceedings of the British Academy,* 25, 1939, pp. 273–300.

Morson, Gary Saul. *Narrative and Freedom: The Shadows of Time.* New Haven, 1994.

Morson, Gary Saul, and Caryl Emerson. *Mikhail Bakhtin: Creation of a Prosaics.* Stanford, 1990.

Muirhead, J. H., ed. *Contemporary British Philosophy.* London, 1925.

Newman, John Henry. *The Idea of a University.* Ed. Frank M. Turner. New Haven, 1996.

Nietzsche, Friedrich. *The Complete Works of Friedrich Nietzsche,* vol. 2. Ed. Oscar Levy. New York, 1964.

Norris, Christopher. *What's Wrong with Postmodernism: Critical Theory and the Ends of Philosophy.* Hemel Hempstead, 1990.

Ogden, C. K. *Opposition: A Linguistic and Psychological Analysis.* Bloomington, 1967.

Orwell, George. *Nineteen Eighty-Four.* New York, 1982.

Parret, H., ed. *Discussing Language.* The Hague, 1974.

Pavel, Thomas G. *The Feud of Language: A History of Structuralist Thought.* Trans. Linda Jordan and Thomas G. Pavel. Oxford, 1989.

Pechter, Edward. "The New Historicism and Its Discontents: Politicizing Renaissance Drama." *PMLA,* 102 (3), 1987, pp. 292–303.

Peirce, Charles Sanders. *Collected Papers of Charles Sanders Peirce,* vols. 5 and 6. Ed. Charles Hartshorne and Paul Weiss. Cambridge, Mass., 1965.

Plato. *Phaedrus.* Trans. R. Hackforth. Cambridge, U.K., 1952.

Popper, Karl R. *Objective Knowledge: An Evolutionary Approach.* Oxford, 1972.

Quigley, Austin E. "Taking the Measure of Theoretical Models." *University of Hartford Studies in Literature,* 17, 1985, pp. 1–12.

———. "Wittgenstein's Philosophizing and Literary Theorizing." *New Literary History,* 19, Winter 1988, pp. 209–37.

Rabinow, Paul., ed. *The Foucault Reader.* New York, 1984.

Rooney, Ellen. *Seductive Reasoning: Pluralism as the Problematic of Contemporary Literary Theory.* Ithaca, 1989.

Rorty, Richard. *Consequences of Pragmatism.* Minneapolis, 1982.

———. *Contingency, Irony, and Solidarity.* Cambridge, U.K., 1989.

———. *Philosophy and the Mirror of Nature.* Princeton, 1979.

Sampson, Geoffrey. *Making Sense*. Oxford, 1980.
Sapir, Edward. *Selected Writings of Edward Sapir*. Berkeley, 1949.
Saussure, Ferdinand de. *Course in General Linguistics*. Ed. Charles Bally and Albert Sechehaye, trans. Roy Harris. London, 1990.
Schechner, Richard. *Performance Theory*. New York, 1988.
Scholes, Robert. *Textual Power: Literary Theory and the Teaching of English*. New Haven, 1985.
Smith, James Harry, and Edd Winfield Parks, eds. *The Great Critics: An Anthology of Literary Criticism*. New York, 1932.
Staten, Henry. *Wittgenstein and Derrida*. Lincoln, 1984.
Stoppard, Tom. *Arcadia*. London, 1993.
Strang, Barbara M. H. *A History of English*. London, 1970.
Tillyard, E. M. W. *The Elizabethan World Picture*. London, 1956.
Trilling, Lionel. *The Liberal Imagination*. New York, 1950.
Vickers, Brian. *Appropriating Shakespeare: Contemporary Critical Quarrels*. New Haven, 1993.
Vološinov, V. N. *Marxism and the Philosophy of Language*. Trans. Ladislav Matejka and I. R. Titunik. New York, 1973.
Warhol, Robyn R., and Diane Price Herndl, eds. *Feminisms: An Anthology of Literary Theory and Criticism*. New Brunswick, 1991.
Washington, Peter. *Fraud: Literary Theory and the End of English*. London, 1989.
Waswo, Richard. *Language and Meaning in the Renaissance*. Princeton, 1987.
Weiss, Peter. *Marat/Sade*. New York, 1969.
Wellek, René, and Austin Warren. *Theory of Literature*. New York, 1956.
Whitehead, Alfred North. *The Aims of Education and Other Essays*. New York, 1929.
Wittgenstein, Ludwig. *The Blue and Brown Books*. New York, 1965.
———. *On Certainty*. Trans. Denis Paul and G. E. M. Anscombe. New York, 1969.
———. *Philosophical Investigations*. Trans. G. E. M. Anscombe. New York, 1969.
———. *Tractatus Logico-Philosophicus*. Trans. D. F. Pears and B. F. McGuinness. London, 1969.
———. *Zettel*. Ed. G. E. M. Anscombe and G. H. von Wright, trans. G. E. M. Anscombe. Berkeley, 1970.
Woodring, Carl. *Literature: An Embattled Profession*. New York, 1999.
Woolf, Virginia. *To the Lighthouse*. Middlesex, 1964.
Yeats, W. B. *Selected Poetry*. Ed. A. Norman Jeffares. London, 1968.

Acknowledgments

Throughout my many years at the University of Virginia, Ralph Cohen convened regular meetings of a "theory group," which was drawn from the faculty of several departments and enriched by a range of visitors from many parts of the United States and from other parts of the world. It was my good fortune to benefit not only from the lively debate among colleagues and guests but also from many conversations with Ralph himself about a variety of literary theories and about theory in general.

My first encounter with the problematics of theory and "theory hope" occurred much earlier, however, and I remain indebted to Peter Shaw, who introduced me at an early point in my education to the work of Wittgenstein and to his cautionary phrase: "We may not advance any kind of theory." Margaret Berry, at about the same time, encouraged my interest in the rapidly developing discipline of linguistics and I am grateful to her for that, and also to John McH. Sinclair, whose constant skepticism about each new linguistic theory has been matched only by his vigorous enthusiasm for coming to terms with the next one. I learned a lot from all three of these scholars about issues in linguistics that remain as central now as they were then to the discipline of literary studies.

My thinking about theoretical issues in a variety of domains has been considerably sharpened over the years by long conversations with John Ellis, whose several books on literary theory have provided models of rigorously sustained logical analysis. His recent readiness to subject to such intellectual scrutiny the theoretical and political orthodoxies of both left and right has served to raise serious questions about the extent to which the politics of polarized interests advances any cause, but just as important is the consequent strengthening of possibilities for productive intellectual exchange across the political spectrum.

Wolfgang Iser, along with his colleagues at the University of Konstanz, has renewed the dimension of literary theory that concerns itself with readers and audiences, and I have benefited considerably from extensive conversations with him over many years, particularly during an extended visit to Konstanz.

The range of views I have encountered in these lengthy exchanges with disparate theorists has significantly enriched my own thinking. In spite of their divergent views on a variety of topics, they share some common perspectives on the status of theories, not so much as a series of machines to think with, but as a set of resources that enable individuals to think for themselves. Though they may well disagree in different ways with the arguments advanced in this book, they will all understand how the project undertaken here is related to their own, and for this I thank them all.

The book has also benefited in innumerable ways, large and small, from conversations with colleagues, friends, and acquaintances, including Michael Levenson, Darryl Gless, Paul Armstrong, Leo Damrosch, Don Hirsch, Rick Waswo, Richard Rorty, Michael Warren, Del Kolve, Michael Halliday, Martin Meisel, David Damrosch, Kathy Eden, Andreas Huyssen, Ed Mendelson, David Kastan, Jean Howard, and Ted Taylor. In developing these arguments, I have also benefited considerably from discussions over many years with my students at the University of Virginia and at Columbia.

Parts of chapter 4 appeared in earlier forms in *New Literary History*, and I am grateful to the editor for permission to reproduce that material here.

My assistant at Columbia, Beth Cornwell, transformed, in a remarkably short period, a variously ordered manuscript into a document of much improved consistency and clarity and for that and for many related acts of kindness I am deeply grateful. I would like to express my appreciation to my research assistant, Jessica Brater, whose rigorous checking of detail reduced citation errors to a minimum, and my thanks go also to the staff at Yale University Press and to Julie DuSablon, whose highly professional work substantially improved the manuscript.

My warmest thanks go to my wife, Patricia, who continues to make everything possible.

New York
December 2002

Index

Abrams, M. H., 19
Altieri, Charles, 140, 237
Anderson, Perry, 243
Aristotle, 11, 244
Armstrong, Paul B., 17, 33–40, 70, 77, 145, 219, 222–23, 227
Augustine, 27, 132–34, 137
Austin, J. L., 122, 234

Bakhtin, Mikhail M., 61–67, 70–74, 76, 79, 153, 157, 166, 181–82, 197–98, 206, 226–28, 233, 238–39, 242–43, 245
Barthes, Roland, xii, xvi, 94, 130, 230, 245
Beattie, James, 124
Bergmann, Gustav, 1, 216
Berlin, Isaiah, 241
Bernstein, Basil, 233, 246
Bhabha, Homi K., 228
Binkley, Timothy, 236
Booth, Wayne C., xi, xv–xvi, 9, 17–20, 23, 32–33, 35–36, 39–40, 157, 163, 200–202, 205, 215–17, 219–20, 222–23, 239, 244–46
Bové, Paul, 222
Brecht, Bertolt, 155, 159, 165–67, 173, 213, 239, 241
Brill, Susan B., 239
Brooks, Cleanth, 166, 191–94, 201, 212, 241, 244–45
Burke, Kenneth, 19

Cantor, Paul A., xvii, 180, 188, 216, 242
Cassirer, Ernst, 11, 218
Cavell, Stanley, 133, 235
Chekhov, Anton, 208, 246
Chomsky, Noam, 81–92, 97–101, 103–6, 110, 112–15, 119, 122–26, 129, 149–50, 159–60, 163, 173, 221, 229, 231, 234–35
Cohen, Ralph, 165, 241
Coleridge, Samuel Taylor, 27
Crane, Ronald S., xiv, 19, 216

259

Culler, Jonathan, 8, 93, 96, 217, 230–31
cummings, e. e., 86

Damrosch, David, 17, 219–20
Darwin, Charles, 48
Davis, Philip W., 78–79, 89, 228
de Man, Paul, 230, 236
Dennis, John, 218
Derrida, Jacques, xii, xvi, 7, 24, 27, 31–32, 92, 97, 131, 140, 143, 161, 176, 181, 197, 220–22, 229–31, 236–37
Descombes, Vincent, 218
Dewey, John, 237–38
Dostoevsky, Fyodor, 61

Eco, Umberto, 94–95, 224, 230
Elgin, S. H., 86–87, 229
Eliot, George, xxi, 216
Eliot, T. S., 14, 165, 218–19
Ellis, John M., 17, 20, 22, 40, 51, 161, 164, 186, 189, 209, 219–20, 223–24, 228, 235, 240–41, 244, 246
Emerson, Caryl, 227, 233

Feyerabend, Paul, 169, 241
Firth, J. R., 57–61, 62–67, 70–71, 73–74, 76, 79, 97–100, 105, 107, 112, 131, 133, 137–39, 142, 193–94, 197, 206, 211–13, 226–28, 231, 233–34, 241, 244, 247
Fischer, Michael, 217
Fish, Stanley, 169, 222, 241–42
Fodor, Jerry A., 88, 229
Forster, E. M., 14–15, 165, 219
Foucault, Michel, xii, xvi, xxi, 158–60, 163, 181–82, 216, 240, 243
Fowler, Alastair, 241
Freud, Sigmund, xii, xvi, 19, 34, 77, 130, 158–59, 181
Frye, Northrop, xvi

Gandhi, Leela, 9, 217, 246
Genet, Jean, 158, 239
Geuss, Raymond, 225
Giddens, Anthony, 243

Goethe, Johann Wolfgang von, 167, 241
Graff, Gerald, xii–xiii, xv, 4–6, 10, 17, 19, 21–24, 27, 36, 39–40, 153, 211, 215–17, 219–20, 222–23, 238, 244, 247
Graham, Keith, 234
Greenblatt, Stephen, 242
Grinder, J. T., 86–87, 229

Haas, W., 142, 223, 235, 237
Halliday, M. A. K., 81, 98–117, 119–23, 125–27, 129, 137, 139, 142, 149–50, 159–61, 163, 173, 197, 201, 206, 208, 211, 231–34, 240, 246
Harrison, Bernard, 88, 229
Hasan, Ruquaiya, 97, 231
Hegel, Georg Wilhelm Friedrich, 130
Henderson, Mae Gwendolyn, 166, 241
Herder, Johann Gottfried von, 11
Herndl, Diane Price, 240
Hirsch, E. D., 81, 194, 228, 245–46
Holmes, Oliver Wendell, 237–38
Howard, Jean, 187–88, 244
Humboldt, Wilhelm von, 229
Hyman, Stanley Edgar, 6, 217

Iser, Wolfgang, 193, 201, 212, 244, 247

Jakobson, Roman, 65–66, 94, 227–28, 230
James, William, 143, 163, 237–38, 240
Johnson, Barbara, 240
Joyce, James, 14, 56, 60, 165, 218–19, 225
Jung, Carl Gustav, xvi

Kant, Immanuel, 11, 18, 130, 219
Kastan, David Scott, 242–43
Katz, Jerrold J., 88, 229
Kress, Gunther, 111–12, 233
Kuhn, Thomas S., 37, 169–74, 241–42, 246

Labov, William, 233
Lacan, Jacques, xii, xvi, 77, 130
Lakoff, George, 90, 97, 229
Lauretis, Teresa de, 243–44
Lawson, Nigella, 241

Lentricchia, Frank, ix–xi, xix, 3, 215–16, 218
Lévi-Strauss, Claude, xvi, 12, 16, 94, 130, 159, 218–19, 230
Locke, John, 27, 238–39
Lyons, John, 220, 229
Lyotard, Jean-François, 240

Mackintosh, James, 238
Malcolm, Norman, 235
Marcus, Jane, 242
Marx, Karl, xii, xvi, 8, 9, 19, 23, 34, 61, 77, 130, 158–59, 181–82, 217
Matejka, Ladislav, 227
McCawley, James, 90, 97, 229
McClintock, Anne, 215
McIntosh, Angus, 232, 234
McKeon, Richard, 216
Medvedev, P. N., 61, 113, 226–27
Meillet, Antoine, 12, 218
Menand, Louis, 237–38
Miller, Arthur, 165, 241
Miller, J. Hillis, 179, 230–31, 236, 242
Mitchell, W. J. T., 157, 220, 235, 239
Montaigne, Michel de, 191, 197–98, 200–202, 227, 232, 244–45
Montrose, Louis, 188, 242–44
Moore, G. E., 238
Morson, Gary Saul, 227, 233, 241

Newman, John Henry, xiii, xxi, 216
Newton, Isaac, 48, 242
Nietzsche, Friedrich, 7, 169, 217, 241, 243
Norris, Christopher, 220, 237

Ogden, C. K., 219
Orwell, George, 14

Pavel, Thomas G., 10, 217–18
Pechter, Edward, 5, 178, 180, 188, 216–17, 242, 244
Peirce, Charles Sanders, 37, 169, 222, 237–38, 241
Plato, 25–27, 167, 197, 245
Popper, Karl R., 169–70, 223, 241

Rabelais, François, 61
Rooney, Ellen, 162–65, 167, 220, 240
Rorty, Richard, 8–10, 76, 127, 216–18, 225–26, 233
Russell, Bertrand, 135, 235

Sampson, Geoffrey, 219, 221, 223
Sapir, Edward, 11, 218
Sartre, Jean-Paul, xvi
Saussure, Ferdinand de, xv, xx, 4, 11–12, 15–16, 30, 43–56, 57–62, 64, 67–75, 76–82, 89–90, 92–94, 96, 99, 104–5, 109, 119, 122–24, 126–27, 129, 149, 157–59, 164, 197, 206, 211, 216, 219, 223–25, 228–29, 233–35, 239, 241–42
Schechner, Richard, 246
Scholes, Robert, 17, 26, 219–20, 222, 242
Shakespeare, William, x, xvi, 4, 180, 182, 186, 194, 217, 221, 243
Spivak, Gayatri Chakravorty, 222, 242
Stanislavski, Constantin, 159
Staten, Henry, 140, 143, 237
Stoppard, Tom, 15, 219
Strang, Barbara M. H., 224
Strawson, P. F., 235
Strevens, Peter, 232, 234

Tillyard, E. M. W., 244
Trilling, Lionel, 9, 217
Tynjanov, Jurij, 228, 230

Valla, Lorenzo, 30–31, 37, 41
Vickers, Brian, 13, 216, 218
Vološinov, V. N., 61–62, 113, 226–27, 245

Wagner, Richard, 165, 192
Warhol, Robyn R., 240
Warren, Austin, ix–xvi, xxi, 165, 186, 194, 215–16, 241, 243
Washington, Peter, 8, 40, 158, 217, 240
Waswo, Richard, 27–31, 39, 198, 219, 221, 223, 235, 245
Weiss, Peter, 183, 243

Wellek, René, ix–xvi, xxi, 165, 186, 194, 215–16, 241, 243
Whitehead, Alfred North, 247
Whitney, Dwight, 72
Whorf, Benjamin Lee, 11
Wilde, Oscar, 167
Wittgenstein, Ludwig, 11, 26, 30–33, 35, 37, 39–42, 77, 112, 127–55, 156–57, 161, 163, 168, 172, 175–78, 184, 198, 200–202, 205–6, 209, 211–13, 218, 220–21, 223, 235–39, 245–47
Woodring, Carl, xvii, xxi, 17, 216, 219
Woolf, Virginia, xx, 216
Wright, Georg Henrik von, 235, 238

Yeats, W. B., 14, 165, 218
Young, Edward, 246